Arguing Counterterrorism is a superb collection of articles giving sustained, cutting-edge, and critical assessment of contemporary counterterrorism policy and practice. Theoretically innovative, empirically rich, and normatively challenging, this landmark volume assesses the current state of knowledge, fills a number of important gaps, and points the way towards new perspectives and understandings, all in clear, accessible language. It exemplifies the growing sophistication and maturity of the critical discourse analytic literature that emerged following the launch of the global war on terror, and deserves the widest possible audience.

Richard Jackson, University of Otago, New Zealand

Challenging the conventional wisdom of much terrorism/counterterrorism literature, Pisoiu and colleagues turn traditional assumptions upside down, looking at pre-9/11 discourse, looking beyond the US for the production of such discourse, considering non-state producers of discourse, and they do so through a hard focus on what is methodologically appropriate. The result? An exceptionally subtle, insightful and thought-provoking text.

Stuart Croft, University of Warwick, UK

The volume brings together a distinct set of critical viewpoints on the subject, written by scholars with diverse academic backgrounds. A necessary and valuable contribution to the burgeoning field of critical terrorism studies.

Arshin Adib-Moghaddam, SOAS, University of London, UK

Arguing Counterterrorism

This book offers a multifaceted, analytical account of counterterrorism argumentation.

Traditionally, existing scholarship in this field of research has taken a selective focus on issues and actors, concentrating mainly on US state discourse after 9/11. However, this approach ignores the fact that there was counterterrorism argumentation before 9/11, and that there are other countries and other actors who also actively engage in the counterterrorism discursive field, both within and outside of the Western world.

Addressing several thematic, chronological and methodological gaps in the current literature, *Arguing Counterterrorism* offers a dynamic perspective on counterterrorism argumentation. Over the course of the volume, the authors tackle the following key issues: first, historical and cultural continuity and change; and second, the phenomenology of counterterrorism argumentation: its nature, instrumentalisation, implications and interactions between the various actors involved. The third theme is the anatomy of counterterrorism argumentation; namely its political, cultural and linguistic constitutive elements. Employing a multi-disciplinary framework, the authors explore these issues through a geographically and historically diverse range of case studies, resulting in a book that broadens the perspective of counterterrorism argumentation analysis.

This book will be of much interest to students of critical terrorism studies, counterterrorism, discourse analysis, security studies and IR.

Daniela Pisoiu is Researcher at the Institute for Peace Research and Security Policy at the University of Hamburg. She has a PhD from the University of St Andrews and is the author of *Islamist Radicalisation in Europe* (Routledge 2011).

Series: Routledge Critical Terrorism Studies
Series Editor: Richard Jackson
University of Otago, New Zealand

This book series will publish rigorous and innovative studies on all aspects of terrorism, counterterrorism and state terror. It seeks to advance a new generation of thinking on traditional subjects and investigate topics frequently overlooked in orthodox accounts of terrorism. Books in this series will typically adopt approaches informed by critical–normative theory, post-positivist methodologies and non-Western perspectives, as well as rigorous and reflective orthodox terrorism studies.

Terrorism and the Politics of Response
Edited by Angharad Closs Stephens and Nick Vaughan-Williams

Critical Terrorism Studies
Framing a new research agenda
Edited by Richard Jackson, Marie Breen Smyth and Jeroen Gunning

State Terrorism and Neoliberalism
The north in the south
Ruth Blakeley

Contemporary State Terrorism
Theory and practice
Edited by Richard Jackson, Eamon Murphy and Scott Poynting

State Violence and Genocide in Latin America
The Cold War years
Edited by Marcia Esparza, Henry R. Huttenbach and Daniel Feierstein

Discourses and Practices of Terrorism
Interrogating terror
Edited by Bob Brecher, Mark Devenney and Aaron Winter

An Intellectual History of Terror
War, violence and the state
Mikkel Thorup

Women Suicide Bombers
Narratives of violence
V.G. Julie Rajan

Terrorism, Talking and Transformation
A critical approach
Harmonie Toros

Counter-Terrorism and State Political Violence
The 'War on Terror' as terror
Edited by Scott Poynting and David Whyte

Selling the War on Terror
Foreign policy discourses after 9/11
Jack Holland

The Making of Terrorism in Pakistan
Historical and social roots of extremism
Eamon Murphy

Lessons and Legacies of the War on Terror
From moral panic to permanent war
Edited by Gershon Shafir, Everard Meade, and William J. Aceves

Arguing Counterterrorism
New perspectives
Edited by Daniela Pisoiu

States of War since 9/11
Terrorism, sovereignty and the war on terror
Edited by Alex Houen

Arguing Counterterrorism
New perspectives

Edited by Daniela Pisoiu

LONDON AND NEW YORK

First published 2014
by Routledge
2 Park Square, Milton Park, Abingdon, Oxfordshire OX14 4RN

and by Routledge
711 Third Avenue, New York, NY 10017

First issued in paperback 2015

Routledge is an imprint of the Taylor & Francis Group, an informa business

© 2014 selection and editorial material, Daniela Pisoiu; individual chapters, the contributors

The right of the editor to be identified as the author of the editorial material, and of the authors for their individual chapters, has been asserted in accordance with sections 77 and 78 of the Copyright, Designs and Patents Act 1988.

All rights reserved. No part of this book may be reprinted or reproduced or utilized in any form or by any electronic, mechanical, or other means, now known or hereafter invented, including photocopying and recording, or in any information storage or retrieval system, without permission in writing from the publishers.

Trademark notice: Product or corporate names may be trademarks or registered trademarks, and are used only for identification and explanation without intent to infringe.

British Library Cataloguing in Publication Data
A catalogue record for this book is available from the British Library

Library of Congress Cataloging in Publication Data
Arguing counterterrorism : new perspectives / [edited by] Daniela Pisoiu.
 pages cm. – (Routledge critical terrorism studies)
 Includes bibliographical references and index.
 1. Terrorism–Prevention. 2. Security, International.
 3. International relations. I. Pisoiu, Daniela.
 HV6431.A7555 2014
 363.325'17–dc23
                                                              2013027205

ISBN 13: 978-1-138-95189-1 (pbk)
ISBN 13: 978-0-415-64083-1 (hbk)

Typeset in Baskerville
by Wearset Ltd, Boldon, Tyne and Wear

For my parents

Contents

Notes on contributors xiii
Acknowledgements xvii

Introduction 1
DANIELA PISOIU AND DAVID SCHEUING

PART I
Roots and cultures 25

1 **The rhetorical origins of the US war on terror** 27
  CAROL K. WINKLER

2 **Western responses to terrorism in the 1970s** 56
  ONDREJ DITRYCH

3 **The power of terrorism frames: responses to non-Islamist lone-wolf terrorism in Europe** 74
  A. MAURITS VAN DER VEEN

PART II
Phenomenology 93

4 **Between insurrection and "reformism": public discourses of twenty-first century Greek armed groups** 95
  ANASTASSIA TSOUKALA

5 **When terrorists talk back** 121
  DANIELA PISOIU AND NICO PRUCHA

6 **Plenty of oxygen: terrorism, news media and the politics of the Australian security state** 141
  DAVID C. HOLMES AND REBEKA SULLIVAN

7 Jihadist terrorism in Europe: what role for media? 160
SYBILLE REINKE DE BUITRAGO

8 Counterterrorism as contested terrain: performative contradictions and "autoimmune disorder" 181
RAMASWAMI HARINDRANATH

PART III
Anatomy 199

9 The elusive essence of evil: constructing Otherness in the coalition of the willing 201
JACK HOLLAND

10 The discourse on political Islam and the "War on Terror": roots, policy implications and potential for change 221
CORINNA MULLIN

11 The multiple contexts of Russian counterterrorism frames: the framing process and discursive field 247
AURÉLIE CAMPANA

12 The hunter and the hunted: metaphors of pursuit, prey and the intractability of difference in post 9/11 American counterterrorism discourse 270
DEBORAH WILLS AND ERIN STEUTER

Index 292

Contributors

Aurélie Campana is Associate Professor of Political Science at Laval University. She holds the Canada Research Chair on Conflicts and Terrorism. She is also a member of the Canadian Research Network on Terrorism, Security and Society (TSAS), a member of the Centre International de Criminologie Comparée (University of Montreal) and a fellow of the Canadian Defence and Foreign Affairs Institute. Her research has focused for years on terrorism in internal conflicts, the diffusion of violence across movements and borders and the Russian discursive counter-terrorism strategies. Her research has appeared in numerous journals, including *Civil Wars, Studies in Conflict and Terrorism* and *Terrorism and Political Violence*. In 2013 she co-edited a book with Gérard Hervouet: *Terrorisme et insurrection: Évolution des dynamiques conflictuelles et réponses des États* (Québec: Presses Universitaires du Québec).

Ondrej Ditrych is Research Fellow at the Institute of International Relations Prague and Assistant Professor at Charles University in Prague. His research focuses on terrorism, transatlantic security and EU external policies. His academic articles have been published in *Security Dialogue, Journal of International Relations and Development*, and *Europe-Asia Studies*.

Ramaswami Harindranath is Professor of Media at the University of New South Wales, Australia. He is the author of *Audience-Citizens* (Sage, 2009), and *Perspectives on Global Cultures* (Open University Press, 2007), and is currently completing a monograph entitled *Southern Discomfort: Reassessing Cultural Imperialism*. His research interests include terrorism and the media; global media, politics and cultures; South Asian media and society; and transnational cultural formations.

Jack Holland (PhD) is Lecturer in International Relations at the University of Surrey. He is the author of *Selling the War on Terror* (Routledge, 2012) and co-author of *Security: A Critical Introduction* (Palgrave, 2013). His research interests lie in American, British and Australian foreign and security policy, particularly during the War on Terror, and in critical approaches in International Relations. He has recently published in journals such as: *European Journal of International Relations*, *The British Journal of Politics and International Relations*, *Millennium Journal of International Studies*, *International Political Sociology* and *The Australian Journal of Political Science*.

David C. Holmes (PhD) is Senior Lecturer in Communications and Media at Monash University, Australia. His publications include *Communication Theory: Media, Technology, Society* (Sage, 2005); with Paul Jones (University of New South Wales) *Key Concepts in Media and Communications* (Sage, 2011); and the following edited collections: *Virtual Politics: Identity and Community in Cyberspace*, (Sage, 1997); and *Virtual Globalization: Virtual Spaces/Tourist Spaces* (Routledge, 2001).

A. Maurits van der Veen is Assistant Professor of Government at the College of William & Mary, Virginia. His research focuses on the role of ideas and beliefs in the study of International Relations, with particular emphasis on the impact of the way policies and issue areas are framed in public debate. He is the author of *Ideas, Interests, and Foreign Aid* (Cambridge University Press, 2011).

Corinna Mullin is Research Associate at the School of Oriental and African Studies (SOAS) and Visiting Assistant Professor in International Relations at the University of Tunis. Her current research is focused on the causes and consequences of the Arab revolutions, the discursive and legal–institutional legacies of the War on Terror in Tunisia and Egypt, the impact of the Arab uprisings on Tunisian and Egyptian foreign policies, and transitional justice in post-revolution contexts. Her research interests also include critical approaches to IR, US and EU foreign policy towards the Middle East, comparative political theory, and political Islam, as well as identity politics. Her book, *America and its Post-'War on Terror' Politics*, will be published by I.B. Tauris in late 2013. She also has recent publications in *Millennium Journal of International Studies* and *Critical Terrorism Studies*.

Daniela Pisoiu (PhD) is Researcher at the Institute for Peace Research and Security Policy (IFSH) at the University of Hamburg. She is the author of *Islamist Radicalisation in Europe: An Occupational Change Process* (Routledge, 2011). She currently researches on subcultural aspects of radicalization and political violence in a comparative perspective and is more broadly interested in social movement theory, terrorism and political violence, critical terrorism studies, political extremism and EU and US security policies.

Nico Prucha is currently completing his PhD at the Department of Near Eastern Studies at the University of Vienna and is also Fellow at the IFSH. His research focuses on textual and audiovisual content analysis of al-Qa'ida activity online, specifically focusing on jihadist Shari'a law interpretation of hostage taking and executions. Recent publications are *Tweeting for the Caliphate: Twitter as the New Frontier for Jihadist Propaganda* co-authored with Ali Fisher (CTC Sentinel, 2013), 'Kangaroo Trials – Justice in the Name of God' in *Jihadism: Online Discourses and Representations (Studying Jihadism)*, vol. 2, edited by Rüdiger Lohlker (Vienna University Press, 2013) and 'Tales from the Crypt: Jihadi Martyr Narratives for Online Recruitment', in *Sacrifice and Death in Modern Islam: History, Ethos and Politics* (forthcoming).

Sybille Reinke de Buitrago (PhD) is Fellow at the Institute for Peace Research and Security Policy at the University of Hamburg and at the Institute for Theology and Peace in Hamburg, Germany. She works on international relations, security policy, and peace and conflict resolution, with a special focus on ideational factors such as identity, self-other constructions, perception and communication processes. She is also lecturer at the University of Lüneburg, Germany. Her publications include the edited volume *Portraying the Other in International Relations: Cases of Othering, Their Dynamics and the Potential for Transformation* (Cambridge Scholars Publishing, 2012); *Threat Images in International Relations: American and German Security Policy on International Terrorism* (Tectum, 2010); and 'The Impact of Psychological-Cultural Factors on Concepts of Fighting Terrorism', *Journal of Strategic Security* (2009).

David Scheuing is a graduate of the Friedrich Schiller University Jena, former intern at the IFSH and currently joining a Master's programme in Peace and Conflict Studies, International Development and Human Geography. He is particularly interested in the fields of terrorism, migration and the construction of marginalized spaces as well as security discourses, the border as social event and political geography/geopolitics. David has also been involved in volunteer work in post-conflict societies around the elections in 2012 (Ghana) and 2013 (Kenya).

Erin Steuter is Professor of Sociology at Mount Allison University. Her recent work focuses on the social construction of the enemy and discourses of dehumanization in contemporary media and politics. She is the co-author of *Pop Culture Goes to War: Enlisting and Resisting Militarism in the War on Terror* (Lexington Books, 2010) and *At War with Metaphor: Media Propaganda and Racism in the War on Terror* (Lexington Books, 2008). She has recently published in journals such as *Media, War & Conflict* and *Journal of War and Culture Studies* and contributed chapters to *Images that Injure: Pictorial Stereotypes in the Media* (Praeger, 2011) and *The Routledge Handbook of War and Society* (Routledge, 2010).

Rebeka Sullivan is a Master of Communication graduate from Monash University whose research examines the relationship between news media and terrorism in Australia.

Anastassia Tsoukala (PhD in Law and Criminal Sciences) is Professor of Criminology at the University Paris 11 and Senior Researcher at the University Paris 5 (Sorbonne); assistant editor of the political science quarterly *Cultures & Conflits* (France) and editor of the Palgrave book series *Transnational Crime, Crime Control, and Security*.

Deborah Wills is Professor of English at Mount Allison University. Her research areas include representations of violence in literature, metaphor and culture, and contemporary gothic fiction. Erin Steuter and Deborah Wills are the authors of *At War with Metaphor: Media Propaganda and Racism in the War on Terror* (Lexington Books, 2008).

Carol K. Winkler is Professor of Communication Studies and Associate Dean of Humanities at Georgia State University in Atlanta, Georgia. Her book, *In the Name of Terrorism: Presidents on Political Violence in the Post-World War II Era* (SUNY Press, 2006), won the 2008 National Communication Association's Outstanding Book Award in political communication. Her scholarship on the rhetoric of counterterrorism has appeared in *Rhetoric and Public Affairs, Argumentation and Advocacy* and *Controversia: An International Journal of Debate and Democratic Renewal*, as well as in several edited volumes.

Acknowledgements

The editor wishes to thank David Scheuing who partook in the initiation of this project, and Andrea Quaden, Henriette Reichwald and Anna Stobbe for their assistance with data collection and copy-editing.

Thanks are due to Andrew Humphrys and Annabelle Harris, who accompanied with dedication and patience the development of this book throughout its many stages. Last but not least, I note my indebtedness to Richard Jackson, editor of the Routledge Critical Terrorism Studies Series, an inspiring scholar and an exceptional person.

Introduction

Daniela Pisoiu and David Scheuing

In a rapidly growing research field and a rapidly evolving political landscape, it has become conventional to initiate one's own discourse on counterterrorism discourse by acknowledging existing achievements, finding points of critique and positioning one's own research as innovative, gap filling, and thus distinguishing itself as an invaluable and necessary piece of the overall academic machinery in the field. This introduction will do the same; it will acknowledge stepping stones, ideas and works that left a mark on us, the contributors to this book. It will also point out the gaps and questions that stirred further questions and the urge to search, explain, present and re-present. But it will also share a rare experience of stepping out of the box and moving beyond the boundaries of an established field, discourse, or "way of doing things." And it will share the joy of discovery.

The original idea of this book was to address some of the blind spots of critical research on counterterrorism discourse, by both zooming in and zooming out of the, by now, classical discussion on the war on terror. Shocked and awed, to paraphrase Fred Halliday (2010), at the realization of the more seriously resonant implications of post-9/11 counterterrorism policy, the academic community has found itself confronted by a series of questions as to how these political actions were possible. In addition, more general questions have been raised regarding the changes that must be undertaken in the ways we think and talk about, as well as deal with, "terrorism." Scholars of Critical Terrorism Studies have reached to a multidisciplinary reservoir of concepts and methods to address the "why," the "how" and the "what to do about it." The quantity of works has increased exponentially in recent years and so has the palette of approaches called to challenge traditional assumptions and paradigms by critical assessments of both counterterrorism policy and its research in the broader terrorism literature.

This newer perspective of study arose from the critique of the processes in which states "write" the war on terror, depicting, naming and narrating a reality that draws its power from the states' discursive weight. This perspective was introduced by Richard Jackson in *Writing the War on Terrorism*

(2005), where he gave the first account of the discursive scheme that enables states to "invent" their opponent terrorist/terrorism and to successfully build up "rational" (or better: rationales of) argumentation for comprehensive security measures. Jackson, using methodological and theoretical resources developed mainly by French post structuralist thinkers such as Foucault and Derrida, paved the path of understanding and analyzing counterterrorism argumentation as a textual system. His work thus enabled the ongoing flood of discourse-analytical scholarship to enter the realm of counterterrorism research and the emergence of the, by now, sizable production of critical analyses of counterterrorism narratives. While by no means intended, a consequence of this initial impetus for critique, namely 9/11, has nevertheless been a focus on US state discourse after 9/11.

One aspect that has attracted much attention is the avalanche of more or less visible measures undertaken by various governments around the world to combat primarily the Islamist terrorist threat – from Guantánamo, military commissions and counter-capture to data retention and wiretapping. The enactment of such measures and other counterterrorism policies has constituted excellent empirical material for the exercise of securitization theory concepts, as prime examples of formulations in which extraordinary circumstances require extraordinary means. Analyses have ranged from the securitization of Islamist activism (Mullin 2011), or of Arab and Muslim communities and countries (Baker 2010), to deeper inquiries into the political culture (Jackson 2011; McCrisken 2011) and the reservoir of rhetoric serving such moves (see for instance the discursive practices of labelling in Appleby 2010; Barrinha 2011 or performativity in de Graaf and de Graaff 2010), to concrete effects on the understanding and practice of democracy and civil liberties (Jackson 2006; Rykkja et al. 2011) and to state terrorism (Blakeley 2010; Jackson et al. 2010). In a broader perspective, research has laid particular emphasis on the construction of the "war on terror" narrative (Clarke and Zalman 2009), the normalization of controversial practices, the framing of terrorist incidents, the demonization of Islam and even the creation of a "new English language," on the effort to impose a certain reading of the terrorist threat landscape, on the background of constructed collective identities, adverse positioning and polarized identities and the exploitation of long established values and self-understandings (see for instance Halliday 2010; Hodges and Nilep 2007; Jackson 2005; Jarvis 2009; Lewis 2005; Stephens and Vaughan-Williams 2009; Talbot 2008).

The idea of this book and its individual contributions has without a doubt built on this corpus of literature. At the same time, contributors have responded to a series of observations as to the limitations of existing scholarship: the fixation on the US counterterrorism discourse, the apprehension of 9/11 as a turning point in counterterrorism discourse, the emphasis on state discourse and the not always overt methodological accounts. Turning this around, we have worked with the assumption that there was a pre-9/11 terrorism discourse; that there are other countries and other actors who also actively engage in the counterterrorism discursive field; and that there needs to be a rigorous methodological account both to substantiate claims and as a means of guidance for further analysis. The contributions of this book offer a varied, dynamic and multilayered perspective on counterterrorism argumentation. Not only is the geographical and historical variety of the case studies unique, but so is the approach to tracing historical, rhetorical and cultural continuity and change, processes and dynamics among the various actors involved and the reflective methodological account. It needs to be said at this point that, in the meantime, a more rigorous focus on research methods can be observed (see for instance Stump and Dixit 2012). Our book is not primarily about methods; it was, however, part of its goal to cover a variety of methods of analysis and also for each chapter to account for its choice and use of methods.

A first overall point to highlight is therefore the diversity of the case studies covered in this book. Without raising the pretence of having covered all relevant countries and regions, we have however managed to significantly enlarge the geographical scope, by including not just the US and the UK, but also Australia, a series of West European countries, India, the Russian Federation and Turkey. Some of the individual chapters also engage in cross-country comparison (Ditrych, Holland, Reinke de Buitrago, van der Veen). A second point, and at the same time, the thematic core of the first part of the book, is the inquiry into counterterrorism argumentation before 9/11, based on the assumption that some of the practices, narratives and resources of the war on terror discourse would display a certain degree of continuity with previous ones. The first part, "Roots and cultures," thus focuses on historical and comparative aspects of counterterrorism argumentation. We approached the relationship between history and discourse along three dimensions: first, each narrative has a history, building blocks, and an evolution in time as well as overlaps with other supportive narratives; second, narratives are themselves embedded in historical contexts, they build upon historical events, wave fragments of historical contingency into the tapestry of the discourse and narrate them in suitable fashion, with the respective interpretations of validity, morality, legality, or identity; and third, the writing of history by discourse. Temporality is central to counterterrorism discourse, concerning the construction of legitimacy (based on precedent and timeless precepts) and of identities with "common past, present and future" (Jarvis 2009: 14–15). Equally important is however also the tracing of particular narratives in time, and how current narratives pave the way for future precedents.

Identifying narration phases, historical fragments and processes of writing necessarily involves resorting to cultural repertoires. The historicalness of counterterrorism argumentation can only be accessed through its cultural backing. In other words, as history in speech is only accessible in an interpreted form, the cultural context presents the instrument through which the processes of interpreting historical events become comprehensible. Without directly focusing on culture as a resource in this part, we still need to regard it as the container, the reservoir of the historical accounts that are being made viable for discourse through their use by culturally informed protagonists. The term "cultures" refers to this understanding, but is also a marker of difference, both in time and in space. As Lewis (2005: 2) notes, "historical and contemporary cultural conditions ... inevitably construct and challenge various models of meaning and meaning-making."

Carol K. Winkler's chapter, "The rhetorical origins of the US war on terror" (Chapter 1), identifies rhetorical framing strategies employed by the Bush administration officials to describe the enemy and the appropriate US response in the war on terror. It recalls historical uses of the same strategic frame, and draws out implications based on comparable outcomes associated with this strategic choice. The chapter demonstrates that the rhetoric justifying the war on terror adopted strategic approaches used by leaders in the early republic (i.e., America's indigenous populations, the Barbary pirates, and the French Revolution), by leaders facing ideologically based threats in the twentieth century (i.e., communism and fascism), and by contemporary Republican presidents responding to terrorism (i.e., Richard Nixon, Ronald Reagan, and George H.W. Bush).

In Chapter 2, "Western responses to terrorism in the 1970s," **Ondrej Ditrych** sets to historicize counterterrorism by looking at its modalities in this particular decade. He first provides a short overview of the political violence that these countries defined as a problem to be resolved through their counterterrorism policies. This is followed by an exposé of the rationality and technologies comprising counterterrorism security apparatuses. Next, he turns to the speech, or discourse of (counter)terrorism as a series of statements enunciated by the First World states in the contemporary debate on the subject in the United Nations. Finally, he explores elements of the discursive formation of terrorism science, which incidentally (but in fact, on the assumption of a constitutive relationship between power and knowledge, not incidentally at all) emerged in the 1970s.

A. Maurits van der Veen, in "The power of terrorism frames: responses to non-Islamist lone-wolf terrorism in Europe" (Chapter 3), focuses on the parliamentary discourse in three European countries (the Netherlands, Norway and Sweden) around the issue of non-Islamist "lone gunmen." Based on the observation that many European policy-makers consciously or subconsciously equate terrorism with acts committed by organized Islamist extremists, the chapter makes three arguments: first, lone-wolf attacks by non-Muslim perpetrators tend not to be characterized as terrorism, even when essentially equivalent to incidents perpetrated by Islamic extremists that *are* seen as terrorist. Second, when such incidents do get classified as terrorist, policy discussions focus as much on Islamist extremism as they do on the actual perpetrator(s). Finally, policy-makers fail to draw lessons from such attacks when subsequently debating counterterrorism.

Apart from historical tracing and positioning, a further important objective of the book has been to overcome the bias towards states and state institutions in the analysis of counterterrorism argumentation. States are not the sole contributors to, or shapers of counterterrorism discourse, and they might even have a less crucial role to play than we think. Part II, "Phenomenology," looks into the nature and process dynamics of counterterrorism argumentation, and aims to capture the diversity, interaction and interrelatedness of the various discourses on terrorism and counterterrorism – the state, of course, but also the media, terror organizations and "terrorists" themselves, and the various components of the "state." We argue that these should not be regarded as an undifferentiated mass, but as a field of interaction and reflection, a discursive "spectacle." This runs against a static, hardened picture of "the state counterterrorism discourse," but opens up the floor to other players, and also opens up the state "black box" by identifying the multiplicity of voices within the state apparatus. It further inquires into how these players interact, react, and are co-constituted by the others, or better yet, by the perception of the others, and in more complex ways than simply "being the opposite of." While not aiming to access the subjective intentions of the various players, the section does go beyond an essentialist view on discourse, by placing articulations, frames and narratives within more "material" notions of interest, power and institutional structure. This part approaches the dynamics of counterterrorism argumentation by setting face to face several actors and their discursive interactions, in various combinations and various contexts: state institutions and media vs guerrilla organizations in Greece; executive institutions and media vs jihadi combatants in Germany; state vs media discourse in Australia; media vs state and jihadi discourse in Western Europe and Turkey; government vs opposition in India.

Anastassia Tsoukala's chapter, "Between insurrection and 'reformism': public discourses of twenty-first century Greek armed groups" (Chapter 4), aims at grasping the nature of the current urban guerrilla movement in Greece. For this purpose it rests upon both a summary account of the media representation of the armed groups and a thematic content analysis of the guerrillas' public discourse (posted on an anti-power site between September 2010 and September 2011). The mixed methods comparative analysis uncovers that, while the propagators of the institutional discourse fuel the image of an unintelligible and essentially subversive urban struggle, today's guerrillas are actually promoting longstanding social demands for democratization of the state and of society in a violent way.

In Chapter 5, "When terrorists talk back," **Daniela Pisoiu and Nico Prucha** enquire into the issues of discursive exchange and co-constitution between government and terrorist organizations in the case of Germany and German jihadi groups. Executive counterterrorism argumentation has so far received significant scholarly attention, while its jihadi pendant has only been approached from the perspective of its ideological and religious roots or recruitment potential, while the interaction between the two has remained largely unexplored. By bringing these two elements together and through the use of frame analysis methodology, the chapter identifies common and divergent narratives, underlying understandings and instrumentalizations of the "terrorist," strategies of agenda arrest, public targeting and persuasion, and traces the dynamics of discursive production and exchange.

David C. Holmes and Rebeka Sullivan, in "Plenty of oxygen: terrorism, news media and the politics of the Australian security state" (Chapter 6), undertake a comparative pre- and post-9/11 analysis of counterterrorism measures and reporting in Australia, including the instrumentalization of the resulting xenophobic effects. They challenge one of the classical principles in counterterrorism policy – taking the broad exposure "oxygen" away from terrorist organizations, by arguing that today, modern states have an interest in the increased reportage of terrorism. Since 9/11 the incidences of international terrorism have increased, but as charted in this chapter, the coverage of such events has increased disproportionately, at times three- or fourfold the degree of coverage that would have obtained for the same number of terrorist fatalities pre-9/11. The chapter explores the "common-interest game" between states and media in promoting fear of terror, as illustrated by the Australian case of the development of counterterrorism measures and new genres of reporting and narrating real and imagined terror.

Sybille Reinke de Buitrago's chapter "Jihadist terrorism in Europe: what role for media?" (Chapter 7) analyzes European media discourse on jihadist terrorism in Western Europe and Turkey. Specifically, it focuses on how seven national print media reported on three attacks in 2010, including offender motives, messages and broader causes; issues of jihadist interest, such as symbolic offences and Western troops in predominantly Muslim countries; and major policy reactions. It finds that media show no clear interest in actually understanding the phenomenon of terrorism and the terrorist perspective, rather tending to replicate official discourse. However, depending on the case and questions analyzed, media have differed, playing either a more active or a more passive role.

Ramaswami Harindranath, in "Counterterrorism as contested terrain: performative contradictions and 'autoimmune disorder'" (Chapter 8), shows how the discourses that underpin counterterrorism policies in India are redolent of the multiple and at times contrasting political interests closely allied to the religious, regional, and linguistic diversity that constitute the Indian nation. Using Butler's notion of "performativity," the chapter examines media and political discourses on counterterrorism in

India as evident in three contexts: the global in the local, the influence of religious politics, and the tensions between the national and state governments. Following Derrida's account of terrorism and counterterrorism as symptoms of "autoimmune disorder" in the body politic, the chapter discusses the ways in which the performative contradictions intrinsic to these discourses have contributed to either undermining the effectiveness of counterterrorism policies or to making them excessively brutal in practice.

Part III of the book, "Anatomy," takes a closer and systematic look at the "bowels" of counterterrorism argumentation. The contributions included here identify, compare and analyze the elements of the script, its cultural resources, and the linguistic toolbox. While the two previous parts aimed, among other things, to contextualize words in their temporal and spatial setting, this part looks at counterterrorism argumentation from a micro-perspective and deals in more detail with specific cultural and linguistic tools and shows how they are instrumentalized in creating coherent counterterrorism narratives. The contributions here deal in particular with the notions of identity and Othering, as well as frames and framing, and with metaphors, which are all critical in understanding the internal functioning of current, and also of previous, counterterrorism argumentation.

The first contribution to this third part, "The elusive essence of evil: constructing Otherness in the coalition of the willing," by **Jack Holland** (Chapter 9), considers the construction of the terrorist Other, in relation to the fractured Self of the Coalition of the Willing. Despite mutual appeals to the essential evilness of enemies during the "war on terror," analyzing the discursive construction of threat and Otherness reveals that divergent understandings of Self-identity inevitably impacted upon a heterogeneous construction of Osama bin Laden's Al Qaeda and Mullah Omar's Taliban, as well as Saddam Hussein's Ba'ath Party. In making this argument the chapter analyzes speeches from political leaders in the United States, Britain and Australia shortly after the events of September 11, 2001.

Corinna Mullin develops a somewhat different perspective on Othering in "The discourse on political Islam and the 'War on Terror': roots, policy implications and potential for change" (Chapter 10). Here, the author explores the discourse on political Islam as it developed in the context of the US declared "war on terror" and, more recently, in light of the "Arab Spring" uprisings. In doing so, she considers the ontological and epistemological roots of the discourse on the Other in modern rationalism, Orientalism and US exceptionalism as well as the ideational and material power that has been generated by its hegemonic diffusion. As this chapter also aims to uncover the complex and dynamic relationship that exists between discourse and policy in the context of the "war on terror," it additionally considers the extent to which this discursive shift has entailed a concomitant shift in policy *vis-à-vis* political Islam.

Aurélie Campana, in "The multiple contexts of Russian counterterrorism frames: the framing process and discursive field" (Chapter 11) argues that the Russian counterterrorism framing process, lacking a clear-cut direction, fails to clearly elaborate a hierarchy of problems and priorities. Based on a micro-discourse analysis of the frames articulated by President D. Medvedev and his Premier, V. Putin, it analyzes how the discursive field in which framing is embedded shapes the process itself as well as its outcomes. It shows that the system of relations between actors and the rules of the game that govern the counterterrorism discursive field, marked by intense competition between actors, tensions and informality, constitute as many mechanisms to prevent frame crystallization, and ultimately leave room for discursive contestation.

Chapter 12, "The hunter and the hunted: metaphors of pursuit, prey and the intractability of difference in post-9/11 American counterterrorism discourse" argues that counterterrorism discourse is deeply embedded in metaphoric frames, shaping a logic of enmity founded in a discourse of intractable difference. **Deborah Wills and Erin Steuter** identify a coherent set of counterterrorism metaphors circulated and ratified in the US political and military speech, analyzing the government's rhetorical framing of the military's task in the war on terror as a hunt for prey, involving "smoking out" and "hunting down" terrorists. The chapter documents the extent of the hunt metaphor, with its reliance on the conflation of enemy and animal, and its expansion from specific enemy figures to Arabs and Muslims at large. Collectively, these have consequences for fomenting conflict. By analyzing and dismantling them, however, giving critical attention to such metaphors offers a means of redirecting such powerful rhetorical tools, subjecting them to a revisionary re-framing that can usefully evolve our discursive lexicon, and create broadened strategies for counterterrorism communication.

Individual contributors to this volume were advised to reflect the core focus of their respective part of the book, and to give a rigorous account of the theories, concepts and methods they relied on. At the same time, leeway was granted in the choice of topic, design, scope, analytical focus, and methodology. This is because we wanted to avoid placing chapters into a straightjacket structure, but rather to celebrate the diversity of writing styles, interests and priorities, so that each chapter could be a unique experience for the reader. Also, along with the respective focus, the contributors were also asked to include aspects related to the other two parts as well. In hindsight, this truly "organic" approach has in fact proven to be natural and necessary. Our initial objective was to broaden the focus of analysis in historical and geographical terms, showing the interrelatedness of various players involved in the counterterrorism argumentation game, and to refine and show in practical terms the use of cultural and linguistic resources in analysis. As the book came together, it became clear that these three dimensions are in fact a central component of any analysis of this kind. This is therefore a second, overarching message in our book. The collection of works as a unitary product shows the gain of "reading" counterterrorism argumentation from our three perspectives: in time, as interaction, and as a web of cultural and linguistic constructs. Depictions of the enemy through metaphors and dichotomies, or the affirmation of national identities, for instance, can only be fully understood by looking at historical precedents and at the continuous process of negotiation of meaning among the various players involved.

Interlude – remembering the myth

Zooming out of the immediate and obvious messages of the book, it is important to point to a second, unintended consequence of bringing together these contributions and to a feature of this, as it were, organic product that emerged out of our individual yet in a sense common efforts to take counterterrorism argumentation out of its box and explore roots, cultures, players and means. This consequence has to do with self-reflection and can be adequately formulated by returning to Barthe's notions of myth and demystifying.

The myth as a "statement," "a system of messaging," and "a way of signifying, a form" (Barthes 1964 [1957]: 85), is appropriate for our purposes because we have a highly intangible "thing" – the counterterrorism discourse, that is mystified, and "all that might be represented by a discourse, may also become myth" (ibid.: 85). Following Barthes, the most crucial aspect of the myth is its ahistoricity. The myth is always pseudo in nature, suggesting (in its own semiological system) that it could be derived naturally, but being in fact highly artificial in construction. What Barthes urges researchers to do is to unveil this "false" naturality, among other things, by demystifying. While necessarily taking an "object" of analysis and in spite of our declared purpose of "multiple perspectives," and precisely while critiquing other peoples' reifications and fetishisms, we need to be alert to the mystification process in which we might be engaging ourselves.

The narration of a "turning point in history" and the creation of a default-like situation in the post-9/11 security environment can certainly qualify as mythological practices. Consider the critique of the hegemonic discourse, of the "they hate our freedom" discourse, the one roughly telling us that terrorism is by definition a matter of non-state actors, individuals and groups who are bent on destroying our Western way of life, barbarians clinging to antiquated societal and political norms, enemies of civilization and progress and indeed, fanatic, irrational and, in extremis, inhumane entities. The critique of this discourse reminds us that terrorism has been and is perpetrated by states as well, with even more disastrous consequences than the one by non-state actors, that terrorism is a tactic employed in the service of political objectives that can be discussed at the negation table, that Western values and systems are not universal and by definition superior and that "they" are not essentially different to "us." And as an umbrella approach, it suggests that we should look deeper into the cultural and linguistic fabric of it all, and into the question of power.

All of this certainly has its pertinence, albeit not always novelty, such as the idea that terrorims is not an end in itself, but rather a means to achieve political objectives. What we are aiming at here, however, goes a step further and is, in a sense, a critique of the critique. Before opening the discussion of theoretical and philosophical approaches, before engaging the material, the tools, the analysis and the conclusions, it is important to reflect on the implications of the very process of critique: in particular, the possibility of falling into the trap of fetishism. What is the counterterrorism discourse? Is there such a thing as *the* counterterrorism discourse? Is it American or Western? Is it something new or is there a particular novelty to it since 9/11? All of these questions will be addressed at large in the reminder of this book. Here, suffice it to draw attention to the danger of creating a counterterrorism discourse Frankenstein, which was never thus intended and which would have never existed were it not for our assiduous work of putting pieces together, making the links and ignoring outliers. At the basis of this new creature is, without doubt, the discourse of the Bush administration, thus far skillfully taken apart and unveiled to its most basic assumptions. But it is also this same critical work that has proclaimed states of emergency, securitization moves and dual identities as its backbone, along with a cohort of straw men in the shape of "the (American) state" and "the (Oriental) terrorist." Could it be that the critics have created something that the administration was never able or willing to create – a hegemonic and by all accounts monstrous counterterrorism discourse? Could it be that, whilst, in our turn, shocked and awed, we focused on a snapshot of eight years and stretched it ad nauseam? That we have ended up ignoring variance and change across and within discourses, and their political, cultural and, indeed, economic underpinnings?

There are the ones who lost their lives on 9/11, there are the ones who deliberately boarded a plane to crash it into a building, there are the ones who stood gazing at smoke and fire, there are the ones who did not notice anything at that day until they switched on their TV, radio, or other device. And there are the ones who shape, influence, and guide our perception of that one single day: governments, international organizations and the media, heavily intertwined to the point of creating a powerful public narration of *one* day as it has seldom been seen in history. And then there are the ones who analyze all this and try to make sense of these other discourses, trace back their roots, expose underpinning power relationships, deconstruct and contest.

This is what, in a sense, all of these contributions are doing; they show historicity, context, continuity and change, difference and interaction. The authors of this volume, through their sensitivity and self-inquiry, have helped to create a meta-level of reflection, not only on the relationship between material and scholar, but also on the way in which we as critical scholars might in fact fight windmills that we created ourselves. The "novelty" of the "war on terror" is put on its head by showing how rhetorical devices can be traced all the way back to the American Revolution (Winkler) and how the articulation of "terrorism" with its current connotations of exceptional threat requiring immediate response, the structuring of current counterterrorism security apparatus and the types of retaliatory state actions can be archeologically recovered in the Western discourse of the 1970s (Ditrych); at the same time, authors also outline the endurance and spread of specific post-9/11 frames (van der Veen), and of basic "readings" at the source of counterterror policies (Mullin; Wills and Steuter); state discourse is depicted as fractured, volatile, and open to contestation (Campana and Harindranath); media turns out to be playing a much more complex role than the assumed "oxygen provider" for the terrorists or mouthpiece for the government (Holmes and Sullivan; Reinke de Buitrago); the "Other" is far from homogeneous, fixed, or new, rather showing splits, fluctuation, while at the same time resting on long-walked pathways of reading and identifying (Holland; Mullin); and there is talk between the state and the "terrorists," albeit highly one-sided (Pisoiu and Prucha; Tsoukala).

Enchiridion

This book is not intended as a general introduction to the study of (counter)terrorism discourse, theory and methods. For excellent and timely introductory books in the matter see for instance Jackson *et al.* (2009) and Stump and Dixit (2012). Our book is meant as a two-pronged effort: on the one hand, to address and demystify some of the, by now, rigidified concepts and assumptions regarding counterterrorism discourse; and, on the other, to open the topic of counterterrorism argumentation to (various) historical and cultural contexts, and take a closer look at discursive interaction, as well as its cultural and linguistic constitutive parts. In a sense, we respond to the appeal for more context as formulated by Toros and Gunning (2009: 107), namely to "place context at the heart of the investigation, restoring a past and a future of terrorism, allowing the concept to evolve along with the world, and embedding (counter)terrorism within its wider socio-historical context of social movements, political, societal and economic structures, non-violent social practices, and the like." The book can also tick off some of the items on the Critical Terrorism Studies research agenda: explore the "ideological, conceptual and institutional underpinnings" of, among others, the practices of counterterrorism; and examine "the origins and evolution of the terrorism discourse in Western societies, and exposing its ontological and epistemological practices" (Jackson *et al.* 2009: 228). We also go beyond, in that we investigate cultural and linguistic depth, as well as the spectacle of counterterrorism argumentation.

Having said all this, it still remains important and relevant to offer here a conceptual roadmap, a short outline tracing and placing some of the concepts with which the chapters operate, as well as some of the broader perspectives and theoretical and philosophical contexts where they are "coming from." This will not be an exhaustive account of schools of thought, theories and methods, but simply orientation points for the reader.

What do we mean by argumentation and what is its relationship to "discourse"? Without going more into the depths of what discourse is, for whom and in what context (we shall approach this at a later point when talking about methodologies), we emphasize the feature of intentionality, an intentionality to sell a story and in this sense persuade, over the logical structure of arguments for instance. We further wish to describe a perspective on the discourse(s) of counterterrorism being not only characterized through linguistic means, but also through its inherent historical embedding, its cultural contextualization, and its phenomenological structure. To further elaborate on this, we draw on Amossy (2009: 252) and understand argumentation as "the use of verbal means ensuring an agreement on what can be considered reasonable by a given group, on a more or less controversial matter," rather than "the art of putting forward logically valid arguments leading to Truth." Here, of crucial importance are the constructive nature of "what is acceptable and plausible," the "dynamism of this exchange" and the embedding in a "cultural framework" (ibid.). Add to this the historical and interactional perspectives – we have the backbone of this book:

> Because the situation of communication and the interdiscourse are embedded in the discourse, context is seen as part of the text. Components like the speaker, the addressee, the place and circumstances of the exchange, the generic framework, the discourse that circulates at the time, are all integrated in the text and constitute an integral part of it. This entails that language is taken not only in its formal, but also in its socio-historical and institutional dimensions.
>
> (Amossy 2009: 256)

Based on the differentiation in Amossy (2009: 254) between argumentative goals and the argumentative dimension of discourse, we focus, to some extent, on the latter; that is, we do not limit ourselves to analyzing discourse that is explicitly aimed at *persuading*, a classic example here being governmental speech in favor of controversial counterterrorism measures. The argumentative dimension of discourse includes here also the quality of "orient[ing] ways of looking at things and interpreting the world without putting forward any thesis" (ibid.). What we want to avoid is a mere linguistic analysis (as complicated and sophisticated as that may become at times). Analyzing counterterrorism argumentation is here not a linguistic effort to establish "fallacies" in the argumentative structure, but an effort to unveil the historical, phenomenological, cultural and linguistic means at its core.

Without going deeper into the intricacies of contemporary constructivism, we begin unrolling the roadmap with two markers: the social construction of reality (Wendt 1999) and the critique advanced by critical constructivists with respect to the constitutive role of discourse with regard to actors' identities and their power relations (Peoples and Vaughan-Williams: 2010: 6). Jackson (2005: 20) reminds us that "discourses form the foundation for the practice by establishing the underlying assumptions, beliefs and knowledge ... words are never neutral; they don't just describe the world, they actually help to make the world." Also: "Because language affects perception, cognition and emotion, it inevitably also affects concrete political action: it has consequences for social processes and structures" (ibid.: 23). A first theme emerges already at this point and this is the question of agency. The field of counterterrorism studies, as opposed to, say, international organizations or norms, is a good opportunity to set two perspectives face to face. One acknowledges the cultural and historical, indeed, social embedding of political practice and discourse. The other represents the apparent strategic and/or self-sufficient moves of individual or institutional players, who not only pursue and push their interests, not only act purposefully, but also appear to manipulate the very cultural arsenal in which they are supposedly embedded. Jackson (2005: 21) notes, for instance, that "Politicians, or more accurately, their propagandists or media relations officers, try to shape public perceptions through the strategic employment of certain words and grammatical formulations." He basically argues that embedding is only a function of persuasiveness:

> [A]dministration officials deliberately deployed language to try to persuade the American people of the logic, reason and rightness of their decisions. At the same time, the language they used drew upon pre-existing and deeply held beliefs, as well as earlier institutional discourses of counterterrorism.
>
> (Ibid.: 27)

Let us glance at securitization theory, which, after all, although concerned with "discourse," deals with securitization moves performed by particular and identifiable actors. Wæver stated (1995: 55):

> With the help of language theory, we can regard "security" as a *speech act*. In this usage, security is not of interest as a sign that refers to something more real; the utterance *itself* is the act. By saying it, something is done (as in betting, giving a promise, naming a ship). By uttering "security," a state-representative moves a particular development into a specific area, and thereby claims a special right to use whatever means are necessary to block it. [Original emphasis]

Ten years later, a well-known constructive critic of the Copenhagen school, Thierry Balzacq (2005), attempts to bring securitization theory back to the "real world" by pointing out the role of the audience, agency and context, whereby agency refers to relations of power. Granted, this is a useful update of the securitization theory, one that brings agency back in the game, but one that, again, leaves out the question of intent. It would most probably be no exaggeration to assert that many, if not all of the analyses of securitization moves *assume* intent, including in more gruesome depictions of the surveillance or torturous state. But is it even possible to access intent? Krebs and Jackson (2007: 36) argue that scholars should "avoid centering causal accounts on unanswerable questions about actors' true motives and to focus instead on what actors say, in what contexts, and to what audiences," because they are skeptical about the possibility of deriving actors' motives (in this case as evidence for "persuasion") from statements.

The contributions to this volume cover this entire range but set specific accents and thus bring perspective and depth to the debate. Tsoukala, somewhat in line with Krebs and Jackson (2007), warns of the methodological difficulties associated with the actor–observer relationship, focuses on the strategic rather than the narrative dimension of the actors' discourse and opts in analysis for the question of "how justified" rather than "why." More on the purposeful agency side, Holmes and Sullivan describe the "common-interest game" of the Australian state and media in provoking fear of terrorism. Winkler argues that administration officials made use of history-laden frames in order to justify targeting specific individuals, groups and states, and in the process deny them due process and sovereignty rights. At the same time, she shows how particular political circumstances lead to adjustments of the rhetorical frames in time. Campana, while noting the idiosyncrasy of discourse and practice at the various levels of government, and, to a certain extent, the underlying interests, also emphasizes power positioning and institutional structure as important explanatory factors for the fractured counterterrorism framing. Van der Veen documents the salience of the organized Islamist terrorism frame on threat assessment and policy-making and shows how policy-makers perpetuate this perception in spite of historical and present-time evidence to the contrary. Ditrych outlines the institutional, ideological and legal constraints on the rationality of state security apparatus from the 1970s until the present day (2013). Wills and Steuter argue that counterterrorism policy is limited by metaphors inscribed in dominant public perceptions of terrorism as conventional rhetorical figures specific to certain discourses. Harindranath and Holland argue that identity and interest are co-constitutive. Holland, while starting off with the common undertaking of the coalition of the willing, documents the decisive effect of different embedded self-perceptions specific to each of the three major members of the coalition. Mullin also starts off with the correlation between identity, interests and practices, and considers agency as embedded in ossified narratives and constrained by more "material" structures, but also challenged by counter-hegemonic discourses.

Related to this and still in the realm of agency is the theme of difference. This refers both to the need to differentiate among various players within "government" (see Campana's and Harindranath's chapters on this), and to the still relatively underexplored discursive dynamic between these players and others: in particular the media as a "meaning making facility" (Lewis 2005: 17) and the terror organizations themselves as participants in the "world of symbolic warfare and symbolic exchange" (ibid.: 26). The explorations in part II, which deal with these aspects, address questions such as: are the media and the state on the same page? How does spectacular violence play into material and electoral calculations? Is the media active in finding out and questioning state discourse? (See here the chapters of Holmes and Sullivan and Reinke de Buitrago). How interested are the state and the terror organizations in listening to each other and how do they re-present each other? (See here the chapters of Tsoukala; Pisoiu and Prucha). Again, the objection of "we cannot know what they think" can be also brought here. Nevertheless, and this should be a relatively solid basis for analysis, comparisons between discourses can be carried out to conclude on whether, at least declaratory, the two sides actually engage in "conversations" of any kind. Further, and this remains a perspective still to be explored, is the question of the ways in which frames circulate among the various speakers as a sort of unconscious learning effect or adaptation. Are certain definitions of situations, labels and pseudo-explanations taken over from player to player and normalized through this dynamic?

A second big theme that we need to engage is that of Othering and identity, this time as a tracing back to postcolonial studies, through poststructuralism and applications in security studies. In his groundbreaking oeuvre *Orientalism* (1978), Edward Said, while embarking on a historical journey of the relations between the West and the Middle East, opened scholarship to the recognition of the processes, effects and problems associated with the production of the Other in scholarly discourse: hegemonic power relationships and identity construction on the basis of a barbaric, subaltern and silenced Other. Oriental is not a descriptive term, but "signifies stereotypical characteristics of the Oriental as mentioned above – exotic, static, irrational, remote, barbaric, primitive and emotional – in binary opposition to characteristics used to describe the West – modern, rational, civilized, advanced, and scientific" (Burney 2012: 29). And these binaries have a function, namely that of identity formation:

> The Orient is the source of its civilizations and languages, its cultural contestant, and one of its deepest and most recurring images of the

> Other. In addition, the Orient ... has helped to define Europe (or the West) as its contrasting image, idea, personality, experience.
>
> (Said 1978: 1–2)

Fabian (1990: 756) states later that it is necessary for anthropologists and ethnographers "to realize that our ways of making the Other are ways of making ourselves. The need to go there (to exotic places, be they far away or around the corner) is really our desire to be here (to find or defend our position in the world)." And while involuntarily building the Western identity, the Oriental is silent, does not have a voice, i.e., is excluded.

From a different perspective, binarism and identity through exclusion have preoccupied the poststructuralists as well. Starting with Saussure's insight that meaning depends on the differences in the structure of the language, difference between signs, Derrida took this thought further, by pointing out the instability of meaning, which is differing and deferring (adding the element of time). Further and more relevant for our identity-Othering complex is the idea of the Western thought securing the instability of meaning through binary oppositions, where the hierarchically superior depends on the inferior one, a meaning secured through exclusion. This parallels the postcolonial thesis of identity formation through binary opposition and exclusion. In security studies, this is reflected in the work of R.B.J. Walker (1993) and his conceptualization of inside/outside, inside meaning safety and security, and outside as insecurity; or of Campbell (1992: 8), who explains it with application to the demonization of the USSR as a means to secure US identity; in *Writing Security*: "The constitution of identity is achieved through the inscription of boundaries that serve to demarcate an 'inside' from an 'outside', a 'self' from an 'other', a 'domestic' from a 'foreign'." A further important point to be brought in is the question of whether identities are in flux or stable. In securitization theory, McSweeney (1996) critiqued the concept of national identity as static. Buzan and Wæver (1997: 246) replied by arguing that "once mobilized, identities have to be reckoned with as something people perceive that they belong to, and act upon as objective, given."

In the context of counterterrorism, scholars have pointed out practices of (securitization and) exclusion of migrants and asylum seekers (Cetti 2010; Huysmans 2006), the identification of the terrorist as the Other *par excellence*, the definition of terrorism as "the product of an 'other' culture," apparent through "the extensive use of discursive collocations such as 'global,' 'international' and 'Islamist terrorism'" (Ortega Breton 2010: 80), and also the "climate of fear" induced by representations of terrorism (ibid.: 82). A well documented theme has been the use of binaries, in particular that of civilization vs barbarism:

> [A]t the core, we still hold on to the perspectival dichotomy between *their* "barbarism" and *our* "civilization," while believing that they are

prone to mad, murderous inhumanity in ways that we don't recognize in ourselves – despite, of course, the historical evidence. Such blindness begins by tabooing their voices and desires, by categorizing their madness, suicides, and killings as qualitatively distinct from ours – in short, by denying "them" a complex subjectivity like ours. [Original emphasis]

(Zulaika 2009: 19)

Of course, simply claiming processes of Othering or pointing out binaries does not lead research very far. What Said meant by introducing this term was to acknowledge certain "knowledge" as being highly artificial, instead of viewing it as being in a fixed, natural state. Beyond that, analysis needs to come up with more intricate and detailed insight into the motivations, intentions and implications of a specific Othering. Othering cannot and should not be regarded as a sufficiently self-explanatory analytical gain; it has to be furthered by the explanation behind the processes or patterns of Othering that can be found at the surface.

Othering and its sub-themes are dully considered by all contributions to this book, from identity formation through difference up to dehumanization and effects in policy-making. Holland engages in an extensive discussion of the identity concept, including the point of state identity as being formed in relation to an "Other." Mullin outlines the identity function of the discourse on a securitized political Islam, which performs a similar function as the violent and irrational Oriental, Arab or Muslim Other in colonial-era discourses. Winkler problematizes the issue of *denial* of identity where terrorists are an amorphous mass and targeted states are themselves terrorist, totalitarian, torturous, and exiled members of the international community. In a similar account of denial of identity, Tsoukala discusses the institutional representation of the guerilla movement as ideologically incoherent, subaltern to previous generations of armed groups and as criminal neo-terrorists. Harindranath diagnoses the *destabilization* of national identity as multi-ethnic, multi-lingual and multi-religious entity, as a result of performative political and media discourses that bring forward religious and structural cleavages.

The theme of "binaries" permeates the book and is historically documented by Mullin, from definitions of the Other in terms of religion, to the binaries of modern-antimodern (democratic, modern and secular states as opposed to rogue and anti-modern states), good/bad Muslim and now good/bad Islamist. Ditrych emphasizes two basic binaries: civilization/barbarism and order/chaos and shows their historical origins as well as their interlinkages with the tropes of "safe-haven" and illness metaphors. Some more nuanced discussions of the binaries theme are present in Holland's chapter, which argues that the construction of the enemy in the Coalition of the Willing has not been simply as binary opposition, but in direct connection to the self-understandings of individual states. Taking this theme further, Wills and Steuter show the critical role of metaphors therein and emphasize the necessity of including *race* in the discussion of the metanarratives of identity and difference, as well as the consequences of binaries – aggressive policies against certain groups. The theme of the dehumanization of the enemy Other is present in Holland's and Ditrych's chapters and is plastically illustrated by Wills and Steuter with regard to the hunt metaphor.

Directly associated with the binaries theme is the one of terrorist motivation. The contributors to this volume show how the Other's motivations are either not addressed at all (Pisoiu and Prucha; Reinke de Buitrago); or *depoliticized* based on their transgression of conventional limits of violence (Ditrych); or how individuals and groups are *assigned* particular and *singular* ideological motivations that can then "justify" repressive measures (Ditrych; Tsoukala; Winkler). Several chapters testify to the subsequent and de facto *exclusion* of the Other from "civilization" and from the rights associated with this membership (Winkler), exclusion from participation in the democratic process (Harindranath; Tsoukala) and from the political system more broadly (Mullin). And they also show the consequences of self-other identity politics: assimilation, removal or extermination (Winkler) and relegation to a state of exception (Mullin and Harindranath). The important theme of hegemonic knowledge is strongly present in three of the chapters (Ditrych; Mullin; Wills and Steuter), as is the normative call for resistance, opening up space for alternative articulations to dominant narratives (Mullin) and for rehumanizing delegitimized groups (Wills and Steuter).

The discussion of general themes would not be complete without the Foucault factor, and this creates a nice bridge towards the discussion of methods. Said himself was inspired by Foucault's notion of discourse. As Burney (2012: 27) finds,

> the hegemonic and stereotypical representation of the Orient by expert Orientalists [–] functions like a discourse that is sedimented and entrenched in written and oral texts. Foucault's theories of discourse and his view that representations and discursive formations are influenced by systems of power is a central argument in *Orientalism*.

We have here already the epistemological, normative and ontological dimensions that help us lead the discussion further towards what discourse is, and what discourse analysis can tell us about relationships of power and emancipation, and, again, the self-other identity. Discourse analysis starts with Foucault. Discourse here is "a regulated set of statements which combine with others in predictable ways" (Mills 2004b: 54), and "should be seen as a system which structures the way that we perceive reality" (ibid.: 55). Discourse analysis "in contrast to formal linguistics, is concerned with applying the notion of structure above the level of the sentence, i.e. taking the analogy of grammatical relations such as subject–verb–object, and applying it to the analysis of longer text." (Mills 2004a: 119–20)

Stump and Dixit (2012) classify discourse analysis in the particular case of terrorism studies into "critical" and "poststructural or Foucauldian." The former, they argue, is concerned with a "normative commitment to emancipation" by uncovering relationships of power, and they find that "The majority of terrorism scholars who use discourse analysis have followed this tradition, under the umbrella of 'Critical Terrorism Studies'" (ibid.: 109). The latter is "not to reveal the ideological underpinnings or to call for emancipation but to illustrate how self–other identities are produced and legitimated within particular discourses," the main representatives of this being the Copenhagen school and Lene Hansen (ibid.: 110). To be fair, the "non-Foucauldians" also start off with Foucault, and yet add a political/normative dimension and a method of analysis. In the words of Mills (2004a: 131), critical discourse analysts, especially Norman Fariclough, have developed a "political analysis of text" and "have integrated Michel Foucault's definition of discourse with a systematic framework of analysis based on a linguistic analysis of the text." Fairclough (1992) himself lists the two elements he took over from Foucault:

> 1. The constitutive nature of discourse – discourse constitutes the social, including "objects" and social subjects; 2. The primacy of interdiscursivity and intertextuality – any discursive practice is defined by its relations with others, and draws upon others in complex ways.
> (Ibid.: 55)

He further explicates the "critical" difference in that considered are not only "discursive structures, but also how discourse is shaped by relations of power and ideologies, and the constructive effects discourse has upon social identities, social relations and systems of knowledge and belief, neither of which is normally apparent to discourse participants" (ibid.: 12).

Similar assumptions and levels of analysis can be seen in the, by now, classical account of critical discourse analysis (CDA) in terrorism studies by Richard Jackson (2005, 2009). He argues that discourse analysis is based, among other things, on the assumption that discourse is "structures of signification which construct social and political realities," productive of subjects and "common sense within particular social groups and historical settings," that are "historically and culturally contingent, intertextual, open-ended, requiring continuous articulation and re-articulation and, therefore, open to destabilization and counter-hegemonic struggle" (2009: 68). This emancipatory commitment to freeing up space for dialogue (McDonald 2009) and the struggle against hegemonic knowledge through deconstruction and counter-narratives are also shared by postcolonial analysis.

Coming back to CDA as a method of analysis, Jackson (2009: 68) outlines the technique in the following way: at the first phase, an examination of "core labels, assumptions, narratives, and discursive formations"; at the second phase, a first-order critique of the discourse "in its own terms," exposing "internal contradictions, mistakes, misconceptions, and omissions," in order to show the "inherently contested and hence political nature of the discourse"; and a second-order critique "reflecting on the broader political and ethical consequences – the wider ideological and historical-material effects – of the representations in the texts."

Poststructuralist discourse analysis is a "process of fixing the meaning of language within particular contexts in an empirical exercise that (a) determines how language constitutes identities and interests; and (b) makes us continuously aware that the 'fixing' and the 'stability' of the language examined is temporary and often an analytical convenience" (Stump and Dixit 2012: 110). The main representatives here are the Copenhagen securitization school and the Paris school – the latter focusing on security practices. Clearly, this separation is a matter of convenience and focus, since, as shown above, both draw on similar assumptions. Further, like the CDA, the poststructuralists also share areas of concern with the postcolonialists, with regard to, for instance the preoccupation with self-other (Copenhagen) or the notion of exclusion (Paris).

Dwelling a bit longer on the securitization school, a series of other roots and points of contact are worth mentioning, since they are also directly relevant to the contributions here in terms of analytical concepts. Coming back to the Wæver (1995: 55) citation:

> With the help of language theory, we can regard "security" as a *speech act*. In this usage, security is not of interest as a sign that refers to something more real; the utterance *itself* is the act. By saying it, something is done (as in betting, giving a promise, naming a ship). By uttering "security," a state-representative moves a particular development into a specific area, and thereby claims a special right to use whatever means are necessary to block it. [Original emphasis]

Security as speech act draws on Austin's (1962) Speech Act Theory, concerning the equivalence of utterances to actions, of utterances to performances. A further parallel is with Butler's notion of performativity. Judith Butler argues in *Gender Trouble* (1990: 25) that "gender is always a doing, though not a doing by a subject who might be said to preexist the deed. [...]. There is no gender identity behind the expressions of gender; that identity is performatively constituted by the very 'expressions' that are said to be its results." Butler herself also draws on Austin's notion of performative utterances or illocutionary acts (*Bodies that Matter* 1993, Austin 1962).

Most of the contributions to this book use discourse analysis as their overall method, with the exception of Reinke de Buitrago, who employs qualitative content analysis, and Campana, van der Veen, and Pisoiu and Prucha, who resort to frame analysis. "Framing" and "frames" are clearly present in all contributions, and are common encounters in the broader literature. Frame analysis as *method*, in itself multifaceted and somewhat differently developed in media studies and political science, is still relatively rare in counterterrorism scholarship. Van der Veen uses frame analysis as developed in political psychology, and differentiates between the cognitive and the strategic dimensions of framing: "frames in thought" and "frames in communication." Frame analysis as developed in the social movement literature can be found in the other two chapters, whereby Campana adds the analytical concepts of "discursive field" and "rules of the game."

Both aforementioned types of discourse analysis have been put to use in the chapters that follow. Holland's chapter is a combination of both. Mullin and Ditrych explicitly use the Foucauldian discourse analysis, the archeological method, with emphasis on intertextuality and policy implications. In some cases we can additionally find specific accents and further developments, as well as cross-fertilization with other methods. Harindranath adds the feminist concept of "performativity" as developed by Judith Butler. Wills and Steuter combine critical discourse analysis with metaphor studies and critical metaphor analysis; here remarkable is also the rare step of evidencing the *effects* of discursive construction – concretely, the adoption of the hunter metaphor by soldiers. An important methodological point is made by Tsoukala, who includes a useful discussion of the limits of discourse analysis imposed by subjectivity, exclusion through temporal delimitation and the choice of the methodological approach.

Finally, we are not going to define terrorism here. As Staun (2010: 403) notes,

> terrorism is a concept, the content of which is dependent on the very definitions made by governments, judicial systems, public debates and to a certain extent, academics. And these definitions differ over time and from country to country ... the concept of terrorism all over the world has a certain initial understanding, but the precise meaning of the term fluctuates enormously over time, country to country and political actor to political actor. Therefore, there is essentially a dead end in researchers searching for the perfect and all-inclusive definition of the content of terrorism.

This is not to say that the definitions of terrorism and counterterrorism are irrelevant. It is to say that, rather than imposing a certain definition here, at the outset of the book, it shall be more rewarding to discover in the various chapters precisely how the understanding of terrorism is "crafted" in each case.

Coda

Thus far we have outlined some theoretical, conceptual and methodological reference points and only brushed at the surface of the individual contributions in this volume, leaving it to the reader to discover the richness of each. This book is an attempt to reach further depth in counterterrorism argumentation analysis, but also broaden the perspectives from which this subject matter can be studied, including by offering a multidisciplinary perspective: political science (government, international relations, comparative politics), criminology, sociology, humanities, communication and media studies. We are tracing rhetorical and cultural continuity, the processes and interest dynamics among the various players involved, the cultural and linguistic toolkit, and we show the implications for policy areas concomitant with and beyond the "war on terror." We invite the reader to let him/herself be guided through each chapter of this book (and its intention), *with the multidimensional perspective in mind*, as it has been unfolded here. We do not abandon the realm of text: we just broaden the perspective using an integrated view to prevent analysis from becoming essentialism, from becoming myth.

And beyond the scholarly effort invested in these chapters, this book draws its soul from an additional source: the individual passions that moved each of us to address things that matter and to make a difference. First and foremost, this book, to paraphrase one of the authors, is a project of the heart.

A final note: we have purposefully not inscribed this book in a particular "tradition." The contributions of this book draw on a variety of traditions, theoretical, philosophical, methodological and, of course, ideological. We celebrate this diversity. We also wish to avoid placing this book in any of the theoretical or ideological camps. As the roadmap has helpfully showed, drawing lines between schools, theories and concepts is difficult, artificial and does not serve any particular purpose as it involves, again, identity through difference and exclusion. We do however gladly join the repeated appeals of the Critical Terrorism Studies scholars for more openness between schools of thought, more exchange and more tolerance.

Bibliography

Amossy, R. (2009) *Informal Logic*, 29(3), 252–67.

Appleby, N. (2010) "Labeling the innocent: how government counterterrorism advice creates labels that contribute to the problem," *Critical Studies on Terrorism*, 3(3), 421–36.

Austin, J.L. (1962) *How to Do Things with Words*, Oxford: Clarendon Press.

Baker, M. (2010) "Narratives of terrorism and security: 'accurate' translations, suspicious frames," *Critical Studies on Terrorism*, 3(3), 347–64.

Balzacq, T. (2005) "The three faces of securitization: political agency, audience and context," *European Journal of International Relations*, 11(2), 171–201.

Barrinha, A. (2011) "The political importance of labelling: terrorism and Turkey's discourse on the PKK," *Critical Studies on Terrorism*, 4(2), 163–80.
Barthes, R. (1964 [1957]) *Mythen des Alltags*, Frankfurt am Main: Suhrkamp.
Blakeley, R. (2010) "Liberal democracies and the globalisation of state terrorism in the 21st century," *Critical Studies on Terrorism*, 3(2), 169–72.
Burney, S. (2012) *Pedagogy of the Other. Edward Said, Postcolonial Theory, and Strategies for Critique*, New York: Peter Lang.
Butler, J. (1990) *Gender Trouble: Feminism and the Subversion of Identity*, London/New York: Routledge.
Butler, J. (1993) *Bodies that Matter. On the Discursive Limits of "Sex"*, New York/London: Routledge.
Buzan, B. and Wæver, O. (1997) "Slippery? Contradictory? Sociologically untenable? The Copenhagen School replies," *Review of International Studies*, 23: 241–50.
Campbell, D. (1992) *Writing Security: United States Foreign Policy and the Politics of Identity*, Manchester: Manchester University Press.
Cetti, F. (2010) "Asylum and the discourse of terror: the European 'Security State'," in B. Brescher and A. Winter (eds), *Discourses and Practices of Terrorism: Interrogating Terror*. Abigdon/New York: Routledge, 58–77.
Clarke, J. and Zalman, A. (2009) "The Global War on Terror: a narrative in need of a rewrite," *Ethics & International Affairs Journal*, 23(2), 101–13.
de Graaf, B. and de Graaff, B. (2010) "Bringing politics back in: the introduction of the 'performative power' of counterterrorism," *Critical Studies on Terrorism*, 3(2), 261–75.
Fabian, J. (1990) "Presence and representation: The Other and anthropological writing," *Critical Inquiry*, 16(4), 753–72.
Fairclough, N. (1992) *Discourse and Social Change*, London: Polity.
Halliday, F. (2010) *Shocked and Awed: How the War on Terror and Jihad have Changed the English Language*, London: I.B. Tauris & Co Ltd.
Hodges, A. and Nilep, C. (eds) (2007) *Discourse, War and Terrorism*, Amsterdam: John Benjamins Publishing Co.
Huysmans, J. (2006) *The Politics of Insecurity: Fear, Migration and Asylum in the EU*, Abingdon/New York: Routledge.
Jackson, R. (2005) *Writing the War on Terrorism: Language, Politics and Counter-Terrorism (New Approaches to Conflict Analysis)*, Manchester: Manchester University Press.
Jackson, R. (2006) "Security, democracy and the rhetoric of counter-terrorism," *Democracy and Security*, 1(2), 147–71.
Jackson, R. (2009) "Knowledge, power and politics in the study of political terrorism," in R. Jackson, M. Breen Smyth, and J. Gunning (eds) *Critical Terrorism Studies. A New Research Agenda*, London/New York: Routledge, 66–83.
Jackson, R. (2011) "Culture, identity and hegemony: Continuity and (the lack of) change in US counterterrorism policy from Bush to Obama," *International Politics*, 48(2), 390–411.
Jackson, R., Breen Smyth, M. and Gunning, J. (2009) *Critical Terrorism Studies. A New Research Agenda*, London/New York: Routledge, 216–36.
Jackson, R., Murphy, E. and Poynting, S. (eds) (2010) *Contemporary State Terrorism – Theory and Practice*, Abingdon: Routledge.
Jarvis, L. (2009) *Times of Terror: Discourse, Temporality and the War on Terror*, Basingstoke: Palgrave.

Krebs, R.R. and Jackson, P.T. (2007) "Twisting tongues and twisting arms: the power of political rhetoric," *European Journal of International Relations*, 13(1), 35–66.

Lewis, J. (2005) *Language Wars: the Role of Media and Culture in Global Terror and Political Violence*, London: Pluto Press.

McCrisken, T. (2011) "Ten years on: Obama's war on terrorism in rhetoric and practice," *International Affairs*, 87(4), 781–801.

McDonald, M. (2009) "Emancipation and critical terrorism studies," in R. Jackson, M. Breen Smyth, and J. Gunning (eds) *Critical Terrorism Studies. A New Research Agenda*, London/New York: Routledge, 109–23.

McSweeney, B. (1996) "Identity and security: Buzan and the Copenhagen School," *Review of International Studies*, 22, 81–94.

Mills, S. (2004a) *Discourse*, London/New York: Routledge.

Mills, S. (2004b) *Michel Foucault*, London/New York: Routledge.

Mullin, C. (2011) "The US discourse on political Islam: is Obama's a truly *post-*'war on terror' administration?" *Critical Studies on Terrorism*, 4(2), 263–81.

Ortega Breton, H. (2010) "Feeling persecuted? The definitive role of paranoid anxiety in the constitution of 'war on terror' television," in B. Brescher and A. Winter (eds), *Discourses and Practices of Terrorism: Interrogating Terror*. Abigdon/New York: Routledge, 78–96.

Peoples, C. and Vaughan-Williams, N. (2010) *Critical Security Studies. An introduction*, London/New York: Routledge.

Rykkja, L.H., Lægreid, Per and Fimreite, A.L. (2011) "Attitudes towards anti-terror measures: the role of trust, political orientation and civil liberties support," *Critical Studies on Terrorism*, 4(2), 219–37.

Said, E. (1978) *Orientalism: Western Representations of the Orient*, London: Routledge.

Staun, J. (2010) "When, how and why elites frame terrorists: a Wittgensteinian analysis of terror and radicalisation," *Critical Studies on Terrorism*, 3(3), 403–20.

Stephens, A.C. and Vaughan-Williams, N. (eds) (2009) *Terrorism and the Politics of Response: London in a Time of Terror*, Abingdon: Routledge.

Stump, J.L. and Dixit, P. (2012) *Critical Terrorism Studies. An Introduction to Research Methods*, London/New York: Routledge.

Talbot, S. (2008) "'Us' and 'Them': Terrorism, conflict and (O)ther discursive formations," *Sociological Research Online*, 13(1). Available at www.socresonline.org.uk/13/1/17.html (accessed June 29, 2013).

Toros, H. and Gunning, J. (2009) "Exploring a critical theory approach to terrorism studies," in R. Jackson, M. Breen Smyth and J. Gunning (eds) *Critical Terrorism Studies. A New Research Agenda*, London/New York: Routledge, 87–108.

Wæver, O. (1995) "Securitization and Desecuritization," in R.D. Lipschutz (ed.) *On Security*, New York: Columbia University Press, 46–86.

Walker, R.B.J. (1993) *Inside/Outside: International Relations as Political Theory*, Cambridge: Cambridge University Press.

Wendt, Alexander (1999) *Social Theory of International Politics*, Cambridge University Press: Cambridge.

Zulaika, J. (2009) *Terrorism: the Self-fulfilling Prophecy*, Chicago, IL: University of Chicago Press.

Part I
Roots and cultures

1 The rhetorical origins of the US war on terror

Carol K. Winkler

Members of the George W. Bush administration justified the US war on terror on the grounds that their country was facing "a new type of enemy" that warranted a new response (e.g., Bush 2001g: 3). In accordance with such thinking, President Bush oversaw many changes, including the largest government reorganization in the past fifty years, expanded law enforcement powers to spy on citizens both at home and abroad, the creation of military tribunals to adjudicate the fates of suspected terrorists, and the authorization of the CIA to conduct harsh interrogation methods for prisoners that today many consider to constitute torture. However, as executive branch officials sought to build both initial and continuing public support for new powers to respond to the new threat, they turned to the past.

The administration utilized historical rhetorical frames to help justify the war on terror. The analogs offered a set of rhetorical resources that, at least during past threatening situations, had proven useful for unifying public support for the actions of the US commander-in-chief. Today, a healthy debate exists regarding both the conditions and the duration of presidential rhetoric's influence on the public (see, for example, Campbell and Jamieson 2008; Edwards 2003; Krebs and Jackson 2007). At a minimum, rigorous studies document that the public communication strategies of the executive branch do drive media framing of issues during times of crisis that, in turn, influence public opinion (Bennett *et al.* 2007). Historical analogs provide a lens for understanding the contours of the administration's public strategy in the US war on terror, as well as a means of assessing the possible short- and long-term implications of relying on those approaches. By examining the rhetorical origins of the Bush administration's war on terror, this chapter hopes to provide a starting framework for understanding the public strategies of enemy construction and response formulation of US terrorism discourse in the twenty-first century.

A few previous studies have addressed historical analogs in relationship to the US war on terror. Mueller (2006) compares Pearl Harbor, the Cold War, nuclear anxieties, and the New World Order to the war on terror in regard to US policies and contextual factors without systematically focusing on the rhetorical justifications for garnering public support. Hodges (2011) conducts a limited analysis of Vietnam, exploring how the Bush administration used that analog to appropriate "containment of an ideological threat" as a rhetorical resource for the war on terror. Jackson (2005) offers the most evocative, systemic analysis of historical analogs by focusing on four recurrent meta-narratives identifiable through his content analysis of the administration's speeches: Pearl Harbor, the Cold War, Civilization vs Barbarism, and Globalization. By integrating several of my previous writings that discuss specific analogs in the war on terror (see Winkler 2002, 2006, 2007, 2008), this study will add to the previous literature by expanding the historical analogs reviewed and their implications, by contextualizing those findings with related archival material from earlier administrations, and by using the analogs to reveal strategic discourse frames in the war on terror.

This chapter will identify rhetorical framing strategies Bush administration officials employed to describe the enemy and the appropriate US response in the war on terror. After initially describing recurrent rhetorical strategies prominent within the enemy and response categories, I will document the approaches used by administration officials in the present day (2013), recall historical uses of the same strategic frame, and draw out implications based on comparable outcomes associated with the strategic choice. This chapter will demonstrate that the rhetoric justifying the war on terror adopted strategic approaches used by leaders in the early republic (i.e., America's indigenous populations, the Barbary pirates, and the French Revolution), by leaders facing ideologically based threats in the twentieth century (i.e., communism and fascism), and by contemporary Republican presidents responding to terrorism (i.e., Richard Nixon, Ronald Reagan, and George H.W. Bush). The decision to focus on this last set of analogs relates to the tendency of Republican presidents to rely on the founding fathers to bolster their conservative points of view and prior research demonstrating that Republican presidents focus on ideologically focused war narratives, rather than individual centric crime narratives in their public discussions of terrorism (Winkler 2006: 200–8).

Depicting the enemy

The contemporary war on terror strived to defeat global terrorism perpetrated by errant individuals (e.g., Osama bin Laden, Richard Reid), extremist groups (e.g., al-Qaeda and associated movements), and "supportive regimes" (e.g., Iraq, the Taliban). Administration officials publicly vilified such individuals, groups, and states to justify to the public that each threat was an appropriate target in the war on terrorism. Two overarching strategic frames dominated the public framing of these enemies: the erasure of individual identity and the erasure of national identity. The two rhetorical frames together positioned the complicated nature of terrorist threat to be unworthy of due process rights commonly afforded individual citizens and to be denied rights of sovereignty commonly afforded internationally recognized nation-states.

Erasing individual identity

Administration spokespersons publicly framed terrorists and those supportive of their cause as undeserving of the rights granted to members of a civilized society. A key rhetorical strategy used to accomplish that objective was to erase such individuals from the public arena by denying them any recognizable personal identity. As the following will demonstrate, the rhetorical approach involved three strategies: stripping rank-and-file terrorists and their supporters of demographic and other indicators of personal uniqueness; focusing on group rather than individual motivations; and emphasizing group-based tactics without public consideration of the actions of specific individuals.

Each of these three strategies was prominent in the rhetoric of the Bush administration after the 9/11 attacks. Official spokespersons denied terrorists and their supporters individual identity by referencing a "global terror network," which encompassed an amorphous mass of mostly nameless participants worldwide (e.g., Cheney 2002). When discussing rank-and-file members of terrorist organizations, Bush rhetorically stripped individuals considered a threat of any identifying characteristics. Treating the terrorists as an amalgamated, nebulous group, Bush (2001a) noted:

> This group and its leader – a person named Osama bin Laden – are linked to many other organizations in different countries, including the Egyptian Islamic Jihad and the Islamic Movement of Uzbekistan. There are thousands of these terrorists in more than 60 countries. They are recruited from their own nations and neighborhoods and brought to camps in places like Afghanistan, where they are trained in the tactics of terror. They are sent back to their homes or sent to hide in countries around the world to plot evil and destruction.

Few names of individuals outside of key leadership positions of relevant terrorist organizations became public. John Walker Lindh, Richard Reid, and names of the nineteen 9/11 hijackers remain isolated exceptions. Even after military and law enforcement officials captured specific individuals suspected of or supporting terrorism, US leaders chose not to release their names or even their countries of origin for years. When released DOD (Department of Defense) photographs showed the detainees at Guantánamo Bay, masks covered identifiable facial features of the specific individuals held in captivity.

Beyond the removal of identifying names or recognizable demographic characteristics, the strategic frame presented all terrorists and their sympathizers as motivated by a single overarching principle. Bush (2001f) was adamant that terrorists "have a common ideology, and that is, they hate freedom and they hate freedom loving people." Official spokespersons specified the terrorists' opposition to free elections, freedom of religion, freedom of speech, and freedom of assembly. By limiting the motivations of terrorists in this way, the nation's leaders presented the war on terror as a cultural conflict between those who were fighting for and against freedom.

Not only did defenders of the war on terror present all terrorists' motivations as the same, but they also reinforced a common set of tactics used by the enemy as well. Bush (2003d) observed that, "terrorists rely on the death of innocent people to create the condition of fear that, therefore, will cause people to lose their will." US officials denounced the methods of the terrorist enemy as "barbaric," "evil," "brutal," "torturous," and "homicidal." Terrorists, rendered nameless and committed to destroying freedom through vile, destructive means, emerged as ill suited for the rights and liberties enjoyed by individuals in civilized societies.

The historical roots of the strategy of erasing individual identity markers of the rank-and-file members of the enemy date back to the days of the United States as an early republic. Portraying the nation's enemies as part of homogenized groups began shortly after the colonists faced indigenous populations upon their arrival in America (Stuckey and Murphy 2001). The final draft of the US Declaration of Independence (1776) demonstrates the approach of treating the enemy as a singular collective when the nation's founders wrote, "the merciless Indian Savages whose known rule of warfare is an undistinguished destruction of all ages, sexes, and condition." Such an enemy frame came without nuance for peaceful tribes or individual Indians refusing to participate in acts of violence to defend their lands; instead, all tribal members emerged as part and parcel of a violent collective undeserving of the rights afforded to citizens in the early republic.

The rhetorical strategy of grouping all non-state terrorists' motivations into a desire for destroying freedom anywhere around the globe, however, did not emerge until Ronald Reagan's tenure as president. Prior to Reagan's term in office, US presidents tried to ignore public discussion of terrorists' motivations altogether, a move even repeated at times during Reagan's own tenure. Historically, presidents routinely adopted various iterations of the public mantra that "nothing could justify acts of terrorism" (e.g., Reagan 1988a: 1231), in an effort to avoid discussions of potential US culpability. When presidents failed to stem further public inquiry into the cause of a particular terrorist act, they shifted to a strategy of minimizing and isolating non-state extremists and their concerns by publicly limiting their depictions to local concerns. Examples include Jimmy Carter's response to inquiries about his decision to admit the Shah into the United States as a precipitating event of the 1979–80 Iranian hostage crisis, as well as Lyndon Johnson's focus on the location of US ships in the 1968 *Pueblo* crisis.

During Reagan's first term in office, however, the conventional practice of portraying terrorists' motivations changed. When first elected to office, Reagan officials publicly framed terrorist acts, particularly those occurring in Central America and Lebanon, as ideological attacks consistent with the parameters of the US Cold War narrative (Winkler 2006: 80–2). The Cold War narrative set the scene in new nations around the globe struggling in the aftermath of World War II to fulfill their promise of self-determination and enhanced freedom. Communists, acting together with terrorists in the narrative, attempted to forestall progress toward freedom, thus necessitating US intervention (Medhurst *et al.* 1990: 22–8). By Reagan's second term, the Cold War narrative's connection to events on the ground became attenuated because high-profile terrorist attacks were occurring, not against fledging democracies, but against US and European personnel (for example, the 1983 attacks on the Marine barracks and US Embassy in Beirut, multiple attacks by Carlos the Jackal in France in the 1980s, and so on). Internal administration polling at the time also showed that a majority of Americans had come to disapprove of Reagan's handling of terrorism. In response, Reagan shifted from portraying the terrorists' motivations as support for communism to opposition to freedom around the globe. Reagan illustrated his revised homogenization approach when he noted,

> ... [W]e must understand that the greatest hope the terrorists and their supporters harbor, the very reason for their cruelty and viciousness of their tactics, is to disorient the American people, to cause disunity, to disrupt or alter our foreign policy, to keep us from the steady pursuit of our strategic interests, to distract us from our very real hope that someday the nightmare of totalitarian rule will end and self-government and personal freedom will become the birthright of every people on Earth.
>
> (Reagan 1985: 899)

The rhetorical shift from the Cold War narrative to a broader attack on freedom eased public skepticism about the linkage between all terrorism and communism.

The rhetorical focus on the barbaric tactics of the enemy in the contemporary war on terror traces back to the nation's early encounters with America's Indian populations. As Robert Ivie notes, "Images of savagery have permeated the rhetoric of war throughout the nation's history, either explicitly or implicitly" (1980: 283). Early Presidents Thomas Jefferson and John Adams considered America's Indian populations as falling low on the savage-to-civilization continuum, rendering members of the tribes unprepared for the responsibilities of citizenship (see Drinnon 1990;

Wallace 1999). Historical anthropologist Anthony Wallace (1999) maintains that the earlier roots of the evolutionary continuum of civilized societies were present in both earlier Scottish and Enlightenment philosophies.

The historical analogs of the new republic and the Reagan administration provide insights into the implications of the emergence of the individual erasure framing strategy. By not adhering to the white male society's norms of civilized behavior, America's indigenous populations lost entitlement to individual rights and liberties afforded the nation's citizens. Mary Stuckey's national award-winning *Defining Americans: The Presidency and National Identity* concludes that the resulting descent by American Indians "into invisibility offered a lesson in citizenship to other Americans and a warning about where history might lead a nation inattentive to those lessons" (Stuckey 2004: 58–9). Stripped of the protections afforded to American citizens, American Indians rhetorically emerged as sub-standard humans deserving of less than a civilized response including up to 30-year-long confinements, trials by non-peer juries, refusals of extradition across state lines, and so on (for more, see Winkler 2002).

A second important implication of individual erasure strategy involves the expansive latitude provided to both the United States and its partners regarding who qualified as an effective target in the war on terror. By presenting the entire collective of global terrorists as conspiring against US interests, the public justification for broad intervention parameters was in place. Just as the leaders of the new republic moved against indigenous populations throughout the original colonies and the Reagan administration deployed military personnel into Lebanon, Grenada, Nicaragua, and El Salvador in pursuit of terrorists, contemporary war on terror leaders justified the expansion of territories appropriate for their assertion of power into Afghanistan, Iraq, and beyond.

Erasing national identity

The scope of the enemy in the war on terror extended beyond individual terrorist and extremist groups. The Bush administration also targeted governments of foreign nation states in its campaign against terror. Rumsfeld outlined the strategy of overthrowing targeted foreign regimes in a memo to Bush as early as September 30, 2001:

> If the war does not significantly change the world's political map, the US will not achieve its aim/There is value in being clear on the order of magnitude of the necessary change. The USG [US Government] should envision a goal along these lines: New regimes in Afghanistan and another key State (or two) that supports terrorism (To strengthen political and military efforts to change policies elsewhere)
> (Office of Secretary of Defense 2001).

To justify the exercise of commander-in-chief powers against foreign governments, officials in the war on terror adopted two strategic approaches for vilifying foreign heads of state: framing regimes as terrorist states and framing them as exiled members of the international community.

Terrorist states

Administration spokespersons moved quickly after the 9/11 attacks to portray regimes harboring terrorists as undeserving of their right to govern. One rhetorical frame used to accomplish that objective was to recast the foreign governments as operating terrorist states, that is, entities that routinely instilled fear into their own internal populations. As will be demonstrated below, the rhetorical approach relied upon two recurrent lines of argument: selected totalitarian regimes were unacceptably oppressive, and their acts of repression targeted the most vulnerable citizens of their nation-states.

To establish that enemy regimes in the war on terror were unacceptably oppressive, US officials portrayed targeted governments as totalitarian rulers with little concern for the liberty, justice, or the social welfare of their citizenries. Rumsfeld (2001d) catalogued numerous instances of Taliban oppression:

> Men are routinely jailed for the most trivial offenses: too short a beard, possession of a television. Religion can be practiced only as Taliban dictate. They have their Ministry of Vice and Virtue, which enforces their rules.... They traffic in opium, worsening the conditions of Muslims throughout the world. At a time when millions of Afghans are starving, in search of food and water, they have disrupted the distribution of international aid, seized warehouses of food intended for the poor, and created catastrophic starvation.

Bush (2003b) provided chilling examples of Saddam Hussein's oppressive assaults on the Iraqi people, including torture, brutality, and the Iraqi leader's practise of cutting out the tongues of those who dissented against his regime's practices.

Beyond depicting the targets in the war on terror as totalitarian regimes, the rhetoric approach also focused on the impact of those terrorist states on the most vulnerable societal members. Administration officials particularly stressed the regimes' tyrannical practices with regard to women and children. Bush (2001e) described the actions of the Taliban, by noting, "Women are executed in Kabul's soccer stadium. They can be beaten for wearing socks that are too thin." He also reminded his audiences that under Taliban rule, "Women are not allowed to attend school" (Bush 2001a). Laura Bush (2001) added offenses against children when she announced, "a world-wide effort to focus on the brutality against women and children by the al Qaeda terrorist network and the regime it supports in Afghanistan, the Taliban." The Bush administration echoed the approach when focusing on the regime of Saddam Hussein. Bush (2002b) catalogued a list of offenses carried out in Iraq: "opponents have been decapitated, wives and mothers of political opponents have been systematically raped as a method of intimidation, and political prisoners have been forced to watch their own children being tortured."

The historical roots of the terrorist state frame date back to the days of the early republic. As the French and American revolutions happened during the same historical time period, comparative assessments between the two transformative efforts are frequent in US presidential discourse, particularly in relation to their contrasting conceptions of liberty, justice and social welfare. US leaders throughout the twentieth century have repeatedly compared the "reign of terror" in the French Revolution with the approach of the American Revolution to underscore themes of "liberty versus enslavement, justice versus injustice, and morality versus immorality" (Winkler 2008: 213). While Robespierre, a noted leader in the French Revolution, touted liberty, justice, and virtue as the divine underpinnings of the revolutionary effort (Tallett 1999), the new French regime, instead, passed laws and took other actions that qualified suspicion as sufficient cause for arrest and prosecution. They also orchestrated a coordinated campaign to undermine the Christian faith within French society (Cobb 1917; Gough 1998; Lucas 1996; Sirich 1971; Tallett 1999). From September 1793 to July 1794, revolutionary leaders in France arrested as many as 300,000 individuals and executed as many as 40,000 citizens perceived to be loyal to the Ancien Régime (Fromkin 1975).

The French revolution functioned as a relevant historical resource for the Bush administration seeking to expose the consequences of regimes uncommitted to liberty, law, or the general well being of their citizenries. Bush (2001e) explicitly used the strategy when he summarized the situation in Afghanistan. He announced, "[The Taliban] regime, and the terrorists who support it ... promote terror abroad and impose a *reign of terror* on the Afghan people" [emphasis added].

The second historical root of the terrorist state frame dates back to strategies utilized during the days of the United States as a new republic. The founding fathers focused on the tribal practices of American Indians as exemplars of those unfit for national governance due to their treatment of their own citizens. Thomas Jefferson focused on the tribe's violence against women and their routine assignment of arduous tasks to female members to illustrate the barbaric nature of America's indigenous populations (Maltz and Archambault 1995). The colonial leaders of the early republic depicted American tribal leaders as lacking the appropriate concern for society's most vulnerable members necessary to govern the broader populace; instead, the tribes' governing bodies became resources to be managed in the new government's pursuit of its own ends (Stuckey 2004).

While both the French Revolution and ongoing struggles with America's indigenous populations provided points of contrast to the founding principles of liberty and rule of law, the activities of Hitler and the Nazis, as well as Stalin and the Communists, served as more recent historical analogs for use in the contemporary war on terror. The Nazis' systematic campaign of exterminating six million Jews, as well as the sick and mentally ill, religious leaders, homosexuals, artists, political leaders, and intellectual leaders, encapsulated for American audiences the potential risks of permitting tyrannical leaders to remain in power (Abzug 1999; Bendersky 1985). Stalin and his communist party functioned as another analog where terrorist leaders meted out unacceptably high atrocities against their citizenries. Historian Roy Medvedev wrote in the Soviet paper *Argumenti i Fakti* that forty million suffered repression under Stalin, including those that were arrested, blacklisted, or moved off their land, while "about 20 million died in labor camps, forced collectivization, famine and executions" (Kellner 1989). Taken together, Hitler and Stalin demonstrated that the bleak future that awaited if totalitarian leaders were permitted to continue their reigns.

To emphasize the magnitude of oppression meted out by terrorist regimes, Bush officials drew explicit parallels between the Taliban and the former Nazi and Soviet totalitarian regimes (e.g. Rumsfeld 2001e). Bush likewise compared Saddam Hussein's leadership cadre to the earlier totalitarian regimes. In his 2002 State of the Union address, for example, Bush (2002a) named Iraq part of the "axis of evil," a reference that recalled the Axis powers from World War II. One year later in a speech delivered in the immediate lead up to the 2003 Iraq War, Bush (2003a) was more explicit: "the ambitions of Hitlerism, militarism, and communism" had returned, and the "ideology of power and domination" had now emerged in Iraq.

Parallels drawn with the French Revolution, American Indian tribal councils, Nazi Germany, and Soviet Communism helped characterize targeted foreign leaders in the contemporary war on terror as totalitarian regimes unworthy of democratic sovereign rights. By depicting the targeted leaders as having little to no concern or respect for their own populations, officials leading the war on terror rendered select heads of the foreign states as unqualified to govern. As in the outcome of each of the four historical analogs of terrorist states, the targeted foreign nation's citizens or the United States had to remove the offending regime from access to governmental control.

Exiled members of the international community

While the terrorist state strategy sought to disqualify selected foreign governments based on their failure to meet internal obligations, the rhetoric used to justify the war on terror simultaneously maintained that such regimes were ill suited to serve as heads of nation-states within the international community. Administration officials worked to exclude selected regimes from the community of nations through rhetorical frames that emphasized how they fell short of internationally accepted community standards of governance. The Bush team relied on two rhetorical approaches to make its case: denying rogue regimes' authentic standing as the leaders of targeted nation-states and holding regimes accountable for terrorist activities in their spheres of influence.

The first approach of withholding governing legitimacy from the targeted regimes surfaced in relation to Afghanistan. Administration officials depicted the Taliban as an occupying power in Afghanistan. US officials repeatedly referred to the regime as "foreign," as "invaders," and as "an illegitimate, unelected group of terrorists" (e.g., Rumsfeld 2001b, 2001d, 2001h). Administration officials publicly degraded the standing of the Taliban regime further by pointing out that it did not control the entirety of Afghanistan. Rumsfeld promised that America would "help the people of [Afghanistan] get rid of the foreign invaders who have come in and taken over a major chunk of your country." A recurrent rationale offered for denying leadership status to the Taliban and its internal terrorist allies was the regime's unstable presence in the nation-state. Bush (2001d) revealed the problem when he noted, "We're adjusting our thinking to the new kind of enemy. These are terrorists that have no borders." Colin Powell (2001a) reinforced the view by noting, "terrorism does not have a geography." Because the Taliban and its internal terrorist allies had no reliable, stable presence in the nation, they could secede from Afghanistan at any moment rendering them illegitimate rulers of the state.

The second strategy of holding nation-states accountable for terrorist groups operating within their spheres of influence also arose in both Afghanistan and Iraq. The Bush team opted to conflate rogue regimes with the terrorists operating within their national territories. In the early days after the 9/11 attacks, Bush rejected a draft of his first address to the nation announcing the war on terror as too vague because it specified that the US would not distinguish between actual terrorists and those who tolerated and encouraged terrorism. While Bush found the terms "tolerated" and "encouraged" too broad, he did, in the final draft, vow that the United States would also pursue foreign states that harbored terrorists (as reported in Woodward 2002: 30). Establishing the clear linkage, Bush (2001b) publicly maintained, "We will make no distinction between the terrorists who committed these acts and those who harbor them." Vice President Dick Cheney also expressed support for the strategy during the administration's internal meetings because he considered it easier to find states than it was to find terrorists such as bin Laden (as reported in Woodward 2002).

Once US officials opted to link targeted states with the terrorists they supported, they maintained that those nation's heads of state should lose their right to govern if they failed to properly police their spheres of influence. Defense Secretary Donald Rumsfeld (2001a) explicitly described the US decision to remove those in power in Afghanistan when he stated,

> [T]he only way that the Afghan people are to be successful in heaving the terrorist network out of their country is to be successful against ... that portion of Taliban and the Taliban leadership that are so closely linked to the al Qaeda. And certainly we are working with the elements on the ground that are interested in overthrowing and expelling that group of people.

Powell (2001b) was also blunt: "the Taliban government must now go, because they are part and parcel to al Qaeda." As the administration reiterated linkages between terrorists and the Taliban, official spokespersons were careful to avoid using terms such as "national leaders," "governing party," or other identifiers that would suggest official status to the Taliban as the ruling party of Afghanistan. During the same period, the Bush administration reinforced the message by bringing diplomatic pressure to bear on Saudi Arabia, the United Arab Emirates, and Pakistan to officially renounce their recognition of the Taliban as the Afghan government within the international community.

The Bush administration targeted the regime of Saddam Hussein using the same rhetorical strategy of holding nations accountable for their spheres of influence as it had utilized earlier with the Taliban. Bush (2003c) insisted, "Iraq is part of the war on terror. Iraq is a country that has got terrorist ties. It's a country with wealth. It's a country that trains terrorists, a country that could arm terrorists." Powell (2003) provided the evidence for the administration's claims by telling the United Nations that al-Qaeda associate Abu Musab Al-Zarqawi was basing his terrorist operations in Iraq. The 9/11 Commission questioned the administration's general claim of Iraq's association with al-Qaeda after it discovered Bush team's supporting documentation was based on the word of an Iraqi National Congress-supplied defector that could not be corroborated. It also found that the training camp served other operational functions in Iraq. The commission therefore concluded that there was no "collaborative operational relationship" between Saddam Hussein and al-Qaeda ('National Commission' 2004: 66). Nevertheless, having publicly rendered both the Taliban and the Iraqi government as harboring and supporting the global terrorist network, US officials publicly positioned them both for removal.

The rhetorical origins of the contemporary war on terror's approach to exiling rogue regimes from the international community traces back to the early days of the early republic. Government officials moved quickly to deny governing legitimacy to tribal leaders in the new nation. The founding fathers had concerns about the new union's ability to work with the tribe's governing councils based on their lack of a stable homeland. Frequent movements by Indian tribes and families produced fluid communities that potentially threatened the fragile new republic. Historian James Wilson described the common practices of the nation's indigenous populations through the experiences with the Alongquins, one tribe encountered on America's eastern coast:

> If you did not like where you were living, you could leave and join relatives somewhere else; whole communities might break away and form their own tribe, or attach themselves to another leader. By the same token, a successful "sachem" [leader in New England] or "werowance" [leader in Virginia] could extend his (or occasionally, her) influence by attracting or conquering a number of smaller groups and forging them into a larger alliance capable of concerted action.
> (Wilson 1998: 2)

The transitory lifestyle of the indigenous populations worried the founders of the new republic. They preferred an agrarian society, which had a more stable relationship with land plots (and thus communities) and was more productive for the nation's longevity than the less enduring practice of hunting performed by Native Americans (Onuf 2000).

The second international community exile strategy of holding targeted governing regimes accountable for supporting or harboring terrorists in their own midst dates back to lessons learned from the United States' experience with the Barbary pirates. From its first few years of existence, the United States faced sustained piracy campaigns from the Barbary States (which today comprise Morocco, Tunisia, Algeria, and Tripoli) who attacked and looted trading ships that entered the Mediterranean Sea (Lewis 2004). From 1776 to 1816, the Barbary pirates held more than 450 Americans hostage to leverage ransom payments from the US government (Irwin 1931). After studying the nation's experience with the Barbary pirates, members of the Reagan administration developed a theory of holding nations responsible for policing terrorism in their spheres of influence. Don Gregg and Doug Menarchik (1985), two of Reagan's National Security Assistants, concluded, "Just as the Barbary powers were held responsible for their piratical actions as well as they actions of independent pirates who exploited the permissive environment, the US could bring pressure to bear on state actors to 'police' their spheres of influence." Holding states responsible for the terrorist actors operating in their environments obviated strategies by foreign leaders to remain noncommittal or to passively resist US interests abroad.

A key institutional factor permitting the Reagan administration to rhetorically link certain foreign states with terrorist groups was the passage of the Export Administration Act of 1979. The US Congress, previously frustrated with Iran's seizure and long-term confinement of fifty-two American embassy personnel beginning on November 4, 1979, passed the act authorizing responses to linkage between foreign states and the terrorists they supported. The act empowered the Secretary of State to create a list of the state sponsors of terrorism who were immediately subject to export controls such as those related to arms, dual-use technologies, and high-cost defense contracts. Those placed on the state sponsor list legally had to have a pattern of supporting terrorism through "logistical aid, provision of weapons and/or training, granting of safe havens, use of diplomatic pouches and/or documentation, and – in some cases-actual targeting [*sic*] and/or provision of information about the selected target" (McFarlane 1984). While the administration retained wide latitude for selecting which nations would qualify as state sponsors of terrorism and for implementing the economic sanctions specified in the act (Dyke 1982), the Reagan administration capitalized on the concept of state sponsorship to create expanded approaches in the fight against terrorism (for example, "Terrorism II" n.d.). Administration officials during the contemporary war on terror built on the Reagan legacy further by making the objective of removing leaders of foreign states an overt activity justified in public to audiences both at home and abroad.

In short, the rhetorical strategy of international exile in the war on terror functioned to justify a change in the standing of ruling regimes of targeted foreign states. The Bush administration rhetorically denied government legitimacy to regimes associated with terrorists by depicting them as part of a group of errant, mobile individuals who threatened the stability and well being of the nations' citizens. The analogs of the Indian tribes and the Barbary pirates reinforced the characterization and foretold the costly outcome of an insufficient response. Depicted as unfit to either rule their own citizens or meet their obligations to the international community, the targeted regimes would and should, from the perspective of US leaders, lose their governing powers in short order.

US response

Having rendered the enemy in the war on terror unworthy of either fundamental individual liberties or the rights of national sovereignty through an orchestrated public communication strategy, US leaders were publicly positioned to exercise wide latitude in their choice of appropriate response strategies. As the following will illustrate, the eventual response strategies that served as roadmap in the war on terror fell into three broad categories: assimilation, removal, and extinction.

Assimilation

Assimilation as a public response option in the war on terror involved three concurrent steps: an offer with specified conditions for a chance to reintegrate into the international community of nations, a refusal to negotiate over those conditions, and a specified short time frame for compliance. Shortly after the 9/11 attacks, Secretary of State Colin Powell (2001a) provided an opening for assimilation to nations previously supportive of terrorists, when he stated, "Perhaps these states [which sponsor terrorism] ... will now come to their senses that it is not in their interest, now that the entire international community is mobilized ... and they'll start to change past patterns of behavior." Bush (2001a) echoed the choice available to all nations, when he explained, "Either you are with us, or you are with the terrorists."

Official spokespersons in the war on terror provided specific sets of public conditions that had to be met if foreign heads of state wished to retain their leadership positions. In a speech delivered to the US Congress, for example, Bush (2001a) issued the following demands of the Taliban if they were going to continue to govern in Afghanistan:

> Deliver to United States authorities all the leaders of al Qaeda who hide in your land. Release all foreign nationals, including American citizens, you have unjustly imprisoned. Protect foreign journalists, diplomats, and aid workers in your country. Close immediately and permanently every terrorist training camp in Afghanistan, and hand over every terrorist, and every person in their support structure, to appropriate authorities. Give the United States full access to terrorist training camps, so we can make sure they are no longer operating.

In the case of Iraqi regime, Bush (2002c) demanded Saddam Hussein disclose and destroy all weapons of mass destruction, end support for terrorism, end persecution of its internal populations, resolve accounts related to lingering personnel issues from the 1990–1 Persian Gulf War, and cease trade outside of the UN oil-for-food program. Failure of either regime to meet the demands, the war on terror rhetoric argued, resulted in its disqualification from the rights of sovereignty and left it vulnerable to forceful measures of removal.

Leaders of the war on terror were also explicit that the imposed demands on the targeted enemy regimes were non-negotiable. Bush (2001a) sent the message to the Taliban clearly when he stated, "These demands are not open to negotiation or discussion. The Taliban must act, and act immediately. They will hand over the terrorists, or they will share in their fate." Prior to the start of the 2003 war, Bush (2002a) sent a similar message to the three "axis of evil" nations – Iraq, Iran, and North Korea. He noted, "We have no intention of imposing our culture, but America will always stand firm for the non-negotiable demands of human dignity: the rule of law, limits on the power of the state, respect for women, private property, free speech, equal justice and religious tolerance." Speaking before the UN, Bush recalled the twelve-year history of the Iraqi regime's failure to live up to the demands embodied in the resolutions passed by the UN Security Council. After adding five new demands to those encompassed by the earlier resolutions, Bush (2002c) provided Saddam Hussein and the Iraqi government only one path to a better future:

> If all these steps are taken, it will signal a new openness and accountability in Iraq. And it could open the prospect of the United Nations helping to build a government that represents all Iraqis – a government based on respect for human rights, economic liberty and internationally supervised elections.

In the war on terror, official statements left no room to avert conflict by diplomatic concessions.

US leaders finally offered limited timeframes for the targeted regimes to implement the actions necessary for them to assimilate back into the global community. Less than one month after the offered choice to the Taliban, Powell (2001b) reported that the regime's time for action had elapsed:

> The president made it clear from the very beginning that if the Taliban regime did not turn over Osama bin Laden and the al-Qaeda organization resident in Afghanistan, that they had essentially designated themselves as a terrorist regime. They did not. And they have to pay the consequences, and the Taliban government must now go, because they are part and parcel to al Qaeda.

Repeatedly, officials stressed that they would not assume additional risks while waiting for targeted foreign leaders to decide. In laying out US plans regarding Iraq, Bush (2001e) explained, "We cannot stand by and do nothing while dangers gather." In the rhetoric of the war on terror, strategies of appeasement, implemented in hopes of obtaining a more hopeful outcome, were considered ill conceived and likely to produce more dangerous outcomes.

Administration officials finally depicted both the Taliban and Iraq as unreliable foreign actors that could not be trusted to meet US conditions. Bush repeatedly chastised the Taliban government for refusing to abide by international norms of denying safe haven and rejecting support to terrorist groups who, left unchecked, would commit future acts of murder worldwide (e.g., Bush 2001a). Going further, various Bush administration officials denounced Saddam Hussein and his government for repeatedly lying regarding Iraq's compliance with the twelve UN resolutions passed in the run up to the 1990–1 Persian Gulf War. In the war on terror, targeted regimes simply lacked credibility as potential partners to defeat the enemy network.

The Bush administration's response strategy of assimilation had as its genesis the rhetoric of the early American republic. In a letter to James Duane, George Washington explained the assimilation approach by noting that the United States should first endeavor to create a boundary between the tribes and the new settlers to facilitate trade between the two. However, Washington (1783) cautioned,

> In establishing the line, in the first instance, care should be taken neither to yield nor to grasp at too much. But to endeavor to impress the Indians with an idea of the generosity of our disposition to accommodate them[.]

US leaders subsequently raised the stakes of assimilation by adding additional demands including the passage of laws that stopped inter-tribal trading and purchases of land without prior approval of the federal government, and others that eliminated communal land holdings by those with at least one-half Indian blood (Report of Committee on Indian Affairs 1783, in Prucha (2nd edn: 1975)).

The contemporary war on terror's public non-negotiation strategy with terrorists and their associated regimes first appeared during the nation's founding, but did not become official US terrorism policy until the years of the Nixon administration. Thomas Jefferson, functioning in his role of Secretary of State during the active period of the Barbary Pirates, lobbied George Washington to stop making payments and, instead, to respond by force. Washington subsequently began lobbying Congress to fund such a strategy. The legislators, however, balked at the high cost of building a navy sufficiently large enough to counter the pirate's threat, so the tribute payments continued (Whipple 1991).

By the early 1970s, the US officially adopted a no-negotiations/no-concessions policy with terrorists. The Nixon administration announced the new stance after the Black September Organization kidnapped the US Ambassador to Sudan Cleo Allen Noel, Jr and US *Chargé d'Affaires* George Curtis Moore during a reception at the Saudi Arabian Embassy in Khartoum. Borrowing from the Israeli's government's response to the kidnapping of nine Israeli athletes at the 1972 Olympic games, President Nixon (1973a) announced the that United States would not "pay blackmail" to obtain the hostages' release. In response, Palestinian Liberation Organization chairman Yasser Arafat approved an order carried out by the kidnappers to execute Noel and Moore ("Seizure of the Saudi Arabian Embassy in Khartoum" 1973). At the memorial service honoring the two public servants, Nixon (1973b) defended the no-concessions policy as a necessary step to deterring future terrorists. Future presidents would consistently embrace the Nixon policy of no-concessions/no negotiations, at least in their public statements.

The war on terror's rhetoric focusing on an abbreviated time frame for diplomacy and assimilation also emerges in the twentieth century.

Throughout the bulk of US history, generic expectations of war rhetoric presumed that the nation's leaders would be cautious in their use of commander-in-chief powers, only invoking them after careful deliberation (see Campbell and Jamieson 2008). Experience with the Nazis in the run up to World War II, however, created a rhetorical resource useful for shrinking the time available for a thoughtful, deliberative approach. At the 1938 Munich Conference, the Nazis received a concession from the British, French, and Italians that Germany could annex and occupy Sudetenland. Rather than assimilate back into the European community, the Nazis capitalized on the delay to amass stronger forces (Bendersky 1985). Memories of the efforts at appeasement reemerged in survey results conducted for the George H.W. Bush administration related to the 1990–1 Persian Gulf War. A memo from Fabrizio, McLaughlin, and Associates to then Chief of Staff John Sununu revealed that replacing the traditional term of US war discourse, "diplomacy," with the coded term that recalled the Nazi experience of World War II, "appeasement," resulted in a twenty-seven point swing in the percentage of the public who favored the use of force to remove Iraqi forces from Kuwait (Fabrizio n.d.).

In short, rhetoric used in the contemporary war on terror draws upon historical analogs related to the American Indians, the Barbary pirates, the Nazis, and the Palestine Liberation Organization (PLO) to create a narrow time frame for enemy states to assimilate back into the global community of nations. Countering the historical practice of terrorists issuing demands to accomplish their political ends, official spokespersons in the war on terror were now making non-negotiable demands on the terrorists and their supporting states. Failure to accede to the demands in short order rendered enemy states vulnerable to escalated response options from the United States and its allies.

Removal

For individuals that refused to meet the US standards for assimilation into the global community, removal became the next response step in the contemporary war on terror. Rumsfeld (2001f) defined America's mission as "to root out the global terrorist networks – not just in Afghanistan but wherever they are[.]" Administration officials reiterated metaphors such as "rooting them out," "draining the swamp," and "smoking them out" to build a public imaginary where removal became an acceptable, necessary reaction to those unwilling to forego terrorist methods. In line with such a framing, US officials implemented a rendition program whereby operatives removed suspected terrorists from their home environments and interrogated them in various locations abroad. Additionally, the United States and its allies relocated 779 captured individuals suspected of terrorism to the Guantánamo Bay Naval Base in Cuba ("Guantánamo Bay Naval Base (Cuba)" 2012). Bush institutionalized the rhetorical framework of removal by signing a Military Order on November 13, 2001 entitled, "Detention, Treatment and Trial of Certain Non-Citizens in the War on Terror." The order granted authority for the Secretary of Defense to remove suspected terrorists to locations in or outside of the United States (2001c).

The strategy of enemy removal first arose when the new republic faced ongoing challenges from the American Indians as it claimed rights to North American territory. In 1803, Thomas Jefferson advocated the strategy of removal in a letter to William Henry Harrison:

> Should any tribe be foolhardy enough to take up the hatchet at any time, the seizing of the whole country of that tribe, and driving them across the Mississippi, as the only condition of peace, would be an example to others, and a furtherance of our final consolidation.
>
> (Jefferson 1803: 23)

In 1830, US President Andrew Jackson signed the Indian Removal Act which made removal the official policy of the United States in order to satisfy the wants of eastern settlers who, in their desire to have more closely accessible land, wanted America's Indians to move west of the Mississippi (Davis 2002). Jackson (1830, as quoted in Richardson 1937) publicly justified the nation's strategy of removal, when he stated:

> Rightly considered, the policy of the General Government toward the red man is not only liberal, but generous. He is unwilling to submit to the laws of the States and mingle with the general population. To save him from this alternative, or perhaps utter annihilation, the General Government kindly offers him a new home and proposes to pay the whole expense of his removal and settlement.
>
> (In Richardson 1937: 522)

Notable examples of the removal strategy included the five-time relocation of the Winnebago tribe, the deadly removal of the Cherokee (which killed up to 40 percent of the tribe), and the multi-step transfer of the Apache tribe across the span of the United States (Fikes 1996; Wilson 1998). In all, American Indians were moved off of more than ninety million acres of their land (Jaimes 1992).

Several of the processes of the removal strategy conducted in the contemporary US war on terror also have their origins in the practices of earlier leadership with regard to the American Indians. Rendition and practices of military tribunals offer reminiscent illustrations. After the capture of Geronimo and three hundred other members of the Apache tribe, the US government initially held the group for six weeks on suspicion of having committed a crime. Afterwards, the prisoners were moved across the United States and the government tried some members of the tribe in front of juries that included none of their peers and others were eventually held for more than thirty years without charging them with a crime (Worcester 1979).

Extermination

For terrorists unwilling to assimilate or move away from lands deemed strategic for US interests, the final strategy in the war on terror was to exterminate the remaining threats. Bush (2001a) announced the intention of the United States to adopt such a strategy when he stated, "the only way to defeat terrorism as a threat to our way of life is to stop it, eliminate it, and destroy it where it grows." The US military reinforced what Rumsfeld (2001g) described as the "campaign to liquidate terrorist networks" by issuing a deck of fifty-two cards with pictures of members of al-Qaeda's action cadre targeted for assassination.

The US government in the war on terror did not explicitly limit those targeted for extermination to those who had previously committed acts of violence against US citizens or their property. Official spokespersons also advocated a preemptive response to those considered future terrorist threats. In 2002, the National Security Strategy document warned that America would, if necessary, "exercise our right of self-defense by acting preemptively against such terrorists, to prevent them from doing harm against our people and our country" (Bush 2002e). While official spokespersons did assert a right to invoke "anticipatory self-defense" (e.g., Rice 2002), they also blurred the public distinction between offensive and defensive approaches to the war on terror. The dual-pronged approach (i.e., simultaneously claiming a right to preempt and casting preemptive actions as defensive) allowed administration officials to justify military intervention for audiences both sympathetic and opposed to preemptive measures in the war on terror (for more, see Winkler 2007).

The US strategy of exterminating threats emerges, once again, during the nation's earliest interactions with the American Indians. When Christopher Columbus and his soldiers first arrived in North America, they killed more than fifty thousand American Indians in their process of settlement (Stannard 1992). By 1851, US Secretary of the Interior Alexander Stuart proclaimed, "The policy of removal, except under peculiar circumstances, must necessarily be abandoned, and the only alternatives left are, to civilize or exterminate them" (as quoted in Stannard 1992: 200). At times, extermination took the form of battles, as in the case where the US seventh Calvary Regiment indiscriminately fired on men, women, and children of the Lakota tribe near the Wounded Knee Creek on December 29, 1890 (Lazarus 1991). At others, biological warfare became the preferred method, as when Captain Simeon Ecuyer, commandant of the Royal Americans at Fort Pitt, provided blankets infected with the smallpox virus as gifts to a visiting delegation of the Pontiac Algonkian Confederacy. Ecuyer's actions resulted in more than 100,000 deaths in the tribe after the disease from the infected blankets spread (Churchill 1994; O'Brien 2008).

The strategy of eliminating key leaders and close action cadre members of the identified enemy has been commonplace in all US wars. The Reagan administration, however, was the first to authorize preemptive actions against state sponsors of terror around the globe. NSDD 138, signed by Reagan on April 3, 1984, authorized the killing of suspected guerrillas and non-head of state officials in foreign countries through preemptory or retaliatory raids. While the directive was open-ended regarding the intended target(s) of the directive, particular focus was placed on the USSR, Iran, North Korea, Libya, Cuba, Syria, and Nicaragua (Simpson 1995). When publicly discussing the directive in the abstract, officials of the Reagan administration maintained that the use of "active defense measures" was necessary to defend US citizens and interests at home and abroad (Office of the Vice President 1986). When applied in specific contexts where Reagan had publicly deployed US military forces, however, public officials blurred distinctions between offensive and defensive war fighting. In his justification of the 1986 US bombing of Libya to the leaders of the US Congress, for example, Reagan presented his response as a necessary defensive response. He referenced the April 5, 1986 bombing of a West Berlin discotheque that injured fifty American servicemen, noting that it was "the latest in a long series of terrorist attacks against United States installations, diplomats and citizens carried out or attempted with the support and direction of Muammar Qadhafi" (Reagan 1988b: 478). Behind the scenes, however, Reagan had authorized numerous offensive, preemptive actions designed to destabilize Qadhafi's regime since the start of his presidency (Vandewalle 2006: 134).

Winning the war on terror

The Bush administration insisted that by using their response strategies of assimilation, removal, and extinction, the United States would win the global war on terror. Governmental officials explained that success was assured due to the divine nature of the mission and a public unified in support of such an approach. Public support, however, depended on public acceptance of certain time tropes that administration officials infused into their public statement.

A key component of that success strategy was to highlight the divine mission of the effort. In his first public speech laying out the foundational principles of the war on terror, Bush (2001a) explained, "The course of this conflict is not known, yet its outcome is certain. Freedom and fear, justice and cruelty, have always been at war, and we know that God is not neutral between them." With divine providence on their side, officials in the war of terror insisted that the United States and those who joined the coalition effort would ultimately prevail.

To succeed in the war on terror, public officials also maintained the necessity of a unified public in support of the effort. Revealing that the American public would have to devote both lives and some of its treasury to the effort, Bush nevertheless called on the public to remain behind the cause of fighting terrorism. Bush (2002a) celebrated the positive results from a unified effort in his 2002 State of the Union address:

> Now America is embracing a new ethic and a new creed, "Let's roll." In the sacrifice of soldiers, the fierce brotherhood of firefighters, and the bravery and generosity of ordinary citizens, we have glimpsed what a new culture of responsibility could look like. We want to be a nation that serves goals larger than self.

With unity, the leaders insisted, the US would achieve inevitable victory in the war on terror.

To facilitate the ongoing public support necessary for success in the war effort, public officials infused variable depictions of time in their public statements in various ways. Stahl (2008) describes how the Bush administration relied, in particular, on three time tropes in the war on terror. The first focused on initiation, a strategy incorporating a repeated set of deadlines and countdowns to demonstrate control over the start times of the overall war on terror and its various subsidiary battles. The second was continuation, where, through the rhetoric of benchmarks and timelines, warfare became both infinite (i.e., endless) and infinitesimal (i.e., perpetually on the verge of ending). The third focused on duration, which in the war on terror used a recurrent figure of the ticking clock that repeatedly stressed the urgency of responding to imminent threats by whatever means the government deemed necessary.

The assumption by US leaders that their cause in the war on terror was divinely inspired has its origins in the American Revolution. Reid illustrates the value of treating the Revolutionary War as a noble cause by pulling four statements from sermons delivered through the period: "faith (1) 'teaches us, to engage in War upon the noblest Principles,' (2) 'enables us to prosecute it with intrepid,' Valor (3) 'secures us the most powerful Assistance and (4) 'assures us of a glorious Reward'" (Reid 1976: 271). The implications of the divine mission expanded beyond the immediate circumstances of the war effort as Reid explains, "the followers are encouraged to believe that the cause was Just and that their sacrifices were not in vain. Furthermore, later generations are encouraged to accept the New Order and to emulate its founders" (Reid 1975: 6). Grounded in the birth of the nation and immersed in the divine, the rhetoric of the war on terror portrayed the positive destiny of America's causes as assured.

Appeals for unified public support for the war effort also date back to the nation's founding moments. Scholars who have theorized the generic elements of war rhetoric have consistently extracted unity appeals related to public support as recurrent substance of presidential justifications for assuming their commander-in-chief powers across all wars (e.g., Campbell and Jamieson 1990; Reid 1976). The Vietnam War, where waning public support for the effort prompted the pullout of US forces and the fall of South Vietnam to northern forces, caused future presidents to conduct internal polling to establish the extent of the public's patience and casualty tolerance for impending war efforts (see, for example, McDaniel 1985; "Historical overview of public support for Korea and Vietnam" n.d.).

Finally, the three tropes of time employed during the contemporary war on terror emerge at various points of US history. Placing conditions, and countdowns during the initiation phase of the war effort, trace back to battles with the nation's indigenous populations. As has previously been discussed, US leaders issued the condition of not "tak[ing] up the hatchet at any time" (Jefferson 1803) as necessary to avoid removal to lands west of the Mississippi River. Presenting the continuation of the war effort as both infinite and infinitesimal, however, had its origins in the 1990–1 Persian Gulf War, when the George H.W. Bush administration first presented the effort in antiseptic terms devoid of visual depictions of the bloody casualties of war (Stahl 2008). The use of the ticking clock in the duration phase of war efforts traces back to the Doomsday Clock, created in 1947 by scientists and engineers who sought to "convey how close humanity is to catastrophic destruction" (Lawrence 2012). The clock, displayed on the cover of the *Bulletin of the Atomic Scientists*, visually represented the risks associated with nuclear dangers by having the hands move closer to or away from the 12 o'clock hour. By pairing the symbolic threat of nuclear destruction with terrorism through the duration trope, public officials invited heightened public concern related to the enemy in the contemporary war on terror.

Concluding remarks

To construct the rhetorical appeals related to the contemporary war on terror, public spokespersons relied on a variety of analogs from US history. Previous strategic choices of the early republic related to the French Revolution, Barbary Pirates, and American Indians served as a key foundation for characterizing both the threat and the appropriate response to terrorism. Another frequently recurrent source for the nation's public communication strategy involved frames first utilized during the presidency of Ronald Reagan. The Reagan era functioned as a critical precursor of the current war's public appeals chiefly because it was the first administration to implement newly passed US laws targeting state sponsors of terrorism. Finally, references to two wars of the twentieth century, World War II and the Cold War, provide rhetorical resources for victorious efforts over formidable foes.

The Bush administration's use of historical analogs in the contemporary war on terror varies considerably across the memorable moments of US history. In the case of the French Revolution, for example, the analog functions simply as the meme "reign of terror," a rhetorical resource that evokes public standards for liberty, justice, and morality without further explication of the historical parallels between the France's revolutionary experience and enemies in the war on terror. In others, such as in the case of the America's Indian analog, multiple lines of arguments from the period frame contemporary discourse. From the characterization of the enemy as unworthy of individual or national identity to the response strategies of assimilation, removal, and extinction, the rhetoric of America's founding fathers in response to the nation's indigenous populations serves as a rhetorical template for justifying the war on terror.

The concentrated focus on the American Indian analog is particularly revealing about the implications of the rhetoric of the war on terror. Just as the founding fathers defined standards of civilized conduct that rendered the American Indians "barbaric savages" unfit for the rights and responsibilities of citizenship, the rhetoric of the contemporary war on terror establishes parameters for civilized conduct by foreign leaders both at home and within the international community that, if violated, might position the foreign regime for removal. The choice of assimilation, removal, or extinction offered to the American Indians with devastating consequences for the tribes again presents itself as a set of incremental steps facing potential targets in the US war on terror. As the experience with the nation's indigenous population attests, the timeframe for implementing the three response strategies can extend to decades. As many aspects of the strategic rhetorical framing of appropriate responses in the US war have made their way into executive orders and even accepted legislation, continued attention to subsequent administrations' terrorism rhetoric remains an imperative.

References

Abzug, R.H. (1999) *America Views the Holocaust, 1933–1945: A Brief Documentary History*, Boston, MA: Bedford/St. Martins.

Bendersky, J.W. (1985) *A History of Nazi Germany*, Chicago, IL: Nelson-Hall.

Bennett, W.L., Lawrence, R.G., and Livingston, S. (2007) *When the Press Fails: Political Power and the News Media from Iraq to Katrina*, Chicago, IL: Chicago University Press.

Bush, G.W. (2001a, September 20) "Address before a joint session of the Congress on the United States response to the terrorist attacks of September 11," *Public Papers of the Presidents*. Available at www.presidency.ucsb.edu (accessed April 24, 2012).

Bush, G.W. (2001b, September 11) "Address to the nation on the terrorist attacks on the World Trade Centers and the Pentagon," *Public Papers of the Presidents*. Available at www.presidency.ucsb.edu (accessed September 13, 2001).

Bush, G.W. (2001c) "Military Order of November 13, 2001," *Federal Register*, 16: 57831–6.

Bush, G.W. (2001d, September 17) "Remarks to employees in the Pentagon and an exchange with reporters in Arlington, Virginia," *Public Papers of the Presidents*. Available at www.presidency.ucsb.edu (accessed April 24, 2012).

Bush, G.W. (2001e, November 10) "Remarks to the United National General Assembly in New York City", *Public Papers of the Presidents*. Available at www.presidency.ucsb.edu (accessed April 25, 2012).

Bush, G.W. (2001f, September 19) "Remarks prior to discussions with President Megawati Sukarnoputri of Indonesia and an exchange with reporters," *Public Papers of the Presidents*. Available at www.presidency.ucsb.edu (accessed April 25, 2012).

Bush, G.W. (2001g, September 16) "Remarks by the President upon arrival," *Public Papers of the Presidents*. Available at www.presidency.ucsb.edu (accessed November 28, 2012).

Bush, G.W. (2002a, January 29) "Address before a joint session of the Congress on the state of the union," *Public Papers of the Presidents*. Available at www.presidency.ucsb.edu (accessed September 13, 2012).

Bush, G.W. (2002b, October 7) "Address to the nation on Iraq from Cincinnati, Ohio," *Public Papers of the President*. Available at www.presidency.ucsb.edu/ws/?pid=73139 (accessed April 24, 2012).

Bush, G.W. (2002c, September 12) "Address to the United Nations General Assembly in New York City," *Public Papers of the Presidents*. Available at www.presidency.ucsb.edu (accessed April 27, 2012).

Bush, G.W. (2002e) "The National Security Strategy of the United States of America," The White House. Available at http://georgewbush-whitehouse.archives.gov/nsc/nss/2002/ (accessed April 27, 2012).

Bush, G.W. (2003a, January 28) "Address before a joint session of the Congress on the state of the union," *Public Papers of the Presidents*. Available at www.presidency.ucsb.edu (accessed April 24, 2012).

Bush, G.W. (2003b, April 25) "Full text of Brokaw's interview with Bush," *New York Times*. Available at www.nytimes.com/2003/04/25/international/worldspecial/25BUSH-TEXT.html?pagewanted=all (accessed April 27, 2012).

Bush, G.W. (2003c. March 6) "The President's news conference of March 6, 2003," *Public Papers of the Presidents*. Available at www.presidency.ucsb.edu (accessed April 24, 2012).

Bush, G.W. (2003d, October 28) "The President's news conference of October 28, 2003," *Public Papers of the Presidents*. Available at www.presidency.ucsb.edu (accessed April 27, 2012).

Bush, L. (2001, November 17) "Laura Bush on Taliban oppression of women," *Washington Post*. Available at www.washingtonpost.com/wp-srv/nation/specials/attacked/transcripts/laurabushtext_111701.html (accessed April 25, 2012).

Campbell, K.K. and Jamieson, K.H. (2008) *Deeds Done in Words: Presidential Rhetoric and Genres of Governance*, Chicago, IL: University of Chicago Press.

Cheney, D. (2002, August 27) "Full text of Dick Cheney's speech," *Guardian*. Available at www.theguardian.com/world/2002/aug/27/usa.iraq (accessed July 21, 2003).

Churchill, W. (1994) *Indians Are Us? Culture and Genocide in Native North America*, Monroe, MA: Common Courage Press.

Cobb, R. (1917) *The People's Armies*, trans. M. Elliot (1987), New Haven, CT: Yale University Press.

Davis, V. (2002) "A discovery of sorts: Reexamining the origins of the federal Indian housing obligation," *Harvard Black Letter Law Journal*, 18, 211–39.

Drinnon, R. (1990) *Facing West: The Metaphysics of Indian-Hating and Empire-Building*, Norman, OK: University of Oklahoma Press.

Dyke, N.B. (1982, March 25) *Memo through Admiral Murphy to Vice President*. Folder, "Narco-Terrorism [3 of 5]," OA/ID 19850, Bush Vice Presidential Records, National Security Archives, College Station, TX: George Bush Presidential Library.

Edwards, G.C. (2003) *On Deaf Ears: The Limits of the Bully Pulpit*, New Haven, CT: Yale University Press.

Fabrizio, T. [n.d.] *Memo to Ambassador Sam Zakhem, Chairman, Freed Task Force*, Folder, "Persian Gulf War 1991 [8 or 11]," OA/ID CF00472. John Sununu, Chief of Staff Files, Bush Presidential Records, College Station, TX: George Bush Presidential Library.

Fikes, J.C. (ed.) (1996) *Reuben Snake, Your Humble Serpent: Indian Visionary and Activist*, Santa Fe, NM: Clear Light.

Fromkin, D. (1975) "The strategy of terrorism," *Foreign Affairs*, 5(4), 683–98.

Gough, H. (1998) *The Terror in the French Revolution*, New York: St. Martin's Press.

Gregg, D. and Menarchik, D. (1985, September 24) "Memo to the Vice President," Folder, "Terrorism [1 of 9]." OA/ID 19849. Bush Vice Presidential Records, National Security Affairs: George Bush Presidential Library.

"Guantánamo Bay Naval Base (Cuba)" (2012, April 19) *New York Times*. Available at http://topics.nytimes.com/top/news/national/usstatesterritoriesandpossessions/guantanamobaynavalbasecuba/index.html (accessed April 24, 2012).

"Historical overview of public support for Korea and Vietnam, with notes on the current Persian Gulf situation" (n.d.) Folder, "Persian Gulf Working Group: Handouts/Articles." OA/ID 03195. Paul McNeill, Office of Communications, Bush Presidential Records. College Station, TX: George Bush Presidential Library.

Hodges, A. (2011) *The "War on Terror" Narrative: Discourse and Intertextuality in the Construction and Contestation of Sociopolitical Reality*, New York, NY: Oxford University Press.

Irwin, R.W. (1931) *The Diplomatic Relations of the United States with the Barbary Pirates, 1776–1816*, Chapel Hill: University of North Carolina Press.

Ivie, R.L. (1980) "Images of savagery in American justifications for war," *Communication Monographs*, 47(4), 279–94.

Jackson, A. (1830, December 6) "Second annual message," in: J.D. Richardson (ed.) (1937) *A Compilation of the Messages and Papers of the Presidents*, Washington, DC: Bureau of National Literature and Art.

Jackson, R. (2005) *Writing the War on Terrorism: Language, Politics and Counter-Terrorism*, Manchester, UK: Manchester Press.

Jaimes, M.A. (1992) "Federal Indian identification policy: A usurpation of indigenous sovereignty in North America," in: M.A. Jaimes (ed.) *The State of Native America: Genocide, Colonization, and Resistance*, Boston, MA: South End Press, 123–39.

Jefferson, T. (1803, February 27) Letter to William Henry Harrison, in: F.P. Prucha (ed.) (1990) *Documents of United States Indian Policy*, 3rd edn, Lincoln, NE: University of Nebraska Press, 22–3.

Kellner, B. (1989, February 4) "Major Soviet papers says 20 million died as victims of Stalin," *New York Times*. Available at www.nytimes.com/1989/02/04/world/major-soviet-paper-says-20-million-died-as-victims-of-stalin.html (accessed April 15, 2012).

Krebs, R.R. and Jackson P.T. (2007) "Twisting tongues and twisting arms: the power of political rhetoric," *European Journal of International Relations*, 13 (1), 35–66.

Lawrence, C. (2012, January 10) "Doomsday Clock a minute closer to the end," ABC News. Available at http://abcnews.go.com/blogs/technology/2012/01/doomsday-clock-due-for-an-adjustment/ (accessed April 27, 2012).

Lazarus, E. (1991) *Black Hills/White Justice: The Sioux Nation versus the United States: 1775 to the Present*, New York: HarperCollins.

Lewis, J.R. (2004) "Savages of the seas: Barbary captivity tales and images of Muslims in the early republic," *Journal of American Culture*, 2, 75–84.

Lucas, C. (1996) "The theory and practice of denunciation in the French Revolution," *Journal of Modern History*, 68(4), 768–85.

Maltz, D. and Archambault, J. (1995) "Gender and power innative North America: Concluding remarks," in: L.F. Klein and L.A. Ackerman (eds) *Women and Power in Native North America*, Norman, OK: University of Oklahoma Press, 230–50.

McDaniel, R.B. (1985, November 25) "Memo to John Poindexter," Folder, "Terrorism & Libya [2 of 6]." Box 91673. Files of Donald Fortier. Ronald Reagan Library.

McFarlane, R.C. (1984, August 15) "Letter to Edwin Meese, III," Folder, "Terrorism, Vol. II 1/1/84–8/31/84 (8404913)." Box 91400, Executive Secretariat, National Security Council: Records. Subject File. Ronald Reagan Library.

Medhurst, M.J., Ivie, R.L., Wander, P., and Scott, R.L. (eds) (1990) *Cold War Rhetoric: Strategy, Metaphor, and Ideology*, New York: Greenwood.

Mueller, J. (2006) *Overblown: How Politicians and the Terrorism Industry Inflate National Security Threats, and Why We Believe Them*, New York: Free Press.

"National Commission on Terrorist Attacks upon the United States" (2004) *The 9/11 Commission Report: Final Report of the national Commission on Terrorist Attacks Upon the United States*, New York: Norton.

Nixon, R.M. (1973a) "The President's News Conference of March 2, 1973," in: J.T. Woolley and G. Peters (eds) *The American Presidency Project*. Available at www.presidency.ucsb.edu/ws/index.php?pid=4123 (accessed June 9, 2011).

Nixon, R.M (1973b, March 6) "Remarks at a ceremony honoring slain foreign service officers," in: J.T. Woolley and G. Peters (eds) *The American Presidency Project*. Available at www.presidency.ucsb.edu/ws/index.php?pid=4132&st=&st1= (accessed June 5, 2012).

O'Brien, C. (2008) *The Forgotten History of America: Little-known Conflicts of Lasting Importance from the Earliest Colonists to the Eve of the Revolution*, Beverly, MA: Fair Winds Press.

Office of the Secretary of Defense (2001, September 30) "Memorandum for the President: Strategic Thoughts," National Archive, George Washington University. Available at www.gwu.edu/~nsarchiv/NSAEBB?NSAEBB358a/index.htm#1 (accessed December 6, 2001).

Office of the Vice President (1986) "Public report of the Vice President's task force on combatting [sic] terrorism," Folder, "Terrorism." OA/ID 14923, Bush Vice Presidential Records, Press Office, George Bush Presidential Library.

Onuf, P.S. (2000) *Jefferson's Empire: The Language of American Nationhood*, Charlottesville, VA: University of Virginia Press.

Powell, C. (2001a) "Secretary Colin L. Powell remarks from Turkish Minister of Foreign Affairs Ismail Cem". Available at http://avalon.law.yale,edu/sept11/powell_brief11.asp (accessed April 24, 2012).

Powell, C. (2001b, October 24) "Secretary of State Colin Powell appears before House International Relations Committee". Available at http://commdocs.house.gov/committees/intlrel/hfa75843.000/hfa75843_0f.htm (accessed April 24, 2012).

Powell, C. (2003, February 6) "Transcript of Powell's UN presentation," CNN. Available at http://edition.cnn.com/2003/US/02/05/sprj.irq.powell.transcript/ (accessed August 1, 2006).

Reagan, R. (1985, July 8) "Remarks at the annual convention of the American Bar Association," *Public Papers of the Presidents*. Available at www.presidency.ucsb.edu (accessed April 25, 2012).

Reagan, R. (1988a, September 22) "Address to the 41st session of the UN General Assembly in New York, NY," *Public Papers of the President, 1986*, vol. 2., Washington, DC: Government Printing Office.

Reagan, R. (1988b, April 16) "Letter to the Speaker of the House of Representatives and the President Pro Tempore of the Senate on the US air strike Against Libya," *Public Papers of the Presidents, Ronald Reagan 1986*, Washington, DC: Government Printing Office.

Reid, R.F. (1975) "Varying historical interpretations of the American Revolution: Some rhetorical perspectives," *Today's Speech*, 235–15.

Reid, R.F. (1976) "New England rhetoric and the French War, 1754–1760: A case study in the rhetoric of war," *Communication Monographs*, 43,259–86.

Report of Committee on Indian Affairs (1783, October 15), in: F.P. Prucha (ed.) (1990) *Documents of United States Indian Policy*, 2nd edn, Lincoln, NE: University of Nebraska Press, 3–4.

Rice, C. (2002, October 1) "Dr. Condoleezza Rice discusses President's National Security Strategy". Available at http://georgewbush-whitehouse.archives.gov/news/releases/2002/10/20021001-6.html (accessed June 1, 2006).

Rumsfeld, D. (2001a, October 8) "America continues strike; New anthrax scare in Florida; MSNBC". Available at www.defense.gov/transcripts/transcript.aspx?transcriptid=2032 (accessed April 24, 2012).

Rumsfeld, D. (2001b, October 7) "Defense Secretary Donald Rumsfeld's news conference with Gen. Richard Myers, Chairman of the Joint Chiefs of Staff, following the US retaliatory strikes in Afghanistan," *Washington Post*. Available at www.washingtonpost.com (accessed April 25, 2012).

Rumsfeld, D. (2001c, October 12) "DOD news briefing – Secretary Rumsfeld and Gen. Myers". Available at www.defense.gov/transcripts/transcript.aspx?transcriptid=2068 (accessed April 24, 2012).

Rumsfeld, D. (2001d, November 13) "Donald Rumsfeld press conference," CNN. Available at http://transcripts.cnn.com/TRANSCRIPTS/0111/13/se.05.html (accessed April 27, 2012).

Rumsfeld, D. (2001e, October 11) "Memorial service in remembrance of those lost on September 11th". Available at www.defenselink.mil/speeches/2001/s20011011-secdef.html (accessed April 24, 2012).

Rumsfeld, D. (2001f, November 1) "September 11, 2001: Attack on America, Statement of the Secretary of Defense," *The Avalon Project*. Available at http://avalon.law.yale.edu/sept11/dod_brief66.asp (accessed April 27, 2012).

Rumsfeld, D. (2001g, October 18) "Special Defense Department briefing re: Operational update on Afghanistan," *Federal News Service*. Available at www.washingtonpost.com/wpsrv/nation/specials/attacked/transcripts/rumsfeld_text101801.html (accessed December 7, 2001).

Rumsfeld, D. (2001h, October 29) Speech: Defense Department Briefing with Secretary of Defense Donald Rumsfeld and Joint Chiefs of Staff Chairman General Richard B. Myers, *Federal News Service*. Available at www.defense.gov/transcripts/transcript.aspx?transcriptid=2226-ok (accessed November 27, 2001).

"Seizure of the Saudi Arabian Embassy in Khartoum" (1973) *Foreign Relations of the United States, 1969–1976, Volume E-6, Documents on Africa, 1973–1976, Document 217*. Available at www.fordlibrarymuseum.gov/library/frus.asp (accessed March 24, 2012).

Simpson, C. (1995) *National Security Directives of the Reagan and Bush Administrations: The Declassified History of US Political and Military Policy, 1981–1991*, Boulder, CO: Westview Press.

Sirich, J.B. (1971) *The Revolutionary Committee in the Department of France, 1793–1794*, New York: Howard Fertig.

Stahl, R. (2008) "A clockwork war: Rhetorics of time in a time of terror," *Quarterly Journal of Speech*, 94(1), 73–99.

Stannard, D.E. (1992) *American Holocaust: The Conquest of the New World*, New York: Oxford University Press.

Stuckey, M. and Murphy, J. (2001) "By any other name: Rhetorical colonialism in North America," *American Indian Culture and Research Journal*, 25(4), 73–98.

Stuckey, M.E. (2004) *Defining Americans: The Presidency and National Identity*, Lawrence, KN: University of Kansas Press.

Tallett, F. (1999) "Robespierre and religion," in: C. Haydon and W. Doyle (eds) *Robespierre*, Cambridge: Cambridge University Press, 92–108.

"Terrorism II: Terrorism Article [2 of 3]." (n.d.) OA/ID 19849, Bush Vice Presidential Records. National Security Archives, College Station, TX: George Bush Presidential Library.

US Declaration of Independence (1776) Available at www.ushistory.org (accessed March 24, 2012).

Vandewalle, D. (2006) *A History of Modern Libya*, Cambridge, UK: Cambridge University Press.

Wallace, A.F.C. (1999) *Jefferson and the Indians: The Tragic Fate of the First Americans*, Boston, MA: Harvard University Press.

Washington, G. (1783) "George Washington to James Duane," in J.C. Fitzpatrick, (ed.) (1931–44) *Writings of George Washington from the Original Manuscript Sources 1745–1799, Vol. 27*, 133–40, Washington: Government Printing Office.

Whipple, A.B.C. (1991) *To the Shores of Tripoli: The Birth of the Navy and the Marines*, New York: Morrow.

Wilson, J. (1998) *The Earth Shall Weep: A History of Native America*, New York: Atlanta Monthly Press.

Winkler, C. (2002) "Manifest destiny on a global scale: The US war on terrorism," *Controversia: The International Journal of Debate and Democratic Renewal*, 1(1), 85–108.

Winkler, C. (2007) "Parallels in preemptive war rhetoric: Reagan on Libya; Bush 43 on Iraq," *Rhetoric and Public Affairs*, 10, 303–34.

Winkler, C. (2008) "Recalling US terrorism history in contemporary presidential discourse," in: H.D. O'Hair, R.L. Heath, K.J. Ayotte, and G.R. Ledlow (eds) *Terrorism: Communication and Rhetorical Perspectives*, Cresskill, NJ: Hampton University Press.

Winkler, C.K. (2006) *In the Name of Terrorism: Presidents on Political Violence in the Post-World War II Era*, Albany, NY: State University of New York Press.

Woodward, B. (2002) *Bush at War*, New York: Simon and Schuster.

Worcester, D.E. (1979) *The Apaches: Eagles of the Southwest*, Norman, OK: University of Oklahoma Press.

2 Western responses to terrorism in the 1970s

Ondrej Ditrych

The aim of this chapter is to contribute to the project of historicising counterterrorism by inquiring into its modalities in the Western European countries in the 1970s. It will first provide a short overview of the political violence that these countries defined as a problem to be resolved through their counterterrorism policies. Second, an *exposé* of rationality and technologies comprising counterterrorism security apparatuses will follow. This *exposé* will also suggest what continuities can be found between those and the relevant current practices. Third, the focus will turn to speech, or *discourse*. Instead of engaging separately with Western European countries one at a time, and drawing on previous research (Ditrych 2013a, 2014), the discourse of (counter)terrorism as a series of statements enunciated by the First World states in the contemporary UN debate on the subject – and a system for their formation and ordering (Foucault 1997: 131) – will be archaeologically recovered and related to the present. The assumption here will be that this discourse reflected – albeit at a generalised level – political positions of the actors concerned, and more importantly, constituted and validated their practices in response to what was defined as the terrorist threat. Last but not least, elements of the discursive formation of terrorism science, which incidentally – but in fact, on the assumption of a constitutive relationship between power and knowledge, *not* incidentally at all – emerged in the 1970s will be critically inquired into, once again with today's 'terrorology' in mind.

Threat

The governments and populations of Western European countries were confronted in the 1970s with a rising wave of political violence that in discursive practice was constructed as 'terrorist'. Western Europe appears to have been one of the areas in the world most afflicted by such violence in this period. From a historical perspective, it was also during this decade that both the number of incidents and the death toll peaked on the continent (Chalk 1996: 45).

Standard explanations for the both temporally and spatially significant occurrence of 'terrorist' violence in Western Europe point to the key role the protest movement of the 1960s played in their emergence (the terrorist groups either turned to violence in frustration caused by the movement's inability to meet its Utopian visions and ultimate disintegration, or were infused with a new revolutionary zeal, even if their agendas were *prima facie* different). They also suggest that environmental factors facilitated the surge and 'invited' foreign terrorists to conduct their activities here. Western Europe is conceived as more vulnerable than other regions because of its relatively limited impediments to free movement (even before 'Schengen-land' came into being), its dense infrastructure (providing a wealth of targets), and the liberal character of its governments constraining their responses to political violence and rendering them weaker, in particular as the terrorist events receive massive public attention due to deep media penetration (Wilkinson 1986 : 190). These explanations can be considered as hypothesised causal patterns, as indeed they are intended. They can also, however, be contextualised as discursive elements of the security apparatus that exercises power to eliminate the problem of terrorism while preserving (neo)liberal freedom of circulation – a quintessential manifestation of what Foucault conceived of as 'security': not the necessary precondition of freedom (as it is bequeathed to us in the Hobbesian myth of the state's security pledge), but rather a constraint, which, however, makes the exercise of freedom ultimately possible since it is constantly threatened by its own conditions of production (Foucault 2007; Lemke 2011: 46).

Three types of political violence typically characterised as terrorism in the 1970s can conveniently be defined. First, there is the violence related to ethnopolitical conflicts, the genesis of which is found in the more distant past, and which was revived in the 1970s (at least in part invigorated by successes of national liberation movements such as FLN, *Front de Libération Nationale*, in Algeria). These include almost notably the conflicts over the state in Northern Ireland and in the Basque Country. PIRA (the Provisional Irish Republican Army) is considered to have been the most destructive of the separatist violent groups, conducting attacks against economic targets and the security apparatus in Northern Ireland (with the peak of its activity there in the early 1970s), and later (from 1972 onward) projecting its activity further to wage the 'English Campaign' with the aim of infusing war weariness among the electorate in the United Kingdom and thus pressure the government to withdraw from Northern Ireland.[1] In Spain, ETA (Euzkadi ta Askatasuma) was the dominant Basque separatist violent force, formed in 1959, launching its violent activity in the late 1960s and coming to the spotlight with the successful attentat against Admiral Carrero Blanco, Franco's designated successor (1973). Like PIRA, it counted among its targets the political establishment, security apparatus and local economic assets (such as tourist resorts); and it also engaged in robberies, rackets and kidnappings to increase funding for its activities.

Second, there is doctrinal violence, aimed at a more fundamental and regionally unspecific transformation of the political order. Generally, groups involved in this violence prove to be more ephemeral than the separatists, operating without a stable territorial and support base and without the capacity to conduct large-scale operations. Most notable among them were the Rote Armee Fraktion (Red Army Faction, or RAF) in Germany (formed in 1970, partly from the earlier Baader–Meinhof group, which was founded in 1968), the Red Brigades in Italy (1970) and, somewhat later, Action Directe in France (1979). Their terrorism is typically linked to the unrest in the 1960s. While, as noted above, it is often portrayed as a frustrated reaction to the collapse of the social movement, the reality was more complex. In the case of Germany, for example, violence seems to have been integrated into the revolutionary strategy at the latest with the shooting of Benno Ohnesorg (1967). Moreover, even before RAF's emergence – not to mention the date of publication of *Das Konzept Stadtguerilla* (1971) – elements in the movement had been fighting in Berlin to establish 'free territories'. The political violence was characterised as 'urban guerrilla' activity before being developed in 1969–70 as a strategy of political struggle against what was perceived as a Fascist state; it however continued to be problematised by the movement's milieu throughout the 1970s either as unjustified, or as understandable (in the face of the preventive 'counterrevolution' by the state) but inexpedient (providing a convenient excuse for governmental militarisation and excess; Gehrig 2011). In terms of tactics, RAF targeted primarily armed forces and police, but also media and the capital, which it identified as sustaining the existing system of exploitation. The RAF's activity peaked in the 'May Offensive' of 1972 (after which its activities became increasingly defensive insofar as the rationale of the attacks turned to securing the release of incarcerated comrades from the prison). In contrast, in Italy the first half of the decade witnessed a surge of reactionary ('black') terrorism – perpetrated by actors linked to the country's security apparatus in what will be posited below as its 'terror–security nexus' – whereas the leftist political violence gained prominence only in the mid-1970s.

Third, there is violence perpetrated by actors with agenda *prima facie* unrelated to Europe, and notably related to the politics of the Middle East. According to Wilkinson, a contemporary terrorologist, approximately 90 percent of all acts of international terrorism in Europe in 1967–77 were perpetrated by Palestinian groups (Wilkinson 1986: 184). The most spectacular of those was undoubtedly the series of events launched after the storming by a Black September commando of the Israeli athletes' dormitory during the Munich Olympics (1972). The live broadcast of the drama, which ended tragically fifteen hours later after the failed rescue operations by German security forces at Fürstenfeldbruck airport, was watched by close to a billion people in more than 100 countries around the world (Taylor 1993).

Such a neat division does not entirely capture the reality, however. Without succumbing to the 1980s and later accounts of a global terrorist conspiracy (possibly orchestrated from Moscow, see Cline and Alexander 1984; Francis 1981; Sterling 1980; for an early criticism of this thesis see Herman 1982), it should be pointed out that intersecting agendas, networks of contacts and cooperative linkages among various groups across the three categories in the 1970s that served as empirical evidence for those accounts indeed existed. At the ideological level, while it is uncertain to what extent the indigenous emancipation movements were infused with leftist doctrines as a consequence of the 1960s student movement, the utopia of ETA or OIRA (the Official Irish Republican Army) in Northern Ireland was distinctly socialist. The actors mentioned above, who were identified with doctrinal violence, in their turn problematised not only the 'Fascist', bourgeois and capitalist systems of organising human relations in the developed world, but also imperialism and the (total) colonial war and therefore their agendas – in particular that of RAF – were effectively internationalised.[2] At the operational level, the groups within the first two categories were not only involved in some degree of cooperation among themselves (PIRA and ETA, RAF and the Red Brigades); they all apparently also received training in Palestinian camps (as had the radicalised German students in the late 1960s). The doctrinal groups moreover provided 'internationals' with operational infrastructure. RAF, for example, seems to have taken part in the planning of the Munich events (among Black September's demands was also the release of five senior RAF members jailed in Germany, including Baader and Meinhof), and German Revolutionäre Zellen participated in the raid on OPEC (Organization of Petroleum Exporting Countries) in Vienna (1975) masterminded by Carlos the Jackal, a freelance terrorist associated with Palestinian groups.

Apparatus

The counterterrorism apparatus, as it developed in the 1970s, may be conceived as consisting of identifiable rationality and technologies. Drawing on Foucault, rationality can be defined as a form of thought producing truth claims that make social reality intelligible through the emergence of commonsense understandings. Technologies then operationalise those rationalities in specific ways (Dean 2010; Foucault 1991).

The rationality of West European security apparatuses in the 1970s, expanded as a result of the problematisation of terrorism as a challenge to the protective power of the state vis-à-vis society at large or of certain segments of it. Those segments of society, which either through management of capital or the exercise of the state's monopoly on legitimate violence sustain the current political and economic order, can be identified as a constant negotiation of the tension between the preservation of the (neo)liberal governmentality and the liberal identity of the government (manifested in its recognition and purported protection of 'civil liberties') on one hand, and the intersubjectively perceived need to meet its security obligation (based on the understanding that *salus populi* is the supreme law of the land and should be the first common good provided by the government) on the other. The concept of 'minimum force' (Chalk 1996: 103) is telling in this respect, insofar as it reflects the aim of controlling the response to protect – in the liberal government's gesture of self-limitation – the liberal values seen as fundamental to the preservation of the *status quo* political order. Resolving this tension in the 1970s was achieved by emphasising the 'legal model' of action (conceiving of terrorism as a crime) as opposed to the 'war model' (even as terrorism could and indeed was conceived, both by those in terrorism science and more widely, as a new mode of warfare).[3] Such a response went far beyond the boundaries of 'normal' politics.

First, this is because special legislation was passed in the 1970s throughout Western Europe (typically around the peak of terrorist activity in the given country), sanctioning technologies that removed the terrorist subject from the realm of law and effectively establishing exception: extrajudicial processes (for example, internment without trial in Northern Ireland in 1971–5, deportations, prevention of entry to the United Kingdom of both UK and Irish citizens suspected of involvement in the 'Troubles', with no review). This special legislation included the establishment of new criminal offences, modifications to standard legal processes (for example, limiting the rights of defence in Western Germany, eliminating juries in Northern Ireland, speedy trial under emergency procedure in Spain); the suspension of *habeas corpus* (the extension of pre-trial detention: this was also used in Northern Ireland and Spain, in order to facilitate gathering evidence, in conditions where the testimonies of witnesses were next to impossible to secure, sometimes using nonstandard interrogation practices,[4] or transferring the onus of proof to the defence); or the extension of criminal investigative powers (access to material held by third parties; broadening of surveillance).

Second, while terrorism was *policed* – in line with the legal model – rather than countered by armies (with the exception of certain spatially and temporally limited contexts),[5] policing was progressively *militarised* in this period. Leaving aside the deployment in counterterrorist operations of traditional paramilitary units in Spain (Guardia Civil), Italy (Carabinieri) or France (Gendarmerie), West European countries in the 1970s witnessed the emergence of special police units (for example Germany's Grenzschutzgruppe 9 (GSG 9), formed in the aftermath of the Munich massacre) – with the notable exception of the UK, where the decentralised system of policing led to the deployment of the army's Special Air Service, the SAS, in Northern Ireland (1976–) instead. These special forces embodied militarisation insofar as they were more isolated from the society and capable of the use of more deadly force than regular police units. In other words, they were trained to conduct surgical but intense strikes to cure the body politic, with their exceptionalist mode of operation and the effective penetration of the war model into the security apparatus, conditioning excesses in the form of extrajudicial killing, torture etc. Furthermore, the war model appears to have also been inculcated into the security apparatus as a result of the unintended consequences of planting the 'stay-behind' networks in Europe, formed and run by US and UK foreign intelligence to be used in case of a Soviet attack (presumably to be followed by occupation of the continent). Whereas conspiracy theories abound concerning those networks (Ganser 2005), it is plausible to assume that while they may not have been integrated into the security apparatus, a terror–security nexus was likely to exist as their involvement in peacetime politics, including their acts of political violence against the left, and possibly even violent acts under a false flag (attributed to left doctrinal groups), were covered, if not conducted in cooperation with, some elements of the apparatus.[6]

While a transnational counterterrorism regime had already been envisaged in the 1930s in the framework of the League of Nations (Ditrych 2013b; Saul 2006; Zlataric 1975), and Interpol did not then serve as a platform for cooperation in political cases as it came to do later,[7] the reasoning that terrorism as a transnational threat demands a transnationalised response was reflected in the emergence of real technologies of such cooperation among West European states in the 1970s. Legal, diplomatic and operational measures were taken. The legal measures entailed the conclusion in the Council of Europe of the European Convention on the Suppression of Terrorism (1977) and in the European Community of the Dublin Agreement (1979), which was meant to ensure unreserved application among member states of the former treaty. However, individual states such as the traditionally liberal and hence in this matter uncooperative Great Britain limited the political offence exception to extradition for trial in other countries in this period, and overall the legal cooperation continued to be hindered by the discretion on whether to extradite, which just as in the earlier Convention for the Prevention and Punishment of Terrorism (1937), was allowed to signatories by an 'exception' clause (art. 13). Diplomatic measures entailed including the issue of state-sponsored terrorism on the agenda of the informal mechanism of European Political Cooperation (EPC).[8] Finally, operational measures entailed founding of the TREVI group of senior state officials in Home Affairs, which facilitated the exchange of intelligence (through a dedicated telex system), compiled a blacklist of persons suspected of involvement in terrorist activities, contributed to the convergence of threat assessments and, perhaps most significantly, served as a platform for socialisation of security professionals in the field.[9]

To conclude, the security apparatus in the Western European countries in the 1970 expanded as a result of the problematisation of terrorism. It included new technologies that betrayed the characteristics of Foucauldean security and biopolitics which, insofar as technological advances permitted, resolved the (neo)liberal dilemma of preserving circulation while securing the legitimacy of the state as a security provider (and parallelled simultaneous development toward less coercive strategies of policing protest; see Della Porta 1998). Surveillance and profiling of populations that are part and parcel of security apparatuses today, which stress governing mobilities through nonintrusive technologies of 'policing at a distance' and risk management (Amoore 2006; Amoore and de Goede 2005) can thus be traced to this period, which witnessed the development of databases shared among national services, such as Personen, Institutionen, Objekte, Sachen (Persons, Institutions, Objects, Things PIOS) in Germany, and generally the computerisation of personal data collection and processing. So can, however, be the parallel *reinforcement* of sovereignty and the (re)emergence of states of exception involving panopticism and decisionism reinscribed in contemporary circulation management (Aradau and van Munster 2007; Bigo 2008: 124; Butler 2006). Like contemporary apparatuses, counterterrorism in the 1970s also involved disciplinary technologies that would, for example, prevent media from passing certain messages while actively disseminating others (on how the 'battle' against terrorism is gradually being won, but individual vigilance is still needed; see Curtis 1984). In this context, it is also worth mentioning that in the milieu of the doctrinal groups, a critique pointing to the role of the penitentiary and mental institutions' system (and thus the complicity of psychiatric science) in the apparatus of suppressing political discontent – to the point of speaking of these disciplinary institutions as new concentration camps where the inmates were subjected to intense sensory deprivation, for example – was rather common in this period (Pekelder 2011). Finally, while the intersubjective construct of national sovereignty impeded transnational cooperation to what was problematised as a transnational problem in Western Europe, the 1970s witnessed the emergence of mechanisms and procedures that later evolved (with the reification of the neoliberal government in the 'Schengenland'), were partly formalised (with the Maastricht Treaty and creation of the Justice and Home Affairs pillar of the European Union, 1992), and further developed in the wake of 9/11 (Bures 2011; Cardona 1992; Deflem 2006).

Discourse

To historicise both the security apparatuses examined above and the current (counter)terrorism argumentation, attention is now turned to the discourse of Western states in the UN where a debate on terrorism was forcefully revived in the aftermath of the Munich massacre (1972). The strategy behind this discourse was to delegitimise non-state revolutionary violence with international linkages (which were indeed asserted with regard to all three categories of terrorist activity defined in the first section).[10] But unlike in the 1930s, when the first robust states' discourse of international terrorism emerged, this discourse was now challenged: interestingly, not so much by the second world states (which seemed to enunciate statements that rather conformed to the current political *status quo*), but primarily by the autonomising states of the third world. Examining the statements articulated on terrorism in the UN in the 1970s, a duality of general orders (rules for their production) can therefore be identified, while the statements made by the states of the first world were often formed in relation/reaction to those of the other order (and *vice versa*).[11]

Terrorism, as defined in the statements articulated in conformity with the first world discursive order was, first of all, directed against the state, attempting to coerce it into a particular action (in the more rational conception),[12] or to undermine its powers so as to bring about a state of general disorder where – and this seems to be really *terrifying* about terrorism – terror is displaced from its constitutional limits and wrestled from its legitimate wielder, the state (in the depoliticised conception, see below). In terms of substance, in continuity with the previous states' discourse of terrorism, assassination and mass bombing were included among terrorist activities, however, the importance of assassination as an attentat was challenged by an increased discursive emphasis on the indiscriminate nature of the terrorist violence. These were compounded by new activities: hostage taking (both protected and unprotected persons) and hijacking (or 'air piracy').

This terrorism was constructed as an alarming phenomenon and an unprecedented threat. Statements abounded about the increasing gravity and frequency of terrorist action; and of violence and terror spreading throughout the world.[13] Medical imagery was mobilised to add urgency to these truth claims, rendering terrorism as a 'plague' or simply a worldwide disease affecting the international body politic and states individually as its constituent units.[14]

By constructing terrorism as an exceptional threat – ironically, using similar discursive patterns witnessed previously, for example in the debate on terrorism in the League of Nations in the 1930s, and later, in contemporary terrorism discourse – political possibilities opened for exceptional responses, some of which were relayed above in the discussion of the 'war model' penetration. An extension of practices related to this model could be furthermore validated by the interdiscursive relationship between terrorism and international humanitarian law in the 1970s (as an international conference held under the auspices of the International Committee of the Red Cross was held in Geneva in 1974–77, resulting in two Geneva Protocols). The translation of humanitarian law discourse, where the concept of terrorism was related to situations defined by the scope of IHL (international humanitarian law), i.e. to the situation of armed conflict, seems to have had a major effect in terms of normalising the construct of the terrorist's victim as 'civilian', even where the particular act to which reference was being made had taken place outside the context of the armed conflict. The terrorist act was therefore rendered more abhorrent by transgressing the norm (of civilised violence) to which soldiers would normally be expected to adhere. Moreover, it could be suggested that a state of war existed in the world – even as this was a *new* kind of war, a 'war without a war' (as a consequence of which, as is the case today, no privileges allowed to the warring party would be bestowed on the terrorist). The war on terrorism was not yet officially declared in political discourse (unlike media discourse in the West, see Sloan 1978), but in the subjectification of the victim of terrorism as 'civilian' it seems to have been implied.

The response to terrorism thus defined had to be immediate. Here, the states of the first world met with fierce opposition as the autonomising third world protested that first, 'underlying causes' of terrorism had to be studied. Even before any such study could be initiated, however, truth claims proliferated on what these underlying causes were: misery, frustration, grievance or despair brought about by colonial, racist and alien regimes. In other words, in this (counter)discourse a causal relationship was established between non-state and state terrorism, 'the most dangerous brand of violence, the most often practiced at the most comprehensive scale'.[15] Such state terrorism, forcibly introduced in the discourse, could stand for a variety of practices: physical repression, denial of political participation, colonial domination, foreign occupation, sustaining poverty, foreign exploitation of natural resources, or systematic destruction of flora and fauna. Furthermore, in other statements, it was not individual 'colonial regimes' (at this time, Israel would be high on the list of such powers) but the entire cruel and unjust international (capitalist) order that was the ultimate cause of (non-state) terrorism.

The states of the first world reacted to this contestation by a variety of discursive tactics such as confining state violence to other debates,[16] questioning the scientific soundness of causal claims made, denying altogether the applicability of 'academic logic'[17] or claiming that while (unidentified) structural causes of non-state terrorism were indeed important, their study would take a long time, whereas action to eradicate it could not, given its exceptional character, be postponed.[18] The most important, however, was what could be termed a discourse of limits. In statements that comprised it, the causes of non-state terrorism were rendered irrelevant, since such terrorism was reprehensible by the sole fact that it transgressed the conventional limits of violence. Since no possible cause could make such transgression legitimate, this was a *status quo* discourse *par excellence*, reifying the existing conventional boundaries of political action and depoliticising terrorism as the discussion of motives was rendered unacceptable. This ban would become more effective only gradually (since the 1990s, numerous General Assembly and Security Council resolutions and states' statements in Ad hoc Committee reports assert that terrorism is criminal whatever its motivation and wherever, whenever and by whomever it is committed, to the point that this position can now be considered hegemonical), because now it was contested by claims that choice of means must be measured against the means of removing injustice that are at one's disposal. Therefore, the debate on terrorism in the 1970s featured an interesting challenge to the limits of political violence that could be deployed to undermine existing structural domination and prevailing notions of (global) justice. While this challenge was not ultimately successful, a consequence was that a general regime of counterterrorism (such as the one envisioned in the 1930s, entailing a fundamental norm on the prohibition of terrorism, establishing procedures for punishment based on the normalisation of particular political orders, and *aut dedere, aut punire* and common surveillance) proved impossible to negotiate and the first world states came to adopt a sectoral approach: implementation of the existing and conclusion of new sectoral treaties that lay the ground for limited particular regimes, including regional ones referred to in the previous section (Strasbourg and Dublin agreements).[19]

The way in which the terrorist subject was constructed in Western discourse can be relayed using the concept of 'basic discourses' – patterns of identity and difference, and association and dissociation, in which the self and the other are constituted (Hansen 2006: 52). Two such basic discourses can be identified: *civilisation/barbarism*, and *order/chaos*. In the first discourse, the terrorist is spatially and temporally situated outside the pale of civilisation since he attacks its values and the civilised mankind as a whole (which also effectively renders him inhuman).[20] In line with the discourse of limits posited above, what makes the terrorist a 'barbarian' is above all the transgression of the established norms of (civilised) violence.

In the second discourse, the terrorist is constructed as a perpetrator of nihilist violence aimed at the destruction of free societies, or the 'murder of the state'. Reinforcing the need for immediate action, it is claimed in the related statements that unless such action is taken, a reign of anarchy, jungle law, or the medieval concept of private war would prevail. In other statements, sometimes related to the discourse of humanitarian law (see above), the new 'war without war' seems already to have been waged, depriving innocent people of their right to be free from fear, which only could be guaranteed by organised governments.[21] The image of the terrorist sowing chaos in the organised (governed) society was amplified by his subjectification as a pirate, related to a particular new manifestation of terrorism: hijacking aircraft.[22] The terrorist could thus be associated with the archetypal and universal crime against order and the transgression of *jus gentium*, which rendered him, as it did the pirate of yore, effectively *hors humanité*. The identification of terrorist with the pirate seems also to have conditioned today's normalised term for a rogue or failed state where terrorism is thriving as a 'safe haven'. Medical metaphors mentioned above could also be mobilised to add vividness to the image of the terrorist as spreading chaos. Terrorism could therefore be constructed as a contagious disease (cancer, plague, or other unspecified epidemic) that threatened to consume the (international) body politic, which had to be cured and immunised as soon as possible – even, in line with the discourse of method, before all causes of the illness were known.

To conclude, many elements of Western discourse as briefly presented here are easily recognisable in contemporary (counter)terrorism speech. The continuities include (ironically) the discourse of alarm (rendering terrorism a new and unprecedented threat), a consequent call for immediate and exceptional action, or the various patterns of depoliticisation and dehumanisation of the terrorist. In the 1970s, this discourse may be seen to (re)emerge as a strategic response to the perceived emergency consisting in the challenge to the political *status quo* both inside the discrete political orders and internationally (as political struggles failed to remain contained to their territorial loci). Because of the divided political field, no hegemony was established in the discourse of states, and no true global prohibition regime emerged. The discourse of the first world states can nonetheless be seen as conditioning concrete national and regional practices of counterterrorism in the West. It can also be seen as related to the truth claims produced in the newly established field of terrorism science.

Knowledge

The 1970s was when the field of Western (not just West European) science of terrorism came into existence. It was formed by a relatively small community of academics from various backgrounds, but with a clear agenda, membership, funding opportunities and some shared causal beliefs and notions of validity (Ranstorp 2006, 2009; Reid 1993). In social terms it can therefore be differentiated from the current field for production of authoritative knowledge about terrorism, which was vastly expanded in the 2000s, partly because of the incorporation of a mass of 'terrorism experts' whose authority seems to depend largely on their proximity to the incumbent structures of power, and who contribute to the acceptance and legitimisation of the governmental discourses by repeating and thus lending authority to their truth claims. That said, and to paraphrase Friedrich Nietzsche, 'terrorology' in the 1970s was born from the spirit of counter-terrorism, which had profound consequences for the field's dominant discursive practice and can be posited at once as a consequence and a vehicle of constitutive relations of power and knowledge.

The field's general *ethos* can be conceived of as liberal and positivist. Its liberal character was manifested in its concern about the future of the Western liberal political order, since this order was claimed to be threatened by terrorism, but also because of the nature of its *response* to terrorism

(Wilkinson 1986). At the same time, the field's ethos was not progressive and emancipatory, but rather favoured the political *status quo* (Gunning 2007; Jackson 2009; Jarvis 2009). More understanding of terrorism would translate into a reduction in terrorist violence, but without the necessity of transforming the existing political order (or changing any of its policies) since this order was not where the causes of such violence were found. The best way to prevent excesses of the security apparatus was to increase its effectiveness. Therefore, the field reflected rather than interrogated the predominant rationality of the security apparatus proposed above.

The better understanding of terrorism that the field as a problem-solving science (Cox 1981) *par excellence* sought to produce was to emerge from the accumulation of truth claims obtained through following the positivist standard of scientific inquiry, privileging quantitative methods and explanatory nomothetic statements as preferred research outcomes. However, in their operation members of the scientific community had to rely on facts that were acquired in ways that fell far short of this positivist standard. Since at the same time the science of terrorism claimed to produce *objective* knowledge, it was not only inconsistent but it also effectively legitimised the reality created by those facts (by and large provided by government agencies) since it endowed them with scientific credentials; or, at the very least, by the use of unreflexive language it reproduced normative assumptions coded into the existing security apparatuses. The procedures of validating power practices in the field of terrorism knowledge identifiable today can also be witnessed – albeit at a smaller scale – in the 1970s.

While the community of terrorism scholars in the 1970s was rather small, no consensus on the definition – i.e. the proper object of study – emerged. This facilitated the field's overreach (Gordon 2004; Silke 2004), since while a ritual of despair that no commonly agreed definition of the subject existed would be often performed in the introduction of terrorism treatises, this would be followed by the production of essentialist, nomothetic and normative statements about the subject whose boundaries were effectively blurred (as they are now). It seems to have been the case even for scholars sceptical of the possibility of a truly scientific and predictive study of terrorism such as Laqueur (2001: 146), who, in spite of his doubts, did not conclude that there was little benefit in subsuming the diverse activities associated with terrorism under one heading and who (his criticism of nomothetic science notwithstanding) made a number of generalising statements about the ineffectiveness of terrorism or the absence of a causal relationship between terrorism and grievance (Laqueur 2001: 220–1). On the other hand, the field – in line with its dominant ethos – did not engage in earnest with state terrorism. Indeed, in another ritual, a number of studies on terrorism made a distinction between state and revolutionary activity. However, after initially establishing such typology, their focus then tended to be exclusively on non-state terrorism (Jackson 2009). When state terrorism is referred to, it seems to be invariably in reference to the *other*, to second world authoritarian dictatorships.

The lack of authentic empirical research notwithstanding, drawing a character sketch of the terrorist was a rather popular endeavor among the 1970s terrorism scholars. In a number of statements, the terrorist emerges as a rational and politically motivated actor (Crenshaw 1981; Jenkins 1974; Shultz 1978). Yet in many others, pointing to his social background but often also his mental health, the terrorist would be characterised as mindless, senseless, irrational, abnormal, sociopathic, narcissistic, paranoid, disturbed or self-destructive (Hacker 1977; Horowitz 1973; McKnight 1974; Russell and Miller 1977); or even as showing pathological features without suffering from any identifiable psychological disorder, a convenient argument relieving the author of the need to summon evidence of the diagnosis (Silke 1998). Such statements could then facilitate strategies of depoliticisation of the terrorist in the political discourse (which also invoked medical imagery, see above) even as both in this discourse and the truth claims generally articulated in the field of terrorism science his political character would, in what could be conceived of as the third ritual, remain to be pointed out.

Finally, while terrorism science in the 1970s does not appear to be significantly disciplined and no paradigmatic theory or competing theories of terrorism can be detected, some conceptualisations were rather established and recurrent. Perhaps the most significant with regard to both the contemporary political discourse and security apparatus on one hand, and the current (counter)terrorism speech on the other, was the concept of terrorism as a new mode of warfare. Like the states' discourse outlined above, terrorism would be constructed as a new and unprecedented threat to the civilised order, a consequence of the terrorist's lack of respect for established norms on the use of violence, the capability of the terrorist to appear and strike anywhere, or society's dependence on modern technology and the terrorist's abuse of this technology to his own advantage, including the (hypothesised) use of weapons of mass destruction (Cameron 2004; Jenkins 1974; Sloan 1978; Wilkinson 1974).[23] In facilitating apocalyptic visions of the future (unless emergency action implicitly conforming to the 'war model' is taken to eliminate the terrorist threat), the concept of terrorism as a new mode of warfare would also prefigure a notion familiar in the academic discourse of terrorism since the end of the Cold War: the 'new terrorism' (for a critical overview of the extensive literature on the subject see Duyvesteyn 2004; Spencer 2006), which also, ironically, constructs terrorist violence as an unprecedented threat due to its unseen lethality (reproducing and amplifying the discourse of CBRN (chemical, biological, radiological and nuclear) terrorism), its indiscriminate character, its (irrational) aim of pure destruction and its potential omnipresence. A significant discontinuity between the concepts of a new mode of warfare and that of a new terrorism seems to lie in the fact that the latter is conditioned on the nexus of terrorism and religion (Hoffman 1993; Jurgensmeyer 2000; Stern 2003) – or better, Islam (Jackson 2007) – which ultimately makes this unfettered and in worldly terms 'inexplicable' violence possible.

In terms of the components of Western security apparatuses, the states' (counter)terrorism discourse and the terrorism science field, which reinforced truth claims produced in the field of political and security professionals in the 1970s, a number of continuities can be identified with the contemporary speech and practice. Pointing out these continuities and the relations of practices in various fields in this period need not be of historical (or even *antiquarian*) interest only. It may also serve (and such indeed was the intent of this chapter) as a contribution to the historicisation and critique (alongside ethical and other interrogations) of what can be posited as a current global terrorism *dispositif* – a heterogeneous assemblage of practices of law, discipline, government and security through which power is exercised in today's politics.

Notes

1 Separatist political violence in Northern Ireland in the 1970s was the domain of not only PIRA, but also (less significantly) of other groups such as OIRA (the Official Irish Republican Army) or INLA (the Irish National Liberation Army). Loyalists/Unionists such as the Ulster Volunteer Force or the Ulster Freedom Fighters also turned to violence, occassionally even against the government (resentful of perceived concessions of the separatists), but mostly as part of the sectarian warfare witnessed by the region.
2 It should not be forgotten in this context to what extent the representations of the Vietnam War had influenced the mobilisation and character of the 1960s movement.
3 The war model was, on the other hand, preferred by the terrorists themselves, who positioned themselves, to take the RAF case, as leading 'resistance' against the 'Fascist state', with obvious historical connotations.
4 The UK reacted to the ruling by the European Court of Human Rights (ECHR) on a case involving the measure (which cited breech of the European Human Rights Convention, art. 5/3) by declaring a public emergency to legitimise it (cf. Bonner 1992). In Spain, the exceptional powers were established by laws passed both by the Frankist and the new democratic government (cf. Jimenez 1992).
5 In Northern Ireland, after the British army initially assumed a broader role in the early 1970s (including the infamous Bloody Sunday, 1972), it remained more involved only in the border areas (underlining the leading role of the Royal Ulster Constabulary, RUC).
6 Chalk (1996: 109) suggests that Italy's Servizio Informazioni Difesa (SID) was involved in protecting, if not stay-behind networks, then certainly right-wing extremists reacting against the challenge to the status quo from the left in the early 1970s.
7 For the history of policing international terrorism, including its rudimentary origins, cf. Deflem (2002).
8 A permanent working group was established in EPC only later (1984), however.

9 From the semantic point of view, it appears that the name of the group was rather heavily loaded. It was at once an acronym (Terrorism, Radicalism, Extremism and International Violence) and a cross-reference to the group's first chairman (A.R. Fontejn) and meeting place (Rome).
10 It was maintained that the debate was organised around international as opposed to domestic terrorism (cf. Doc. A/9028/1973, Report of the Ad hoc Committee), and because of this effective internationalisation the statements about terrorism are taken to be relevant to both forms, with less attention being paid to the recurrent securitising truth claims about terrorism as a threat to the international political order in the discourse of alarm (see below).
11 In what follows, statements made by West European states are given only as illustrations of the first world discourse. Statements were produced in this discourse however also by other states in the geographical first world and their allies in the geographical third world.
12 Doc. A/C.6/SR.1369 (1972), Minutes of the Sixth Committee, statement by Italy.
13 Doc. A/RES/3034 (1972); A/AC.160/1 (1973), statements by Austria, Belgium, Germany, Italy, or Spain.
14 Doc. A/PV.2142 (1973), statement by Austria.
15 Doc. A/AC.160/1 (1973), debate in the Ad hoc Committee, statement by Syria.
16 Cf. Doc. A/AC.160/L.3 (1973), Draft Report of the Ad hoc Committee; A/32/37 (1977), Report of the Ad hoc Committee; A/AC.160/SR.7 (1977), Minutes of the Ad hoc Committee.
17 Making an analogy between terrorism and war, Belgium pointed out that the special committee on the question of defining aggression had never been asked to consider its causes: in this attempt to make war illegal, its causes were of no consequence. Doc. A/C.6/SR.1365.
18 Cf. Doc. A/AC.160/1 (1973); A/PV.2037 (1972); A/PV.2125 (1973); A/C.6/SR.1355 (1972); A/C.6/SR.1357 (1972); A/C.6/SR.1367 (1972); A/9028 (1973).
19 Cf. Doc. A/AC.160/WG/R.2 (1979), a working paper by the United Kingdom for the Ad hoc Committee.
20 Doc. A/9028 (1973), Report of the Ad hoc Committee, proposal by France; A/AC.160/1 (1973), observation by Austria to the Ad hoc Committee; A/C.6/34/SR.6 (1979), Minutes of the Sixth Committee, statement by Spain; A/AC.160/1 (1973), observation by Portugal to the Ad hoc Committee; A/PV.2037 (1972).
21 Cf. Doc. A/C.6/SR.1359 (1972), statement by Portugal, who invoked the authority of Hedley Bull to strike the point; A/C.6/SR.1365 (1972), statement by Belgium; A/AC.160/1 (1973), observation by Austria to the Ad hoc Committee; A/AC.160/SR.6 (1977), Minutes of the Ad hoc Committee, statement by Austria.
22 The identification of aircraft hijacking with piracy may have been conditioned on the terrorist and the pirate both roaming spaces characterised by a void of sovereign power (at least until the conclusion of treaties of the ICAO (International Civil Aviation Organization), at the Hague and the Montreal conventions). At the same time, the subjectification was not inevitable since in the traditional understanding, embodied also in Geneva Convention on the High Seas (1958), piracy tended to be defined as an act of one vessel against another (rather than a forcible takeover of one vessel by those on board) and related to strictly private ends (cf. Glaser 1973: 833).
23 Jenkins, who coined the concept of terrorism as a new mode of warfare, was himself sceptical of the use of nuclear weapons by terrorists. Drawing on his other famous metaphor, terrorism as theatre, and convictions about the terrorist's rational character, he would instead claim that 'terrorists wanted a lot of people watching, not a lot of people dead' (Jenkins 1975).

References

Amoore, L. (2006) 'Biometric Borders: Governing Mobilities in the War on Terror', *Political Geography* 25(3), 336–51.
Amoore, L. and de Goede, M. (2005) 'Governance, Risk and Dataveillance in the War on Terror', *Crime, Law and Social Change* 43(2–3), 149–73.
Aradau, C. and van Munster, R. (2007) 'Governing Terrorism Through Risk', *European Journal of International Relations* 13(1), 89–115.
Bigo, D. (2008) 'Security: A Field Left Fallow', in M. Dillon and A. Neal (eds) *Foucault on Politics, Security and War*, London: Palgrave Macmillan, 93–114.
Bonner, D. (1992) 'The United Kingdom Response to Terrorism', *Terrorism and Political Violence* 4(4), 171–205.
Bures, O. (2011) *EU Counter-Terrorist Policy: A Paper Tiger?* London: Ashgate.
Butler, J. (2006) *Precarious Life: The Powers of Mourning and Violence*, London: Verso.
Cameron, G. (2004) 'Weapons of Mass Destruction Terrorism Research: Past and Future', in A. Silke (ed.) *Research on Terrorism: Trends, Achievements and Failures*, London: Frank Cass, 72–90.
Cardona, M. (1992) 'The European Response to Terrorism', *Terrorism and Political Violence* 4(4), 45–254.
Chalk, P. (1996) *West European Terrorism and Counter-Terrorism*, New York: St. Martin's Press.
Cline, R. and Alexander, Y. (1984) *Terrorism: The Soviet Connection*, New York: Crane Russak.
Cox, R. (1981) 'Social Forces, States and World Orders: Beyond International Relations Theory', *Millenium* 10(2), 126–55.
Crenshaw, M. (1981) 'The Causes of Terrorism', *Comparative Politics* 13(4), 377–99.
Curtis, L. (1984) *Ireland: The Propaganda War*, London: Pluto Press.
Dean, M. (2010) *Governmentality: Power and Rule in Modern Society*, London: Sage.
Deflem, M. (2002) *Policing World Society: Historical Foundations of International Police Cooperation*, Oxford: Oxford University Press.
Deflem, M. (2006) 'Europol and the Policing of International Terrorism: Counterterrorism in a Global Perspective', *Justice Quaterly* 23(3), 336–59.
Della Porta, D. (1998) *Policing Protest: The Control of Mass Demonstrations in Western Societies*, Minneapolis, MN: University of Minnesota Press.
Ditrych, O. (2013a) 'From Discourse to Dispositif: States and Terrorism between Marseille and the 9/11', *Security Dialogue* 44(3), 223–40.
Ditrych, O. (2013b) 'International Terrorism as Conspiracy: Debating Terrorism in the League of Nations', *Historical Social Research* 38(1), 200–10.
Ditrych, O. (2014) *States' Discourse of Terrorism: A Genealogy*, London: Palgrave.
Duyvesteyn, I. (2004) 'How New is the New Terrorism?' *Studies in Conflict and Terrorism* 27(5), 439–54.
Foucault, M. (1991) 'Questions of Method', in G. Burchell, C. Gordon and P. Miller (eds), *The Foucault Effect: Studies in Governmentality*, Chicago, IL: Chicago University Press, 73–86.
Foucault, M. (1997) *Archaeology of Knowledge*, London: Routledge.
Foucault, M. (2007) *Security, Territory, Population: Lectures at the Collège de France (1977–1978)*, London: Palgrave.
Francis, S. (1981) *The Soviet Strategy of Terror*, Washington: Heritage Foundation.
Ganser, D. (2005) *NATO's Secret Armies: Operation Gladio and Terrorism in Western Europe*, London: Routledge.

Gehrig, S. (2011) 'Sympathizing Subcultures? The Millieus of West German Terrorism', in M. Klimke, J. Pekelder and J. Scharloth (eds) *Between Prague Spring and French May: Opposition and Revolt in Europe: 1960–1980*, New York: Berghahn Books, 233–50.

Glaser, S. (1973) 'Le terrorisme international et ses divers aspects', *Revue internationale de droit comparé* 25(4), 825–50.

Gordon, A. (2004) 'Terrorism and Knowledge Growth: A Databases and Internet Analysis', in A. Silke (ed.) *Research on Terrorism: Trends, Achievements and Failures*, London: Frank Cass, 104–18.

Gunning, J. (2007) 'A Case for Critical Terrorism Studies?' *Government and Opposition* 42(3), 363–93.

Hacker, F.J. (1977) *Crusaders, Criminals, Crazies: Terror and Terrorism in Our Time*, New York: W.W. Norton.

Hansen, L. (2006) *Security as Practice: Discourse Analysis and the Bosnian War*, London: Routledge.

Herman, E. (1982) *The Real Terror Network: Terrorism in Fact and Propaganda*, Boston, MA: South End Press.

Hoffman, B. (1993) *'Holy Terror': The Implications of Terrorism motivated by a Religious Imperative*, Santa Monica, CA: RAND.

Horowitz, I.L. (1973) 'Political Terrorism and State Power', *Journal of Political and Military Sociology* 1(1), 147–57.

Jackson, R. (2007) 'Constructing Enemies: "Islamic Terrorism" in Political and Academic Discourse', *Government and Opposition* 42(3), 394–426.

Jackson, R. (2009) 'Knowledge, Power and Politics', in R. Jackson, M. Breen Smyth and J. Gunning (eds) *Critical Terrorism Studies: A New Research Agenda*, London: Routledge, 66–83.

Jarvis, L. (2009) 'The Spaces and Faces of Critical Terrorism Studies', *Security Dialogue* 40(1), 5–27.

Jenkins, B. (1974) *Terrorism: A New Kind of Warfare*, Santa Monica, CA: RAND.

Jenkins, B. (1975) *Will Terrorists go Nuclear?* Santa Monica, CA: RAND.

Jimenez, F. (1992) 'Spain: The Terrorist Challenge and the Government's Response', *Terrorism and Political Violence* 4(4), 110–30.

Jurgensmeyer, M. (2000) *Terror in the Mind of God: The Global Rise of Religious Violence*, Berkeley, CA: Berkeley University Press.

Laqueur, W. (2001) *A History of Terrorism*, New Brunswick: Transaction Publishers.

Lemke, T. (2011) *Foucault, Governmentality and Critique*, London: Paradigm.

McKnight, G. (1974) *The Terrorist Mind*, Indianapolis, IN: Bobbs and Merrill.

Pekelder, J. (2011) 'The RAF Solidarity Movement from a European Perspective', in M. Klimke, J. Pekelder and J. Scharloth (eds) *Between Prague Spring and French May: Opposition and Revolt in Europe: 1960–1980*, New York: Berghahn Books, 251–66.

Ranstorp, M. (2006) *Mapping Terrorism Research: state of the Art, Gaps and Future Direction*, London: Routledge.

Ranstorp, M. (2009) 'Mapping Terrorism Studies after 9/11: An Academic Fields of Old Problems and New Prospects', in R. Jackson, M. Breen Smyth and J. Gunning (eds) *Critical Terrorism Studies: A New Research Agenda*, London: Routledge, 13–33.

Reid, E. (1993) 'Terrorism Research and the Diffusion of Ideas', *Knowledge and Policy* 6(1), 17–37.

Russell, C. and Miller, B. (1977) 'Profile of a Terrorist', *Studies in Conflict and Terrorism* 1(1), 17–34.
Saul, B. (2006) 'The Legal Response of the League of Nations to Terrorism', *Journal of International Criminal Justice* 4(1), 78–102.
Shultz, R. (1978) 'Conceptualizing Political Terrorism: A Typology', *Journal of International Affairs* 32(1), 7–16.
Silke, A. (1998) 'Cheshire-Cat Logic: The Recurring Theme of Terrorist Abnormality in Psychological Research', *Psychology, Crime and Law* 4(1), 51–69.
Silke, A. (2004) 'An Introduction to Terrorism Research', in A. Silke (ed.) *Research on Terrorism: Trends, Achievements and Failures*, London: Frank Cass, 1–29.
Sloan, S. (1978) 'International Terrorism: Academic Quest, Operational Art and Policy Implications', *Journal of International Affairs* 32(1), 1–5.
Spencer, A. (2006) 'Questioning the Concept of "New Terrorism"', *Peace, Conflict and Development* 8(8), 1–33.
Sterling, C. (1980) *Terror Network: The Secret War of International Terrorism*, New York: Holt, Rinehart and Winston.
Stern, J. (2003) *Terror in the Name of God: Why Religious Militants Kill*, New York: HarperCollins.
Taylor, P. (1993) States *of Terror: Democracy and Political Violence*, London: Penguin.
Wilkinson, P. (1974) *Political Terrorism*, London: Macmillan.
Wilkinson, P. (1986) *Terrorism and the Liberal State*, New York: New York University Press.
Zlataric, B. (1975) 'History of International Terrorism and its Legal Control', in M.C. Bassiouni (ed.) *International Terrorism and Political Crimes*, Springfield, IL: Charles C. Thomas, 474–86.

3 The power of terrorism frames

Responses to non-Islamist lone-wolf terrorism in Europe

A. Maurits van der Veen

On July 22, 2011, Anders Behring Breivik bombed government buildings in Oslo, and then carried out a mass shooting at Utøya island in Norway. His acts resulted in a total of 77 deaths. As many have noted, before Breivik had been apprehended, most commentators were sure that organized Islamic extremists were behind the terrorist attacks (Gjørv 2012: 22). After he had been identified, on the other hand, a number of observers argued that he was not a terrorist after all, but a mass murderer (e.g., Orr 2011). Perhaps most strikingly, the Norwegian government's official report on Breivik's attacks allocated more space to the possible threat posed to Norway by organized Islamic extremists than to the threats represented by actors similar to Breivik.

This pattern of reactions is neither accidental nor unique to Norway; I argue that it is due to the international dominance of a particular framing of terrorism, not only among the general public, but also among policy-makers. This frame links terrorism to Islamist extremists organized in international networks. This chapter analyzes the influence of this frame across several cases where it is clearly inappropriate, identifying a cross-national pattern that has not previously been noted. Specifically, the chapter focuses on three cases of attacks by non-Muslim, solo assailants after 2001: the 2002 murder of Pim Fortuyn in the Netherlands, the 2003 murder of Anna Lindh in Sweden, and Breivik's attacks in Norway.

These cases were selected for several reasons. First, none of the three countries had direct experience with Islamist terrorism at the time of these attacks, but each had some prior experience with the type of attack studied here. This makes them comparatively unlikely to be hosts to a strong organized Islamist terrorism (OIT) frame. Second, the three attacks cover a wide range of possible scenarios, from a nearly random assault with no advance planning (Sweden), through political assassination (Netherlands), to a mass attack (Norway). If the OIT frame is evident in each case, therefore, this tells us something about the scope of its influence. Finally, all three of these countries are stable democracies of long standing; they ought to be less vulnerable than some newer or less stable democracies to demagoguery or rhetorical hype such as might be associated with the strategic use of the OIT frame.

I argue that, notwithstanding this lack of direct experience with Islamist terrorism, a strong OIT frame has nevertheless shaped reactions to the three incidents in question. Specifically, attacks that are not perpetrated by organized Islamist extremists tend not to get characterized as terrorism, even though they do not differ in any meaningful sense from comparable incidents perpetrated by Islamic extremists that *are* characterized as terrorism. Second, when such incidents *do* get classified as terrorist acts, policy discussions will focus as much on Islamist extremism as they do on the actual perpetrator(s). Finally, lessons from such incidents are likely to be incorporated imperfectly, if at all, in counterterrorism policy, thus affecting reactions to subsequent terrorist incidents.

I develop the argument in two stages. First, I briefly discuss the relevant literature on the framing of counterterrorism policy, offering some context for the arguments made here. In addition, in order to establish the empirical relevance – or rather, lack thereof – of the OIT frame, I review the historical experiences with terrorism in each of the three countries. The second part of the chapter analyzes the policy debates that followed the incidents in question in each of the three countries. Here, I focus specifically on official government reports and on debates within the national parliament. The emphasis throughout is on policy-makers debating issues with one another, rather than trying to sell a particular story to the public, in order to establish that the framing we observe is not simply a matter of populist expediency – in which case it might not affect policy choices – but rather reflects how policy-makers themselves see the issue.

Framing and counterterrorism

The literature on responses to terrorism continues to expand rapidly.[1] In recent years, scholars have increasingly emphasized the importance of national discourse and perceptions in shaping reactions to terrorism. Among others, the role of authorities and the media in defining and framing the issue has become a fertile subject of study (e.g., Spencer 2012). For example, Tsoukala shows that French and British authorities have defended emergency counterterrorism measures by appealing to sovereignty-related arguments over civil liberties and human rights (Tsoukala 2006). Related arguments have been made for other countries (Baker 2003; Heller *et al.* 2012; Meyer 2009: 652).[2]

As one might expect, ideational factors help account for cross-national variation in counterterrorism (Perliger 2012). Thus, Katzenstein argues that "different conceptions of self and other" account for the divergent framing of the 9/11 terrorist attacks in the United States (war), Germany (crime), and Japan (crisis) (Katzenstein 2003: 733). Similarly, Meyer emphasizes the central importance of cross-national variation in threat perceptions to counterterrorism policy in the European Union (Meyer 2009; see also Rees and Aldrich 2005).

More generally, we know from the extensive literature on framing in political psychology that the way people think about an issue has a significant impact on their policy attitudes and choices (Chong and Druckman 2007a; Druckman 2010; Goffman 1974), as well as on their choices of frames in attempting to persuade others (Chong and Druckman 2007b; Entman 2004; Zald 1996). As a result, outcomes will be shaped both by the deliberate choices of particular frames to push a policy initiative, and by decision-makers' individual, internal framing of a policy – what Chong and Druckman call "frames in communication" and "frames in thought," respectively (see Druckman 2010).

If framing – and, in particular, the importance of national experiences to the salience of particular frames – indeed has the impact scholars attribute to it, we should expect significant and persistent divergence across countries in the shape of their counterterrorism policies. Indeed, Nohrstedt and Hansén find that there has been comparatively little convergence in counterterrorism policies across the European Union (EU) since 2001, despite pressures towards convergence arising from similar international (from the United States) and supranational (from the EU) entities (Nohrstedt and Hansén 2010). On the other hand, some evidence suggests that national experiences and collective identity are not as important to the shaping of counterterrorism policy as they might be in some other issue areas. For example, these same authors also find that EU nations *have* converged in their codification of what constitutes terrorism, even where countries have little experience with terrorist attacks on their own soil (Nohrstedt and Hansén 2010).[3]

In fact, one particular frame regarding terrorism has become salient in many countries. It links terrorism to organized Islamist extremism, and this, in turn, to incompatibilities between Western and Islamic values (Jackson 2007). Its prominence is not altogether surprising. After all, prior to Breivik's attacks, the three modern terrorist events that loomed largest in the minds of most Europeans were undoubtedly the September 11, 2001 plane hijackings and crashes in the United States, the March 11, 2004 train attacks in Madrid, and the July 7, 2005 subway attacks in London. These were also the attacks with the highest victim death toll: 2,976 in the United States, 191 in Madrid, and 52 in London. More importantly, in all three events the perpetrators were part of an organized group of Islamist extremists.

On the other hand, it is far from obvious that incompatibilities between Western and Islamic values lie at the root of these attacks (and others similarly associated with Islamist extremists). Moreover, it is not the case that all attacks perpetrated by extremists claiming to act in the name of Islam are the result of organized group planning. Finally, such extremists are hardly the only perpetrators of terrorist attacks in recent years (Europol

2012). Few political leaders would deny these basic facts. However, it is possible that they nevertheless remain influenced, perhaps subconsciously, by the salience of the OIT frame (cf. Greenwald 2011). If so, this may well have negative effects on the quality and effectiveness of counterterrorism policy. In fact, several scholars have identified the strength of this frame as one of the causes of policies that overreact to certain terrorist incidents perpetrated by Islamist extremists, for instance by singling out all Muslims for heightened scrutiny (e.g., Pantazis and Pemberton 2009).

In this chapter, I focus on a different implication: the salience of the OIT frame can also be expected to undermine the ability of policy-makers to learn from and react to instances of terrorism perpetrated by non-Islamic, non-organized "lone wolves." As noted earlier, we should expect to observe three things. First, such incidents will tend not to get characterized as terrorism, even though they do not differ in any meaningful sense from comparable incidents perpetrated by Islamic extremists that *are* characterized as terrorism. This is problematic because it means that policies in place to respond to terrorist attacks may not be invoked or activated. Second, when such incidents *do* get classified as terrorist acts, policy discussions will focus as much on Islamist extremism as they do on the actual perpetrator(s); as a result, some potential lessons to be learned may not be discovered. Finally, and relatedly, such incidents will not form part of the national experiences that inform subsequent reactions to terrorism.

Before analyzing the implications of the OIT frame, it is necessary first to eliminate one possible explanation for its salience that would undermine my argument. Counterterrorism policies seek to maximize a polity's ability to prevent terrorist attacks; to foil or interrupt attacks that are not prevented; and to prosecute the perpetrators in such a way as to minimize their political impact. Ideally, all this should be accomplished as efficiently (cheaply) as possible. It is conceivable that the salience of the OIT frame aids in this goal by offering a valuable heuristic shortcut. If this were the case, its salience would need to be driven by the historical experiences of and current threats faced by the countries studied here. If, on the other hand, neither past experience nor present threats justify the salience of the frame, this further supports my argument.

Experiences with terrorism in the Netherlands, Sweden, and Norway

Public perceptions notwithstanding, organized Islamist terrorism is quite rare in Western countries, and is dwarfed in impact by separatist terrorism (Europol 2010, 2011, 2012). This is true not only for the most recent period, but also going back several decades (Engene 2011; Kundnani 2012; Nesser 2008: 924). In the particular countries under study here, the Netherlands, Sweden, and Norway, Islamist extremists have not been prominent.

In the Netherlands, terrorism has caused 28 deaths since 1970 (22 victims and six perpetrators). The most visible instances of terrorism prior to the turn of the century were several train hijackings in the mid-1970s perpetrated by Moluccan extremists. One such hijacking ended with three deaths in 1975; another, two years later, resulted in the deaths of two hostages and six hijackers. Comparatively little political violence has taken place in the Netherlands in the three decades since. The IRA committed several attacks, including (probably) the assassination of the British ambassador in 1979, as well as the killing of several British soldiers in 1988 and of two Australian tourists in 1990. The Revolutionary Anti-Racist Action group (RaRa) bombed a number of buildings and monuments between 1984 and 1993, but no one was ever wounded in their actions. A few other organizations have bombed or threatened symbolic buildings or political leaders, but again without causing injury or death.[4] As of 2002, the year Fortuyn was murdered, there had been no violent incidents associated with Islamic extremism.

In Sweden, groups with terrorist tendencies have been associated with the white power and anarchist (and similar) milieus (Reinfeldt *et al.* 2011). In 1975, a branch of the Red Army Faction (RAF) occupied the West German embassy in Stockholm. Two embassy officials and two perpetrators died in the attack. In the mid-1980s four Palestinians were sentenced for participation in a number of bombings in Sweden, Denmark, and Amsterdam. Swedish Prime Minister Olof Palme was killed in 1986, in a still-unsolved shooting. Finally, in 1991–2, a right-wing extremist shot 11 dark-skinned people, killing one.

In Norway, lastly, most terrorist activity has been associated with right-wing extremism. Neo-Nazi groups and sympathizers have attacked a leftist bookstore (1977), a Labor Day parade (1979), and a mosque in Oslo (1985). In addition, Israeli commandos killed a Moroccan waiter they mistakenly believed to be a prominent Palestinian activist in 1973, and an unknown assailant attempted to kill the publisher of the Norwegian translation of Rushdie's *Satanic Verses* in 1993.

Overall, even before Breivik's attacks, all three countries had had more exposure to right-wing and racist violence than to Islamist terrorism (Kundnani 2012: 33–4). All three countries had also experienced one or more "lone-wolf" incidents perpetrated by individual actors without any systematic connection to organized terrorist groups. Although such attacks appear to have become more prevalent in recent years, lone-wolf terrorism remains comparatively understudied (but see Bakker and de Graaf 2010; Pantucci 2011; Spaaij 2010). Be that as it may, in each of these three countries policy-makers could draw on their own national experiences with such attacks. Moreover, insofar as lone-wolf attacks empirically constitute a prominent threat in each of these countries, one might have expected political actors to react accordingly in terms of rethinking counterterrorist policy. Instead, as we shall see, the organized Islamic terrorism frame affected reactions in each case.

Reacting to lone-wolf, non-Islamic attacks: three case studies

In each of the three cases analyzed below, a tendency to think of terrorism primarily as organized Islamist terrorism produced the effects predicted: a tendency not to classify an incident as terrorist in nature, an emphasis on organized Islamist terrorism when the incident is nevertheless seen as terrorist, and a failure to derive potentially relevant lessons for counterterrorism policy. In the case of the murders of Pim Fortuyn and Anna Lindh, the second of those implications is mostly absent, since the incidents were almost never discussed as terrorist; in contrast, this second effect is particularly notable in the case of Breivik's attacks, which *were* widely characterized as terrorist in nature.

The murder of Pim Fortuyn (Netherlands, May 6, 2002)

Pim Fortuyn was killed on May 6, 2002, at the height of a national election campaign. The precise motives of his killer are unclear, but in his confession he pointed to Fortuyn's opinions about weaker groups in society, his polarizing effect on Dutch politics, and his likely political power after the elections (Netherlands 2002). Volkert van der Graaf, the perpetrator, appears to have acted alone and was arrested almost immediately. A little less than a year later he was sentenced to 18 years in prison. Most Dutch politicians identified the murder as an act of political assassination rather than terror (de Jong 2012). Nevertheless, although Van der Graaf's primary purpose appears to have been assassination rather than terror, the justification offered in his confession does imply that other similar Dutch leaders might have reasons for some fear about their safety. Moreover, the murder is included in the standard datasets of terrorist incidents (e.g., Engene 2007).

Although it was the first notable political assassination in the Netherlands in over 300 years, it was accepted with relative equanimity. It produced no major new legislation to deal with such threats, and the main conclusion authorities drew was that the Dutch system of surveillance and protection of prominent public figures needed to be strengthened and more centrally coordinated (Commissie van den Haak 2002). About one month after Fortuyn's death, the government set up an independent commission, chaired by H. F. van den Haak, to research the circumstances surrounding Fortuyn's security and protection. Although the commission's mandate was framed entirely in terms of the government's failure to protect Fortuyn, who had received several death threats over the preceding months (cf. *Handelingen* 2002a), its inquiries inevitably ventured into an assessment of the source and nature of those threats (Commissie van den Haak 2002).

Although the word terrorism occurs numerous times in the Van den Haak report, this is generally by way of distinguishing what happened to

Fortuyn from terrorism. For example, the report notes that protecting individuals is not, in principle, the job of the international security service (Binnenlandse Veiligheidsdienst, BVD), although in cases of terrorism this could become part of its task. It also discusses how Fortuyn reacted to the 9/11 terrorist attacks (Commissie van den Haak 2002: 44127ff.). Ironically, it notes that Fortuyn himself explicitly propagated the OIT frame: "Islam ... is an aggressive ideology. And terrorism is therefore intrinsic to it" (quoted in Commissie van den Haak 2002: 175). Finally, the report cites the conclusion of an official investigation into threats Fortuyn received during the election campaign, which was that "there is no indication of a terrorist threat against Mr. Fortuyn" (Commissie van den Haak 2002: 271). Nowhere does the report suggest that Fortuyn's murder was an instance of terrorism, or that it offers any real lessons for counterterrorism policy.

The debate in parliament about the Van den Haak report, on December 19, 2002, concentrated on the responsibilities of the Dutch state to protect those who may face death threats, regardless of their origin. It ran across the morning and afternoon sessions of the Chamber of Representatives, occupying 57 pages in the parliamentary record. Strikingly, not one speaker mentioned the word "terrorism." The single occasion when the notion of terrorism reared its head was when representative Herben, Fortuyn's successor as leader of the Lijst Pim Fortuyn (LPF, Fortuyn's political party), argued, "an Al Qaeda suicide murderer is not going to warn you that he is coming" (*Handelingen Tweede Kamer* 2002b: 2723). He did so even though there was no evidence that any of the threats Fortuyn had received prior to his demise had originated from organized Islamist extremists.

In sum, the Dutch case displays each of the three patterns predicted: it is not classified as an act of terrorism, the lone instance when terrorism comes into play features a reference to Al Qaeda, and policy-makers do not derive any lessons for counterterrorist policy. Even expanding the system of surveillance and protection did little to prepare the Dutch government for its next experience with political violence, the murder of Theo van Gogh two years later, on November 2, 2004. This murder *was* committed by an Islamist extremist, and it is striking how differently policy-makers responded. Van Gogh, another major public figure with no official political position, was murdered by Mohammed Bouyeri, who fired seven bullets, making sure Van Gogh was dead by also stabbing him several times with a large knife. Bouyeri then attached an open threat to Dutch parliamentarian Ayaan Hirsi Ali to the body with the same knife.[5]

As was the case with Fortuyn, this murder was the act of a single extremist, with no obvious plans to kill other people – Bouyeri had hoped to die a martyr in the process of being apprehended. Yet in a drastic departure from the reactions to Fortuyn's murder, nearly every commentator immediately identified this as an act of terrorism. Moreover, the Dutch

Parliament held an emergency debate on the murder just nine days later, again in contrast to the far more subdued reaction in 2002. The debate was opened by Geert Wilders, expressing his anger that Van Gogh had been murdered in barbaric fashion by a "Muslim terrorist" (*Handelingen* 2004: 1278). Wilders is well known for his ideas about Islam and terrorism, so his judgment is not surprising. However, every other participant in the debate, across the entire political spectrum, characterized the murder as an act of terrorism as well. In addition, the debate itself was all about terrorism; not, as had been the case after Fortuyn's murder, about the protection of public figures. Strikingly, the murder of Pim Fortuyn was mentioned just twice in the entire debate, both times by a representative of his political party, the LPF.[6]

In another departure from the reactions to the Fortuyn murder, the government also announced a thorough overhaul of its anti-terrorism legislation. The debate on this new legislation took place several months later, on February 9, 2005. It was a lengthy debate, lasting more than 12 hours, and featured contributions of speakers from every political party represented in the Parliament as well as from three government ministers. Once more, it is striking how little reference speakers made to prior terrorist incidents in the Netherlands. The debate included no references at all to the terrorist attacks of the 1970s, and just a single reference to the Fortuyn murder (Van der Veen 2007).

Interestingly, terrorism scholars, too, have tended to downplay or even ignore the relevance of the Fortuyn murder for counterterrorism policy. For example, Bakker argued in 2005 that the severe reaction of the Dutch to Van Gogh's murder can be explained by the fact that the Netherlands has "so little experience with terrorism" (Bakker 2005), mentioning neither the Fortuyn murder nor the incidents in the 1970s. More recently, a thoughtful and thorough report on Dutch counterterrorism policy reviews the Van Gogh case in some detail, but fails even to mention the Fortuyn case (Eijkman *et al.* 2012).

The murder of Anna Lindh (Sweden, September 10–11, 2003)

On September 10, 2003, Sweden's foreign minister, Anna Lindh, was attacked with a knife inside a department store in central Stockholm, by Mijailo Mijailovic, a Swede of Serbian origin. She succumbed to her injuries the next day, on the second anniversary of the September 11 attacks in the United States. The murder took place towards the end of a referendum campaign on Sweden's adoption of the European Union's euro currency, in which Lindh had played a leading role. The perpetrator, Mijailovic, had been captured on camera, and was apprehended two weeks later. He was sentenced to life in prison. During his trial, Mijailovic confessed to the murder, stating that he had not felt well, and had heard voices in his head. He had not planned to attack Lindh until he saw her.

On the other hand, he claims to have been driven by a general hatred of the political establishment, and had wanted to kill another politician the day before (Dragic and Holmén 2011).

If terrorism requires specific premeditation, Lindh's murder likely does not qualify; indeed, it is not included in standard terrorism databases (Engene 2007; National Consortium for the Study of Terrorism and Responses to Terrorism (START) 2012). On the other hand, its impact on the Swedish public was considerable, and no different from what it would have been if the murder had been planned. Moreover, authorities initially believed the murder *had* been planned, and suspected the assailant of having neo-Nazi ties (Osborn 2003). That fact alone makes the incident worthy of consideration.

As in the Netherlands with the Fortuyn murder, the immediate reaction was one of bewildered calm. Despite the possible symbolism of the date of the attack, it was not seen as an instance of terrorism. Opening the new year of the Riksdag (the Swedish Parliament) a few days later, the Speaker made no reference to possible motives behind the attack, and simply called for greater openness and transparency in the Swedish political system (Riksdagens Protokoll 2003a: §2, speaker 2). That same afternoon, the King addressed the Riksdag with a similar message, albeit with an implicit reference to one possible motive, emphasizing the importance of Sweden's active efforts to support and strengthen the United Nation's role in conflict resolution, reconstruction, and peace-building (Riksdagens Protokoll 2003b: §1, speaker 2).

The greatest concern among Swedish authorities was that they would fail to capture the perpetrator and that the murder would remain unsolved, as continued to be the case for Olof Palme's murder 17 years earlier (Carlshamre 2003). Once this fear proved ungrounded, there was no discussion of new legislation or policy measures to deal with the threat to public figures. Despite the successful resolution of the case, the memory of Anna Lindh remains alive among the Swedish public. For example, on December 4, 2012, a popular Swedish television crime show dedicated much of its program to her murder (Veckansbrott 2012).

It is, therefore, all the more striking that any possible lessons for counterterrorism policy remain completely ignored. Eric Rönnegård, a retired police chief, has argued that the Swedish police lack the manpower, resources, and a well-prepared command structure to respond to such crisis situations quickly and successfully (Rönnegård 2012b; see also Rönnegård 2008). Moreover, in a response to the aforementioned television broadcast, he explicitly drew a link between lessons from Lindh's murder and Sweden's preparedness for possible future terrorist incidents (Rönnegård 2012b). Significantly, in an implicit concession that Lindh's murder does not appear to carry much weight in this respect among Swedish audiences, he linked shortcomings within Sweden's police force to similar shortcomings in Norway that emerged after the July 2011 attacks in that country, hoping that that case *will* be seen as a source of important lessons (Rönnegård 2012a).

As was the case with the Netherlands, Sweden experienced another terrorist incident some years after the Lindh murder. On December 11, 2010, an Islamist suicide bomber blew himself up in central Stockholm, fortunately killing only himself. Taimour Abdulwahab was a Swede of Iraqi origin who had lived in the United Kingdom for more than a decade. He appears to have traveled to Sweden on his own initiative, without any organized support. Immediately prior to blowing himself up, he emailed messages to the Swedish media and police authorities threatening the Swedish public that "now your children, daughters, and sisters will die just like our brothers and sisters and children die" ("Hot mot svenskar i mejl" 2010). This incident clearly distinguished itself from the Anna Lindh murder in that many more people could have died, and the general public was the target. On the other hand, there were some obvious similarities, most obviously in terms of the location of the attack.

By coincidence, the government published a report on violent Islamist extremism just a few days later (Säkerhetspolisen 2010). Although this was a companion report to an earlier report on violent extremism among white power and anarchist movements, the Stockholm bombing inevitably placed an extra emphasis on Islamist terrorism. A lengthy debate in the Riksdag followed on January 26, 2011. Significantly, no speakers drew lessons from the Lindh murder, even though several noted the importance of greater police resources as well as a better command hierarchy for crisis responses.[7]

In sum, we observe in Sweden, as in the Netherlands, a disinclination to classify a political murder as an act of terrorism, as well as a failure to draw any lessons that might be relevant for counterterrorism. Since Lindh's murder was never discussed as terrorist, however, we cannot observe whether those who might have seen it as such would have been inclined to focus on organized Islamist terrorists – something Mijailovic quite obviously was not.

The attacks by Anders Behring Breivik (Norway, July 22, 2011)

The worst terrorist incident in the modern history of the Nordic countries took place on July 22, 2011, when Anders Behring Breivik exploded a large bomb outside government offices in Oslo, drove to the Utøya vacation camp north of Oslo, and opened fire on members of the Social Democratic party's youth organization who were staying there for a retreat. Eight people died as a result of the Oslo bombing, and 69 died at Utøya. Both in terms of preparation – Breivik had been building the bomb for several weeks, and had been planning the attacks for as long as two years – and in their destructive impact, these attacks clearly distinguish themselves from the Dutch and Swedish cases. On the other hand, the perpetrator was, once again, a non-Islamist loner.

As the attacks were taking place, and before the perpetrator had been identified, authorities and journalists alike assumed that they were the work of organized Islamist extremists (Gjørv 2012: 22). Indeed, the main debate was over which Islamist group was responsible (Mudde 2011). Moreover, immigrants and Muslims in Oslo were subjected to verbal threats and insults as the day wore on, and a few were apparently even assaulted (Gjørv 2012: 22). Strikingly, it took some news sources more than a day to correct their initial faulty reporting regarding the perpetrator (Humphrys 2011). In fact, of course, Breivik was a right-wing extremist worried about a Muslim take-over of Europe. He never denied responsibility for his acts, arguing that they were brutal but necessary in order to send a message to those in Norway he saw as complicit with this take-over. After a trial that lasted from April until June 2012, Breivik was found guilty in August, and sentenced to life imprisonment.

Shortly after the attacks, the government appointed a commission to document and investigate both Breivik's actions and the responses by police and other authorities. The 22 July Commission published its report a year later, in August 2012 (Gjørv 2012). Among others, it pointed out that right-wing extremist acts are less likely to be identified as terrorist in nature than are similar acts perpetrated by Islamist extremists (Gjørv 2012: 51). Breivik's attorney, Geir Lippestad, offered an example of this in practice, arguing in late 2011 that Breivik was different from "political terrorists," as an illustration of which he offered "an Al Qaeda terrorist who drives a car into a building" (Vikås and Mosveen 2011).

Of course, the scale and nature of Breivik's attacks made it essentially impossible to see this as anything other than terrorism. This shifts the focus to the second implication of my argument: that reactions should emphasize organized Islamist terrorism, even though Breivik was an anti-Islam loner. Indeed, this tendency was on ample display in the 22 July Commission's report, Chapter 4 of which represented an attempt to extract from the recent history of political violence and terrorism those incidents and lessons most relevant to the events of July 22 (Gjørv 2012: 45). The emphasis throughout this chapter on Islamist extremism is striking, especially in light of Breivik's identity. At the beginning of the chapter, for example, a one-page overview of the history of politically motivated violence in Norway lists a number of incidents, none of which had anything to do with Islamist extremism. However, this overview finishes with a claim that Norway's risk of becoming the target of a terrorist attack has grown in recent years in particular because of extreme Islamism (Gjørv 2012: 46). A far lengthier section on extremist Islamist terrorism immediately follows, pointing out, among other things, that the security police warned the government in 2007 that they thought it more than 50 percent likely that Norway would experience an attempt at a terrorist attack by extreme Islamist groups in the next three to five years, whereas it deemed right-wing extremists "not ... a real threat against vital national interests" (Gjørv 2012: 49, 51).[8]

The same incongruous emphasis on the Islamist threat is evident in statements by political leaders. For example, Justice Minister Storberget gave an official statement to Norway's parliament, the Storting, on November 10, 2011 regarding the government's response to the attacks, with preliminary ideas about new policies and procedures that might need to be implemented. In it, he argued that, despite the events of July 22, "extremist Islamists represent the most serious terrorist threat against Norway and Norwegian interests" (Stortingstidende 2011: 340). He received some pushback on this claim both at the time and in a follow-up debate on March 8, 2012, from several parliamentarians; even these, however, gave credence to the severity of the Islamist threat.[9]

The third implication of my argument is that the strength of the organized Islamist terrorism frame undermines a polity's ability to learn optimally from a particular incident. It is too early to arrive at any firm conclusions on this count, but some preliminary evidence suggests that this prediction holds even in a case as extreme as Breivik's. First, in his official response to the 22 July Commission report, prime minister Stoltenberg did allow that the government might have been too focused on the terror threat from extremist Islamic groups, blaming this on the risk assessments from the security police mentioned earlier (Stortingstidende 2012b: 4595). However, he largely ignored the fact that better intelligence about the source of the threat would have had little bearing on the response by the authorities once Breivik's attacks began. In this regard, too much of a focus on improving intelligence estimates may well detract from the incorporation of insights derived from the actual experience of responding to Breivik's attack. Second, and perhaps even more strikingly, in a letter to the Storting dated October 26, 2012, new Justice minister Faremo announced that the terrorist threat from Islamist extremism continued to be the primary focus of the police, and that little had happened to change assessments of the terror threat from right-wing extremists (Faremo 2012: 12). It is possible, of course, that the Norwegian security police knew something Europol did not (cf. Europol 2012), but it is difficult to see such a conclusion as anything other than evidence of the strength of the OIT frame.

Conclusion

Numerous commentators have identified the prominence in the mass media of a frame identifying terrorism with organized Islamist extremism. In fact, while the perpetrator(s) of terrorist attacks remain unidentified, it has become common to assume they are Islamists. As noted above, in the Norwegian case the authorities joined media outlets in jumping to this conclusion. More generally, even the most respected news sources reflect the power of the OIT frame. The *New York Times*, for example, in discussing initial reports of the Norwegian case that focused on "Islamic militants" argued, "There was ample reason for concern that terrorists might be responsible," as though non-Islamic extremists would somehow not be terrorists (Mala and Goodman 2011). Later, as Breivik's trial approached, the paper identified him as a "confessed mass killer" rather than a terrorist ("Norway: Killer of 77 was insane during rampage, prosecution says" 2011).

One might assume that, unlike media commentators, government officials are too careful to get trapped into the OIT frame. The present study shows that this is not the case. While it is true that explicit invocations of the OIT frame are rare among government officials, especially in policy debates, the evidence presented here makes its influence quite clear. As we saw especially in the Dutch and Swedish cases, incidents that are (or would be) characterized as terrorist in nature when committed by Islamist extremists are not identified as terrorist when the perpetrator is not Muslim. Moreover, these incidents are largely ignored in subsequent counterterrorism policy debates, even when they might offer valuable insights and lessons. Meanwhile, the Breivik case shows most clearly that when the terrorist label cannot be rejected, the OIT frame still shapes debates and policy reactions alike.

Terrorism scholars increasingly identify right-wing extremism as no less an enduring threat than Islamist extremism (e.g., Lambert and Githens-Mazer 2010: 79). After Breivik's attacks, this trend is likely to strengthen. At the same time, other scholars have begun to question just how serious a threat Islamist extremism really constitutes (e.g., Mueller and Stewart 2012). On the other hand, responses by many political leaders to Breivik's attacks – in Norway as well as in other countries (e.g., von der Dunk 2011) – demonstrate that their perceptions have not caught up with the scholarship, or even with empirical evidence.

This chapter demonstrated the impact of the organized Islamist terrorism frame on policy debates; the logical next questions are how this frame came to exercise such a hold on policy-makers, and under what conditions this hold might be weakened. Answering those questions goes beyond the scope of the chapter. At present, the literature offers one main suggestion: salient frames are most likely to change or be dislodged at times of crisis or shock, such as the 9/11 terrorist attacks. However, Breivik's attacks arguably should have been a larger shock to the Norwegians. The fact that the OIT frame appears to remain strong among Norwegian leaders indicates that other factors are at work. It seems likely that ongoing debates about the presence, role, and influence of Muslims in Europe come into play as well (cf. Klausen 2005). Given the impact of the OIT frame on the shaping of counterterrorism policy demonstrated here, it will be well worth investigating its origins and persistence more thoroughly.

Notes

1 It remains, of course, dwarfed by the literature on terrorism itself. Both literatures are hamstrung in part by the difficulty of settling on a generalizable and value-neutral definition of terrorism (Crelinsten 1998; Staun 2010).
2 An emerging literature on "performativity" directly connects framing by government officials to policy successes and failures. Thus, De Graaf and De Graaff argue that "it is not necessarily the policy measures and their intended results as such, but much more the way in which they are presented and perceived that determine the overall effect of the policy in question" (de Graaf and de Graaff 2010: 261; see also de Graaf 2011).
3 Indeed, since certain terrorist threats are international in nature, it would be puzzling if authorities completely ignored the experiences of other countries in this respect.
4 See (De 21 doden die Theo van Gogh voorgingen 2005) for a list of attacks and deaths. It is worth noting that Germany's experiences with the Rote Armee Fraktion (the Baader–Meinhof Group) were extensively reported in the Dutch media, providing some additional indirect exposure to terrorism.
5 Hirsi Ali went into hiding and did not reappear in the Dutch parliament for more than two months.
6 (*Handelingen* 2004: 1,286–7). Even the speaker of the socialist party (SP) – not a party usually associated with the Islamist terrorism frame – explicitly characterized Van Gogh's murder as an act of terrorism because it was the planned murder of a person for his opinions and statements, with the intent to scare others who believe in freedom of expression (*Handelingen* 2004: 1,292). The same, of course, can be said regarding Fortuyn's murder.
7 For example, Social Democrat Sven-Erik Österberg (Riksdagens Protokoll 2011: §1, speaker 4). No speakers mentioned former police chief Rönnegård either.
8 Tellingly, among a number of large-scale terrorist incidents the Commission deemed relevant, the report also describes Bouyeri's murder of Van Gogh (Gjørv 2012: 51), while omitting numerous attacks by right-wing lone wolves – including the series of shootings in Sweden in 1991–2 mentioned earlier.
9 Grande (Stortingstidende 2011: 340). In the follow-up debate see, for example, Klinge of the Center Party (Stortingstidende 2012a: 2548).

References

Baker, N. V. (2003). "National security versus civil liberties," *Presidential Studies Quarterly*, 33(3), 547–67.
Bakker, E. (2005) "De gevoelde bedreiging: Nederland te gemakkelijk in de ban van terrorisme," *Duitslandweb*. Available at www.duitslandweb.nl/dossiers/archief/RAF/Balans/Edwin+Bakker.html (accessed May 21, 2013).
Bakker, E.and de Graaf, B. (2010) *Lone Wolves: How to Prevent this Phenomenon*. The Hague, NL: International Centre for Counter-Terrorism.
Carlshamre, M. (2003) "Vansinniga spekulationer," *Dagens Nyheter*, September 18. Available at www.dn.se/ledare/signerat/vansinniga-spekulationer (accessed May 21, 2013).
Chong, D. and Druckman, J. N. (2007a) "Framing theory," *Annual Review of Political Science*, 10(1), 103–26.
Chong, D. and Druckman, J. N. (2007b) "A theory of framing and opinion formation in competitive elite environments," *Journal of Communication*, 57(1), 99–118.

Commissie van den Haak (2002) *De veiligheid en de beveiliging van Pim Fortuyn: Feiten en verantwoordelijkheden*, 's Gravenhage, NL: Sdu Uitgevers.

Crelinsten, R. D. (1998) "The discourse and practice of counter-terrorism in liberal democracies," *Australian Journal of Politics & History*, 44(3), 389–413.

"De 21 doden die Theo van Gogh voorgingen" (2005) *Elsevier*, July 9. Available at www.elsevier.nl/web/1041957/Dossiers/Terreur-in-Nederland/De-21-doden-die-Theo-van-Gogh-voorgingen.htm (accessed October 10, 2012).

de Graaf, B. (2011) *Evaluating counterterrorism performance: A comparative study*, London: Routledge.

de Graaf, B. and de Graaff, B. (2010) "Bringing politics back in: The introduction of the 'performative power' of counterterrorism," *Critical Studies on Terrorism*, 3(2), 261–75.

de Jong, S. (2012) "Zo reageerden politici op de moord op Pim Fortuyn," NRC.nl, May 6. Available at www.nrc.nl/nieuws/2012/05/06/eerste-reacties-van-politici-na-dood-pim-fortuyn-in-op-6-mei-2002/ (accessed May 21, 2013).

Dragic, M. and Holmén, C. (2011) "Mijailovic talar ut: Det är dags att sanningen kommer fram," *Expressen*, August 28. Available at www.expressen.se/nyheter/expressen-avslojar/mijailovic-talar-ut-det-ar-dags-att-sanningen-kommer-fram/ (accessed May 21, 2013).

Druckman, J. N. (2010) "What's it all about? Framing in political science," In G. Keren (ed.) *Perspectives on framing*, New York, NY: Taylor & Francis, 279–302.

Eijkman, Q., Lettinga, D., and Verbossen, G. (2012) *Impact of counter-terrorism on communities: Netherlands background report*, London, UK: Institute for Strategic Dialogue.

Engene, J. O. (2007) "Five decades of terrorism in Europe: The TWEED dataset," *Journal of Peace Research*, 44(1), 109–21.

Engene, J. O. (2011) "Terrortallenes tvetydige tale," *Samtiden*, 4, 60–71.

Entman, R. M. (2004) *Projects of Power: Framing News, Public Opinion, and US Foreign Policy*, Chicago, IL: University of Chicago Press.

Europol (2010) TE-SAT 2010: Terrorism situation and trend report: Europol.

Europol (2011) TE-SAT 2011: EU terrorism situation and trend report: Europol.

Europol (2012) TE-SAT 2012: EU terrorism situation and trend report: Europol.

Faremo, G. (2012). "Redegjørelsene om regjeringens oppfølging av 22. juli kommisjonens rapport – spørsmål i forbindelse med komitebehandlingen," October 26. Oslo, Norway: Det Kongelige Justis- og Beredskapsdepartement.

Gjørv, A. B. (2012) *Rapport fra 22. juli-kommisjonen*, Oslo, Norway: Informasjonsforvaltning.

Goffman, E. (1974) *Frame Analysis: An Essay on the Organization of Experience*, Cambridge, MA: Harvard University Press.

Greenwald, G. (2011) "The omnipotence of Al Qaeda and the meaninglessness of 'terrorism'," *Salon*, July 23. Available at www.salon.com/2011/07/23/nyt_17/ (accessed May 21, 2013).

Handelingen (2002a). Handelingen van de Tweede Kamer der Staten Generaal, 2001–2002. Kamerstuk 28374: "Aanslag op de heer W.S.P. Fortuijn." No. 5: "Verslag van een algemeen overleg" (June 12). 's Gravenhage, The Netherlands: Sdu.

Handelingen (2002b). Handelingen van de Tweede Kamer der Staten Generaal, 2002–2003. 36ste vergadering (December 19). 's Gravenhage, The Netherlands: Sdu.

Handelingen (2004). Handelingen van de Tweede Kamer der Staten Generaal, 2004–2005. 22ste vergadering (November 11). 's Gravenhage, The Netherlands: Sdu.

Heller, R., Kahl, M., and Pisoiu, D. (2012) "The 'dark' side of normative argumentation – The case of counterterrorism policy," *Global Constitutionalism*, 1(2), 278–312.

"Hot mot svenskar i mejl" (2010), *Svenska Dagbladet*, December 11. Available at www.svd.se/nyheter/inrikes/hot-mot-svenskar-i-mejl_5802959.svd (accessed May 27, 2013).

Humphrys, E. (2011) "Your 'terrorists', our 'lone wolves': Utøya in the shadow of 9/11," *Journal of International Relations Research*, 1(1),72–80.

Jackson, R. (2007) "Constructing enemies: "Islamic terrorism" in political and academic discourse," *Government and Opposition*, 42(3), 394–426.

Katzenstein, P. J. (2003) "Same war – different views: Germany, Japan, and counterterrorism," *International Organization*, 57(4), 731–60.

Klausen, J. (2005) *The Islamic challenge: Politics and religion in Western Europe*, Oxford, UK: Oxford University Press.

Kundnani, A. (2012) "Blind spot? Security narratives and far-right violence in Europe," The Hague: International Centre for Counter-Terrorism.

Lambert, R. and Githens-Mazer, J. (2010) *Islamophobia and anti-Muslim hate crime: UK case studies 2010*, London, UK: European Muslim Research Centre.

Mala, E. and Goodman, J. D. (2011) "At least 80 dead in Norway shooting," *New York Times*, July 23. Available at www.nytimes.com/2011/07/23/world/europe/23oslo.html?pagewanted=all (accessed May 27, 2013).

Meyer, C. O. (2009) "International terrorism as a force of homogenization? A constructivist approach to understanding cross-national threat perceptions and responses," *Cambridge Review of International Affairs*, 22(4), 647–66.

Mudde, C. (2011) "Extremisten tonen noodzaak vrij debat," *Volkskrant*, July 29. Available at www.volkskrant.nl/vk/nl/3184/opinie/article/detail/2822641/2011/07/29/Extremisten-tonen-noodzaak-vrij-debat.dhtml (accessed May 21, 2013).

Mueller, J. and Stewart, M. G. (2012) "The terrorism delusion: America's overwrought response to September 11," *International Security*, 37(1), 81–110.

National Consortium for the Study of Terrorism and Responses to Terrorism (START) (2012) "Global Terrorism Database," College Park, MD.

Nesser, P. (2008) "Chronology of Jihadism in Western Europe 1994–2007: Planned, prepared, and executed attacks," *Studies in Conflict and Terrorism*, 31(10), 924–46.

Netherlands, O. M. (2002) *Verklaring Volkert van der G*, The Hague, Netherlands: Openbaar Ministerie.

Nohrstedt, D. and Hansén, D. (2010) "Converging under pressure? Counterterrorism policy developments in the European Union member states," *Public Administration*, 88(1), 190–210.

"Norway: Killer of 77 was insane during rampage, prosecution says" (2011) *New York Times*, November 30, A12.

Orr, D. (2011) "Anders Behring Breivik's not a terrorist, he's a mass-murderer," *Guardian*, July 27. Available at www.guardian.co.uk/world/2011/jul/27/breivik-not-terrorist-insane-murderer (accessed May 27, 2013).

Osborn, A. (2003) "Swedish police explore neo-Nazi links of Lindh murder suspect," *Guardian*, September 18. Available at www.guardian.co.uk/world/2003/sep/18/thefarright.politics (accessed May 27, 2013).

Pantazis, C. and Pemberton, S. (2009) "From the 'old' to the 'new' suspect community: Examining the impacts of recent UK counter-terrorist legislation," *British Journal of Criminology*, 49(5), 646–66.

Pantucci, R. (2011) *A typology of lone wolves: Preliminary analysis of lone Islamist terrorists*, London, UK: International Centre for the Study of Radicalisation and Political Violence.

Perliger, A. (2012) "How democracies respond to terrorism: Regime characteristics, symbolic power and counterterrorism," *Security Studies*, 21(3), 490–528.

Rees, W. and Aldrich, R. (2005) "Contending cutures of counterterrorism: Transatlantic divergence or convergence?" *International Affairs*, 81(5), 905–23.

Reinfeldt, F., Ohlsson, B., and Ask, B. (2011) "Krafttag mot den våldsbejakande extremismen," *Dagens Nyheter*, August 5. Available at www.regeringen.se/sb/d/7395/a/173111 (accessed May 27, 2013).

Riksdagens Protokoll (2003a) September 16. Morning session. Available at http://uk-mg5.mail.yahoo.com/neo/launch?.rand=ahcphg8d8j9vc# (accessed October 3, 2013).

Riksdagens Protokoll (2003b) September 16. Afternoon session. Available at http://www.riksdagen.se/sv/Dokument-Lagar/Kammaren/Protokoll/Riksdagens-protokoll-2003042_GR092/ (accessed October 3, 2013).

Riksdagens Protokoll (2011) January 26. Available at http://www.riksdagen.se/sv/Dokument-Lagar/Kammaren/Protokoll/Riksdagens-protokoll-2011126_GZ0962/ (accessed October 3, 2013).

Rönnegård, E. (2008) *Kris i ledningen för svensk polis: Mordet på Anna Lindh inget undantag*, Stockholm, Sweden: Jure Förlag.

Rönnegård, E. (2012a) "Även Sverige behöver lära av 22 juli-kommissionen," newsmill.se, August 15. Available at www.newsmill.se/artikel/2012/08/15/ven-sverige-beh-ver-l-ra-av-22-juli-kommissionen (accessed May 21, 2013).

Rönnegård, E. (2012b) "SVT skyler över polisens misstag vid Anna Lindh-mordet," newsmill.se, December 7. Available at www.newsmill.se/artikel/2012/12/07/svt-skyler-ver-polisens-misstag-vid-anna-lindh-mordet; (accessed May 21, 2013).

Säkerhetspolisen. (2010) *Våldsbejakande islamistisk extremism i Sverige*, Stockholm, Sweden: Säkerhetspolisen.

Spaaij, R. (2010) "The enigma of lone wolf terrorism: An assessment," *Studies in Conflict and Terrorism*, 33(9), 854–70.

Spencer, A. (2012) "The social construction of terrorism: Media, metaphors and policy implications," *Journal of International Relations and Development*, 15(3), 393–419.

Staun, J. (2010) "When, how and why elites frame terrorists: A Wittgensteinian analysis of terror and radicalisation," *Critical Studies on Terrorism*, 3(3), 403–20.

Stortingstidende (2011) November 10. Topic 2: Redegjørelse av justisministeren og forsvarsministeren om angrepene 22. juli 2011. [Speech by the Justice minister and the defense minister about the attacks on 22 July 2011].

Stortingstidende (2012a) March 8. Topic 1: Innstilling fra Den særskilte komité om redegjørelse fra justisministeren og forsvarsministeren i Stortingets møte 10. november 2011 om angrepene 22. juli. [Report from the special committee about the speech by the Justice minister and the defense minister in the Stortingsmeeting 10 November 2011 about the attacks of 22 July].

Stortingstidende (2012b) August 28. Topic 1: Redegjørelse av statsministeren og justis- og beredskapsministeren om regjeringens oppfølging av rapporten fra 22.

juli-kommisjonen. [Speech by the Prime Minister and the justice and defence minister about the governments reaction to the report of the 22 July commission].

Tsoukala, A. (2006) "Democracy in the light of security: British and French political discourses on domestic counter-terrorism policies," *Political Studies*, 54(3), 607–27.

Van der Veen, A. M. (2007) "Framing anti-terrorism policies: Debates in the United Kingdom and the Netherlands," Athens, GA: University of Georgia, Department of International Affairs.

Veckansbrott (2012) December 4. Available at www.svtplay.se/video/891561/del-8-av-10 (accessed December 8, 2012).

Vikås, M. and Mosveen, E. (2011) "Lite som minner om en politisk terrorist," *Verdens Gang*, December 2. Available at www.vg.no/nyheter/innenriks/22-juli/artikkel.php?artid=10024307 (accessed May 27, 2013).

von der Dunk, T. (2011) "Von der Dunk: 'Breivik trok logische consequentie uit Wilders' retoriek'," *Volkskrant*, September 5. Available at www.volkskrant.nl/vk/nl/6178/Thomas-von-der-Dunk/article/detail/2891848/2011/09/05/Von-der-Dunk-Breivik-trok-logische-consequentie-uit-Wilders-retoriek.dhtml (accessed May 27, 2013).

Zald, M. N. (1996) "Culture, ideology, and strategic framing," in D. McAdam, J. D. McCarthy, and M. N. Zald (eds) *Comparative perspectives on social movements: Political opportunities, mobilizing structures, and cultural framings*. New York, NY: Cambridge University Press, 261–74.

Part II
Phenomenology

4 Between insurrection and "reformism"

Public discourses of twenty-first century Greek armed groups

Anastassia Tsoukala

The violent shocks inflicted on Western political systems by the current systemic crisis of capitalism reflect an ongoing struggle on a global scale between the financial classes and political power (Laskos and Tsakalotos 2012), the effects of which are being felt particularly strongly in southern Europe. In these countries, with their long traditions of defiance of state authority, the convulsions of politico-economic power have generated wide-ranging reactions within society which have, in turn, provided a wider base of legitimacy for militant movements.

While certain new forms of peaceful protest, such as the Indignant movement, represent one aspect of this popular awakening, the growing power of violent militant groupings is visible in a proliferation of attacks of varying scale and intensity. Given that engagement in armed struggle has always been characterized by its specific national context (Bonelli 2011), the recourse to repertoires of violent action that we see today varies noticeably from one country to another due to complex historical and cultural factors that are beyond the scope of this chapter. However, the entire current generation of guerrillas shares a common willingness to inscribe their action within an international framework. We are witnessing the emergence of an urban guerrilla phenomenon that is multi-faceted and multi-layered, in which attacks may be carried out in isolation or, equally, be explicitly connected to events in other countries in the name of a solidarity that may be based on real personal contacts, or may be entirely independent of these, having developed in a purely virtual space where links are formed between guerrillas who have never physically met. It is still too early to be able to say for sure whether this international focus suggests a weakness in these armed groups' domestic social base, as was the case in France and Germany during the 1980s, or whether it demonstrates the influence of the deterritorialized Al Qaeda model, reflects the processes of globalization, or simply reveals a desire for power, real or imagined. Since it is not possible, then, to discern what meaning these groups place on their action through the study of their operational methods alone, we can only hope to gain a clearer picture of their motivations and intentions through an analysis of their own discourse.

The adoption of a discourse analysis-based approach to questions relating to armed groups remains a relatively uncommon methodological choice in academia. While the urban guerrilla campaigns, which marked various European countries from the 1960s to the 1980s, did give rise to numerous studies of the motives and organizational structures of the main armed groups of this period, analyses of the public discourse of political violence have only started to proliferate in the wake of the attacks of September 11, 2001 (Featherstone *et al.* 2010; Graham *et al.* 2004; Hodges and Nilep 2007; Jackson 2007; Lazar and Lazar 2004; Leudar *et al.* 2004; Merola 2008; Mythen and Walklate 2006; Steinert 2003; Tsoukala 2004, 2006, 2008a, 2009). Yet, in spite of the massive use of the Internet by twenty-first century guerrilla fighters, discourse analysis has been applied almost exclusively to the pronouncements of politicians and other representatives of established society. Analyses of the discourse of armed groups have remained significantly less numerous (Broek 2004; Tsfati and Weimann 2002; Weimann 2006). It is thus important to try to grasp the nature of the urban guerrilla movement in southern Europe through an analysis of the public discourse of fighters in one of the countries in question, namely Greece, for two reasons: as well as shedding light on certain aspects of a movement that is believed to be representative of current tendencies in Europe, this study will widen the literature documenting a so far under-explored theme. As this discourse has been produced in constant interaction with the media coverage of urban guerrilla activities, the analysis of the former will go hand-in-hand with a brief analysis of the way in which mainstream media have sought to represent this form of political violence.

The current upsurge in urban guerrilla activity

The popular uprising which shook Greece in 2008 following the murder of a teenager by an on-duty police officer has been the subject of much analysis, both in academia (Astrinaki 2009; Karamichas 2009; Kotronaki and Seferiades 2010; Mentinis 2010; Mowbray 2010; Pechtelidis 2011; Petropoulou 2010; Sevastakis 2010, 2012; Sotiris 2010) and within the protest movement itself (Indymedia 2009a, 2009b). In hindsight, this mass revolt against the established order seems to represent a crystallization of popular exasperation, due both to the long history of arbitrary repression by the police and to the worsening economic situation of a population increasingly at the mercy of an ever-expanding neo-liberalism.

The paths of protest opened up in 2008 appealed to a significant section of Greece's youth who, in calling for the democratization of the state and of society "right here, right now," not only became conscious of their own power and of the fact that the state's authority had "limits and fissures" (Pechtelidis 2011: 460), but also came to realize the impossibility of achieving reform through these protests. Reinforcing young people's disillusionment in the face of the imperviousness of the political system to the demands of social movements (ibid.: 459), this realization of the impotence of popular democracy was accompanied by growing approval for more radical action (Geka 2012), in particular among a faction of this younger generation who had already taken part in the student protest movement of 2006–7, and had come to see violence as a legitimate mode of intervention in the public arena, a means of legitimate self-defense against the violence of the state security apparatus (Anders 2011). Rooted in this climate of general disenchantment and growing dissatisfaction with conventional modes of collective action, the social unrest of 2008 strengthened those armed groups that were already active and created many new ones. The most emblematic groups of this period – Revolutionary Organization Fire Cells Conspiracy (FCC), Sect of Revolutionaries (SR), Revolutionary Organization 6 December (6D)[1] – would now act in parallel with a loose assortment of groupings engaged in a variety of violent activities of lower intensity,[2] but which nevertheless fall into the category of "terrorism" as defined by article 187A of the Greek Penal Code.

At first glance, these groups seem to have much in common with earlier armed organizations, the most active of which having been Revolutionary Organization 17 November (17N),[3] Revolutionary People's Struggle (RPS)[4] and Revolutionary Struggle (RS).[5] Whatever their ideological differences, the members of these earlier organizations had shared a common political vision, namely the overturning of liberal democracy through a popular uprising, and the establishment of a new political and social order based on Marxist/anarchist principles. While the pursuit of this revolutionary objective was a feature these guerrillas shared with their European counterparts of the 1960s–1980s (Della Porta 1995; Ruggiero 2010; Sommier 1998, 2008; Steiner and Debray 2006), the degree of support they enjoyed within society was not. For a long time, their attacks seemed justified in the eyes of a significant section of the population (*Eleftherotypia* 2002a, 2002b; Sakellariou 2003), who saw these as acts of popular justice in the face of the violence of the dictatorial regime and the interference of the United States in the country's internal affairs. However, the subversive potential of armed struggle was progressively eroded by the growth of materialistic values, the rise of individualism, and an increasing wealthy society from the 1980s onwards, along with the post-bipolar decline of Marxism. While an acknowledgement of this declining influence can be read between the lines in a recent text written by one of the imprisoned members of 17N (Koufodinas 2012), the present political and economic situation seems to have given a new lease of life to an urban guerrilla movement that had been weakened both through its growing social isolation and through the dismantling of its most emblematic organization.

It might thus have been tempting to see the current generation of guerrillas as the inheritors of this long tradition of opposition to the established order. Indeed, such an approach would have echoed the hegemonic discourse of the media and the police who, by vaguely describing as "neo-terrorism" the urban guerrilla movement that emerged following the dismantling of 17N in 2002 (*Ethnos* 2009a), uncritically place the new generational and organizational features of this movement within a logistical and ideological continuum (*Ethnos* 2009b), without giving any consideration to the potentially fundamental differences between the guerrillas of today and their predecessors. With the exception of a few isolated voices of dissent (Koufodinas 2009; Sevastakis 2009), public debate is thus dominated by the idea that the motives and objectives of both the former and the latter have essentially remained the same across the decades. In the absence of any publicly voiced counter-arguments, it is impossible either to confirm or disprove the validity of this representation or, consequently, to assess the political benefits that would flow from the construction of such an image of political violence as static and completely cut off from the historical development of the country. An analysis of the public discourse of present-day guerrilla fighters would undoubtedly help us begin to answer these questions, but before embarking upon such an approach, we must first resolve a number of ethical and methodological issues.

Remarks on the analysis

Ethical considerations

When focusing on this public discourse, an awareness of the ethical questions posed by this methodological choice is crucial. Do we have the right to speak in the name of others? On what epistemological basis can we claim to interpret acts committed by individuals who, having fully undertaken the risks involved in their decisions, intervene in the political arena through violence for reasons which, while they may vary, can be seen in the final analysis to stem from an existential quest for the absolute? Should we not also admit, like R. De Giorgi (in Lambropoulou 2004: 235), that we may well be unable to identify the origins of any urban guerrilla movement?

These questions go beyond the subjectivity inherent in any analysis of public discourse insofar as they concern an uncomfortable confrontation between the inevitable coldness of an external gaze and the existential tumult experienced by those who cross the line into revolt in order to give meaning to their own lives. While the fundamental nature of this actor–observer relationship will never be purged of its dark aspects, the burden of this interaction can be lifted somewhat if the discourse in question is treated not as the narrative of individual actors' personal choices, but rather as a strategy of individual/collective positioning within the political field. By moving away from the question of why things are done, to focus instead on how they are justified, this analysis aims solely to elucidate the ways in which these guerrillas seek to legitimate their past or future actions by adopting various argumentative strategies.

It is clear, then, that the imaginary dialogue on which an analysis of this discourse is necessarily predicated encounters a major obstacle in the form of the difficulty, if not impossibility, of locating gaps that might allow us to read the frontiers between what can and cannot be said, and between what actors are able to grasp or want to communicate, and what their observer is in turn able to grasp or wishes to reveal. The words and silences of both parties are related as much to personal limits as to political choices. For, in such a situation, the narcissistic ego of the guerrilla who seeks to justify direct intervention in the political field collides with the narcissistic ego of the observer, who intervenes indirectly in this same field by reacting to the guerrilla's action with a view to molding interpretations of this action. In this double game of shifting political communication, there can be no truly "neutral" position. Both parties desire, in a more or less authoritarian manner, to impose their own vision of the world through, respectively, the tangible violence of a physical act, and the subtle violence of an epistemological construction. Seen in this light, the discourse analysis proposed here places the two parties on an equal footing, since the observer's role is limited to examining the interpretative schemas put forward by the guerrillas themselves, treating the latter as political actors rather than individuals. This approach does not seek to construct a discursive substitute for the discourse of guerrilla fighters, but rather to examine critically the latter to grasp the modes of its construction and, by extension, its coherence.

Methodological remarks

There can be no doubt that such an approach would require the juxtaposition of two sets of discourse in order to reveal the ways in which the media function as a channel for the production and dissemination of a particular ideology, in the Gramscian sense of the term, but also as agents seeking to increase their own economic, social and symbolic capital, to use Bourdieu's terminology. However, owing to limitations of space, it will not be possible to carry out a full comparative study here or, for the same reason, to include an analysis of the public discourse of previous generations of guerrillas. Consequently, I will only present certain key points of the discourse produced by what I will from now on term the propagators of institutional discourse (police officers, journalists, academics), as it appeared in the so-called quality press between September 2009 and November 2011, along with a thematic content analysis of 78 texts written by guerrilla fighters and posted on https://athens.indymedia.org between September 1, 2010 and September 1, 2011. These fall into the following categories: theoretical texts (TT), communiqués (COM), letters from guerrillas in prison (PL) or in hiding (LH), transcribed radio interviews (INT), messages of solidarity (MS) and political declarations made in court (PDC).⁶ The analysis of these texts will occasionally make reference to previous or later texts if the content of these helps to illustrate the argument. While the choice of the period of reference for the institutional discourse examined here necessarily follows the pattern of attacks and arrests, that of the discourse of the guerrillas is linked to the unpredictable nature of an urban guerrilla campaign. Given the increasing speed with which the FCC was being dismantled from November 2010 onwards, the choice of the period to be analyzed was informed by the hypothesis that public discourse becomes more revealing when it is forced to take up a position under pressure. Rather than simply analyzing the messages disseminated by the members of a guerrilla movement in full swing, I have sought to capture the discourse produced when some of its members begin to encounter difficulties (sequences of attacks alternating with waves of arrests, followed by time spent in hiding, acts of solidarity, the end of the first cycle of FCC's activity, and so on).

The present analysis will examine the texts posted on the aforementioned site in the period under study, with the exception of two extremely brief communiqués and those texts that were written by members of earlier armed organizations. I have also chosen not to include a communiqué from the 6D (posted on April 21, 2011). The richness of this text, in terms both of its analysis of the (inter)national political and economic situation and of its (re-)positioning of the guerrilla movement in relation to current political challenges, contrasts so strongly with the content of the other texts from the same period that it stands no comparison with them. Moreover, since 6D has only posted one text on the aforementioned site in the period under study, I have judged that this communiqué is not representative of the guerrilla discourse to be analyzed here. Out of the texts that have been kept, 36 are anonymous or bear the signatures of various groups (31 in total), which occasionally act in concert; 31 are signed by FCC, occasionally acting in concert with others; and 11 are signed by individual anarchists.

It is clear that any analysis of these texts will inevitably be partial, in both senses of the term. As well as being subjective, as already mentioned, it seeks to capture a discourse that is doubly collective in the sense that it is both the product of a collective editorial effort, and a distillation of the discourse produced by various groups which differ not only in the objectives they have set themselves and the methods they employ to achieve these ends, but also in the social and cultural capital of their members. This analysis is also truncated in that, owing to its temporal delimitation, it not only excludes the discourse of those actors who did not make public statements during the period under study, but also, given its professed aim to interpret an evolving collective discourse, it can only hope to draw provisional conclusions, which are merely indicative of an ongoing process. A final limitation is imposed by the choice of analytical perspective, which restricts the study to a single facet of the discourse in question, namely the modes of justification used with respect to the urban guerrilla campaign. Certain elements are thus left out of the analysis, such as, for example, issues related to the narcissistic focus on a hedonistic, dominating and authoritarian ego within society, the spectacularization of the urban guerrilla movement, or the impact of prison life on the perception of armed struggle by fighters in detention.

The urban guerrilla movement and the press

As noted above, the media coverage of the twenty-first century guerrilla movement remains distinctive in that, while it acknowledges the generational renewal of these armed groups, it emphasizes the organizational continuities between the guerrillas of today and their predecessors without ever posing in any serious manner the question of possible (dis)continuities between what is routinely referred to as "neo-terrorism" and earlier armed groups. Consistently formulated in a practically static manner by the propagators of institutional discourse, the representation of the guerrilla movement is based on three sets of arguments focusing, respectively, on the incoherence, the subalternity and the criminal nature of "neo-terrorism."

Incoherence

Reprising one of the usual modes of the social construction of threat, namely the dissociation of the "threatening figures" from their historical context (Tsoukala 2008b), the propagators of institutional discourse make a point of not placing attacks carried out by these young guerrillas in the social and political context of the country. Whereas, as will be shown below, the guerrillas explicitly connect their acts to the functioning of society and the state apparatus, their attacks are invariably presented as "incoherent" (*Ethnos* 2009b) or, at any rate, as acts in which "it is difficult to decipher messages or objectives" given that their "targets are random, chosen on the spur of the moment according to emotional criteria, innocent victims who, for whatever reason, find themselves caught up in senseless attacks"[7] (Vidali 2010). The attacks are therefore threatening not so much for the harm they cause to the social order as because, far from carrying a clear political meaning, they are the reflection of "an absurd truth," which remains "incomprehensible for the majority of the population" (Yatromanolakis 2009). Faced with this threat, the reaction tends to be either to ask rhetorical questions about this ill-defined evil that is poisoning the country's youth (Panoussis 2010), or to attribute the emergence of these "neo-terrorists" to non-political factors of a psychological or cultural nature. It is thus suggested that engagement in armed struggle is characteristic of the immoderate behavior of (post-)adolescents (Rigopoulou 2010), whose crossing of the line separating thought from concrete action is made easier either by the presence of a collective imagination filled with the violence of historical exploits from the past (Vima 2010d), or by the persistent grip of the logics of antagonism within Greek society (Vidali 2009).

Even when the new urban guerrilla movement is explicitly linked to the uprising of 2008, the attacks it mounts are not invested with any meaning, since the propagators of institutional discourse refuse to attribute any political sense whatsoever to the violence of the rioters, or even to acknowledge the intrinsic lawmaking function of violence (Benjamin 1921). No consideration is given to Hannah Arendt's remark (2000: 123) that "when our sense of justice is offended, and where there is reason to suspect that conditions could be changed and are not, violence is the only possibility of setting the scales of justice right again." It is, rather, claimed that "violence without a cause has led people to join, also without a cause, groups which are involved in violent phenomena" (Vima 2011b). In other instances, a connection between the urban guerrilla movement and the uprising of 2008 is drawn only in order to criticize parents for being too indulgent, suggesting that the young guerrillas were introduced to political violence "when adults justified fury, approved of violent reactions, applauded acts of extremism; when parents encouraged their children to take on the role of protagonists, a role that they themselves could no longer perform; when society failed to set acceptable limits, through love and discipline, on their behavior," thus creating "terrorists without a cause, motiveless revolutionaries, criminals who are unaware of the gravity of their acts," a generation "who have come to believe in the impossible, who have tried to become something which does not exist" (Vima 2010c).

This insistence on the alleged incomprehensibility, if not irrationality, of these attacks is in turn predicated on a twofold argument that takes as its starting-point the absence of any theoretical framework sufficiently developed to explain why individuals take up armed struggle (*Ethnos* 2009b) – and then proceeds to transform supposition into objective reality. The lack of theoretical sophistication visible in the guerrillas' declarations is thus assumed, unjustly, to reveal an absence of ideological underpinnings. It is stated, for instance, that the new armed groups "lack any theoretical or ideological ground" (*Ethnos* 2009b), whereas their communiqués are considered to be "ideologically empty" (Vima 2010a). Always framed in a very summary fashion, this denial that the armed struggle possesses any ideological basis nonetheless remains curtailed, for it is itself based on incomplete reasoning. While the urban guerrilla movement is presented as lacking any coherent ideological ground, the definitional vacuum thus left is not filled by any alternative explanatory schema attributing a different meaning to these attacks or, on the contrary, explicitly defining them as pathological in nature. Placed in the domain of the non-signified, the origins of these attacks float around within a restricted political space, circumscribed on the one hand by what can be attributed to "personal initiatives" and, on the other, by what might give rise to "ad hoc" actions (*Ethnos* 2009b).

Subalternity

This consistently vague representation of the ideological underpinnings of the urban guerrilla movement facilitates the projection of an image of continuity between earlier armed groups and those of today. Never explicitly described as such, ideological continuity is assumed to be real as a logical deduction from an organizational continuity that is presented as fact by the police, even if it has yet to be conclusively proved. In any case, this continuity is perceived in terms of an unequal relationship between the generations, the young guerrillas occupying a subaltern position with respect to their elders – an image which, in turn, implicitly reinforces the hypothesis of ideological continuity between the two.

This supposed continuity is first established between the new generation of guerrillas and the RS. Although the political theses of the RS, which are elaborated in numerous texts besides the organization's communiqués (Gournas *et al.* 2011; "Sinelefsi gia tin ipothesi tou Epanastatikou Agona" 2012a, 2012b), clearly correspond to the revolutionary profile of previous armed organizations, the propagators of institutional discourse look no further than the date of the group's appearance (2003) in order to place it alongside contemporary armed groups as an integral part of "neo-terrorism." This identical labeling of guerrillas belonging to different generations and, as will be shown below, adhering to different political theories, allows the police to assert that numerous links exist between the FCC and the RS. Allusions to links of personal comradeship forged at some unspecified past date (*Ethnos* 2011) go together with lengthier descriptions of operational links established through the presence of "liaison guerrillas" (Vima 2011a; 2011c). It is thus stated that "officers from the anti-terrorist branch believe that the FCC's strategy has been influenced by the RS" (Kathimerini 2010b); that the groups have undertaken joint operations (Vima 2011c); or that the FCC has long been considered as "an organization made up of 'apprentice' terrorists, under the guidance of the RS, whose members provided them with the explosives needed for bomb-making" (Nea 2011), protected this younger generation (Nea 2010), while always leaving sufficient "space for the need for initiative and self-respect" felt by the young guerrillas (Vima 2010a). The continuation and further intensification of the FCC's activity long after the dismantling of the RS has, undoubtedly, dealt a serious blow to the credibility of these accounts, but has not yet given rise to any alternative representations.

This focus on the subaltern position of the young generation of guerrillas is backed up by the idea that the influence of their elders could even go beyond the supposed role of the RS and stretch further into the past as part of an attempt to "re-establish a 'restored' version of the climate of terrorism of the 1970s–1980s" (*Kosmos tou Ependyti* 2010b). Based exclusively on police sources, which have never been officially verified, the subalternity of the current generation of armed groups is presented as self-evident, as can be seen simply from the titles of articles which regularly announce, for instance, that "[The police] are looking for weapons and mentors" (Vima 2011a), or "The old generation are guiding the neo-terrorists" (*Ethnos* 2009a). The theory of inter-generational influence is found in various slightly different versions, all of which, however, agree regarding the recruitment of young guerrillas by "older and more experienced individuals with a background in anti-establishment/anarchist circles" (Kathimerini 2010a), who had been members of now defunct armed groups, and have handed down their experience to the younger generation (Vima 2010b, 2011a). Sometimes contradictory, sometimes mutually corroborating, these police-manipulated accounts are filled with detailed descriptions, one of the functions of which is to lend them greater credibility:

> Police investigations are focusing on a man of around 60, who is thought to have been one of the founder members of the post-dictatorship terrorist organizations and to have more recently established neo-terrorist groups. ... He managed to evade detection when the 17N and the RPS were being dismantled.
> (*Ethnos* 2009a)

> It seems that the consolidation [of the FCC] has been the work of a man of about 40 – a former cadre of Popular Revolutionary Action and Armed Revolutionary Action – and of a man of similar age, who was one of the leaders of the Revolutionary Cells group which was active between 1997 and 2001.
> (Vima 2010b)

> The FCC was created by two individuals attached to the anti-power movement who, in 2007, had been involved in a bank robbery. The group was then reinforced by members of Popular Will and Popular Revolutionary Action who brought their expertise with them. ... It appears that the group was later influenced by an individual ... who was formerly one of the leaders of the Revolutionary Brigade.
> (Vima 2011a)

The criminal nature

This image of an urban guerrilla movement whose ill-defined ideological profile implicitly aligns it with earlier armed groups, which in any case are supposedly keeping a benevolent eye on these young fighters, is complemented by an insistence on the movement's links with the more traditional criminal underworld (*Ethnos* 2009a). Relying mainly on information provided by the anti-terrorist branch, but also taking into account the fact that some communiqués contain messages of solidarity with criminals on the run (COM, February 8, 2011), journalists routinely state that today's guerrillas "collaborate closely with organized crime" (*Kosmos tou Ependyti* 2010b). In stressing that such links were rare in the past, they point out that a process of osmosis between the criminals and guerrillas, for example through the supply of weapons and stolen vehicles, has become systematic since the early 2000s (Vima 2010a).

The frequently repeated media version of these links dismisses entirely the notion that this alleged collaboration might also be, to some extent, the result of certain ideological affinities, whether underlying or established in a prison setting, in line with a long tradition of blurred boundaries between outlaw figures, whether they are engaged in underworld activities or political violence (Hobsbawm 2000). Hence, even when it is acknowledged that this exchange is a result of contacts established in prison between guerrillas and common criminals, it is always concluded that:

> these criminals legitimize their illegal behavior through ideology, and receive support and justification for their lifestyles and actions from individuals involved in anti-power movements, while the guerrillas receive convenient "logistical support" – and even the services of professional killers – from these criminals.
>
> (Vima 2010a)

Along with the arguments regarding the incoherence and subalternity of the new generation of guerrillas, this depreciatory image of an urban guerrilla movement whose political aura has become tarnished through its dealings with organized crime serves further to discredit these armed groups which, allegedly, lack political awareness, act under outside influences and, according to police sources, are made up of "young hotheads, lacking any moral principles or concrete objectives, who have turned in an ill-defined and uncontrollable manner against society" (*Kosmos tou Ependyti* 2010a).

The urban guerrilla movement from the guerrillas' perspective

Thematic content analysis of the texts under study reveals that the justification given for the current urban guerrilla movement is based on the application of an ideologically determined system of interpretation to the interactions between guerrillas, society and the state. For the sake of practicality, this analysis will be illustrated here by a selection of extracts that can be considered representative of the whole.

Ideological positioning

A comparison of the texts written by the guerrillas of the past (Chalazias 2003; Epanastatikos Laikos Agonas s.d.; Epanastatikos Laikos Agonas 2003; Gournas *et al.* 2011; 17 Noemvri 2002) with those produced by the current generation reveals a huge gulf in terms of the latter's very limited theoretical development of the rationale for armed struggle and the simplified character of their analysis of the (inter)national political and economic situation. These particular features of more recent guerrilla discourse can be attributed to two factors. First, although the involvement of the older generation cannot be ruled out, the arrests that have been made indicate that we are talking about individuals who, in most cases, were less than 25 years old at the time of their arrest. Their comparatively young age, which by definition precludes their having fully completed their further education, may explain somewhat the lack of conceptual sophistication found in their discourse. Second, their adoption of certain positions influenced by individualist anarchism suggests that the comparative simplicity of their discourse may well be the result of deliberate choices by guerrillas who have broken free of the ideologies and practices of earlier leftist political formations (Newman 2010a).

In either case, in order to analyze the stance adopted by this new generation, a stance that focuses on the emergence of the individual as a political actor deserving the right to influence the development of society, and on the rejection of any revolutionary objective, it is necessary to take a step back from the day-to-day reality of these young people and attempt to distinguish their ideological framework more clearly. While I assume here that they are familiar with the work of the US individualist anarchists, such as Josiah Warren and James L. Walker, and also that they have been influenced by many different contemporary authors, such as Guy Debord, Raoul Vaneigem and Hakim Bey, I consider that the basis of their ideology can only be analyzed with reference to the thought of Max Stirner (1845/1907). With his "universal condemnation of 'ontological culture'" (Koch 1993: 332), Stirner enjoys emblematic status among the founders of individualist anarchism, and serves as an explicit or implicit frame of intellectual reference for any study of post-anarchism. Without seeking to play down the influence of contemporary authors on the formation of the guerrillas' intellectual outlook, in particular with respect to the celebration of hedonism, the desire for immediacy and the rejection of consumer society, I will thus approach the question of their ideological position with particular reference to Stirnerian thought.

Following this line of analysis, it becomes clear that the focus on the reforming capacity of the individual, mentioned in 20.5 percent of the texts studied, is contrasted with a wider society that is perceived as apathetic, if not an active vector of vile values. The labeling of the individual as a "revolutionary subject" (PL, March 4, 2011) is accompanied by declarations of belief in the existence "of a creative ego, able to resist everything that fails to allow its expression, able to confront the devouring mass of individuals who fear everything that is different" (COM, February 11, 2011). Radically opposed to "the majority of this society of passive morons contemplating the spectacle of their own psychical and corporeal death" (COM, January 5, 2011), this revolutionary subject, which is alone elevated to the status of "Man" (ibid.), is placed above all other concerns. In the name of its unique ability to constitute, in itself, its own directing principle, it claims the absolute right to obtain "self-satisfaction and the realization of one's own desires" (PL, December 25, 2010) by embracing modes of (possibly violent) opposition, in order to "become the actor of [its] own history" (COM, April 1, 2011).

This individualistic vision of political action, which takes the ego as the privileged locus of political power, dismisses any idea of concerted collective action with a view to achieving an objective shared by, or imposed upon, a wider community. Revolutionary action is seen as "independent of mass approval" (PDC, July 6, 2011), and the guerrillas seek "to carry on with the war [whether they are] surrounded by social movements or not" (COM, April 13, 2011). This action is inscribed in a "right here, right now," which is referred to in 10.2 percent of the texts studied as the only possible setting for action. The rejection of the future as a spatial–temporal site of projection for human action, and the consequent rejection of revolution as an objective legitimizing present and future action, places little reliance on arguments reprising critiques of the inability of communism's social liberalism to free the individual, or of the inability of classical anarchist theories to oppose effectively the idea of the state and the principle of state authority (Newman 2001; Stirner 1845/1907), or indeed of the need to reconsider anarchist notions of power and the individual in the light of post-structuralist theory (Koch 1993; May 1989; Newman 2010b). The young guerrillas justify their stance in the name of a passion for life which, unable to accept the constraints of time, and searching for a context which would allow the individual to lead a meaningful existence and achieve self-fulfillment, cuts out any intermediary stages and brings its manifestation forward into the present. The vague statement that "the 'objective conditions' seem to us too abstract, and we do not intend to remain inert while waiting for them to 'ripen'" (COM, January 20, 2011) thus goes hand-in-hand with the rejection of a Marxist-style revolution since, "[given that] class consciousness is dead ... we are not going to take on the job of awakening the people" (COM, November 25, 2010). Now freed from the "vision of social revolution" (ibid.) as a frame of reference for their militant action, these guerrillas are able to "remove the so-called revolutionary subject of the oppressed proletariat from [their] vocabulary" (ibid.) and declare that "revolution is an existential fight ... the absolute rejection of the status quo" (PDC, July 6, 2011).

Although FCC identified itself as distinct from all earlier armed groups as long ago as 2009 (COM, February 14, 2009), this new urban guerrilla phenomenon only started to be explicitly defined as an anarchist–individualist movement in 2010 (TT, May 19, 2010). As the dismantling of FCC progressed, along with the arrests in parallel of numerous isolated guerrillas, the need to affirm the ideological identity of these imprisoned fighters, and to inscribe their struggle in the historical process of their country, led to a proliferation of references to the "new" urban guerrilla movement. Opposed "to state and society alike" (TT, November 25, 2010), the latter "is an integral part of the individualist anarchist and nihilist tendency of the anti-power movement" (PL, April 6, 2011), which "does not seek to form an avant-garde leading the masses, the people and society in the right direction" (PDC, July 6, 2011).

While individualist anarchism is sometimes seen as being hostile to any idea of solidarity (Fabbri 1903), this image of guerrillas acting as "lone wolves" is not necessarily contradicted by their frequent interventions in public debate. Aiming to rally a vaguely defined audience to the cause of armed struggle, the communication strategy they have implemented should be seen as "'propaganda' with a view to selecting individuals who have yet to discover their individualist-anarchist temperaments, or at least creating an intellectual environment favorable to their development" (Armand 1911). Certain active guerrillas with nihilistic inclinations seem to have similar objectives when they berate anarchist circles, which, in the face of the mass arrests of numerous guerrillas, appear "stunned, defeatist and disorganized" (COM, March 24, 2011). Extended beyond national boundaries, this search for like-minded individuals leads to increasing numbers of expressions of solidarity with foreign guerrillas (found in 25.6 percent of the texts studied) and, in particular, gives rise to calls for the creation of an international network of groups and individuals sharing the same desire for revolt (PL, November 25, 2010).

However, substituting this "struggle for the destruction of the values, symbols, relations and morality generated by this world" (LH, November 12, 2010) for social revolution means that these groups pose no meaningful threat to the regime, since they seek to inspire numerous individual revolts rather than an uprising of the masses. They clearly state their "opposition to the fetichization of the masses and the obsessive attachment to the idea that the crowd is at the heart of any revolution" (PDC, July 6, 2011). The insurrection they call for, then, to use Stirner's terms, aims not so much to overturn the established order as to offer a way out for individuals who wish to escape the constraints of this order and become masters of their own destinies:

> The Revolution aimed at new arrangements; insurrection leads us no longer to let ourselves be arranged, but to arrange ourselves, and sets

no glittering hopes on "institutions". It is not a fight against the established, since, if it prospers, the established collapses of itself; it is only a working forth of me out of the established. If I leave the established, it is dead and passes into decay.

(Stirner 1845/1907)

This rejection of any revolutionary objective in favor of the "revolutionary transformation of society through social revolt" (COM, September 12, 2010) does not, however, provide an entirely coherent ground to these groups' stance, as this inscription of action in the immediate present does not dissociate it completely from the eschatological tendency that underlies any revolutionary vision. The utopian temptation does not appear in its messianic form of a "redeeming revolution" which, by transposing into the political domain the belief of apocalyptic religion in the triumph over evil, justifies the recourse to violence in the name of a need to perfect humanity, or at least to save it from damnation (Goyard Fabre 1987: 54ff.; Gray 2007). Rather, this rejection of the revolutionary perspective shifts its utopia from a dream of an ideal future society to the destruction of society as it now exists. Although the urban guerrilla movement consistently denies its utopian character,[8] as is clearly shown by its recurring use of the time-honored formula "the day will come," in fact it embraces a form of metaphysical utopianism in that the use of violence is justified by its desire to change the course of history by force, on the basis of a deep conviction that it alone knows what really constitutes the common good and personal fulfillment.

Relations with society

Unlike the public discourse of earlier guerrilla organizations, whose demands were strictly political in nature, the discourse of the current generation also contains an element of social critique that is striking insofar as, often adopting a plaintive tone, it rejects society not so much for its inherent propensity to dominate individuals, as for its imperfections. The citing of a long list of social ills as the justification for armed struggle, however, is a departure from Stirnerian thought since, even though these young guerrillas turn to the logic of destructive action in order to free themselves from the yoke of society, their behavior seems to be the result of a deep incompatibility between the dominant values of society and their own, and not of any constraints placed on their fulfillment by the very existence of society itself. The scarcity of explicit criticism of "the dominant civilization" (COM, July 7, 2011), along with the absence of the attacks usually directed at anarchists by primitivists (Sheppard 2003), further suggest that the influence of primitivist theories on their thinking is weak, and that their critique is fuelled mostly by the alienating nature of the consumer society itself (Debord 1967).

Present in 20.5 percent of the texts studied, the critique of society denounces in a fierce way "a world in which injustice, exploitation and money reign supreme" (COM, January 17, 2011). It condemns the breakdown of human relations (COM, November 27, 2010) and the degradation of non-material values in a society in thrall to materialism and focused purely on frenetic consumption, gorged on a constant flow of superficial and politically manipulated information from the media (COM, March 5, 2011), which is aimed at the "moronic grin of TV-addicted people, and the mindless gaze of the insatiable consumer" (PL, May 20, 2011). Noting the grip of "alienated relations" on society (PL, December 25, 2010), the guerrillas build their existence around the position they take up in relation to this state of affairs. As a result, their opposition to social alienation is unequivocally placed at the heart of the process by which the identity of all those who seek to assert themselves as autonomous individuals and intervene forcefully in the public sphere is forged.

From this perspective, taking direct action is seen as a way out in the face of the existential crisis caused by living in a society that is perceived as vile and alienated. Of the texts studied, 12.8 percent describe how "the loneliness, the emptiness, the mediocrity, the submissiveness" produced by a "life spent cooped up in apartments, bombarded by TV advertising, exposed to thousands of CCTV cameras, and being constantly harassed by the police" (PL, March 4, 2011), in a society dominated by "easy options, informing, thoughtless complicity, and the sterile consumption of intellectual and material detritus, presented as the absolute incarnation of happiness" (TT, November 7, 2010), cannot fail to provoke "fury and hatred against a weathering daily existence" (COM, November 27, 2010). Conceived of in these terms, armed struggle becomes more than anything a form of resistance to the generalized decay of a "herd-society" (COM, March 24, 2011). Held aloft as an "affirmation of our existence, an ally of the authentic side of life" (COM, November 25, 2010), it is a "response to the existential emptiness imposed by contemporary consumer culture" (PL, March 1, 2011), and the only possible reaction to the "false dreams of a future without hope" (COM, October 16, 2010). Far from leading to a dynamic of future collective action, then, armed struggle satisfies a need to release pressure that has built up on an individual level. In the opposition thus established between the ego and society, there is no promise of final victory. Armed struggle takes on the aspect of a war fought day-to-day and in a constantly evolving manner against various forms of domination (Newman 2001) in the full knowledge that "the final destination of all those who resist is prison" (INT, November 2, 2010). Consequently, "active rupture, ruthless daily war, powerful awareness, opposition to today's way of life, critical analytical thinking and radical revolutionary action" (TT, November 7, 2010) do not take the positive form of destructive/creative action, but rather the negative form of desperate action, which "preaches revolutionary nihilism and antisocial anarchy" (PL, December 25, 2010).

When looked at in this way, the categorical rejection by the guerrillas of the "voluntary servitude of the majority of society" (PL, March 1, 2011), and their refusal to make any compromises in a "world [which] has no room for [their] dreams and desires" (COM, February 11, 2011), become the central means by which a system of values structured around human dignity can be expressed. Referred to in 17.9 percent of the texts studied, these "last bastions of human existence, dignity and moral values" (COM, March 12, 2011) are what guides the steps of these young guerrillas, who feel called to "take [their] lives in [their] hands and press forward with honor, dignity and courage to the end, to the revolution" (LH, November 7, 2010). While this insistence on human dignity is reminiscent of J. Burton's theory (1997: 10ff) of the human limits of the malleability of individuals who, if confronted with the risk of alienation, may turn to violence in order to protect the nucleus of their identity, it also attributes a moral foundation to armed struggle that makes any hesitation unthinkable – for the preservation of human dignity now becomes the last non-negotiable refuge of identities imperiled by the alienating effect of their environment.

Placed at the heart of the guerrillas' militant stance, the assertion of this moral basis for their action may appear perplexing, not so much because it could dissociate them from Stirnerian individualist anarchism, but rather because it employs a different frame of reference. One could, admittedly, consider that the focus on this moral ground is compatible with the position taken by Stirner who, while condemning morality and all its attendant obligations, passes a positive value judgment on certain moral properties of the individual who is his own master (Leopold 2002). However, insofar as moral values serve to separate the guerrillas from the rest of society, by referring to such values they also dissociate themselves from Stirnerian theory, which totally rejects the binary opposition between the moral essence of individuals and the immoral and corrupting power of their environment (Newman 2001). If we take the anti-power stance of this discourse to be genuine, we can attribute this inconsistency to the overall influence of classical anarchist theories, which assert the existence of just such a dichotomy between the dominant morality of society and that of anarchist struggle and solidarity. This hypothesis is, however, unsettled by the presence of religious references which, while few in number, remain perplexing since they crop up regularly over the years in the discourse of this young generation who, no doubt owing to the all-pervading power of the Greek Orthodox Church, have still not managed to "break the tyranny" of religion (Stirner 1845/1907) and free themselves from the mindset it imposes upon them. It is thus possible, when paying homage to a guerrilla killed by the police in March 2010, to wish him a "safe journey"[9] and to imagine him speaking with other guerrillas killed in combat (COM, March 22, 2010), or to declare that one can "see him Up there, in the company of others, rare and beautiful, drawing up Plans" (COM, March 11, 2011).

The ambivalence in the guerrillas' relation to religion is all the more difficult to discern because it reflects a similar ambivalence in anarchist circles more generally, as suggested by the long absence of anti-clerical texts from the main anarchist newspapers *Diadromi Eleftherias* and *Babylonia*, as well as the declarations of an anarchist in hiding who denounces prisons, which are "full of souls in revolt" (Karakatsani 2009), or the inclusion of a fetus in a list of the dead from an arson attack on a bank on the fringes of a demonstration (Syspeirosi Anarchikon 2011b). It is therefore unsurprising that this "burden" of religion[10] should also have its part to play in determining the guerrillas' repertoire of action. Although, in a time of deep economic crisis, the property of the Greek Orthodox Church is still not subject to tax, it is rare for a church to be the target of an attack. It is also revealing that, when the members of FCC listed targets that were common to militants of all anarchist movements, they did not include churches among the "public buildings, public security agents and symbols of wealth" to be attacked (COM, May 19, 2010).

Attitudes towards the state

The ideological gap between the theoretical bases of the current urban guerrilla movement and Stirnerian theory, or even classical anarchist theory, appears even wider when one considers the way in which the state is perceived. The product of an existential malaise rather than a political vision in the classical sense,[11] the urban guerrilla movement is undoubtedly eager to proclaim its anarchist credentials, but one has to admit that these claims cannot be taken at face value. In spite of its radical appearances, the guerrillas' discourse is characterized by the absence of any demands for the abolition of the state and its institutions. Rather than putting forward any vision of individual liberalism, or of radical political liberalism, the guerrillas are happy simply to criticize liberal democracy. Repeating the aforementioned pattern with respect to their critique of society, their political critique does not bring the political system as such into question, but rather denounces its deviations from its ideal type, as if the imperfections in the functioning of the state apparatus were what originally spurred these young people to turn to the repertoire of violent action.

Found in 28.2 percent of the texts studied, the criticisms leveled at the regime concern the routine violation by the oppressive state apparatus of numerous constitutionally protected rights and liberties. As well as disillusioned comments that "democracy is counter-attacking and taking its revenge" (COM, February 20, 2011) and that "the democratic façade of the regime is collapsing under the pressure of resistance" (COM, February 18, 2011) to reveal "the hideous face of totalitarianism" (PL August 16, 2011), there are also denunciations of abuses and cruelty by the police, the pursuit, arrest and trial of numerous anarchists for their opinions, and the systematic impunity enjoyed by police officers, who are accused of being arbitrary in the execution of their duties.

There can be no doubt that any objective observer would be hard-pressed to argue with the validity of these criticisms. The violent repression of demonstrations in a climate where the police act with practical impunity is not regularly denounced only by the guerrilla movement (PL, March 1, 2011) but also by Greek and international human rights organizations, reporters' organizations and even the Order of Physicians in Athens (Amnesty International 2010, 2011; Hellenic League for Human Rights 2011; Human Rights Watch 2011; Reporters Without Borders 2010; *Eleftherotypia* 2010b). Criticism of the violent arrest and pre-trial detention of anarchists on the basis of no evidence, or even reasonable suspicion whatsoever (PL, March 1, 2011), is often vindicated by the subsequent acquittal of the individuals in question. Given that the introduction of exceptional measures in the context of anti-terrorism legislation has authorized, among other things, the holding of trials without juries, away from regular courtrooms, and implied implicit approval of serious breaches of procedure, the description of these trials as a "parody" of justice (COM, March 12, 2011) only serves to echo the severe criticisms leveled at them from jurists and scholars (Manoledakis 2006; Milonas 2004). The political nature of some rulings has even been denounced by the Greek parliament's Special Permanent Committee on Institutions and Transparency (*Eleftherotypia* 2010a). Finally, the bitter observation that "justice is the web of a spider which captures and devours small prey, while leaving the big snakes free to crawl across it and control it" (COM, January 5, 2011) is sadly confirmed by academic studies, which reveal that existing class inequalities are reflected at every level of the criminal justice system (Sorvatzioti 2011).

This unexpected, albeit backhanded defense of the institutions of liberal democracy is accompanied by a virulent critique of the media (found in 10.2 percent of the texts studied). Journalists are described as "lackeys of power, dealing in disinformation and trickery and molding opinion to serve their masters" (COM, December 11, 2010), and accused of being a "sub-branch of the anti-terrorist brigade and the state security services" (COM, January 20, 2011), which "seeks to sow fear among fighters … and rebuild the image of an all-powerful state" (PL, April 12, 2011). Yet, as we have already seen regarding similar criticisms of failures of the rule of law, these accusations against those who:

> trample on the freedom and dignity of our comrades by printing the lies of the police and then embroidering them with scenarios taken straight from their imaginations, who sit in judgment and pass sentence by destroying reputations and lives even before state justice takes its turn to do the same[,]
>
> (COM, January 17, 2011)

do in fact correspond to the conclusions of academic studies of media coverage of the urban guerrilla movement (Panoussis 2005).

Concluding remarks

This analysis of the public discourse of Greek guerrillas brings to light a reality that is considerably more complex than the police and the media, or indeed the guerrillas themselves, would care to admit. Firstly, it is clear that, in contrast to the ideas promoted by the prevailing institutional discourse, this generation of "neo-terrorists" are not the bearers of a revolutionary project in the traditional sense of the term because they do not aim to overturn the established order. While it is true that, in resorting to various forms of violent action, these groups challenge the authority of the state – all the more so given the degree to which this authority has been shaken by the current economic and political crisis – this challenge is nonetheless diluted by the inconsistencies visible in the conceptual framework surrounding it. These young guerrillas seem to use anarchist discourse almost as a mask behind which to hide their deep existential malaise and their disappointment in the face of the failures of liberal democracy, rather than wholeheartedly embracing an anti-state, and possibly antisocial stance. Besides, in so doing, they have already come under fire from certain anarchist quarters (Syspeirosi Anarchikon 2011a). Since the absence of a solid ideological underpinning to their actions rules out any ambitions this urban guerrilla movement might have had to hegemony, even at the level of freely associating individuals, the movement's political impact is ultimately divorced from its public discourse.

Put in other terms, if there is a real questioning of the established order, it only manifests itself in the implicit demand – which is also somewhat paradoxical given the profile of those making it – that the political regime, and society as a whole, should conform to their own guiding principles. By adopting violent methods in order to advance the demands for democratization made in vain by the youth uprising of 2008, today's guerrillas are moving away from Stirner's postmodern thinking on politics (Assoun 1986/2001: 1107) and taking on the mantle of a classical liberalism that is still struggling to free itself from the "burden" of religion. This, by definition, means that they do not threaten the central pillars of the state or of Greek society. It is clear that these conformist aspects of the urban guerrilla movement undermine any prospect of subversive revolt. It is not surprising then that it is the older generation, applying hindsight to their past militancy (Koufodinas 2012), that are opening up new anti-establishment paths by their suggestion to patiently move towards the creation of autonomous spaces and the multitude of local revolts which are characteristic of post-anarchism (Amster 2012; Newman 2010b).

Uncovering the complexity of the contemporary urban guerrilla movement in this way also sheds new light on how institutional discourse seeks to discredit this armed struggle by playing down its political dimension and also concealing its "reformist" tendencies. Even if we presume that this discourse, which is to a large extent manipulated by the police, may reflect the shortcomings in the analytical abilities of the officers of the anti-terrorism branch, who seem to have been initially reassured by the image of these "baby terrorists" (Nea 2010; Vima 2010b),[12] we cannot possibly explain why the increasing radicalization of this urban guerrilla movement has not caused a shift in the media representation of the phenomenon. Hence, it is this dual aspect of an institutional discourse, which is both static and misleading, that can lead one to suspect that it also serves other, undeclared purposes. Clearly, its attempts to deny any meaning to the urban guerrilla movement by presenting its actions as incomprehensible, or by linking them to organized crime, are in line with one of the key objectives of the ongoing threat construction process. The less any given behavior corresponds to a register of familiar actions, the less likely it is to produce feelings of identification between those adopting it and the rest of society, and the less sympathy is liable to be felt when the former are subject to repression (Tsoukala 2008b), the easier it then becomes to "open up a gap in legitimacy between the institutionalized practice of physical coercion in the name of protecting public order, and the practices of protest or opposition" (Braud 1993: 16). The implicit attribution of meaning to the urban guerrilla movement through the suggestion that today's guerrillas are still pursuing the objective of Marxist-style revolution sought by their predecessors, even though the very basis of such a project is now obsolete, further reinforces this process by rendering their actions so unintelligible that they will, by definition, lack any spontaneous popular support.

Yet the dissemination of the idea that this guerrilla movement is essentially subversive, opposed to liberal democracy, goes beyond the usual mechanisms of the social construction of threat. It allows the authorities to dismiss the demands for democratization that underlie the actions of this movement, and consequently sidestep any debate regarding a system of power that unquestionably lacks respect for the rule of law. The objectives of the anti-terrorist campaign thus seem to some extent to concern not so much the protection of liberal democracy as the continuation of a system of power that denies *de facto* the very principles of the regime that it claims to defend. By inverting the perspective from which this political violence is usually examined, then, we see that, beyond the apparent aspects of this discourse and the questions of public security it raises, the actions of these guerrillas not only reveal the complexity of the ways in which the founding principles of democracy are articulated, how they are applied in the functioning of the state apparatus, and how they are perceived by the people, but also highlight the right of the people to demand that the terms of the social contract be respected as the basis for consensus within democracy.

Notes

1 FCC (active since 2008) was partially dismantled between 2010 and 2011. No members of 6D or SR have been arrested to date.
2 FCC, SR and 6D claim to have carried out murders and bomb attacks; other groups have carried out only minor attacks.
3 Active between 1975 and 2002 (date of dismantling).
4 Active between 1975 and 1995 (date of unilateral cease-fire).
5 Active between 2003 and 2010 (date of dismantling).
6 All the following references can be accessed on the website https://athens.indymedia.org (browse by date). Website last accessed on June 20, 2011.
7 This and all following citations from Greek sources are the author's translations.
8 The denial of the utopian aspect inherent to certain political projects is, by definition, visible at the heart of the thinking of those who promote them. Thus E. Reclus (1896/2009: 31) considered that "our new world is rising up around us ... it is by no means a pipe-dream ... but has already revealed itself in many guises." On the (in)ability of political actors to perceive and acknowledge the possible utopian aspects of their programmes, and to question the use of terror which their implementation would necessarily entail, see Papaïoannou (1978).
9 Message appearing on a poster mourning his death, March 2010.
10 The term "burden" (original French: *pesanteur*) is understood in the sense given to it by J.-P. Piotte (1970/2010: 207) with reference to the persistence of dominant ideological schemas.
11 According to N. Sevastakis (2009), the basis of these guerrillas' action is rooted in metapolitics owing to its existentialist character and its having broken away from "the historical identities of all leftist tendencies."
12 So-called because of their youth and the minimal danger posed by their early attacks.

References

17 Noemvri (2002) *I prokirikseis 1975–2002*, Athens: Kaktos.
Amnesty International, Annual Report: Greece (2010). Available at www.amnesty.org/en/region/greece/report-2010 (accessed May 10, 2012).
Amnesty International, Annual Report: Greece (2011). Available at www.amnesty.org/en/region/greece/report-2011 (accessed May 10, 2012).
Amster, R. (2012) *Anarchism Today*, Santa Barbara, CA: Praeger.
Anders, G. (2011) *Via Nai i Ochi. Mia anagkaia sizitisi* [Violence: Yes or No? A necessary discussion], Athens: Eleftheriaki Koultoura.
Arendt, H. (2000) *Peri Vias* [On Violence], 2000: Athens: Alexandria.
Armand, E. (1911) "Petit Manuel Anarchiste Individualiste," in: S. Faure (ed.) *Encyclopédie Anarchiste*. Available at www.panarchy.org/armand/armand.html (accessed June 5, 2012).
Assoun, P.-L. (1986/2001) "Stirner Max," in: F. Châtelet, O. Duhamel and É. Pisier (eds) *Dictionnaire des œuvres politiques*, Paris: PUF., 1101–7.
Astrinaki, R. (2009) "'(Un)hooding' a Rebellion: The December 2008 Events in Athens," *Social Text*, 27(4101), 97–107.
Benjamin, W. (1921) *Ya mia kritiki tis vias* [Critique of Violence], 2011: Athens: Eleftheriaki Koultoura.
Bonelli, L. (2011) "De l'usage de la violence en politique," *Cultures & Conflits*, 81–2, 7–15.

Braud, P. (1993) "La violence politique: repères et problèmes," *Cultures & Conflits*, 9–10, 13–42.
Broek (Van den), H. (2004) "BORROKA – the legitimation of street violence in the political discourse of radical Basque nationalists," *Terrorism and Political Violence*, 16(4), 714–36.
Burton, J. (1997) *Violence Explained*, Manchester: Manchester University Press.
Chalazias, C. (2003) *I ideologia tou Epanastatikou Laikou Agona. Ta keimena*, Athens: Ellinika Grammata.
Debord, G. (1967) *La société du spectacle*, Paris: Gallimard.
Della Porta, D. (1995) *Social Movements, Political Violence and the State*, Cambridge: Cambridge University Press.
Eleftherotypia (2002a) "Ti 'vlepame' gia 17N prin apo 2 chronia," August 5.
Eleftherotypia (2002b) "Aristera – Deksia kai tromokratia," August 10.
Eleftherotypia (2010a) "Vouli kata dikaiosinis gia diafthora," November 1.
Eleftherotypia (2010b) "Dakrigona kai xilo ek promeletis," December 12.
Epanastatikos Agonas (s.d.) *Prokirikseis 2003–2009*, s.l.
Epanastatikos Laikos Agonas (2003) *Antipliroforissi I, II, III*, Athens: Grafes.
Ethnos (2009a) "I palia genia kathodigei tous neotromokrates," February 22.
Ethnos (2009b) "I palia froura analamvanei drasi stin Antitromokratiki," October 31.
Ethnos (2011) "Mia organosi me vari oplismo pou etoimazotan gia kanoniko polemo," March 20.
Fabbri, L. (1903) "L'individualismo stirneriano nel movimento anarchico," *Il Pensiero* 7–8–10. Available at http://athens.indymedia.org/front.php3?lang=el&article_id=357182 (accessed June 5, 2012).
Featherstone, M., Holohan, S. and Poole, E. (2010) "Discourses of the War on Terror: constructions of the Islamic Other after 7/7," *International Journal of Media & Cultural Politics* 6(2), 169–86.
Geka, M. (2012) "La construction sociale de la citoyenneté chez les jeunes Grecs," in: P-D. Galloro and A. Mouchtouris (eds) *Jeunesse et discrimination*, Perpignan: PUP, 201–23.
Gournas, K., Roupa, P., and Maziotis, N. (2011) *Keimena apo ti filaki*, s.l.: s.n.
Goyard Fabre, S. (1987) "Thomas More et l'Utopie," in: T. More *L'utopie*, Paris: Flammarion, 31–65.
Graham, P., Keenan, T. and Dowd, A-M. (2004) "A call to arms at the end of history: a discourse-historical analysis of George W. Bush's declaration of war on terror," *Discourse & Society*, 15(2–3), 199–221.
Gray, J. (2007) *Black Mass. Apocalyptic Religion and the Death of Utopia*, London: Allen Lane.
Hellenic League for Human Rights (2011) "Lefta gia chimika pantos iparchoun," June 29. Available at www.alfavita.gr/artro.php?id=37795 (accessed May 22, 2012).
Hobsbawm, E. (2000) *Bandits*, London: Weidenfield & Nicolson.
Hodges, A. and Nilep, C. (eds) (2007) *Discourse, War and Terrorism*, Amsterdam: John Benjamins.
Human Rights Watch (2011) "Greece: inquiry on police abuse a positive step," July 6. Available at www.hrw.org/en/news/2011/07/06/greece-inquiry-police-abuse-positive-step (accessed May 22, 2012).
Indymedia (2009a) "Aftapates ton anarchikon," February 18. Available at http://athens.indymedia.org/front.php3?lang=el&article_id=992429 (accessed June 14, 2011).

Indymedia (2009b) "I phantasiaki thesmisi tis exegersis," November 9. Available at http://athens.indymedia.org/front.php3?lang=el&article_id=1102253 (accessed June 14, 2011).

Jackson, R. (2007) "Constructing enemies: 'Islamic terrorism' in political and academic discourse," *Government and Opposition*, 42(3), 394–426.

Karakatsani, K. (2009) "Anarchiki eimai, zitiana den eimai," *Kiriakatiki Eleftherotypia*, November 22.

Karamichas, J. (2009) "The December 2008 riots in Greece," *Social Movements Studies*, 8(3), 289–93.

Kathimerini, I (2010a) "Vomves me kathodigites," November 4.

Kathimerini, I (2010b) "Analipsi efthinis apo Pirines," November 26.

Koch, A. (1993) "Poststructuralism and epistemological basis of anarchism," *Philosophy of the Social Sciences*, 23(3), 327–51.

Kosmos tou Ependyti (O) (2010a) "Neotromokratia me osmi parakratous," July 24–5.

Kosmos tou Ependyti (O) (2010b) "Idou ta evrimata stis yafkes," December 11–12.

Kotronaki, L. and Seferiades, S. (2010) "Sur les sentiers de la colère: l'espace-temps d'une révolte," *Actuel Marx*, 48(2), 152–65.

Koufodinas, D. (2009) "Chreiazetai polli skepsi prin apo kathe enopli drasi" (interview), *Proto Thema*, February 28.

Koufodinas, D. (2012) "Mia machi me ti mnimi". Available at http://athens.indymedia.org/front.php3?lang=el&article_id=1401743 (accessed May 27, 2012).

Lambropoulou, E. (2004) "Tromokratia kai peri tromokratias" (round table), *Epistimi kai koinonia*, 12, 219–48.

Laskos C. and Tsakalotos E. (2012) *Apo ton Keynes sti Thatcher. Choris epistrofi*, Athens: Kapsimi.

Lazar, A. and Lazar, M. (2004) "The discourse of the New World Order: 'outcasting' the double face of threat," *Discourse & Society*, 15(2–3), 223–42.

Leopold, D. (2002) "Max Stirner," *The Stanford Encyclopedia of Philosophy*. Available at http://plato.stanford.edu/archives (accessed May 9, 2012).

Leudar, I., Marsland, V. and Nekvapil, J. (2004) "On membership categorization: 'us,' 'them' and 'doing violence' in political discourse," *Discourse & Society*, 15(2–3), 243–66.

Manoledakis, I. (2006) *I aponomi dikaiosinis se periodo krisis*, Athens: Sakkoulas.

May, T. (1989) "Is Post-structuralist political theory anarchist?," *Philosophy and Social Criticism*, 15(2), 167–82.

Mentinis, M. (2010) "Remember remember the 6th of December: a rebellion or the constituting moment of a radical morphoma?," *International Journal of Urban and Regional Research*, 34(1), 197–202.

Merola L. (2008) "Emotion and deliberation in the post-9/11 media coverage of civil liberties," *Democracy & Society*, 5(2), 7–9.

Milonas, I. (2004) *Ipothesi 17N*, Athens: Proskinio.

Mowbray, M. (2010) "Blogging the Greek riots: between aftermath and ongoing engagement," *Resistance Studies Magazine*, 1, 4–15.

Mythen, G. and Walklate, S. (2006) "Communicating the terrorist risk: harnessing a culture of fear?," *Crime, Media, Culture*, 2(2), 123–42.

Newman, S. (2001) "War on the state: Stirner and Deleuze's anarchism," *Anarchist Studies*, 9(2), 147–64. Available at http://theanarchistlibrary.org (accessed June 14, 2011).

Newman, S. (2010a) *The Politics of Postanarchism*, Edinburgh: Edinburgh University Press.
Newman, S. (2010b) "Post-anarchism and power," *Journal of Power*, 3(2), 259–74.
Panoussis, I. (ed.) (2005) *I diki tis 17N apo tis stiles ton efimeridon*, Athens: Sakkoulas.
Panoussis, I. (2010) "Poioi einai oi pragmatikoi apodektes," *To Vima*, November 7.
Papaïoannou, K. (1978) *Lénine ou l'utopie au pouvoir*, Paris: Spartacus.
Pechtelidis, Y. (2011) "December uprising 2008: universality and particularity in young people's discourse," *Journal of Youth Studies*, 14(4), 449–62.
Petropoulou, C. (2010) "From the December youth uprising to the rebirth of urban social movements: a space–time approach," *International Journal of Urban and Regional Research*, 34(1), 217–24.
Piotte, J.-P. (1970/2010) *La pensée politique de Gramsci*, Quebec: Lux.
Reclus, E. (1896/2009) *L'anarchie*, Paris: Mille et une nuits.
Reporters Without Borders (2010) "Unacceptable police violence," December 9. Available at http://en.rsf.org/greece-unacceptable-police-violence-09-12-2010,39000.html (accessed May 22, 2012).
Rigopoulou, P. (2010) "I via erchetai apo psila," *To Vima*, November 7.
Ruggiero, V. (2010) "Armed struggle in Italy," *British Journal of Criminology*, 50(4), 708–24.
Sakellariou A. (2003) *"17 Noemvri": I organosi*, unpublished Master dissertation, Athens: Panteio University.
Sevastakis, N. (2009) "Enas orismenos neoanarchismos," *Eleftherotypia*, April 11.
Sevastakis, N. (2010) "O Dekemvris kai i martiria tou," *Kiriakatiki Avgi*, December 5.
Sevastakis, N. (2012) *I tyrannia tou aftonoïtou*, Athens: Enthemata Avgis.
Sheppard B.O. (2003) *Anarchism vs Primitivism*. Tucson: See Sharp Press. Available at http://libcom.org/library/anarchism-vs-primitivism (accessed May 22, 2012).
"Sinelefsi gia tin ipothesi tou Epanastatikou Agona" (2012a) *Oi politikes topothetiseis ton sintrofon pou dikazontai gia tin ipothesi tou Epanastatikou Agona sto eidiko dikastirio tou Koridallou*, s.l.: s.n.
"Sinelefsi gia tin ipothesi tou Epanastatikou Agona" (2012b) *Meres mnimis kai agona*, s.l.: s.n.
Syspeirosi Anarchikon (2011a) "Epanastatiki prooptiki, antartiko polis kai anarchia," *Diadromi eleftherias*, 101.
Syspeirosi Anarchikon (2011b) "Stou kremasmenou to tsardi den milane gia skoini," *Diadromi eleftherias*, 110.
Sommier, I. (1998) *La violence politique et son deuil*, Rennes: PUR.
Sommier, I. (2008) *La violence révolutionnaire*, Paris: Presses de Sciences-Po.
Sorvatzioti, D. (2011) *I "ftocheia" tis dikaiosinis*, Athens: Kapsimi.
Sotiris, P. (2010) "Rebels with a cause: the December 2008 Greek youth movement as the condensation of deeper social and political contradictions," *International Journal of Urban and Regional Research*, 34(1), 203–9.
Steiner, A. and Debray, L. (2006) *RAF. Guérilla urbaine en Europe occidentale*, Paris: L'Échappée.
Steinert, H. (2003) "The indispensable metaphor of war: On populist politics and the contradictions of the state's monopoly of force," *Theoretical Criminology*, 7(3), 265–91.
Stirner, M. (1845/1907) *The Ego and Its Own*, New York: Benjamin R. Tucker. Available at www.lsr-projekt.de/poly/enee.html#secondii3 (accessed May 24, 2012).

Ta Nea (2010) "Pistevan oti me ton E.A. eixan exarthrosei kai tous Pirines," November 4.

Ta Nea (2011) "Lernaia Hydra oi Pirines tis Fotias," January 19.

Tsfati, Y. and Weimann, G. (2002) "www.terrorism.com: Terror on the Internet," *Studies in Conflict & Terrorism*, 25(5), 317–32.

Tsoukala, A. (2004) "Democracy against security: the debates about counterterrorism in the European Parliament, September 2001–June 2003," *Alternatives: Global, Local, Political*, 29(4), 417–39.

Tsoukala, A. (2006) "Democracy in the light of security. British and French political discourses on domestic counterterrorism policies," *Political Studies*, 54(3), 607–27.

Tsoukala, A. (2008a) "Defining terrorism in the post-September 11th era," in D. Bigo and A. Tsoukala (eds) *Terror, Insecurity and Liberty*, London: Routledge, 49–99.

Tsoukala, A. (2008b) "Boundary-creating processes and social control," *Alternatives. Global, Local, Political*, 33(2), 139–54.

Tsoukala, A. (2009) "Terrorist threat, freedom, and politics in Europe," in: P. Noxolo and J. Huysmans (eds) *Security and Insecurity: Community, Citizenship and the "War on Terror"*, Basingstoke: Palgrave Macmillan, 71–88.

Vidali, S. (2009) "Poios trefei ti via?" October 4.

Vidali, S. (2010) "I krisi, o fovos kai I tromokratia," July 25.

Vima, To (2010a) "Pos oi anarchikoi piran ta opla," August 1.

Vima, To (2010b) "Ta mistika ton Pirinon tis Fotias," November 7.

Vima, To (2010c) "Tromokrates choris aitia," November 7.

Vima, To (2010d) "Thimata tis kiriarchis ideologias," November 7.

Vima, To (2011a) "Psachnoun opla kai kathodigites," March 15.

Vima, To (2011b) "Oi goneis kai ta mora tis tromokratias," March 16.

Vima, To (2011c) "I agnosti simachia Pirinon kai Epanastatikou Agona," November 6.

Weimann, G. (2006) "Virtual disputes: the use of the Internet for terrorist debates," *Studies in Conflict and Terrorism*, 29(7), 623–39.

Yatromanolakis G. (2009) "I pragmatiki apeili," *To Vima*, October 4.

5 When terrorists talk back

Daniela Pisoiu and Nico Prucha

'In the end, every President talks to the bad guys' is the title of an op-ed by Leslie H. Gelb (2008) on Vice-President Cheney's famous statement, 'We don't negotiate with evil; we defeat it'. Gelb goes on to outline how US Presidents have, in fact, negotiated with scores of states and leaders deemed 'evil' but at one time or another strategically useful, or 'the lesser evil'. Talking to terrorists can be flipped either way: as a way of ending protracted conflicts, or as a means of legitimizing their goals and especially means, and, perhaps, even thus encouraging others to undertake such tactics in their confrontations with the state. Most contemporary authors seem to agree on two things: that states should talk to terrorists, and that the reasons why this does not happen more often relate to limited framings of the 'terrorist'. Zulaika (2009: 4), for instance, has argued that there is no communication between states and 'terrorists' because 'the counterterrorist loses interest in the intellectual premises, subjective motivation, and political goals that underlie and guide terrorist actions; his only concern is how to react against utterly dangerous, secretively sinister actors that he does not know.' In fact, the very use of the term 'terrorist' arguably limits the available policy options. Toros (2008: 422) shows how:

> Reducing a group or movement to its terrorist acts, which often do not even represent the main activity of the group, limits the group's possibilities of being anything but a 'terrorist group'. It also limits how the state can engage with such groups, putting decision makers in a 'policy straightjacket'.

This is the policy side of things, the negotiating table. Apart from and beyond this however, governments and terrorists communicate all the time, albeit indirectly. Whether or not governments, as Zulaika (2009) argues, continue to ignore the humanity of the terrorists and therefore fail to engage in direct dialogue, the incorporation of the concept 'radicalisation' in counterterrorism strategies has meant, among other things, increased attention to the jihadi narrative. This is because 'de-radicalising' individuals and 'countering' radicalization could not go around the ideational framework legitimizing and supporting behaviour. Obviously, the preoccupation with jihadi narratives is primarily driven by the hope of deconstructing and delegitimizing particular ideological framings, and therefore decreasing recruitment (Al Raffie 2012), rather than 'communicating' with terrorists in any meaningful way, i.e. addressing 'their' concerns. Sedgwick (2012) has recently offered an insightful analysis of the narrative structure of the British Prevent strategy to assess the extent to which it addresses jihadi themes. He argues that the counter-ideology ('the West is not at war with Islam', the differentiation between extremist and moderate Muslims and the promotion of democracy) has little chance of succeeding, because it contests jihadi themes that are, in fact, widely accepted among Muslims: that Muslims around the world suffer because of the actions of non-Muslims, the equivalence of a just and fair society with Islam and Shari'a, and the differentiation between Muslims and non-Muslims. He concludes that it is the means that should be countered, namely: the use of force in general, and that it can be assumed to lead to success; the use of force against civilians; and the killing of Muslims in the process.[1]

Clearly, with a few exceptions, such as the UK or Denmark, most European countries do not in fact have a counter-radicalization strategy in the form of countering jihadi narratives. That is, in most cases, including Germany (the focus of this chapter), the state does not directly engage the other's discourse. Nevertheless, and beyond the context of targeted deconstruction programmes, governments and terrorists talk, if not to each other, most certainly *at* each other. One might picture this as a virtual debate room, where each side throws its arguments in communiqués, televised appearances, videos, and so on. Jihadis (broadly defined here as militant actors subscribing to the ideology of Al Qaeda (AQ), including the use of terrorist tactics) use modern media to communicate and to issue their demands, clarify their motivations, and explain the legitimacy of their actions, primarily to sympathizers and potential supporters, but also to governments and state actors in general. The Internet is their primary and global communication platform, where they issue statements and hold 'press conferences' (Prucha 2010b: 18) in a similar self-perception that governments claim to be reserved for themselves. This then enables a virtual interaction between the two players, where jihadi actors, empowered by the Internet, can directly respond to claims made by governments and vice versa. An obvious example here is the case of hostage and kidnapping cases, where 'terrorists' issue demands to 'state representatives' and embed their narrative and justifications into a greater framework. The government response, while demanding the release of hostages, employs narratives as well, emphasizing the human rights angle and the illegitimacy of their counterparts' actions in general. Another space of virtual interaction and at the same time the focus of this particular piece is the broader issue of Western engagement in Afghanistan and the jihadi retaliation there, as well as in the form of terrorist attacks on European soil. Assumedly, both sides will attempt to argue for the legitimacy of their cause and means, and support their claims through 'empirical' evidence, as well as broader cultural and normative frames. But are they also addressing each other's arguments in more concrete ways? Are they engaging in contestation? How are they using the 'cultural toolkit' to increase the chances of being persuasive? Are these tools partially similar? This is particularly interesting in the case of homegrown jihadis addressing not only their brothers in battle, but also their communities at home and the broader population. Are there any overlaps between the frames, or perhaps even changes in rhetoric as a reaction to the other's arguments?

This chapter attempts to shed some light on these questions by examining a concrete example of discursive interaction between the German government and German homegrown jihadi groups. We aim to identify the themes and the underlying frames within governmental and jihadi narratives in this particular period in time, compare them for similarities and differences, and spot possible mutual effects of this interaction. In doing so, we use the methodological instrumentarium of framing theory, and consequently structure our analysis along the framing of the problem, the cause of the problematic situation, including the construction of the enemy, and the use of the cultural kit in order to ensure resonance with the audience. Before going into the body of the analysis, we offer some background on German jihadi media productions, as well as some methodological considerations.

Communicating jihad

Jihadi propaganda has been an effective tool for incitement, radicalization, and recruitment ever since the armed struggle in Afghanistan against the Soviet Red Army in the 1980s. Own media departments were developed in the 1980s and deployed in the early 1990s in Bosnia (Prucha 2013a), the Caucasus and other war zones around the world. Current jihadi videos are made and produced professionally. Regardless of the main language of the video, the theological narrative is coherent and backed by primarily Arabic ideologues whose writings can be easily found and accessed online. A typical video starts by portraying grievances or the suffering of Muslims, who have to endure occupation (*ihtilal*) and discrimination by either Zionist and/or Crusader military powers. Grievances are fuelled by the narration of 'agents' ('*umala*), and 'apostates' (*murtaddun*) who actively support the 'war against Islam' and are thus excommunicated (*takfir*) from Sunni Islam (Prucha 2013b). Following this are usually bloody and gory scenes, showing for example the aftermath of drone strikes in Pakistan, with body parts and killed children. 'Praiseful hymns' (*nashid*) or 'encouraging battle songs' (*huda'*) (Holtmann 2013) are an important emotional and theological part played during film sequences that justify the militants' acts as necessary and as a divine obligation. Following the classical 'an eye for an eye' (al-Azdi 2012) guideline, martyrdom operations in general as well as various militant responses are sanctioned and framed as a 'just war', and rhetorically demarked by religious keywords and sentiments. Typically, the next key notion consists of a sermon, held by a preacher: a scholar (*shaykh*), a fellow fighter (*mujahid*) or an *al-shaykh al-mujahid*, whose words are backed by his personal commitment on the front lines.

While the quantity of non-Arabic jihad videos is inferior to the one of Arabic language videos, due to historical reasons and the dominance of Arabs in jihadi media centers (El Difraoui 2010), German jihad videos have become an essential part of the overall global and multilingual Al Qaeda media landscape. The German language videos have been produced and published online by several jihadi groups, such as the Islamic Movement of Uzbekistan (IMU), the German Taliban Mujahideen (DTM),[2] or AQ's main media outlet as-Sahab. In terms of content, while the core structure of the German language videos is broadly the same, a series of adaptations for the German audience are noticeable, such as hymns and battle songs in German. Out of the various types of videos available (sermons, military operations, martyrdom notes, and so on), we have limited our search to videos where the content, the preacher or specific sequences are more specifically related to German foreign policy, mainly its participation in Afghanistan under NATO command. Out of these, we decided to focus on one particular video, 'A Call to the Truth' (*Ruf zur Wahrheit*), disseminated online on 24 September 2009. This choice was motivated by both circumstantial and thematic factors. Starting with the latter, the video addresses in great detail a series of political issues and events, speaks directly to Muslims but also to the broader population in Germany and engages statements made by German politicians. The NATO involvement in Afghanistan, the partnership with Israel, but also the issues of 'targeted killings' and the 'Adler mission'[3] are central besides the usual jihadi doctrinal sermons and pseudo-theological explanations. Second, the video, the first public appearance of the DTM, was released before the German parliamentary elections, shortly after a similar one had been released by a German AQ member, Bekkay Harrach (a.k.a. Abu Talha al-Almani) on 18 September 2009, in an apparent attempt to influence the results. Germany had been referred to and/or cautioned before in jihadi video messages, but never directly threatened with imminent attacks as retaliation for the engagement in Afghanistan, as in these two videos. The film, approximately 30 minutes long, starts by showing training sequences and shooting exercises, followed by the lengthy monologue of an individual called Ayyub Almani (the German), later identified as the German national Yusuf Ocak from Berlin (Steinberg 2013: 155). Almani is sitting in a classical jihadi video set-up: on the ground with a heavy machine gun, a

Pulemyot Kalashnikova, in front of him. The scene is symmetrical, with an artillery shell and a Kalashnikov rifle frame on either side, and behind him a large black banner of the Taliban, stating 'Islamic Emirate Afghanistan'.

Additionally, to complete the picture of the reference points used in such videos and therefore to better compare and assess their resonance, an additional video was considered, *Böses Vaterland* (Evil Fatherland), released on 9 February 2012, and dated 13 December 2011, in Waziristan, Pakistan. The video was produced and disseminated by the Jund Allah Studios, the media wing of the IMU, and mainly features two German–Moroccan brothers, Mounir and Yasin Choukha, who act as the German language media facilitators. The brothers are from Bonn and known in jihadi circles by their respective *noms de guerre* Abu Adam and Abu Ibrahim al-Almani. The video could perhaps be termed as a sequel to *Ruf zur Wahrheit* as it focuses on similar elements. The main actor featured in the video is Mounir Chouka (Abu Adam), who gives a sermon-styled talk after a lengthy introduction. The statements are filled with religious connotations and references, with the intent to inspire German-speaking Muslims in the Diaspora to either join the IMU or undertake 'lone-wolf' attacks in their country of residence.

The introduction of the video summarizes the most evident notions by aligning several sequences of statements made by German politicians. The mashed sequences start with a short excerpt from a speech made by the German Chancellor Gerhard Schröder on 11 September 2001: 'I have assured the American President George Bush of Germany's unrestricted solidarity'. This statement is then followed by sequences of several terror attacks, reminding the audience of the jihadi counter-actions against Western countries that are all contributors to the troop deployment in Afghanistan.

Framing and data selection

In their habitus and manifestation, government as well as 'terrorist' discourses refer to certain principles of belief, or state norms, symbols, wordings and sources with the intention of resonating with their target or random audience. As members of their respective societies, or religiously influenced cultures, they operate from 'within' in crafting public messages and framing their narratives, sanctioning violence and defining 'justice' and 'values'. It is as if:

> the form in which the significant symbols are embodied to reach the public may be spoken, written, pictorial, or musical, and the number of stimulus carriers is indefinite. If the propagandist identifies himself imaginatively with the lives of the subjects in a particular situation, he is able to explore several channels of approach.
> (Lasswell 1927: 631)

Persuasion as a function of resort to the 'cultural kit' has long established itself as a major category of analysis in the context of social movement mobilization, and recently also in that of government discourse. Crawford (2009: 119) notes: 'All political arguments occur in a context of belief and culture', and further,

> if an argument can be understood within the lifeworld and the dominant discourse ... it has a much better chance of being persuasive. Arguments can also be *framed* by their proponents to fit with existing dominant beliefs, actors, and identities, and within existing social structures. [Original emphasis]
>
> (Crawford 2009: 118)

Frame analysis as *method* has been developed in the social movement literature and works with a series of major categories: diagnostic and prognostic framing (statement of problem and solution), as well as several resonance criteria clustered around frame credibility and salience (Benford and Snow 2000; see also Pisoiu 2012).

In order to contextualize the video in the domestic political discourse, but also to be able to capture any potential changes in government rhetoric after the release of the video, we searched political statements for a time period of six months before and six months after the release (between 1 April 2009 and 1 March 2010). The criteria for the search of political statements were derived from the video itself, namely the main themes addressed: the German mission in Afghanistan; the scandal of the airstrikes in Kunduz resulting in the destruction of two hijacked fuel trucks and many civilian casualties; the alliance with the Uzbekistani regime and the massacre of Andijan. The text search was performed on the official websites of the Chancellor's Office (Kanzleramt) and relevant ministries (Defence, Interior, External Affairs); additionally, statements of the former Defence Minister Struck and the newspaper *Der Spiegel* were searched, as they were explicitly mentioned in the video. The total number of texts found was 118 and the number of speakers was more than five, given the change in government that occurred during this time period: Angela Merkel (Chancellor), Franz Josef Jung, Karl-Theodor zu Guttenberg (Ministers of Defence), Wolfgang Schäuble (Minister of the Interior), Frank-Walter Steinmeier, Guido Westerwelle (Ministers of Foreign Affairs), and Peter Struck (former Defence Minister). Overall, no major differentiations in positioning could be observed among the various speakers, with the exception of isolated instances of person-specific formulations.

References to the video itself were not made at all in this period in official governmental discourse. In fact, the broader reactions and interpretations of the video were few and focused on one aspect only, namely the nature and probability of a concrete threat through a terror attack on

German territory. Only one regional intelligence office briefly commented on the video in its annual report: they mentioned the critique of the German politicians and media, the Adler Mission, the beefing up of German combat actions in Afghanistan, and in particular the fuel trucks bombing scandal, and the depiction of the former Minister of Defence as 'a criminal, a case for the executioner'.[4] Also:

> Additionally, emphasizes the speaker, the participation of German troops in the Afghanistan operation justifies the transfer of the jihad to Germany and makes an attack on Germany all the more attractive for the Mujahideen. Obviously, in order to increase the validity of the video message, pictures of the Brandenburger Tor in Berlin, the Skyline of Frankfurt am Main, the Oktoberfest in Munich, the Hamburg railway station and the Dome in Cologne are displayed
>
> (VSB Hessen 2009: 32).

Here, the intelligence office interpreted the pictures of various buildings as targets, whereas it appears from the video that these only illustrated points made in the video. Press comments interpreted the pictures in a similar way, as 'possible targets' (Musharbash and Gebauer 2009).

Problem and solution

The framing of the problem–solution complex, as formulated by the two parties in the texts analysed, is largely the same: their own actions constitute self-defence, prompted by the other party's initial aggressive acts. Jihadis argue that their attacks are sanctioned by the occupation of Islamic territories and the overall 'war against Islam'. The government argues that the 'mission' in Afghanistan occurs because of previous terror attacks and in order to prevent new ones that might emerge from the same country. This latter narrative does not change after the release of the video and can be summarized as 'terrorists could also strike here in Germany. This is why we got involved [in Afghanistan]' (Steinmeier 2009b). What does change is the delineation of the 'enemy', something that can only be said to run against the intended objective of the video. Concretely, the 'terrorism hotbed' frame, which was voiced both before and after the video, slightly moves in focus from 'terrorists' to 'Taliban'.

The overall political objective in Afghanistan is 'an Afghanistan that can ensure its own security, an Afghanistan that effectively prevents its regions from again becoming the home of international terrorism' (Merkel 2009a).

> [After the release of the video] Afghanistan under the Taliban and Al Qaeda was the hotbed of the 9/11 terror attack. Further attacks followed. It applied then and it applies now: the mission of the Federal

Army in the framework of the international NATO mission was and is in the most urgent interest of the security of our country.

(Merkel 2010a)

While the government rhetoric does not address terrorist grievances in any way, nor does it attempt to discredit their formulations, the video is replete with concrete and evidenced contestations of government rhetoric. For example, a memorable quote along the lines of self-defence is taken apart in the video. Ayyub Almani focuses on a specific statement made by former Minister of Defence Peter Struck (2002–5) after 9/11: 'Theoretically, one could indeed say that the security of the Federal Republic of Germany is also defended in Hindu Kush' (Struck 2002). With an inset of the Minister showing in the upper right corner of the screen, Almani attempts to turn the self-defence argument on its head:

> [R]emember, *your borders are not being defended in Hindu Kush. Rather, due to your involvement here against Islam an attack against Germany is tempting for us Mujahideen.* So you may taste some of the suffering that the innocent Afghan people must endure day by day. That is why your matter of security is a mere illusion and it is only a question of time before jihad tears down the German walls. [Emphasis added]

Another focus of intense contestation concerns aspects of the 'solution': the actual activities carried out in the context of the mission. While the German mission in Afghanistan was officially declared to have nation building and reconstruction objectives, Almani questions both its overall success and the true intentions of the German government: 'Where are the bridges and schools you promised, where?', and elaborates: 'You are being lied to directly in your face with terms such as reconstruction and peace mission; but with bombs and ammunition no country is reconstructed.'

With regard to the overall objective, we can observe one of the rare instances where government rhetoric actually changes after the release of the video.[5] Initially, democratization was prominent on the list of objectives to be reached in Afghanistan: 'In the end, it is about convincing people of our values of a free society. Only this way can we stabilize crisis regions in the long term' (Schäuble 2009a). Almani, after expressing serious doubts about German democracy at home, can envision only *shari'a* for Afghanistan: '[b]ecause the only law between the creator and the creatures is that of the creator himself, which is the *shari'a*'. The official discourse does not go so far, but does tune down the applicability of democracy to this region:

> I have long ago already reached the conclusion that Afghanistan, especially given its history and [cultural] imprint, is not suitable for a showcase democracy according to our standards ... The question of

human rights must be incorporated, without ignoring the grown cultures in Afghanistan.

(zu Guttenberg 2009b)

The task in Afghanistan did not and will not consist of establishing something like a form of state there according to our model. It consists of preventing a strengthening of the Taliban there, as terror and with it danger for our own security comes from the Taliban.

(Merkel 2010b)

Framing the enemy

There are several dimensions to the framing of the 'enemy', many of which common. Both parties engage in criminalization and de-legitimization. Just as the government speaks out for human rights and justice, the jihadis reserve the key moral humanitarian principles as their main motivation. The parties to the conflict address one another as criminals and depict themselves as the ones morally obliged to act on behalf of the civilians, who are the main victims of the conflict.

We are dealing with cynical and ruthless enemies, for whom human rights do not count. They abuse the civilian population as human shields and even shoot at paramedics.

(Jung 2009a)

This [the Afghanistan mission] was and is approved by the Afghani government, and we know how many simple Afghanis ask us, again and again, not to leave them alone in their fight against the Taliban.

(Merkel 2009a)

[After the release of the video] The people in Afghanistan support the foreign troops and see much success with the reconstruction of the country. They reject the brutal and the inhuman terrorists and radical Taliban and they wish the continuation of our help with their fight for a livable future.

(Jung 2009b)

The Taliban terrorize their own people and they fight the international protection troops ISAF [International Security Assistance Force] in a brutal and perfidious way ... The Afghanis are proud and freedom-aware. They will not yield to terror.

(zu Guttenberg 2009a)

In the video, the German army is portrayed as yet another Crusader force at work against Muslim civilians while the government leaders in Berlin are labelled as henchmen of the United States. Delegitimization is performed on the jihadi side through the contestation of democracy, which 'in Germany itself is not functioning'. The government labels the jihadis as undemocratic and non-liberal:

> The purpose of Islamist terrorism is the weakening of the liberal constitutional state and the shortening of the freedom spaces that it guarantees. The closed Islamist worldview blatantly rejects the open society with its liberal values and constitutional principles, as they constitute the guiding principles of Western democracies.
>
> (Schäuble 2009b)

In the video, the speaker Ayyub Almani turns the tables on the official view by illustrating how the government betrays its own values and principles, lies to its people, and does not care for their security. They, and not the Mujahideen, are traitors and the 'real terrorists'. Almani emphasizes the hypocrisy of the German government with regard to respect for human rights and illustrates it by its cooperation with the government of Uzbekistan: 'your government has even become an ally of Uzbekistan. This is a state on the same page with North Korea und Burma, renowned for their crimes against humanity.' With a shocked expression, Almani says that in these countries 'you can get locked up and tortured for having your own opinion'. This cooperation as well as the Adler Mission is proof for Almani that the government is driven by an evil force to wage its war against the Muslim population in Afghanistan, while keeping the truth hidden from their own people ('with your own media being silent about the dead'). In his view, the media is an ally of the government in this deceit, partaking therefore in the 'war against Islam': 'our motivation is to expose the hypocrisy and falsity of your media, of your government, of your politicians, of your coward troops.'[6]

Almani offers Germany a way out by framing it as a US 'vassal' and in essence then a 'partner in crime', but not as the initiator. Germany could still redeem itself by pulling out of the war. Almani exploits the fact that Germany had not been directly affected by attacks and was not the primary enemy like the US, France, the UK and Israel. Almani appeals to reason by questioning the German political decision to support the US and the UK in the hopeless attempt to impose democracy in Afghanistan, and thereby play the mere role of 'vassal, sacrificing their own soldiers'.

The German government also seems to allow the Taliban a way out, following the release of the video, by differentiating between the 'good Taliban' and the 'bad Taliban':

> I do not rule out the possibility of involving certain forces of the Taliban in an overall solution. The conditions are that they, among other things, renounce armed conflict.
>
> (zu Guttenberg 2010)

It is about separating the hard fundamentalist terrorist core from the followers – young men, who often cannot read or write, and are often, due to economic hardship, ready to take up arms for a few dollars.

(Westerwelle 2010)

Two years later, the jihadi narrative changes. As pictured in the *Böses Vaterland* video, Germany has missed its chance to redeem itself. Abu Adam emphasizes that the German Federal Republic is now an integral part of the 'enemies of Islam', which justifies any revenge mission to be carried out in Germany. Evidence of this includes the deployment of unmanned drones, the killing of the German jihadi Abu Askar from Hamburg by a US drone, the failure of reconstruction efforts in Afghanistan and the persecution of Muslims in their home countries:

the truth is that the German government has from the first second on been sitting with the Americans in the same boat.... The truth is, no matter where the Americans are fighting Muslims in the world, in Somalia, Palestine, or here in Waziristan, the German government is active on the same level, if not by greater means.

Finally, the framing of the vassal is turned around, in that Germany is the 'employer' of the Americans, sending prisoners outside their own judicial system for interrogation and torture.

Resonating frames

Empirical credibility

Empirical credibility, the use of empirical evidence to substantiate claims, appears relatively sparsely in governmental discourse. This type of argument is mainly used to illustrate the danger posed to Germany through the occurrence of several terror attacks:

Afghanistan under the Taliban and Al Qaeda was the hotbed of the 9/11 terror attack.... After 9/11 came other devastating attacks in Europe, in Madrid and London. Also Germany – we know this – is a target. The plans of the Sauerland Group have been fortunately thwarted; they could have had disastrous consequences. The training of these attackers occurred in Afghanistan. This is why one should not confuse the causes: the Afghanistan mission is our reaction to terror – it came from there – and not the other way around.

(Merkel 2009a)

Empirical credibility is used far more amply in the jihadi narrative in support of their delegitimization attempts. The classical example of the failure of other nations to occupy Afghanistan also appears here. In 2009, after eight years of German participation in the NATO mission, Almani claims, 'you and your Uncle Sam can never win this war. On this soil the Brits and the Russians were crushed; and now the American crusaders and the Germans are being annihilated.' In addition, two particular incidents are put forward as proof of the government's hypocrisy: the first was the NATO airstrike on two fuel trucks ordered by a German officer, Oberst (Colonel) Georg Klein. The initial reaction of the Minister of Defence, Franz Josef Jung, was to justify the action as necessary, given the 'substantial danger to the German soldiers', since the Taliban had 'threatened several times to plan attacks against the troops before the elections'. The Ministry also assured the public that 'The protection of civilians has the highest priority for the Federal Armed Forces' (*Spiegel* 2009a). On the same day, however, information was communicated by the regional Afghani government and local people that civilians were among the victims. Nevertheless, Jung continued with the denial of civilian victims: 'According to the information I possess at this time, only terrorist Taliban were killed during the mission carried out by the US plane' (Jung in *Spiegel* 2009b).

As it later turned out, there were civilian casualties among the victims, the operation had not been carried out according to NATO standards (i.e. there was no second intelligence source) and the troops were not in a situation of immediate danger. The media labelled this as 'the end of innocence' (*Spiegel* 2009c). Later, after a lengthy inquiry, Merkel eventually apologized in 2010, after Jung and other two officials had resigned. Before these steps were taken, however, the video had already been released and the incident utilized appropriately. Almani does not conceal the fact that 'we had hijacked two fuel trucks' but claims that the Taliban's sole intention was 'to share the content with our brothers and sisters'. The reaction of the German army led to an 'enormous massacre among the civilian population … More than 120 women, children, and civilians were lying torn up in pieces on the streets.' All this is then framed as evidence that the German government and the Bundeswehr (Federal Army) in Afghanistan are in fact the true criminals and murderers. Additionally, the incident could also be used as evidence that the Western forces are in fact not protecting the civilian population, as they claimed, a conclusion that the German media also shared: 'The big reconstruction project Afghanistan that promised peace, democracy and prosperity has failed.... That people do not feel protected is the main reason for the failure of the West in Afghanistan' (*Spiegel* 2009c).

A second incident is used in the jihadi narrative to substantiate the claim that the German state itself does not rise to the standards it attempts to impose on others. Almani mentions the massacre of Andijan (Uzbekistan) in 2005, where families had protested the arrest of 23 businessmen as alleged Islamic extremists (BBC 2005) and later freed them by force, which then triggered a massive army response:

Hundreds of people were massacred in open streets in Andijan. Allegedly the whole world, including Germany, was outraged. Nevertheless, the German government, after just three months, invited Suki Almatov, a man like an SS-officer, for treatment in a special clinic in Hannover to ensure the friendly relationship.... Through these actions, you are violating your own principles.

(Don't) mention the war

The 'war' theme is a very difficult terrain in Germany, not least due to the historical experiences of the two World Wars, but also considering the strong peace movement in the country, as well as the general lack of popular support for military missions. Indeed, 'almost 70 percent of the Germans are against the mission of the Federal Army in Afghanistan' (*Spiegel* 2009d). The video takes up this theme of war and engages first of all in a systematic attempt to delegitimize and contest the official narrative, as well as the one presented in the media. Almani states from the very beginning and as the main motivation behind the release of the video: 'we are seeing here what you [the people] will never perceive, where your sources of information [the media] are simply lying.' Other than argued by government sources, 'Germany is at war, but the people are in slumber', while Minister of Defence Franz Josef Jung (2005–9) is labelled as 'minister of war'.

On the government side, before the release of the video, politicians were at great lengths to deny the occurrence of 'war':

> War usually takes place between two states. But in Afghanistan we are fighting against terrorism together with the government there. And we support the civilian reconstruction. This is a dangerous combat operation, but not a war.
> (Steinmeier 2009a)

> It is a 'stabilisation mission', where troops are also confronted with 'concrete combat situations'.
> (Jung in Gebauer and Szandar 2009)

Interestingly, after the video is released, the formulations increase in creativity, whereby war *is* being waged, but against the German army, rather than by it: 'In parts of Afghanistan there are without doubt war-like situations ... the Taliban are waging a war against the soldiers of the international community' (zu Guttenberg 2009a). The tone of the media, especially after the fuel truck incident, is clearer and more radical. In an article titled 'A German crime', *Der Spiegel* finds that on 4 September, the German people have had to give up their self-image of a nice, peace-loving nation, 'cured of war', and to learn that Germany is waging war and does not even keep to its own rules (*Spiegel* 2010).

Related to the issue of war, both sides make concrete references to Germany's Nazi past. Almani equates the acts and the rules of engagement of the Bundeswehr in Afghanistan to the Wehrmacht of the Nazis. As Abu Adam would later repeat in the video *Böses Vaterland*, Almani claims: 'Germany is in a state of war.... Just as back then during the annihilation of the Jews'. In this video, the reasoning of the German jihadis is based on a firm belief in the recurrence of a Nazi-style annihilation of Muslims instead of Jews, with a similar attempt to cover up their intentions. The government's interpretation is, as expected, different. It uses the reference to National Socialism to emphasize the importance of the freedom–security complex: 'Only when the state provides sufficient security, can people really realize their chances in an open society. Freedom and security are therefore no opposites, but two sides of the same medal' (Schäuble 2009b).

Values, symbols and performance

While in the previous sections certain commonalities, overlaps, and common terrains of contestation could be outlined, this is the section where the two narratives part. The official discourse consistently resorts to national and international legal principles, the obligation to protect and the interdiction to 'act alone':

> We are in Afghanistan because we protect the security of our citizens. This is our duty and our constitutional mandate. In the words of the Preamble of our Basic Law: 'In the awareness of its responsibility before God and the people, animated by the will, as equal member in a united Europe to serve the peace of the world.' In Afghanistan we serve the peace of the world, in that we fight the evil of terrorism to its root.
>
> (Jung 2009a)

> Germany is in the service of peace in the world ... is a defensive democracy; we protect our citizens, their life and their integrity ... Germany stands in this world in firm alliances and partnerships: going it alone in foreign policy is not an option.
>
> (Merkel 2009a)

> [After the release of the video] [The new threats] challenge us at home, but also outside the borders of our country.... Freedom and security are not opposites for the new federal government; they belong together. The state has to guarantee both, be it the protection of personal data in the new communication technologies, or Germany's contribution to international security.
>
> (Merkel 2009b)

The jihadi discourse also employs key symbols, norms and values in order to sanction and justify their actions. Jihadi actions and operations are first of all backed by invoking religious sources, notably suras of the Qur'an, stories of Prophet Muhammad (*hadith*), or by quoting historical scholars such as Ibn Taymiyya (1263–1328) in order to underline the credibility of the definition and interpretation of specific keywords and concepts. Abu Adam references this scholar in the video *Böses Vaterland*, for example, to amplify his statements and to depict the Mujahideen as the ones who are rightfully guided and thus the only 'true' Muslims: 'if the enemies of God knew what we carry in our hearts, the satisfaction and happiness, they would combat us only on this basis'.

Symbols such as the notorious 'black banner' or flag (*raya*), used by jihadi groups to delineate their presumed socio-religious authority as well as the conviction of being 'soldiers of God' (*jund allah*), are a further main element. Almani, in the video *Ruf zur Wahrheit* is sitting in front of such a black banner, in this case the flag of the Afghan Taliban, which has the sword as a key visible element like most jihadi flags. The latter can be related to the famous saying 'the foundation of religion is a book leading the right way with a sword assisting' (*qawam al-din kitab yahdi wa-sayf yansur*), attributed to Ibn Taymiyya, which is often used by jihadis to legitimize their fight (Lohlker 2013: 65–89). The use of fire, a reference to the 'hellfire', is also a recurring visual element. For example, the same video concludes with a collage of a picture of the Minister of Defence, Jung, the logo of the Bundeswehr and a coffin covered by the German flag. This collage is overlapped by flames, simulating the 'fires of hell', reserved for all non-Muslims and apostates. The visualization underlines the jihadi conviction that any individual belonging to the Crusader states at war with Islam, or any of their allies, will be punished in the afterlife.

Jihadis consider themselves as the only 'true' Muslims who, by their operations and deeds, bear witness in an active stance to enforce the oneness of God (*tawhid*), fully committed to 'elevate the word of God' within the mental framework of the fight against non-Muslim enemies. The Mujahideen propagate to combat all forms violating the principle of *tawhid*, first and foremost those who exchange the proper conduct of religion for worldly means. The commitment to this universal fight, often portrayed as a 'conflict of the program of truth (*haqq*) versus the program of falsehood (*batil*)' (al-'Utaybi 2006; Meijer 2007), is central to the identity of Islamist militant actors. *Ruf zur Wahrheit* is such a reference to the 'truth'. Most Muslims, particularly the diaspora in Western countries, dwell in the unchanged status of sin, while the Mujahideen, by their contribution to *jihad* and by undertaking the migration (*hijra*), have 'cleansed' themselves of such sin and neglect. Any jihadi operation, however, can cleanse any individual who wants to redeem him/herself and become such a true Muslim as well. This is a core message that should reach and inspire other German Muslims at home to join the fight.

Conclusion

How do governments and terrorists converse virtually? Are they addressing similar frames and are there any changes subsequent to this interaction? As we have seen in the analysis above, jihadis selectively engage governmental discourse, and thereby attempt to deconstruct and delegitimize it, by making extensive use of empirical credibility frames. The government, as expected, does not directly address the jihadi discourse at all. The main focus in discourse is made up of various normative and to a lesser extent empirical references meant to legitimize the German engagement in Afghanistan. In terms of common frames and framing strategies, the actors depict each other as the aggressor, and themselves as the protector of the civilian population, righteous actors in a situation of self-defence that sanctions and validates violence. Both actors make reference to the historical past, yet for different purposes and with different interpretations. There are, however, also clear differences, particularly concerning the use of the 'cultural toolkit'. Some notable changes could also be observed subsequent to the interaction, yet most probably not as a consequence of it, but rather owing to developments 'on the ground'. In the jihadi discourse, Germany develops from being a mere ally of the US into one of the main enemies and therefore a legitimate target for future attacks. The officials gradually abandon the democratization objective, feel forced to allow for the 'good Taliban' and have to confront the long avoided idea of 'war'. The latter theme could be identified in the analysis as a rare instance of gradual discursive convergence, and as a prime example of the jihadi version of 'hearts and minds' campaigning, no doubt supported by the 'local' cultural and political expertise of the German Mujahideen.

Notes

1 It must be noted that the jihadis have, for their part, been keen on propagating their 'lessons learned' from relentless suicide-bombing attacks in Algiers in 2007 (Prucha 2010a), and indiscriminate bombings in Iraq and Pakistan, and have in the meantime issued theological conditions and 'rules of engagement' to protect Sunni Muslims.
2 IMU joined AQ in around 2007, after prior hostilities between the groups and apparently at the initiative of German fighters and media activists within IMU (Steinberg 2013). The DTM used to be a detachment operating on the Afghan–Pakistani border and composed exclusively of German fighters. The group dissolved after the death of its key members (Steinberg 2012).
3 The Adler Mission was a common German–Afghani operation carried out in the summer of 2009 that was meant to chase away Taliban forces in the North of Afghanistan.
4 All translations from the German language are our own.
5 However this might also be due to the overall discourse expressing scepticism with regard to the democratization of Afghanistan, as well as to the mission's repeated failure to achieve this.

6 The jihadi media, with its professional and multi-lingual media departments, have been repeating this key sentiment as the only truthful and legitimate source of information.

References

Al-Azdi, A. (2011) 'Al-Qistas al-'adl fi jawwaz qatl atfal wa-nisa' al-kuffar; mu'aqiba bi l-mithl', Ansar al-Mujahideen Forum. Available at as-Ansar.com/vb (accessed 29 June 2013).

Al Raffie, D. (2012) 'Whose Hearts and Minds? Narratives and Counter-Narratives of Salafi Jihadism', *Journal of Terrorism Research*, 3(2). Available at http://ojs.st-andrews.ac.uk/index.php/jtr/article/view/304 (accessed 29 June 2013).

al-'Utaybi, A. (2006) 'al-Furqan bayna 'l-haqq wa-l butlan, Minbar tawheed wa-l jihad', Available at http://tawhed.ws/r?i=f3dkkksv (accessed 30 June 2013).

BBC (2005) 'How the Andijan killings unfolded', 17 May. Available http://news.bbc.co.uk/2/hi/4550845.stm (accessed 8 March 2013).

Benford, R. and Snow, D. (2000) 'Framing Processes and Social Movements: An Overview Assessment', *Annual Review of Sociology*, 26, 611–39.

Crawford, N. (2009) 'Homo Politicus and argument (nearly) all the way down: persuasion in politics', *Perspectives on Politics*, 7(1), 103–24.

El Difraoui, A. (2010) *Al Qaida par l'image ou la prophétie du martyre. Une analyse politique de la propagande audiovisuelle du jihad global* (PhD dissertation, Sciences Po, Paris).

Gebauer, M. and Szandar, A. (2009) 'Murads Rache', *Spiegel Online*, 27 July. Available at www.spiegel.de/spiegel/print/d-66208530.html (accessed 8 March 2013).

Gelb, L.H. (2008, 27 April) 'In the End, Every President Talks to the Bad Guys', *Washington Post*. Available at http://articles.washingtonpost.com/2008-04-27/opinions/36808535_1_bad-guys-president-talks-evil-empire (accessed 30 June 2013).

Holtmann, P. (2013) *The Use and Genre of Huda' (encouraging battle songs) versus Anashid (praiseful hymns) in Jihadi Propaganda and in Jihadi Death Rites*, unpublished manuscript, forthcoming.

Jung, F.J. (2009a) 'Rede des Bundesministers der Verteidigung anlässlich der Trauerfeier in der Evangelischen Stadtkirche Bad Salzungen', 2 July. Available at www.bmvg.de/portal/a/bmvg/!ut/p/c4/NY3bCoJAFEX_aC6BdHkzIoiiXoKy-Fxn1OB5xZuTM0SD6-DRwb9gva8GWLznVmxGtYQzedPIpsxJ3xVsUbrTCoc-fIQDg4YSGWDZYNQ_5nIxADVmgHb-Mi5hGQc71NElFRTcZ_2hChbidHPuazC kQZPPC8DJ5xWkuGA4k-EHczGYgmIrCSmdKHvdJqif6u7-f0slFqdboeb-7J3Lv0BwsxxHg!!/ (accessed 8 March 2013).

Jung, F.J. (2009b) 'Rede des Bundesministers der Verteidigung, Dr. Franz Josef Jung, anlässlich der Trauerfeier in Fulda', 12 October. Available at www.bmvg.de/portal/a/bmvg/!ut/p/c4/NY3BCoJAFEX_aMYBLWpXRNKi2mW2kVGf4xNnRt-48DaKPTwPvhbs5B658yblOT2g0o3e6l0-ZV7gv36K0kxEWHQYGwtEKA6FqsWoZij-bgBiwRjM6E1axCIBcqF2SiJoa0u7T-QBNNzsyW85qEJV3wMsyOMZ5DWn-2JAZP3C9kJJqJwFrmkTodIxWtUd9tdk0f6SaOL7fzXQ7WHn4zw3tH/ (accessed 8 March 2013).

Lasswell, H. (1927) 'The Theory of Political Propaganda', *The American Political Science Review*, 21(3), 627–31.

Lohlker, R. (2013) 'Religion, Weapons, and Jihadism: Emblematic discourses', in R. Lohlker (ed.), *Online Discourses and Representation*, Vienna: V&R Unipress, 65–89.

Meijer, R. (2007) 'Yusuf al-'Uyairi and the Making of a Revolutionary Salafi Praxis', *Die Welt des Islams – International Journal for the Study of Modern Islam*, 47 (3–4), 422–59.

Merkel, A. (2009a) 'Regierungserklärung von Bundeskanzlerin Merkel zu den aktuellen Ereignissen in Afghanistan', 8 September. Available at www.bundesregierung.de/Content/DE/Regierungserklaerung/2009/2009-09-08-regerkl-merkel-afghanistan.html (accessed 8 March 2013).

Merkel, A. (2009b) 'Regierungserklärung von Bundeskanzlerin Merkel im Wortlaut', 10 November. Available at www.bundesregierung.de/Content/DE/Regierungserklaerung/2009/2009-11-10-merkel-neue-Regierung.html (accessed 8 March 2013).

Merkel, A. (2010a) 'Regierungserklärung zum Afghanistan-Konzept der Bundesregierung von Bundeskanzlerin Merkel', 28 January. Available at www.bundesregierung.de/Content/DE/Regierungserklaerung/2010/2010-01-28-merkel-erklaerung-afghanistan.html (accessed 8 March 2013).

Merkel, A. (2010b) 'Afghanistan – es geht um unsere Sicherheit', Interview mit: Angela Merkel, 31 January. Available at www.bundesregierung.de/Content/DE/Interview/2010/01/2010-01-31-interview-merkel-wams.html (accessed 8 March 2013).

Musharbash, Y and Gebauer, M. (2009) 'Video-Botschaft: Taliban drohen Deutschland mit Anschlägen', *Spiegel Online*, 25 September. Available at www.spiegel.de/politik/ausland/video-botschaft-taliban-drohen-deutschland-mit-anschlaegen-a-651464.html (accessed 8 March 2013).

Prucha, N. (2010a) 'A Look at Jihadis' Suicide Fatwas: The Case of Algeria', Research Institute for European and American Studies. Available at www.rieas.gr/images/prucha.pdf (accessed 29 June 2013).

Prucha, N. (2010b) *Die Stimme des Dschihad – Sawt al-Gihad – al-Qa'idas Erstes Online Magazin*, Hamburg: Verlag Dr. Kovac.

Prucha, N. (2013a) 'Arab Foreign Fighters in Bosnia – the Roads to Europe', in G. Hauser, F. Kernic and S. Gareis (eds), *The European Union – a Global Actor?*, Opladen, Berlin, Toronto: Budrich Publishers, 334–50.

Prucha, N. (2013b) 'Kangaroo Trials – Justice in the Name of God', in: Rüdiger Lohlker (ed.), *Jihadism: Online Discourses and Representations, Studying Jihadism*, vol. 2, Vienna University Press.

Schäuble, W. (2009a) 'Sicherheit in der global vernetzten Welt, Rede von Bundesminister Dr. Wolfgang Schäuble im Rahmen der Vortragsreihe zur "Deutschen und Europäischen Sicherheits- und Verteidigungspolitik"', 2 June. Available at www.wolfgang-schaeuble.de/index.php?id=30&textid=1311&page=1 (accessed 8 March 2013).

Schäuble, W. (2009b) 'Freedom vs. Security: Guaranteeing Civil Liberties in a World of Terrorist Threats, Rede von Bundesminister Dr. Wolfgang Schäuble im Rahmen der Bucerius Summer School on Global Governance', 26 August. Available at www.wolfgang-schaeuble.de/index.php?id=30&textid=1327&page=1, (accessed 8 March 2013).

Sedgwick, M. (2012) 'Jihadi ideology, Western Counter-ideology, and the ABC Model', *Critical Studies on Terrorism*, 5(3), 359–72.

Spiegel (2009a) 'Dutzende Tote in Afghanistan Bundeswehr wollte mit Luftangriff Selbstmordattentat verhindern. Afghanistan: Blutiger Angriff gegen Taliban', 4 September. Available at www.spiegel.de/politik/ausland/dutzende-tote-in-afghanistan-bundeswehr-wollte-mit-luftangriff-selbstmordattentat-verhindern-a-647081.html (accessed 8 March 2013).

Spiegel (2009b) 'Afghanistan Tanklastzug-Attacke zwingt Minister Jung in die Defensive', 5 September. Available at www.spiegel.de/politik/ausland/afghanistan-tanklastzug-attacke-zwingt-minister-jung-in-die-defensive-a-647224.html (accessed 8 March 2013).

Spiegel (2009c) 'Afghanistan, Das Ende der Unschuld' 14 September. Available at www.spiegel.de/spiegel/print/d-66886599.html (accessed 8 March 2013).

Spiegel (2009d) 'Schatten auf der Lichtgestalt', 14 December. Available at www.spiegel.de/spiegel/print/d-68167751.html (accessed 8 March 2013).

Spiegel (2010) 'BUNDESWEHR, Ein deutsches Verbrechen', 1 February. Available at www.spiegel.de/spiegel/print/d-68885074.html (accessed 8 March 2013).

Steinberg, G. (2012) 'Die Elif-Media-Informationsgruppe und die Deutschen Taliban Mujahidin', in: G. Steinberg (ed.), *Jihadismus und Internet: Eine deutsche Perspektive, Stiftung Wissenschaft und Politik (SWP)*. Available at www.swp-berlin.org/de/publikationen/swp-studien-de/swp-studien-detail/article/jihadismus_und_internet.html (accessed 29 June 2013).

Steinberg, G. (2013) *German Jihad: On the Internationalization of Islamist Terrorism*, New York: Columbia University Press.

Steinmeier, F.W. (2009a) 'Interview von Außenminister Frank-Walter Steinmeier mit der Welt am Sonntag (Auszug)', 12 July. Available at www.auswaertiges-amt.de/DE/Infoservice/Presse/Interviews/2009/090712-BM-WamS.html (accessed 8 March 2013).

Steinmeier, F.W. (2009b) 'Rede von Bundesaußenminister Steinmeier zu den Ereignissen in Afghanistan', 9 September. Available at www.bundesregierung.de/Content/DE/Rede/2009/09/2009-09-08-rede-steinmeier-afghanistan.html (accessed 8 March 2013).

Struck, P. (2002) 'Pressekonferenz am 5 Dezember 2002 mit Bundesminister Dr. Peter Struck zur Weiterentwicklung der Bundeswehr', Berlin, 5 December. Available at www.bmvg.de/portal/a/bmvg/!ut/p/c4/NY3BCsIwEET_KGkOFetNUUEPetR6KWmypItNUjabevHjTYXOwBzmDYx8yeKgZ3SaMQY9yqdsDe76j-j97ITHgImBMHvhIJkBzcDQ_dkMxIAWXQ4urcMuAXKnmroWliYoTWLK5i0fy5MFYWIAXpIhMJZ0pDmSmCLxuJBMVIhAK9tKHQ-Vqlap72bbXk9NqS638110O3u9_-L2Ycw!!/ (accessed 8 March 2013).

Toros, H. (2008) '"We Don't Negotiate with Terrorists!": Legitimacy and Complexity in Terrorist Conflicts', *Security Dialogue*, 39(4), 407–26.

VSB Hessen (2009) 'Verfassungsschutz in Hessen. Bericht 2009. Hessisches Ministerium des Innern und für Sport. 2., überarbeitete Auflage', Available at http://starweb.hessen.de/cache/hessen/vsbericht2009.pdf (accessed 8 March 2013).

Westerwelle, G. (2010) 'Vieles ist besser geworden in Afghanistan', 30 January. Available at www.bundesregierung.de/Content/DE/Interview/2010/01/2010-01-30-interview-westerwelle-sz.html (accessed 8 March 2013).

zu Guttenberg, K.T. (2009a) 'zu Guttenberg: Kriegsähnliche Zustände in Teilen Afghanistans', 3 November. Available at www.bundesregierung.de/Content/DE/Interview/2009/11/2009-11-03-interview-guttenberg-bild.html (accessed 8 March 2013).

zu Guttenberg, K.T. (2009b) 'Afghanistan ist keine Vorzeige-Demokratie nach unseren Vorstellungen', Interview with Karl-Theodor zu Guttenberg, 28 December. Available at www.bundesregierung.de/Content/DE/Interview/2009/12/2009-12-27-interview-guttenberg-bams.html (accessed 8 March 2013).

zu Guttenberg, K.T. (2010) 'Schutz durch Ausbildung', 28 January. Available at www.bundesregierung.de/Content/DE/Interview/2010/01/2010-01-28-interview-zu-guttenberg-zeit.html (accessed 8 March 2013).

Zulaika, J. (2009) *Terrorism: the self-fulfilling prophecy*, Chicago, IL: University of Chicago Press.

6 Plenty of oxygen

Terrorism, news media and the politics of the Australian security state

David C. Holmes and Rebeka Sullivan

The British Prime Minister, Margaret Thatcher once quipped that media coverage is the "oxygen of terrorism." The way to manage terrorism, according to this view, is to withdraw reportage of it. One suspects there may be something to this thesis, when, following the news of fatalities in a bombing incident, we read of multiple groups all wanting to take responsibility. Of course, to suggest that media attention is a singular source of motivation for terrorist groups is rather simplistic. The political terrorism that Thatcher wanted to manage had deep historical momentum deriving from the Northern Ireland conflict that well preceeded the mass media in Britain. But, even if it is not always their main motivation, modern terrorist acts increasingly address national or global audiences; in this they share a mutual interest with news organizations that profit from the increased reportage of terrorism. And, as argued later in this chapter, there can also be political benefits for governments in increased reportage of terrorism. By feeding the press with revelations about security threats and the need for counterterrorism measures, especially in the periods leading up to elections, governments accrue more political capital within electorates. Conversely the media construction of a threat or security crisis enhances the attention cycle, with breaking news and official announcements tapping into audience anxieties about terror.

Two economists. Bruno Frey and Dominik Rohner, in a seven-year study of high profile press coverage, *Blood and Ink! The Common-Interest-Game between Terrorists and the Media*, suggest that there is at least a two-way set of interests involved in the media/terrorism relationship. They argue that mass media and terrorist groups help each other out. For every act of terror, the circulation and profits of newspapers increase, and terrorist groups get publicity, feeding further acts of terror in an escalating cycle of violence and spectacle (Frey and Rohner 2006).

Their study concentrated on two well-respected international broadsheets, the *New York Times* (*NYT*) and *Neue Zürcher Zeitung*, a high-quality Swiss newspaper. Their methodology was simply to count references to "terror" and "terrorism" between 1998 and 2006 whilst measuring such journalism against actual occurrences of international terror.

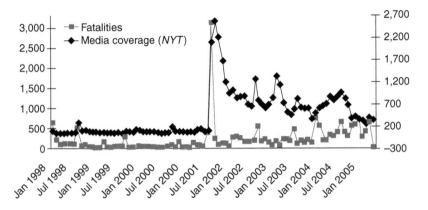

Figure 6.1 Terrorist fatalities and media coverage (monthly data, January 1998–June 2005) (sources: MIPT (Memorial Institute for the Prevention of Terrorism: mipt.org); *NYT*).

Note
The scale to the left corresponds to the number of fatalities from terrorist attacks, whereas the scale to the right represents the media coverage of terrorism in *NYT*.

Frey and Rohner's conclusions, arrived at after putting these figures through some very clinical equations that economists use, was that representation and reality interact in a more or less mechanical way, i.e. that media coverage unambiguously *causes* terror and vice versa. The study makes no attempt to contextualize the possibility that acts of terror may be responses to other political or military events (the election of a militaristic leader, or the invasion of sovereign territory, for example).

Be it as it may, the above graph does show that, whilst post-9/11 incidences of international terrorism increased in the four years following the event, the coverage of such events had increased disproportionately, at three or four times the degree of coverage that would have obtained for the same number of terrorist fatalities pre-9/11.

When we add electronic media into the equation, where our screens can be interrupted by blanket-feed coverage from CNN for days about an incident, it can certainly be argued that mass media raise the tempo of insecurity, and induce fears about personal and collective safety.

The latter outcome of insecurity is often expressed as an escalation of xenophobia toward "outsiders," a trend, we argue in this chapter, that is promoted by governments and news organizations for different ends. Electorally, governments are able to benefit from the "climate of fear" that is produced by an increase in the reportage on terrorism, whilst commercially, media organizations are able to increase audience share by turning to genres of "moral panic," disaster and spectacle in programming outside of regular news formats.

Reportage of terrorism in Australia

In Australia, the reportage of terrorism in the seven years following 9/11 largely followed global trends, but began to decline after 2008. A Factiva database search of all major Australian newspapers (*The Australian, The Sydney Morning Herald, The Age, Herald Sun, Sunday Herald Sun, Sunday Age, The Australian Magazine*), using "terrorism" as a keyword revealed that a sample in mid-2008 returned a much higher reportage of this issue than for the same sample period just prior to September 11, 2001.

The first search yielded a total of 79 articles mentioning the word in a period of two months before September 11, 2001. In the two months after, the total escalated to 2,556 articles mentioning the word "terrorism," as was expected. The last search, between the dates of June 20 and August 20, 2008 yielded a result of 372 articles mentioning terrorism. Whilst the reportage of terrorism had declined since 9/11, seven years on, it was still higher than it was before 9/11.

As will be argued, the increased level of reportage correlates with the increased level of response on the part of the Australian government, in the form of anti-terrorism legislation, since 2001. However, the level of reportage did not correlate with the level of terrorist activity that directly affected Australian security. According to Christopher Michaelsen (2005: 321) the level of threat that Australia faced at that time did not warrant the introduction of laws that "significantly curtail civil liberties and fundamental freedoms" in Australia.

He also noted in 2004, that "In light of the [Australian] Government's heavily publicized campaign to promote 'public awareness' on 'terrorism' and 'national security'," it is not surprising that a large majority of Australians indeed believed that a devastating terrorist attack on Australia is just a matter of time. According to an opinion poll published in *The Sydney Morning Herald* in late April 2004, 68 percent of Australians expected terrorists to strike on Australian soil within a few years.

Whilst terrorism and counterterrorism have been researched extensively since 2001, the news media framing of such developments has not. Nor has the dynamic relationship between the actions of terrorists, the counterterrorist measures of states and the news media reportage of this relationship been explored in great detail. It is too simplistic merely to say that there is a causal relationship between the three, instead it will be suggested in this chapter that there is a direct link between the way that the news media "frames" and portrays terrorism and the ways in which governments of democratic, Western societies react through the introduction and implementation of counterterrorism measures. Politicians and policy-makers may themselves fear terrorist activity according to advice they receive from security organizations. But they also fear being seen not to take terrorism seriously when fear, real or imagined, is created within news audiences.

In Australia, as in many nations since 9/11, the fear of "outsiders" breaching national borders has heightened. In Australia a commercial network reality series, *Border Control*, a drama about the surveillance of Australia's northern coastline, was the highest rated television program of 2006. This program was an extremely highly promoted "audience-magnet" for the Channel Seven free-to-air television network in Australia, which took the ratings lead in 2006 for overall audience share. In 2007 a range of similar programs were tried on other commercial networks. Since this time there have been a number of programs trialed on the Australian small screen, though not all were specifically about the threat to Australia. Some programs such as *Homeland*, aired on the Channel Ten network in 2012, depict a soldier defecting from the American army and possibly being converted to terrorism. Shows such as this keep the possibility of "the terrorist" in the minds of the viewers. According to Cynthia Banham of *The Sydney Morning Herald*,

> Popular culture tends to reflect how we see ourselves – and how we want to see ourselves. So what do these two TV series [*Homeland* and *24*] tell us about how the US's approach to terrorism has shifted in the decade since September 11, 2001? ... *24* was a great show – pacey and addictive – but also insidious for how it normalised behaviour so contrary to everything we believed in before the war on terrorism started. The program changed as America – and we, as allies in that war – changed.
>
> (Banham 2012)

Banham continues in regard to *Homeland*'s references to US President Barack Obama saying that there have been changes to the way that he has handled counterterrorism measures. Torture is no longer US policy, American military has extracted itself from Iraq, yet at the same time Guantánamo Bay still remains open and laws created allowing US citizens to be held indefinitely without charge at Guantánamo. "It's debatable how much – based on what has been shown so far on Australian TV – one can draw from *Homeland* about shifts in US attitudes to dealing with terrorism." Either way, it can easily be said that there is a definite preconditioning of the audience, whether this is to the effect of highlighting the "other" in society or an acceptance of counterterrorism measures, no matter in what country these kinds of shows are aired (see Banham 2012).

The social currents that such programming produces enhance the power of the modern security state in unprecedented ways, enabling it to control the places where people can assemble and subject them to searches at airports and public venues.

However, apart from analyzing the way terrorism reportage benefits prevailing governments, the preoccupation of modern states with security must be thought of as an emerging and possibly enduring trend that deserves greater understanding. In the remainder of this chapter we will explore not the relation between terrorism and the media, but rather a "common-interest game" between states and media in promoting fear of terror.

"Presentism" in media reportage of terrorism

The "tempo of insecurity" that the reportage of terror can create is largely divorced from an historical appreciation of terror and its representation. To an ever greater intensity media consumers have been persuaded of the historicism of living not in *an* age of terror, but *the* age of terror. In the aftermath of 9/11, terror in Australia was portrayed as much more ubiquitous, random and devastating than it has ever been. However, the crucial background that is absent from such reportage is the dramatic decline in sources of political violence and military conflict around the globe over the past 40 years. When there are fewer wars and political violence to report, new organizations seize upon whatever source they can to recycle ritualistic narratives about disaster and conflict.

According to the Human Security Report (Human Security Report 2005a), commissioned by the University of British Columbia, armed conflicts around the globe have diminished dramatically over the past 60 years, and we tend not to hear about them unless a new one is starting up. Ninety-five percent of the world's armed conflicts are internal to nations, with wars between nations being very rare. When they do happen, they receive extraordinary coverage like the 2006 Israel–Lebanon war. The report also points out that casualty rates in wars are far lower than they were 50 years ago: in 1950, the rate was 38,000 and in 2002 only 600. Since 1992, the decline in armed conflict began plummeting further, by 40 percent up until 2003, with the most deadly (over 1,000 fatalities) declining by 80 percent.

Three major reasons can be advanced for the demise of modern warfare:

1 The disappearance of all colonial/anti-colonial warfare that dominated the 1950s, 1960s and 1970s.
2 The abrupt end to the Cold War, which was feeding so-called "proxy wars" in the third world, conducted by the US and USSR.
3 Despite relentless attacks from world media over selected failure in resolving conflicts, the United Nations (UN) has been a vital institution in coordinating peace-building, peacekeeping and conflict prevention.

Since the end of the Cold War, UN missions to end conflicts and prevent wars from starting have increased six-fold. Also the number of states affected by UN sanctions has ballooned ten-fold (Human Security Report 2005a: 8–9).

The decline in inter- and intra-state forms of warfare is perhaps one of the key explanations for why terrorism has become so newsworthy. Without major geo-political conflict to deal with, news organizations fill the prime-time void with real or imagined stories about terrorism, where they have interests in common with terrorists themselves.

It *is* true that international terrorism is the only form of political violence in the world that is actually increasing (see Figure 6.2). However, most casualties have occurred since the invasion of Iraq and Afghanistan by the US and its allies. Furthermore, in these cases, either the conflict is directed toward the foreign invasion or violence continues between groups who disagree over how to respond to it. As with the anti-colonial conflicts of the 1950s, the invasion of sovereign land, rather than religious or ideological differences, still proves to be a primary source of conflict.

Furthermore, the figures on international terrorism since 9/11 are contradictory. In 2004, the US state department released a report – "Patterns of Global Terrorism 2003" – claiming that the 2003 total of 190 international terrorist attacks was the lowest since 1969, and that such attacks had declined by 45 percent between 2001 and 2003 (United States, Department of State 2004: 1) Such figures, which define an act of terror as an attack on "civilians and military personnel who at the time of the incident were unarmed and/or not on duty," were advanced by White House spokespersons as evidence that the US was winning the war against terrorism. However, for the US State in particular, making distinctions between civil/military, armed/unarmed has become difficult to sustain, as the number of American military casualties mounted to the point of producing civil unrest in the United States.

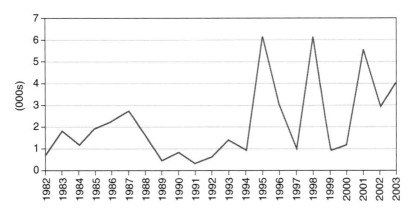

Figure 6.2 Casualties from international terrorism, 1982–2003 (source: Human Security Report 2005b: 44).

Note
Annual casualties (including deaths) from international terrorist attacks have increased dramatically since the 1980s.

The politics of terror and citizenship in Australia post-9/11

In Australia however, a relatively unique set of circumstances unfolded. In the six years immediately following 9/11, Australia had one percent of the troops that the US had in Iraq and only two casualties, both the result of military accidents.

Because of this, many have questioned why terrorism had become such a preoccupation for the Australian news media, policy-makers and legislators when it so rarely affects the lives of Australians, and when Australia itself has been spared a bombing incident. As charted by a number of analysts (Ayson and Ball 2006; Wright-Neville *et al.* 2004), the levels of actual security threats in Australia have been historically quite low.

Nevertheless, in the six years following 9/11, the Howard Liberal government passed 54 separate security related and anti-terrorist acts of parliamentary legislation. A further six items of anti-terrorism legislation were passed between 2007 and 2012 in the Rudd and Gillard periods of Labor Government, a significant slowing down from the conservative government rule where there was new legislation introduced on average every seven weeks.

One explanation for this legislative surge can be found with the Bali Bombings of October 2002, in which 88 Australians died and many more were injured. This event was the deadliest single episode of terror in Indonesia's modern history, and in Australia it became a disaster marathon in the press for several weeks. Post-mortems of the Bali bombings brought attention to the existence of radical terrorist groups in Indonesia and to members of the group convicted of the bombings, Jemaah Islamiah. While prior to the bombings, the names of such groups were virtually unknown in the Australian press, after the bombing, awareness of their existence fueled the thesis that terrorism was getting closer to Australian soil.

Justifications of counterterrorism in Australia became heavily politicized in a way that Goodin has analyzed in other nations to have been exploited to instil fear in the citizenry (see Goodin 2006). In the years immediately following 9/11, it was remarkably easy for Howard's Conservative–Liberal government to persuade Australians of the necessity of counterterrorism planning, a phenomenon that is much more tangible and concrete than terrorism itself. One way in which this was achieved was by setting up a National Security Hotline in 2002, where appeals were made to Australian citizens to report behavior that put National security at risk.

The Hotline was introduced as part of the "Be Alert, Not Alarmed" campaign that commenced at the same time, but which did little to actually specify the kinds of suspicious behavior to watch out for. Australian Journalism Studies academic Diana Bossio argues that this ambiguity served the interests of the state in winning acceptance of its legitimate control over the security intelligence:

> Part of the Australian government's domestic contribution to the global "war on terror" is the ongoing "Be Alert, Not Alarmed" campaign. The $15 million advertising and public relations initiative was intended to inform an increasingly insecure nation of how to report potential terrorist activities to appropriate authorities. The pervasive ambiguity that surrounds this campaign suggests much about the political benefits and effects associated with governmental communication of risk. Government communication often highlights state reliance on the oppositional discourse of threat and protection. The projection of fearful "realities" are [sic] balanced with the state's evidence of its ability to control the unanticipated. Yet, in this constructed "drama of the everyday", audiences receive no indication of what to "be alert" for, nor why these advertisements are needed if there is nothing to be alarmed about. Risks are strategically deployed at politically beneficial times to legitimize the actions of incumbent authorities. Government communications strategies are produced to elicit social acceptance of these actions through the presentation of idealized narratives of individuals working within a collective national identity to defeat "terror".
>
> (Bossio 2005)

Certainly 9/11 and Bali have paved the way for successive Australian governments to assert greater control over the citizenry through measures that have seen a decrease in civil rights.

Central to establishing such bio-political control has been the patrolling of the Australian national border, both physically and psychologically within news narratives. The obsessions with boat arrivals, "illegal immigrants" and "queue jumpers" by conservative politicians and newspapers had set the scene for future policies on citizenship in Australia and the future rights of asylum seekers, culminating in the implementation of the Citizenship Test. This Citizenship Test, and other new anti-terrorism laws, was aimed at those attempting to enter Australia with the intent of terrorist activity, but would have a more extensive impact on those who wish to enter as migrants seeking to join family in Australia, or asylum seekers.

There did not seem to be any need for a Citizenship Test in Australia until after the 2001 attacks. There were talks of implementing such a test, but it was never brought to fruition. However, post-2001, this was a different story. The circular dynamic of public opinion, the news media and successive governments demonstrated a common interest in stricter controls on who could enter the country.

For example, an article by James Button (2006) in *The Sydney Morning Herald* describes how:

> A new Australian citizenship test, announced by the Howard Government this week, could be much tougher, potentially testing not only

English language but knowledge of Australian history, institutions and values. It is likely to be based on the British model, and follows similar tests introduced in Europe in the past year. However silly, tough or harsh some aspects of the tests might seem, their introduction reflects growing alarm over a cluster of issues: globalisation, national identity, mass immigration and terrorism.

As the parliamentary secretary for immigration, Andrew Robb put it, when launching a discussion paper on the test: "The whole issue of terrorism ... in combination with globalisation has created a sort of general anxiety amongst not only the Australian community but other communities, and a threat to their identity" (Button 2006).

The very existence of asylum seekers has been portrayed by politicians and the Australian press as a threat to sovereignty, state power and the "Australian way of life." Asylum seekers were not to be trusted, and were often castigated as people of low morals not worthy of Australian citizenship, as in the case of those refugees involved in the so-called "children overboard" incident.

In the early afternoon of October 6, 2001, about 100 nautical miles north of Christmas Island, the HMAS *Adelaide* intercepted SIEV 4 (Suspected Illegal Entry Vehicle 4), a vessel carrying 223 passengers seeking asylum and crew. It was alleged by the Australian government at the time that, as the boat was ordered to leave Australian waters, some of the asylum seekers threw their children overboard. This incident, portrayed in the news media as a factual occurrence complete with pictures of children in the water, was used by the Howard Government of Australia to secure an election victory (Ferguson *et al.* 2005: 120), as at the time Prime Minister Howard was seen to be acting in the best interests of the country by turning away "illegal aliens," again another way of saying the "other," who would go so far as to endanger the lives of their children. After the election, it was established that the report of children having being thrown overboard was fictional (Manne 2002). The relevance of this incident here is the connection between terrorism and countering an "outside threat" no matter what the consequences. In this case it is argued that the consequences are seen most notably in the area of human rights – especially in regards to those who are seen as the "other" in society, including asylum seekers and those of Arabic and Muslim backgrounds (Norris and Inglehart 2003). In this way, the Howard Government solidified the Australian policy against outsiders: "zero tolerance." This can also be seen in the Australian government's implementation of a Citizenship Test to be taken by travelers to Australia before entrance into the country is granted.

The children overboard scandal, as well as the 2002 and 2005 Bali bombings, which involved Australians, induced an "acceleration of expenditure on human technological security measures at and beyond the border" (Shuja 2006: 52). The Australian government enacted 54 new pieces of anti-terrorism legislation between 2001 and 2006, most of which were passed in haste and without the opportunity for debate and refinement. In fact the then-Prime Minister John Howard called a media conference to declare that there was a "potential terrorist" threat and that certain parts of the 2005 Anti-Terrorism Bill had to be rushed through parliament within a day (Head 2006).

Another example of the way in which news media were supplied with stories of a potential threat occurred one week after Howard's media conference. During this time, heavily armed police and intelligence personnel raided homes in Sydney and Melbourne and arrested 19 Muslim men (Head 2006). According to Bloodworth (n.d.), the news media discourse that surrounded this incident was enough motivation to induce a trial-by-media phenomenon.

The September 11 attacks were especially significant in Australia, as they cemented a particular ideological belief about Muslims living in Australia.

The 2005 Cronulla riot in Sydney is a typical example of the outcome of a post 9/11 climate of fear. It illustrates how Muslims within Australian communities were immediately targeted at those who looked "different" from the norm (Anglo-Australian), but looked very much like those portrayed as the perpetrators of the 2001 attacks. These riots were aimed at Lebanese youth in the beachside town of Cronulla. This was no accident. According to an Australian Broadcasting Corporation online transcript of the radio show *PM*: "There's been widespread condemnation after reports of thousands of Anglo-Australians singing Waltzing Matilda while Lebanese youths were being hunted down and bashed at the beachside suburb" (Vincent and Iggulden 2005). It can be said that this event made the unspoken fear of the "other" in society the subject of an open debate and made the climate of suspicion official. This scenario was not only limited to Australia, however. Similar scenes were played out in America and the United Kingdom, where those who once lived peacefully next to their Muslim neighbours turned on them, simply out of the suspicion that they were somehow "involved" in the attacks or "with" the terrorists.

One common factor in almost all of the attacks that occurred in Australia, America and the United Kingdom after September 11, 2001 was the fact that those who were attacked had some physical resemblance to the terrorists of 9/11 portrayed in the news media, or similar dress (which showed that they were of the Muslim faith). In one case in America, those who were not Muslim also paid the price of the constant news reportage of "the stereotypical" terrorist. Goodstein and Lewin of the *New York Times* stated in 2001:

> Frightened by a wave of violence and harassment, Sikhs across the country are struggling to explain to an uncomprehending public that despite their turbans and beards, they are not followers of the Taliban and not in any way responsible for last week's terror attacks.

This is but one example of the climate of fear, of not only an attack from without, like September 2001, but also of an attack from within, as was shown by the example of the London bombings of July 7, 2005.

According to a study by Gary Bouma *et al.* (2007), there has been a marked increase in the "mistaken Islamophobia" as a result of the September 11, 2001 attacks "where people, incorrectly assumed to be Muslim, have also been targeted. Communities affected by this phenomenon have been non-Muslim Arab, Lebanese, Indian, Sikh, Pacific Islander and African communities."

Andrew Padgett and Beatrice Allen (2003) argue that, during times of crisis, Western mass media are faced with an irreconcilable paradox: the simultaneous demand for, and denial of, a fear-inspiring "other" (the Soviet Union, Al Qaeda, and so on). This paradigm of "otherness" was overcome in the post-Cold War and pre-9/11, as the US media was able to demonize "others" at home – in the war on drugs, for example. The fact that the news media frames "terrorism," more specifically counterterrorism, in terms of both war and crime at the same time, allows the government to introduce anti-terrorism legislation with greater ease.

Counterterrorist legislation since 9/11

The establishment of the "Be Alert, Not Alarmed" campaign, the Citizenship test, the politicization of boat arrivals and the increased emphasis on the social sorting of Australian citizens were key factors in the broadening of the powers of the Australian Security Intelligence Organisation (ASIO) since 2001. Mimicking the kinds of reforms being introduced in the UK and the US, ASIO was bestowed with the power to detain and interrogate anyone indefinitely, without access to legal representation. In addition, a list of deemed terrorist organizations was drawn up, and the Attorney General was bestowed with the power to act personally to ban any political organization judged to have terrorist affiliations.

A search on the Australian Parliamentary Library website revealed that the Australian Government did not have any laws in place specifically relating to terrorism at the time of the 2001 attacks in the US (Australian Parliamentary Website).

Within the first few months after September 11, 2001 the Australian Government began introducing new legislation, most of which was rushed through Parliament, under the guise of increasing the protection of the average citizen. At the time, the Howard Government proposed numerous changes to Australian legislation that were to be introduced if the Howard was voted into office again. On November 1, 2001, the Howard Government was reinstated and introduced the Security Legislation Amendment (Terrorism) Bill 2002 [no. 2], the Suppression of the Financing of Terrorism Bill 2002; the Criminal Code Amendment (Suppression of Terrorist Bombings) Bill 2002; the Border Security Legislation Amendment

Bill 2002; and the Telecommunications Interception Legislation Amendment Bill 2002.

The Security Legislation Amendment (Terrorism) Bill defined a "terrorist act" as a criminal act in such broad terms as to implicate all manner of political and industrial events. For example, since 2002, a trade union strike can be deemed a terrorist act if "serious" property damage occurs. The Bill defines as terrorist:

> an action or threat of action ... done with the intention of advancing a political, religious or ideological cause and with the intention of coercing, or influencing by intimidation, the government or State or Territory or foreign country or intimidating the public or a section of the public.
>
> (Australian Government 2002)

This act was just the start of a raft of legislative changes: the 54 security-related acts that have been passed since 2002. These include the power to detain suspects for seven days without charge and without the detainee being given rights to legal representation. Hocking argues that this power alone brings about a condition of universalized surveillance, where any member of the population is a potential suspect (Hocking 2004: 233).

Legal and journalistic framing of the war on terror

The formulation of counterterrorism legislation needs to be considered in relation to the US call for a war on terror: a "war" that is conducted both domestically and as a matter of foreign policy.

According to Robert Hardaway (2004: 117), the legal aspects of the war on terror can be divided into three categories: international law relating to the law of war and the use of force; domestic law relating to internal national security; and international and domestic law relating to the legal rights of detainees captured in the war on terror. These three categories in Hardaway's view relate specifically to US domestic and foreign policy; however these categories can also serve as a model for the types of laws implemented in Australia.

The media framing of terrorism in terms of war (Hocking 2003: 359) suggests that no democratic country can go to war without significant public agreement about what course of action the elected government should take. This clearly does not apply to the US-led war on terror commencing in 2001, as the public disapproval at the time of the war being called did not stop it from going ahead. The revelation two years later in 2003 that the impetus for calling a war – to eradicate WMDs in Iraq – was unfounded created a legitimization crisis for the US at the time, which made it even more important for politicians to control news about the success of the war.

One of the strategies taken to enhance such control by both the US and Australia was regulating the access of journalists to military theaters of war.

Embedded journalists were to be shown only what the state wanted them to see and denied access to operations that were purported to be operationally sensitive or dangerous for journalists to be there. But such regulation could also be applied to situations regarded as too politically sensitive and work to optimize forms of reporting that presented allied participation in the most favorable light.

Public acceptance/approval of the war on terror is connected to the framing of information pertaining to terrorism in the news media. If terrorism is framed in such terms as "imminent threat" and "war on terrorism," then the public will not only become aware of the so-called imminent threat, but will be more willing to accept a course of action to combat this imminent threat. However, Stabile (2001) contends that this is not always the case and connects the generalization made by scholars that the public as a whole shows acceptance and support for stringent law and order measures to the mistake of seeing audiences as a "monolithic mass" vulnerable to the news media's messages and incapable of any but the most reactionary responses. Specifically, "the appearance of consent may lead members of the public (not to mention the media and politicians) to behave as if the consent did exist" (Stabile 2001: 266).

There is a difference, however, between the news media describing terrorism in terms of a "war," frame and their describing it in terms of a "crime" frame. These two frames have been recognized by some theorists (Baker 2003: 2; Hocking 2003: 358) as the basis for public approval for the counterterrorism measures proposed by democratic governments around the world in the wake of 9/11. To these can be added a "vengeance" frame, which was dominant in the years immediately following 9/11.

According to Edy and Meirick (2007: 136):

> The "vengeance frame" makes the group responsible for attacks on individuals. Because the group is guilty, inflicting harm on group members who may have played no direct role in the attacks is morally acceptable. Indeed there may be an "eye-for-an-eye" logic behind the relative willingness of those subscribing to this frame to inflict civilian casualties in Afghanistan. A "pure war" frame describes an attack on a group by a group, creating an "us-versus-them" evaluation that justifies military action on grounds of self-defense[.]

A "war-crime frame" invokes its own unique moral judgment. Like the war frame, it defines its user as a member of a wronged group; however, it identifies not a general "enemy" but specific "criminals" responsible for the wrong.

Criminalization of terrorism vs the legitimization of war

Whilst the phrase "war on terror" has paired these two terms together, it should be observed that terrorism should not be equated with war. As a particular form of violence, terrorism must be separated from other forms, and defined in its own right. According to Noam Chomsky, "Terrorism is the use of coercive means aimed at civilian populations in an effort to achieve political, religious, or other aims" (Chomsky 2001: 57). Terrorism cannot be shown to be a legitimate form of warfare because there is nothing legitimate about its execution. A terrorist attack consists of terrorists attacking unarmed civilians. There is nothing to suggest that there is any chance of retaliation from those who are attacked by the terrorists. The very word "terrorism" is used here as a way of demarcating and separating this form of violence from other more commonly known forms such as legitimate warfare. Walter Laqueur (1978) explains further:

> War, even civil war, is predictable in many ways; it occurs in the light of day and there is no mystery about the identity of the participants. Even in civil war there are certain rules, whereas the characteristic features of terrorism are anonymity and the violation of established norms.
> (Laqueur 1978: 3)

Acts of terrorism are different from other acts of violence, such as conventional war. Terrorism is different in the way its victims are defined. In war, violence is carried out between two sides (usually) that are both armed, wear uniforms, fight on behalf of a state, and conduct themselves according to the laws of war and international laws such as the Geneva Convention.

It must be stated here, though, that President George W. Bush never framed the war on terrorism as a war on Arabs and Muslims. In fact, Bush denounced violence against Muslim – and Arab – Americans, saying: "Those who feel like they can intimidate our fellow citizens to take out their anger don't represent the best of America, they represent the worst of humankind, and they should be ashamed of their behavior" (Norris *et al.* 2003: 146). Democratic governments involved in the "war on terror" do not see themselves as simply embarking on a "war" campaign – otherwise all that would be occurring in the war frame would be two sides fighting each other in the same way as in the two World Wars. Instead, the governments involved introduce, as part of their counterterrorism measures, legislation allowing government officials and agencies such as ASIO (Hocking 2004) more power to monitor, surveil, detain and prosecute individuals or groups in an effort to preempt and prevent rather than simply contain the aftermath. The counterterrorism measures undertaken by democratic governments in this case must involve some sort of legal foundation to be able to embark on such actions – connecting the ideas of the terrorist and terrorism with the idea of crime and criminal legislation.

Without the connection to counterterrorism measures, legislation and the labeling of the terrorist as criminal, the "war on terror" would be chasing an arbitrary enemy. Connecting terrorism with criminality means that, in the minds of the public, the laws implemented that allow for increased surveillance and control of individual citizens are completely warranted because, as in the case of the London bombings on July 7, 2005 *any* citizen can be a terrorist. If the government can give shape and form to terrorism by giving terrorists a "face" the enemy is no longer abstract and amorphous because there is no realistic sense in which a war can be fought against such an amorphous and diverse entity (Gupta 2002: 28).

Criminalization, then, is the way that government security agencies can introduce increased forms of control. By connecting terrorism to crime, rather than simply to war, those who are caught can be charged in the same manner as any other criminal and sentenced according to the same laws.

However, the problem with this arises when the law is ignored and those who are suspected of terrorist activity are not dealt with under the law – like the inmates of Guantánamo Bay for example – as David Hicks once was. Another Australian, Jack Thomas, who did not technically commit any acts of crime, was nevertheless deemed a criminal, based on new anti-terrorism legislation and the publicizing of the criminalization of particular behaviors for preemptive reasons (and even the allocation of stereotypical nicknames such as "Jihad Jack") in the news media.

According to Wilson and Weber (2008: 128), examples of how human surveillance capacities have been deployed in Australia include overseas networks of federal police tasked with monitoring and disrupting people-smuggling activities and "enhanced coastal surveillance coupled with military interdiction at sea". These measures may be related specifically to border security, but this is one major area where security has been increased in the fear that terrorists may enter the country, especially as refugees. It is a well-known fact that Australia's policy of interning refugees in detention camps upon arrival in Australia arises from the perception that these refugees are in some way a potential risk to society, and, as stated above, in such a train of reasoning, they are reduced to criminals and, therefore, treated as such.

Terrorism and privacy

The fact that terrorism is now a perceived threat, even in Australia, has changed the ways in which surveillance and privacy are viewed (Bloss 2007). According to Bloss, there has been a progressive shift toward police surveillance over individual privacy rights (Bloss 2007: 208). "Money laundering" and terrorism, also implicated in the American "war on drugs", are becoming increasingly difficult areas of the "war on terror" to regulate. According to Shields (2005), the electronic transfer of funds, for example, aids terrorist groups in fulfilling their terrorist acts, as they need money to finance the acquisition of guns, bomb materials, and even training. He argues that new communications technologies have added new concerns for "Law enforcement agencies and regulatory authorities, as well as many policy-makers and journalists" who "have expressed alarm that developments in information and communications technology (ICT) have provided terrorists, drug traffickers, pedophiles and the like with unnerving new capacities and opportunities to commit crimes and evade law enforcement" (Shields 2005: 484).

Surveillance, as first described by Bentham, is a way of preempting undesired behavior, a kind of "universalized surveillance" (Hocking 2004: 233). Surveillance, therefore, not only preempts, but also prevents terrorist acts from occurring. This idea of surveillance as a preemptive measure is connected to the very heart of the reason for the implementation of the anti-terrorism legislation in Australia. Wilson and Weber (2008) describe the preemptive measures in place in Australia for detecting possible threats at Australia's borders and making sure they do not enter the country. These preemptive measures are a form of social sorting (Wilson and Weber 2008: 125; Lyon 2002: 13), where certain characteristics, behaviors, associations and even Internet browsing and credit card purchase history (Shields 2005) can be scrutinized and interpreted as qualities alluding to possible future risks to society (Baruh 2007: 188).

Australia legally monitors people who are deemed "risky" in society, and has dataveillance legislation in place to allow government agencies such as ASIO or the Australian Federal Police (AFP) to engage in such monitoring. Some of the legislation introduced since 9/11 pertaining to detection, detention and dataveillance include the ASIO Legislation Amendment Act 2003, which amends the Australian Security Intelligence Organisation Act 1979, to ensure that ASIO has the ability to collect effectively the information necessary to prevent a terrorist act (Australian Government 2003). Specifically related to surveillance and new media there is the Surveillance Devices Act 2004, which establishes the procedures for authorities to obtain warrants and authorizations (emergency and tracking device use) for the installation and use of surveillance devices in relation to criminal investigations, and most importantly also for terrorism-related investigations (Australian Government 2004). Lastly, there is now the Australian Federal Police and Other Legislation Amendment Act 2004, which amends the Australian Federal Police Act 1979 and the Crimes Act 1914 (Australian Government 2004).

According to David Luban (2005), the balance between security and civil liberties is not easily found: "[t]he trade-off between security and civil liberties might represent a judgment that we fear our own government less than we fear terrorists" (Luban 2005: 245). The aforementioned effects of terrorism legislation and government power, are, according to Luban, necessary if one is to feel safe from terrorism, but on the other hand, there is no reason why the government should be trusted if what Goldstone (2005) suggests above is the result of a trade-off between security and civil liberties. The theory by Norris *et al.* (2003: 4), that there is a "critical shift in the predominant news frame used by the American mass media for understanding issues of national security," can be used as a framework for what happened simultaneously with the Australian mass media post-9/11. It can be said that this shift in the perception of terrorism has occurred at the state level and is filtered through the news media – which in turn filters it through the public – creating the ideology that citizens are at an increased risk of becoming victims of terrorism – just like 9/11. This is a myth according to Norris *et al.*, but this myth leads to the acceptance of increased counterterrorism legislation and surveillance. Therefore, it can be seen how the media's framing of terrorism to create the need for "civil protection" reinforces this perception in both the public and the political arena.

This chapter has shown that the media framing of terrorism as an "imminent" threat has opened up the Australian public to the concept of counterterrorism and risk preemption. As we have shown, both politicians and news media organizations have a "common interest" in promoting fear of terror. The Australian public becomes used to the rhetoric of "war" and "counterterrorism" in the news media, and when the government introduces new legislation in the name of countering terrorism, it is passed with little opposition (Hocking 2003). In turn, the news media in Australia has benefited from the heightened levels of fear in being able to command greater audience attention and sell more newspapers.

References

Australian Government (2002) Security Legislation Amendment (Terrorism) Act 2002, part 5.3 – Terrorism Division 100 – Preliminary 100.1 Definitions. Australian Government Printing Service. Available at www.nationalsecurity.gov.au/agd/www/nationalsecurity.nsf/Page/Publications (accessed July 19, 2007).

Australian Government (2003) ASIO Legislation Amendment Act 2003. Australian Government Printing Service. Available at www.nationalsecurity.gov.au/agd/www/nationalsecurity.nsf/0/660EDAE0E8068AD9CA256FCC00126731?OpenDocument (accessed July 19, 2007).

Australian Government (2004) Australian National Security. Available at www.nationalsecurity.gov.au/agd/www/nationalsecurity.nsf/AllDocs/826190776D49EA90CA256FAB001BA5EA?OpenDocument (accessed July 19, 2007).

Australian Parliamentary Website. Available at www.aph.gov.au/library/intguide/law/terrorism.htm (accessed July 10, 2009).

Ayson, R. and Ball, D. (2006) *Strategy and Security in the Asia-Pacific*, Crows Nest, NSW: Allen & Unwin.

Baker, Nancy (2003) "National security versus civil liberties," *Presidential Studies Quarterly*, 33(3), 547–68.

Banham, Cynthia (2012) "New War Emerges, as seen on your television," *Sydney Morning Herald*. Sydney, Available at smh.com.au (accessed February 10, 2012).

Baruh, Lemi. (2007) "Read at your own risk: shrinkage of privacy and interactive media," *New Media and Society*, 9(2), 187–211.

Bloodworth, Sandra (n.d.), *Socialist Alternative Website*, available at www.sa.org.au/index.php?option=com_k2&view=item&id=5475:howard%E2%80%99s-terrorism-witchhunt&Itemid=562 (accessed July 1, 2008).

Bloss, William. (2007) "Escalating US police surveillance after 9/11: an Examination of causes and effects," *Surveillance and Society*, Special Issue on "Surveillance and Criminal Justice" Part 1, 4(3), 208–28.

Bossio, D. (2005) "Be Alert, Not Alarmed: Governmental communication of risk in an era of insecurity," presented at the Annual Meeting of the Australian and New Zealand Communication Association, Christchurch, New Zealand, July 4–7.

Bouma, Gary D., Pickering, Sharon, Halafoff, Anna and Dellal, Hass (2007) *Managing the Impact of Global Crisis Events on Community Relations in Multicultural Australia: Background Report*. Prepared for the School of Political and Social Inquiry, Monash University, and Australian Multicultural Foundation for Multicultural Affairs Queensland and Department for Victorian Communities. Available at www.multicultural.qld.gov.au (accessed August 5, 2009).

Button, James (2006) "You Don't Get In That Easily," September 23, *The Sydney Morning Herald*. Available at www.smh.com.au/news/world/you-dont-get-in-that-easily/2006/09/22/1158431897985.html?page=fullpage (accessed July 5, 2009).

Chomsky, Noam. (2001) *September 11*, Crows Nest, NSW: Allen & Unwin.

Edy, Jill, A and Meirick, Patrick (2007) "Wanted, dead or alive: media frames, frame adoption, and support for the war in Afghanistan," *Journal of Communication*, 57, 119–41.

Ferguson, I., Lavalette, M. and Whitmore, E. (2005) *Globalisation, Global Justice and Social Work*, Adington: Routledge.

Frey, B. and Rohner, D. (2006) *Blood and Ink! The Common-Interest-Game between Terrorists and the Media*, Working Paper no. 285, Institute for Empirical Research in Economics, University of Zurich. Available at http://ideas.repec.org/p/zur/iewwpx/285.html (accessed May 20, 2007).

Goldstone, R. (2005) "The tension between combating terrorism and protecting civil liberties". *Human Rights in the "War on Terror"*. New York: Cambridge University Press.

Goodin, B. (2006) *What's Wrong with Terrorism*, London: Polity.

Goodstein L and Lewin T (2001) "Victims of mistaken identity, Sikhs pay a price for turbans," *New York Times*, September 19. Available at www.nytimes.com/2001/09/19/national/19HATE.html (accessed June 23, 2013).

Gupta, S. (2002) *Replication of Violence: Thoughts on International Terrorism after September 11th 2001*, London: Pluto Press.

Hardaway, Robert (2004) "The role of the media, law and national resolve in the War on Terror," *Denver Journal of International Law and Policy*.

Head, M. (2006) "Australia: anti-Muslim 'terror plot' unravels," World Socialist Web Site, International Committee of the Fourth International, November 11. Available at www.wsws.org/en/articles/2006/11/asio-n11.html.

Hocking, J. (2003) "Counterterrorism and the criminalisation of politics: Australia's new security powers of detention, proscription and control," *Australian Journal of Politics and History* 49(3), 355–71.

Hocking, J. (2004) *Terror Laws: ASIO, Counter-terrorism and the Threat to Democracy*, Sydney, UNSW Press.

Human Security Report (2005a) Human Security Report 2005. Available at www.hsrgroup.org/docs/Publications/HSR2005/2005HumanSecurityReport-Overview.pdf (accessed September 30, 2013).

Human Society Report (2005b) Figure 1.14 in "Graphs and Tables 2005." Available at www.hsrgroup.org/human-security-reports/2005/graphs-and-tables.aspx (accessed September 30, 2013).

Laqueur, W. (1978) *Terrorism*. London: Weidenfeld & Nicolson.

Luban, D. (2005) "Eight fallacies about liberty and security," *Human Rights in the "War on Terror"*, New York: Cambridge University Press.

Lyon, David (2002) "Surveillance as social sorting," in D. Lyon (ed.), *Surveillance as Social Sorting*, Hoboken, NJ: Taylor & Francis.

Manne, R. (2002) "How Tampa sailed into 2002," *The Age*. Available at www.theage.com.au/articles/2002/12/29/1040511254630.html (accessed June 27, 2008).

Michaelsen, C. (2005) "Anti-terrorism legislation in Australia: A proportionate response to the terrorist threat," *Studies in Conflict and Terrorism*, 28(4) (July–August), 331–9.

Norris, P. and Inglehart, R. (2003) "Public opinions among Muslims and the West," in P.Norris, M. Kern and M. Just (eds) *Framing Terrorism: The News Media, the Government, and the Public*, New York: Routledge, 203–28.

Norris, P., Kern, M. and Just, M. (2003) "Framing terrorism," in P.Norris, M. Kern and M. Just (eds) *Framing Terrorism: The News Media, the Government, and the Public*, New York: Routledge, 3–26.

Padgett, A. and Allen, B. (2003) "Fear's slave: The mass media and Islam after September 11," *Media International Australia: Culture and Policy*. No. 109. November. Available at www.uq.edu.au/emsah/mia/issues/miacp109.html+Tampa+children+overboard+media+coverage&hl=en&ct=clnk&cd=5&gl=au (accessed June 27, 2008).

Shields, Peter. (2005) "When the 'information revolution' and the US security state collide: Money laundering and the proliferation of surveillance," *New Media and Society*, 7(4), 483–512.

Shuja, Sharif. (2006) "Australia's response to terrorism in the Asian region," *National Observer*, 70, 9–60.

Stabile, C. (2001) "Conspiracy or consensus? Reconsidering the Moral Panic, *Journal of Communication Inquiry*, 25(3), 258–78.

United States, Department of State (2004) "Patterns of global terrorism 2003." Available at www.state.gov/documents/organization/31912.pdf (accessed June 23, 2013).

Vincent and Iggulden 12 December 2005, *PM* "Cronulla locals search for answers over race riots."Available at www.abc.net.au/pm/content/2005/s1529417.htm (accessed August 5, 2009).

Wilson, D. and Weber, L. (2008) "Surveillance, risk and preemption on the Australian border,"*Surveillance and Society*, 5(2), 124–41.

Wright-Neville, D. Vicziany, M. and Lentini, P. (2004) *Regional Security in the Asia-Pacific 9/11 and After*, Cheltenham/Northampton: Edward Elgar.

7 Jihadist terrorism in Europe
What role for media?

Sybille Reinke de Buitrago

What role do media play in discourse on terrorism and, here specifically, jihadist terrorism? Do media possibly attempt to understand terrorism and terrorists, in terms of terrorists' perspectives, or do they rather tend to replicate the existing official, that is, policy-making discourse on terrorism? And how active or passive are media in playing a critical role, in terms of covering different perspectives, uncovering problematic aspects or giving their own spin when reporting on jihadist terrorism in Western Europe?

While attention has typically been paid to official state discourse on counterterrorism, media discourse on terrorism has been much less analyzed. This chapter is attempting to provide some insights into this direction. Thus, this chapter asks if media actually discuss motives of jihadist terrorists and if jihadist interests get any attention and, if so, in which manner. Also of interest is whether or not there are differences among national media discourse, or if there is a common, cross-European media discourse. This chapter presents results of a qualitative analysis of media coverage of three jihadist terrorist attacks in Europe in 2010 in major print media in France, Germany, Italy, the Netherlands, Spain, Turkey and the United Kingdom.

The results presented here are based on outcomes of a research project on jihadist terrorism. The project is based in Germany and has cooperated with research institutions in six other European countries, namely France, Italy, the Netherlands, Spain, Turkey and the UK.[1] The inclusion of seven countries offers an interesting comparison of national media discussion, and one that goes beyond a purely Western European one. In each country, two major and nationally representative newspapers were selected: Germany – *Frankfurter Allgemeine Zeitung* and *Süddeutsche Zeitung*; France – *Le Monde* and *Le Parisien*; Italy – *Corriere della Sera* and *La Repubblica*; Netherlands – *Volkskrant* and *NRC Handelsblad*; Spain – *El País* and *El Mundo*; Turkey – *Hürriyet* and *Sabah*; and UK – *The Financial Times* and *The Guardian*. These papers represent the media discourse in their respective country due to their circulation, national standing and their ideational spectrum from more liberal to more conservative.

For a comparable context, three jihadist terrorist attacks in Europe in 2010 were chosen, and media discourse was analyzed for a period of three weeks after each attack. The selected cases have a clearly established jihadist motivation or background, but they are different in type regarding the target, means applied and/or (planned or actual) damage: the attack on Danish cartoonist Kurt Westergaard on January 1, 2010, the Yemen cargo plane plot on October 29, 2010, and the suicide attack in Stockholm on December 11, 2010. In the Westergaard case, a man entered Westergaard's house by force, trying to kill him with an axe. Westergaard was already under police protection due to earlier threats and was able to flee to a constructed "panic room" in his house and alert police. The attacker was then brought into custody. In the Yemen cargo plane plot printers with explosive material were sent over much of Europe before being found in Great Britain. Though no explosion occurred, the incident raised great alarm in Europe and beyond. Finally, in Stockholm the offender ignited a car bomb and then tried to ignite his explosives belt, which went off early, killing himself and injuring two persons nearby. The offender most likely aimed for greater damage, as the attack occurred during the Christmas shopping season and near a central commercial street. Even though the three attacks did not achieve their intended damage, they had a considerable impact – thus, and for better reading here, they are referred to as attacks, and not attempted attacks.

The analysis includes all media articles relating to the attacks (a total of 349, and on average 45 to 50 articles per country) and is conducted as qualitative content analysis. It applies categories, or thematic dimensions, based on existing literature and previous research about discourse on terrorism: The first refers to offender motives, messages and broader causes. The aspect of motives refers to whether or not media discuss any motivations leading the offender(s) to conduct the attack or for engaging in jihadist terrorism in general, thus, whether media either interpret or speculate on possible motives or only report on these when stated by the offender(s); the aspect of messages refers to whether or not media reflect on any messages or demands that were communicated by the offender(s) before, during or after the attack; and the aspect of broader causes refers to whether or not media discuss any broader or root causes that may lie behind the attack or the involvement in terrorism, such as political, social, religious or biographical factors. Next, the focus lies on specific issues of terrorist concern, such as Western troops in predominantly Muslim countries, symbolic offences, and relations between Europe/the West and the Muslim world/Islam. Thus, the second dimension relates to whether or not the presence of Western troops in predominantly Muslim countries like Afghanistan plays a role in media discourse – this would at least seem to be of jihadist concern.[2] The third dimension refers to media discourse regarding symbolic offences to Islam or Muslims, such as the Muhammad cartoons in Western media. And, the fourth dimension tries to capture media discourse about the relationship between the West and Europe on the one side and the Muslim world and Islam on the other side. Finally, a fifth dimension aims to grasp the major reactions that media discuss after each attack, in terms of legislation, surveillance, technical measures, social measures and foreign policy.[3] The dimensions differ in breadth, while some also overlap, for example motives and causes. Proceeding in this manner enables the analyst to capture the nuances in media discourse. In addition, while a media analysis leads to rich results, only key findings can be presented here. Depending on the degree of specificity of results, the chapter refers to national media discourse (for example French media or France Report) or to specific newspapers.

The selection of different types of attack can enable insights regarding whether there is a shared cross-European media discourse, or national media discourse differs. As media discourse on terrorism is still a fairly scant subject of scientific research, and although the inclusion of a greater number of attacks would certainly offer more solid results, important insights about the connections between the type of terrorist attack and resulting media discourse can be drawn. The analysis has actually shown that each attack has led to a particular cross-European discourse: the Westergaard case to a value-oriented discourse, the Yemen cargo plane plot to a discourse of control, and the Stockholm attack to a broader and less defined discourse. But before delving into the results, the role of the media is briefly discussed.

The role of media

When taking a look at how media influence societies today, including the political sphere, we can recognize media's significant power – at least in societies with a free press and other civil and political liberties. Media shape public and, to some degree, political discourse by reporting events. More specifically, media select and take up specific issues, interpret them in a specific manner and link them with a particular context – they zoom in on certain facets and thereby ignore or minimize others. The process of what to report on and what not, in the context of short time spans and little space, necessarily leads to a particular perspective being offered. This is also the case when media report on terrorist acts; also here, media give different amounts of attention to the acts themselves, to offenders, to possible motives and to the ramifications, and engage in a selection process.

Communication is highly important in the understanding of terrorism (Archetti 2013: 33–34), especially the ways in which we, or the media, communicate about terrorism. For example, Sutter points to the dynamics of media's self-referencing and acts of self-exposure and self-portrayal, as found in television, which can also be partially found in newspapers. In trying to be the first to cover an event, for example, media necessarily engage in various degrees of interpretation and speculation as well as a media competition. In the process of reporting, media content is further spread, interpreted and adapted (Sutter 2010: 34, 44). Media thus position themselves as active players in public discourse. But Flood *et al.* speak of media being both entwined with the larger consensus regarding terrorism, and caught between their role in providing full information on events and upholding national values (2012: 250), an aspect that is supported by the results of this analysis. Interestingly, Flood *et al.* further find that reports on terrorism have an Islamist coloring, that is, they tend to include references to Islamist violence (ibid.: 189–191), and also this aspect is partially, though very implicitly, found in the results offered by this chapter.

The relationship between media and terrorism (see for example Bassiouni 1981; Laqueur 1976; Martin 1985; Nacos 2002; Wilkinson 2006) plays out in both needing one another: simply put, media needs events to report on and terrorists want attention. Archetti argues, however, that the relationship between media and terrorism can vary and range from various degrees of unwanted support-lending by media, simply by giving terrorists attention in media coverage, to problematic or irresponsible coverage; but who exactly influences whom in what manner in the study of the media–terrorism nexus is still not clear (2013: 37–40, 55). Since any media outlet aims to be the first to report on a story, media tend to sensationalize and present views in a dramatic manner to assure public attention (Combs 2013: 169–170). When seen in this light, it becomes especially clear that terrorists often profit from media reporting on and broadcasting their acts, in terms of generated attention and amplification. Media coverage of terrorist acts can even serve as a showcase for terrorism, illustrating how to conduct attacks and inspiring others (ibid.: 171–173). To counter some of these negative effects, Combs – in terms of a media–government nexus – argues for media possibly needing to cooperate with the government to work out guidelines regarding limits on access to events and information, and on when to release what kind of information, so that the need for security and the need for full coverage can be balanced. In addition, reporting should be non-inflammatory and impartial (ibid.: 185–186).

The media–terrorism nexus can then also be seen from the active versus passive role. One is active media communication about terrorism and terrorists; the other is a more passive role of media, in terms of media reflecting society and its discourse. In their active role, media offer views on terrorism, terrorist acts and terrorists. There is the intent to inform and, to some degree, shape views of the public and policy-makers. This quality, as Sutter (2010: 17) and Combs (2013: 170) point out, relates to the role of media in a country in general, but also the already stated aspect of media competition and the resulting tendency to sensationalize. This tendency is related to an inherent drive to generate resonance. The media is thus a significant contributor to public opinion, and can even influence the policy arena. The active role of media is also seen in social constructivism (Berger and Luckmann 1967).[4] Seen through this lens, humans produce and reproduce their particular social reality in social interaction and communication; media then co-construct social reality. On the other hand, media can also play a more passive role. Aside from an active intent to inform, there is a deeply rooted cultural framework at work. Here, media function as a reflection of society, of what it thinks and how it reacts to events. Included are the national self-image[5] and self-understanding. It is argued here that seeing media as a reflection of society implies that journalists write based on the assumptions and values of their society and its cultural framework. Differentiating between passive and active media roles in practice is difficult, however, for they tend to mingle and overlap, as this media analysis also shows.

Furthermore, whether passive or active, and in agreement with Le (2006: 10–12), journalists also write from a historical framework, as part of their cultural frame. References to history allow readers more easily to connect current events to those of the past. In this manner new facts are integrated into existing individual and collective knowledge. News reporting is thus framed, and references to the past serve to analyze as well as dramatize current events. Frames present an important concept in media discourse. The concept of a frame or a news frame can be used when speaking about the definition of an issue or event in media, this definition also being shaped by a society's organizational principles (Glaab 2007; Goffman 1974: 10ff.). An event, such as a terrorist attack, is portrayed in a particular manner, offered with selected facts and placed in the context of particular values, thereby resulting in or offering one particular interpretation over an alternative one. News recipients are thus presented with a specific portrayal or framing of this event and its context (see also Entman 1993, 2010; Goffman 1974: 21), where news frames facilitate certain interpretations over others (Norris *et al.* 2003: 10–11). Framing is also a dynamic and complex process and depends on many factors (de Vreese 2005). Even for an informed audience, that has access to multiple news sources, framing has a strong impact, as shown in numerous studies (see for example Entman 2010; Glaab 2007; Linsky 1986; Lomax Cook *et al.* 1983; Nacos *et al.* 2011; Pritchard 1992; Puglisi 2004). In addition, the human tendency to use mental short cuts and filters in information processing, so as to process new facts and information with as little effort as possible, explains why framing has such a strong impact (see also Fiske and Taylor 1991).

Media discourse on jihadist terrorist attacks

Taking up the question whether media actually aim to understand terrorism and the terrorists' perspectives or rather tend to replicate existing official discourse on terrorism, this section presents the media discourse on the three jihadist terrorist attacks along thematic dimensions. The related question of how active or passive media are in covering these events, and whether or not media actually debate different points and offer different views, is also discussed.

The dimension of motives for attacks, messages and broader causes

In the Westergaard case, media do not express a real interest in understanding terrorism or the terrorist behind the act when discussing offender motives, messages and causes. For example, media discuss neither the motives for the attack in a detailed manner, nor the biographical factors of the offender. When *motives* and *causes* are mentioned, they are intertwined here – thus, all media mention revenge as both the likely motive and cause, as the offender called for revenge and blood during the attack. Media also report on Al Qaeda having called for the killing of such cartoonists, but disagree on the offender having links to Al Qaeda in East Africa and the Somali terrorist group Al-Shabaab (France Report; Germany Report; Netherlands Report; Spain Report). However, broader causes for the offender engaging in terrorism are not discussed. The aspect of the offender acting rationally or irrationally only plays a role in UK media: the offender may have had a rational motive, because he felt offended, but he proceeded irrationally, because he chose violence for his response. In terms of *messages*, media discourse indirectly expresses the offender message that such cartoons will have consequences for the cartoonist. But media argue against the validity of such consequences, for although they express some awareness that cartoons of the Prophet Muhammad are offending to Muslims, they highlight freedom of expression as a Western value that must be defended. UK media go further by portraying the offenders as having attacked the Western value of democracy, and call to defend Western values. Here, the attack is clearly seen in a larger context, the offender aims are enlarged, and core Western values are seen to be in danger. UK media also speak of a clash of cultures, stating that Western and Islamic values are in conflict, and that Western values are right and overall valid. Thus, media take an active role in this case by giving their own spin and highlighting the value of freedom of expression and the need to defend it. Of course, freedom of expression and freedom of the press are also in the interest of Western media. Although to a lesser degree, also Turkish media are part of this discourse. Thus, freedom of expression, and this freedom being under attack, is highlighted above all other aspects of the attack. Freedom of expression is of course part of the broader Western value system that also finds attention in media discourse. Media thus generally position themselves as active player in the defense of freedom of expression and Western values in general.

The Yemen case is discussed in a more sober manner; there is no explicit reference to values or to a clash of values, for example. Even the terrorist aims of achieving great damage are stated soberly. Thus, offender *motives* of increasing and maximizing damage are mentioned. According to French, German, Italian and Turkish media, the offenders have tested security arrangements at Western airports to find gaps and then conduct larger attacks with maximum damage. But German media also debate the possibility of timing an explosion for an exact time and place, as packages cannot be tracked exactly. Broader or root *causes* are mentioned, but not further discussed. For example, the presence of the US military in Afghanistan and Yemen is only briefly stated in Italian and UK media. German media see the lack of education and the poverty in Yemen as issues exploited by terrorists to gain recruits. UK media add unemployment and low economic growth as well as depleting water resources leading to violence in Yemen, but also the governmental inability to control its territory, all of which Al Qaeda is exploiting. The biographical background of offenders is not discussed. Regarding offender *messages*, and the point of offender (ir)rationality, only UK media refer to it. They see the goal-oriented proceeding as a sign for offenders having acted rationally. However, while one source argues for offenders having acted irrationally in wanting to send an effective message to the US and Europe, it describes Al Qaeda as rational in building effectiveness: "The group is brilliant in amplifying its message" (UK Report; Boucek November 1, 2010). In this case, media concentrate on fact-reporting and play a much less active role; only the interpretation of the offenders being irrational in aiming to send a message to the US and Europe with such an attack points to a somewhat active position. Discourse is also rather unemotional and does not touch much on values. Thus, media take a more passive role here. Media do not aim for an understanding of terrorism or the terrorists, for motives are not discussed in depth, biographical factors find no attention at all, and also broader causes are only repeated from general knowledge but not elaborated or debated.

Also, in the Stockholm case, media discourse shows no interest in understanding terrorism or the offender's view. In this case, the offender had actually sent a threatening letter and email before the attack. Thus, *motives*, *causes* and *messages* play some role in media discourse, but this likely because of the offender's threatening letter and email, for there is no in-depth discussion. In terms of motives and broader causes, which are entwined here, media briefly mention Sweden's participation in Afghanistan and the Swedish support for the Muhammad cartoon by the Swede Lars Vilks. UK media add that in general social and economic conditions can also be facilitators of violence, and that terrorist action is a natural response to Western presence in Iraq and to the Western position in the Middle East conflict (Watt and Norton-Taylor 2010); a clear link to the particular attack or the offender is not made, however. As cause, a German newspaper sees Islamist centers playing a role in radicalization processes (*Frankfurter Allgemeine Zeitung* 2010e). French news speak of the offender having been instigated by the Islamic State of Iraq (Al Qaeda's branch in Iraq), which had called for action against such cartoonists. And a Turkish news source mentions that the offender's youngest child, a baby boy, is named

Osama (*Hürriyet Gazetesi* 2010), which seems to point to the offender's strong interest in Al Qaeda. But a UK source also plays the threat of lone perpetrators down, as, although one can hardly defend against them, they tend to be less successful due to a lack of technical skills (Watt and Norton-Taylor 2010). As *message*, German media report on the offender having called for jihad against Sweden, but also Europe. UK news quote his statements: "Now will your children, daughters and sisters die the same way our brothers and sisters die. Our actions will speak for themselves. As long as you don't end your war against Islam and degradation against the prophet and your foolish support for the pig Vilks" (Borger 2010), as stated in one way or another by all national media. But despite the offender's threatening letter and email, a real debate was not initiated and media showed no clear interest in the offender or why he undertook this attack. Regarding the active versus passive role of the media, here media (although not all national media) seem to assume a middle position, being slightly more active in offering their own views than in the Yemen case, but less so than in the Westergaard case, expressed in the points regarding Islamist centers, offender instigation or the limited danger of lone perpetrators. The particulars of the attack and some points in the offender statements seem to have touched on the Western way of life in general and thus provoked responses.

The dimension of Western troops in predominantly Muslim countries

Media discourse on this dimension neither expresses an interest in understanding terrorism or the offenders nor an active role in interpreting, raising criticism or questioning policy. The expectation that the aspect of Western armed forces in predominantly Muslim countries such as Afghanistan or Iraq would be significant in media discourse, as this is an issue of jihadist concern (see also Bakker 2006; Nesser 2006), was not fulfilled. Only brief references are made. For example, in the Westergaard case a German news source mentions the deteriorating situation in Afghanistan, and states that the West cannot retreat to some panic room the way Westergaard did (*Frankfurter Allgemeine Zeitung* 2010a). Regarding the Westergaard and Yemen cases, French and UK media mention foreign troop presence in Afghanistan and Yemen only in connection with radicalization in general. The Stockholm case differs due to the pre-attack offender statements about the Swedish military engagement in Afghanistan as one of the motives for the attack. Media thus refer to this point but do not discuss it. Thus, while terrorists would seem to be interested in a Western debate about Western troops fighting in predominantly Muslim countries, especially when this debate leads to a criticism of such engagement and demands to pull out troops, the analysis shows that media are not interested in initiating such a debate.

The dimension of symbolic offences

Media discourse in the Westergaard case expresses a limited struggle over ideas and a deeper discussion on the extent of Western freedom of expression, and the possible limits and potential consequences of crossing these limits. Yet, there is no real interest in understanding terrorism or the offender. Rather, media discourse remains self-centered and illustrates only very limited awareness that people in Muslim countries are very critcal of the Muhammad cartoons. Discourse is framed by the dominant value of freedom of expression, and media call for the defense of freedom of expression and, by extension, Western values of freedom and democracy in general (Germany Report; Italy Report; Netherlands Report; Spain Report; UK Report). While Italian media also speak of Western hostility to Islam and of editors being aware that such cartoons offend Muslims, they too emphasize the value of freedom of press and opinion as well as the need to defend these, especially following terrorist attacks. Turkish media highlight the offensive nature of the cartoons, yet couple it with Westergaard's statement on the cartoons being linked to the freedom of expression. They seem to weigh both equally, if not giving priority also to freedom of expression. Dutch media compare the attack to other cases, such as the Dutch politicians Geert Wilders and Hirschi Ali or the filmmaker Theo Van Gogh. Here, both the need to defend freedom of speech and the issue of possible boundaries of freedom of speech find attention, especially when it comes to religion, but also the question of who can really decide what is insulting to others and what is not (Netherlands Report; *Trouw* 2010), the latter being similar to views in German media. For example, minor voices in German media are more cautious and argue that an open debate is only possible in an atmosphere of respect and tolerance (Herrmann 2010). Dutch media also mention a Danish survey, which shows that 84 percent of the Danish agree with the decision of Danish media not to republish the Westergaard cartoons for security reasons. Furthermore, there seems to be a Western inability to fully comprehend Muslim reactions to and their deep offence from such cartoons. For example, the chief editor of the newspaper who printed the cartoons expressed great surprise about public reactions to them, as stated in a German news source (Klein 2010). Some see only little comprehension of how much Islam influences Muslims, even in the West (Hannemann January 4, 2010; Kreye January 4, 2010). At the same time, however, German media call on the West not to give up its values for fear of attacks, arguing that the West must practice complete freedom of expression. Overall, while the extent of Western values, such as freedom of expression, are to a small degree questioned or nuanced here, the focus remains on the self, the West. Freedom of expression and freedom of the press are of course in the media's own interest and essential for media's functioning. It should not surprise then that a Western value such as freedom of expression, and freedom of the press, is the strongest theme in media discourse. Media are also active here in upholding national values. But in this case media also express a debate; rather than only sensationalizing, media also reflect on the notion of rights and limits to rights. Media discussion in the Westergaard case thus has a strong normative side, expressing parts of Western identity, norms and values. As such, media express also a more active and slightly more critical and reflective role.

However, in the Yemen and Stockholm cases media discourse shows no discussion of symbolic offences. The Yemen case has not led to any explicit reference to symbolic offences such as the cartoons in any national media. Instead, other aspects are discussed, as shown in the next sections. And while in the Stockholm case all national media report on the offender's statements about the cartoons (by the Swede Lars Vilks, and by extension those of Westergaard) and the Swedes' support of the cartoonists as another reason for the attack, there is no discussion or reflection on these statements. Media here fulfill only their reporting role, but do not engage in a debate or offer different views.

The dimension of the relationship between the West/Europe and the Muslim world/Islam

In the Westergaard case, media, somewhat, discuss the relations between the West and Europe on the one side and the Muslim world and Islam on the other side. In this relationship, media discourse expresses the dominance of Western values, such as freedom of expression, and the need to uphold them. Existing links between the West and Muslim countries, such as migration, are mentioned only as background and not as expression of commonalities. Media discussions can be divided into two main perspectives, both of which show a more active media role. One highlights the divisions between the West and Islam, in terms of culture and values. An example is the stated opposition of free societies and Islamist terrorists, where the latter comes with implicit references to Islam. A German news source sees:

> some fundamental values [as] irreconcilable. Freedom and democracy are by no means ways of life that are considered the highest level of human development in the Islamic world. The separation of church and state is not provided for. But even more emotional is the relationship between religion and the state on one side, and freedom of expression on the other side.
> (Kreye 2010, translated by author)

Such statements polarize Western and Islamic values, which can result in the construction of barriers in Western–Muslim relations. The other perspective focuses on the value of an open debate and how best to lead it.

Here, a German news source calls on the West to maintain tolerance and refrain from trying to force its own Western values onto others and thereby risk itself becoming fundamentalist. Assuming the supremacy of Western values could only be detrimental precisely to these Western values of democracy and debate (Steinfeld 2010). Fear is also not a useful guide, as it only hinders open debate (Herrmann 2010). Furthermore the existence of misinterpretations and antipathies in Western–Muslim relations are mentioned (France Report; Germany Report; UK Report). Media discourse expresses calls to differentiate among Muslims, since many Muslims are said to pursue their life without violence. But also the idea is expressed that Muslims need to understand Western values without overreacting. A further aspect in media discourse is the integration of Muslim immigrants in the West, particularly in Denmark. German media place some blame on Danish policy and society, while arguing that some Muslim immigrants may actually pursue terrorist aims. Dutch media call for the safeguarding of Western values within a frame of co-existence. Finally, Turkish media refer to the continuing struggle between the West and religiously inspired terrorism. All in all, media discourse, with the call both for more differentiation among Muslims and for Muslim tolerance, reflects Western society, the value of tolerance and tradition of debate, but also Eurocentric thinking. The tendency is not to distinguish among terrorists, and to a lesser degree also not to distinguish among Muslims. In some instances, terrorists and Muslims are not clearly separated and are placed in close context – thereby, all Muslims could come to be seen as *potential* terrorists – echoing the previously stated Islamist coloring of terrorism in news coverage. The lack of differentiation has already led to resentment, to harassment of Muslims, and to the idea that Muslims are more interested in their Islamic identity than in trying to integrate into Western societies.[6] The discourse on integration needs, views on the existence and impact of distinct values and the calls for differentiation thus also evidence the more active role of media here. Media here position themselves as active players in public discourse on terrorism, generally upholding own (Western) values, while also calling for improved integration of immigrants, in particular Muslims, and balanced views of Muslims.

In the Yemen case, the issue of the West/Europe's relationship with the Muslim world/Islam plays no explicit role. At the most, a German news source mentions that although there are differences among groups such as tribes in Yemen and Al Qaeda, both have negative views of the US (*Frankfurter Allgemeine Zeitung* 2010c). Here, media neither show interest in understanding terrorism nor play an active role.

Neither has the Stockholm case led to an in-depth discussion of relations between the West/Europe and the Muslim world/Islam. This aspect is only briefly referred to in some national media. Thus, German, Spanish and Turkish media express an overall tone of not blaming all Muslims for the act of an individual, since not all Muslims support terrorism. That the

Luton mosque attended by the offender publicly rebuked him for his abnormal views on Islam also finds attention (Germany Report; Spain Report; Turkey Report). Additionally German media report on the Swedish political debate regarding the possible dangers of Islam in Sweden and on the failure of Sweden's political right to use the attack for their own goals (*Frankfurter Allgemeine Zeitung* 2010f). That Al Qaeda now seems to seek more mature, disciplined and selfless recruits for a "conspired community of Muslim holy warriors" against today's Western and Western-influenced world is further stated (Croitoru 2010, translated by author). Italian media see a conflict between the violence and Sweden's relatively free society, with its openness to accommodating people from various backgrounds. Dutch media add that Swedish policy towards Islam is both open-minded and mild. Thus, while media remain centered on the West, not showing interest in understanding terrorism or the offender, media play a somewhat active role. This somewhat active position is expressed in the point of not blaming all Muslims for the act of one and the aspects regarding free societies and open-mindedness. Albeit only to some degree, media do express their own views here. The attack was likely seen to present an attack on (Western) values, and it thus naturally provoked a response in terms of leading to some debate regarding values and how to uphold them.

The dimension of reactions

In discussing reactions to the Westergaard case, media focus on the West, Western values and social measures such as the need for improved integration. Thus, German media mention that immigrants do not integrate well in Denmark, and media in Italy argue that improved integration is necessary to prevent salafism from spreading (Kepel 2010), and report on the Danish government taking such steps after the cartoons' publication (Ginori 2010). There is only indirect reference then to integration possibly reducing the marginalization of immigrants and thereby radicalization. In addition, UK media call on their government to utilize both soft and hard power to prevent Islamic political parties from influencing Western law, though liberty must be upheld. UK media also state that the apparent inability of governments to prevent jihadist terrorism directly may have fostered indirect, and publicly supported, action, such as a Swiss referendum against minarets or the French ban of wearing burkas in public. A French news source also reports on Danish political parties debating the need for stricter legislation in dealing with foreigners (Truc 2010). In terms of technical measures, only proposals regarding more Internet controls to prevent the spread of radical views and the blocking of Internet sites with radical violent content are reported by French media. Thus, in discussing reactions to the attack, the focus in media discourse lies on ways of protecting Western societies from terrorists and radical individuals and views. Media play a partially active and critical role, exemplified by the call to use both soft and hard power and by the interpretation regarding indirect nationalist actions. Both of these points are interesting; the call to use hard power also points to governments needing to take a tougher stance, and the interpretation on indirect nationalist actions both supporting a tough stance and expressing a rather negative evaluation of government effectiveness in currently dealing with terrorism.

In the Yemen case, media discourse focuses on control and surveillance, along with some legislative measures needed for increased surveillance. All national media converge on the need to close national and international security gaps in air cargo and the need for greater control of cargo flights overall (France Report; Germany Report; Spain Report). Specific surveillance and technical measures mentioned by most national media include the banning of all unaccompanied cargo from Somalia and Yemen, hand luggage restrictions and increased passenger profiling, such as no-fly lists for suspected terrorists. However, Dutch media mention the existing disagreement between the US and Europe on passenger privacy legislation. A German news source adds that politicians have long ignored this danger with the argument that terrorist attacks using air cargo would be unrealistic (*Süddeutsche Zeitung*, 2010). German media see the dilemma of security officials that it is hardly possible to know where and from whom to expect the next attack and thus how to prepare, as well as the lack of common security standards in air cargo, which leads to gaps that can be exploited by terrorists; they call for more tailored approaches, with control rigor depending on the safety rating of the country of origin. Some national media also highlight the difficulty of balancing security and costs, as a complete control of air cargo would incur enormous costs (Germany Report; Netherlands Report; UK Report). One option is to zero in on the "unknown small-parcel senders" and check packages already at postal stations (*Frankfurter Allgemeine Zeitung* 2010d, translated by author). But the question of balancing state control and civil rights such as data protection also find attention (*Frankfurter Allgemeine Zeitung* 2010b). In this case, media discourse shows a focus on control, the West and protecting Western countries by closing security gaps. In this, media do take a somewhat active role. Media not only report on and call for the need to improve air cargo control, but actually discuss and debate the difficulties in providing air cargo security, as well as the high costs of doing so. Also the balancing of security and civil liberties is debated in media, evidencing a more active role.

In the Stockholm case, similar to the Westergaard case, it can be argued that media discourse indirectly refers to the benefit of reducing marginalization and radicalization through social measures. The need for improved integration especially is stated by national media, as many immigrants live in immigrant quarters, have no job and are behind in school (Germany

Report; France Report; UK Report). German media discuss possible school and youth campaigns to prevent radicalization, as well as terrorism-exit programs and the role of Islamist centers in radicalization. French media see worth in encouraging terrorist defection.

Media show a more active role when discussing the balancing of security and civil liberties. Thus, in mentioning a new Swedish wiretap law for Internet and telephone connections, which would give greater control to the Swedish secret service, German media warn against too much state control. German media furthermore discuss the need to monitor Al Qaeda communication and Internet propaganda, as well as the role of prosecutions in changing terrorists' motivations. Some national media, however, highlight the impossibility of having all information or total control, or of preventing all terrorist attacks, seeing openness in Swedish society as a value to be promoted (Germany Report; France Report; Spain Report; UK Report). Furthermore, Italian media promote the value of freedom of the press; they also argue that terrorists can use any issue as an excuse for their acts, implicitly arguing against reducing civil liberties. Thus, media take a more active role, not only reporting but also debating different courses of action, especially on balancing security and civil liberties. Media reflection is also evident in views on the adverse living conditions of immigrants and on the programs necessary for preventing or reducing radicalization. Finally, the recognized impossibility of preventing all attacks might actually counter any calls for much tougher reactions to attacks.

Conclusions

The role of media reconsidered

On the posed question of whether media are actually interested in understanding terrorism, terrorist acts and terrorists, or they tend to replicate official discourse, and the linked question on whether they are passive or active, the analysis has led to mixed results. Regardless of the thematic dimension, media do not show a real interest in understanding the phenomenon of terrorism, the terrorist acts or the perpetrators behind the cases analyzed. While media discourse regarding the dimension of policy reactions is focused on the West and not on understanding terrorism or the terrorists, discourse on the Westergaard and Stockholm cases makes implicit references to the benefit of reducing marginalization and radicalization. But these very indirect references do not evidence a clear interest in the terrorist offender. Placing much interest in understanding the terrorist(s) is likely also considered taboo, as media do not want to showcase terrorism. Thus, in the analyzed cases, media discourse expresses no efforts to understand terrorism and the offenders' perspectives or to offer an alternative view on these.

However, depending on the attack case and the thematic dimension, media discourse at times expresses an active media role, with some degree of an active role in about half of the dimensions per case, as detailed below. When broken down for the cases analyzed, media in the Westergaard case played a more active role overall, in the Yemen case a more passive role overall, and in the Stockholm case a slightly more active than passive role. When broken down for the dimensions, however, there is no clear pattern: but in the dimension of Western troop presence in predominantly Muslim countries media play a passive role in all three cases, and in the dimension of policy reactions media play a role that is more active than passive in all three cases. In the other three dimensions, the media role differs for each case and dimension, without a discernible pattern. Clearly, different attacks also evoke and relate to different issues. Depending on the type of target, the means of attack and the damage caused, a different discourse seems to result (this finding is taken up in more detail below). But different attacks likely also touch us as humans, including journalists, in distinct ways. We may relate to the victim(s) sooner in some instances than others, especially when individualized and personalized. And we may feel in more or less danger of such an attack coming closer to our home and possibly affecting us directly one day, again depending on the particulars of an attack.

Furthermore, we find the aspect of ethnocentrism and media discourse reflecting the Western cultural framework. While this Western framework was less strong in Turkish media, the Turkish media discourse still did not present a contrast. Perhaps the best example both for the Western cultural framework expressed in media and the active role of media is the highlighting and dominance of the Western value of freedom of expression, as in media discourse on the Westergaard case. While freedom of expression is, as already stated, in the specific interest of media themselves, here media clearly position themselves as active players. The applied frame of freedom of expression subsumes and thereby minimizes other aspects of the case, for example the offender having been angered by the Mohammed cartoons, and the offensive potential of such cartoons. Thus, while feelings of offense from the Mohammad cartoons may even be partially comprehensible by people in Europe and the West, the frame of freedom of expression as dominant frame in news coverage sidelines possible empathy or solidarity in thought. The fact that only a minority of views further limit freedom of expression also illustrates how dominant the frame of freedom of expression is. News recipients are thus presented with the interpretation that such symbolic offences perhaps do not represent the best or most thoughtful of Western actions, but that they must be tolerated by those who are offended due to the value of freedom of expression. When media thus cover a terrorist attack under the frame of freedom of expression, they shape the interpretation of such an attack, and of needed countermeasures and policy. Moving back to a more

Jihadist terrorism and the role of media 175

general level, media then are active players in contributing to our understanding and in creating social reality in our societies. And although the public reception of media discourse has not been part of this analysis, the details of this would be very interesting to examine in future research.

Thus, if media contribute to our interpretation of events, the need for responsible journalism is clear. This analysis of media discourse on the three cases then points to the following needs, which are brief but nevertheless can represent useful starting points: The Westergaard case shows that it is important not to get caught in an emotionally charged discussion with value oppositions and clash-of-civilization aspects. Both an oppositional framing of issues or policies fostering such opposition should be avoided. The Yemen cargo plane plot highlights that simply applying more controls will not automatically result in more security. As the analysis also discovered a readiness towards a frame of control, civil liberties must be especially guarded in reacting to or covering such an attack. The Stockholm case shows that the greatest benefit may lie in improved integration, so that fewer people in a society are or feel marginalized and fewer can become susceptible to radicalization. To further foster an open and tolerant society, it could be useful if media also report and illustrate examples of successful integration.

Future research: attack types and discourse in Western media

An insightful result that was initially not anticipated refers to the nexus of attack type and the resulting media discourse. The question that requires expanded analysis is then: Which type of attack leads to which type of discourse? The relevance of this question lies in the possibility that terrorists learn from media discourse when planning their next attacks. If it were found that certain attacks tend to lead to certain discourses (and via discursive meaning-making that affect policy), then terrorists could actually learn to concentrate on a type of attack when aiming for a specific response. And while this chapter's focus is not on policy, initial insights to guard against such trends can be derived.

What the results of the media analysis have shown is that attacks such as the Westergaard case – a lone offender against a single person perceived to have committed a grave offence – seem to lead to a *value debate*. While the West, as the results of the analysis show, defends its values, a value debate shows a struggle between values that are perceived to be different or even opposing. Deeply held convictions, based on cultural socialization, are active and shape the views of responses to perceived threats. In part, this is a debate about principles, with a tendency to divide and/or highlight existing differences. Such a value debate can easily facilitate a position of "us versus them," and such division can to some extent be found within Western society, as the issue of self-criticism also arises. While media discourse on this case has shown that Western society overall maintains its values, a possible starting point for initiating a more fundamental debate within the West on values and rights and how far to go to defend them is exposed. Thus, if terrorists aim to promote or create a division within Western society, by utilizing Western self-criticism, they are more likely to choose an attack like the one on Westergaard. Likewise, if terrorists want to accentuate or foster a division between the West and the Islamic world, attacks that arouse a debate on values seem especially suitable. When 84 percent of the Danish in a survey agree with Danish media that the cartoons by Westergaard (and by extension also similar ones) should not be published again for fear of attacks, then such an attack would seem partially effective, in terms of both instilling a fear of punishment in the population and revenge for a felt offence.

If, however, terrorists aim to shake the security apparatuses of Western countries as well as to raise costs associated with the provision of security, then an attack like the Yemen cargo plane plot may be their first choice. As results of the media analysis show, the Yemen cargo plane plot has led to a *discourse of control*, with a clear emphasis on surveillance and control as well as on required changes and adjustments in legislation. Other issues are mostly ignored in the discussions. Such an attack calls for security officials and security experts to improve measures and coordination, aspects that shape media discourse accordingly. It also touches on the need for improved international cooperation. Furthermore, this particular attack has shown that terrorists can create great disturbances and large-scale effects with a relatively small amount of financial and human resources. Al Qaeda even advertised the limited expenditure on this low-cost attack afterwards, expressing pride in having created such transport disruption at such a low cost.[7] It is also significant that with this attack the terrorists have succeeded in getting the West to publicly recognize and state aloud that it is impossible to control all cargo, that air cargo is indeed the weak link in security and that the costs needed for full control of all cargo are too great. One may conclude that air cargo remains an attractive target for terrorists.

The attack in Stockholm, on the other hand, has mostly led to a *broader discourse*, less defined by an overarching theme. Discourse focused on the need to improve the integration of immigrants and maintain an open society, social and economic aspects, views of the self versus views of Muslims, as well as on calls for more differentiation of Muslims and Islam, and some legislative measures relating to the appropriate amount of state control. The broader and more general discourse that has resulted in this case may imply that neither individual terrorists nor organized terror groups or networks will find carrying out another such attack attractive according to their utility calculations (also based on the fact that the attack was not successful). However, as the offender in Stockholm was a single person without any clear network ties, the possibility of a lone individual, having becoming sufficiently radicalized, deciding one day to commit an attack, will always be there. Thus, while the lone terrorist offender may further engage in such types of attack, it would seem less attractive for a terrorist group or network.

The initial findings regarding attack type and discourse require further research for substantiation, and this chapter has laid some groundwork for such research. In addition, the insights offered here regarding the media role in framing and interpretation, in particular on terrorist incidents, serve as a useful contribution to the debate on media and terrorism/counterterrorism.

Notes

1 The project "Technical prevention of low-cost terrorism" is conducted at the Institute for Security and Prevention Research (Institut für Sicherheits- und Präventionsforschung/ISIP), Hamburg University, Germany. The project is funded by the German Federal Ministry of Education and Research. ISIP is grateful both for the funding and to the cooperation partners: Centre de Recherches Sociologiques sur le Droit et les Institutions Pénales, Centre National de la Recherche Scientifique, France; Università Cattolica del Sacro Cuore, and Transcrime, Italy; University of Leiden, Centre of Counterterrorism Studies, the Netherlands; University of Barcelona, and Judicial System and Human Rights Observatory, Spain; Bahcesehir University, Strategic Research Center, Turkey; and Chatham House, International Security Programme, UK. Research includes interviews with national security agency and law enforcement officials. The author wishes to thank project manager Michael Fischer and previous reviewers for their constructive and helpful comments.
2 Nesser found the Iraq War to be one important motive for jihadist terrorists, with the war being the main focus in online discourse of jihadists and their supporters (2006: 324). The war in Afghanistan is added by Bakker (2006: 2).
3 The coding was conducted manually, and validity was assured by discussing results with other researchers.
4 For different constructivist strands, see also Katzenstein *et al.* (1998); Krell (2004); Kubálková *et al.* (1998); Wiener (2006); and Weller (2005).
5 For more on images and national images, see Boulding (1956, 1996) and Scott (1965).
6 See for example Pew Research Center (2005); and while the US was not included in this study, the following illustrates the same dynamics: *USA Today* (2006).
7 According to *Inspire*, an Internet magazine run by Al Qaeda in the Arabian Peninsula (AQAP), the attack cost only $4,200.

References

Archetti, C. (2013) *Understanding Terrorism in the Age of Global Media*, Basingstoke and New York: Palgrave Macmillan.
Bakker, E. (2006) *Jihadi Terrorists in Europe*, Den Haag, Netherlands Institute of International Relations Clingendael.
Bassiouni, M.C. (1981) "Terrorism, law enforcement, and the mass media: perspectives, problems, proposals," *Journal of Criminal Law and Criminology*, 72(1), 1–51.

Berger, P.L. and Luckmann, T. (1967) *The Social Construction of Reality*, London: Allen Lane, Penguin Press.
Borger, J. (2010, December 13) "Stockholm Bombing: authorities ponder impossibility of policing lone jihadists," *Guardian*, p. 1.
Boucek, C. (2010, November 1) "Yemen needs more than our military support," *Financial Times*, p. 11.
Boulding, K.E. (1956) *The Image*, Ann Arbor, MI: University of Michigan Press.
Boulding, K.E. (1996) "National Images and International Systems," in G.R. Weaver (ed.) *Culture, Communication and Conflict: readings in intercultural relations*, Needham Heights, MA: Simon & Schuster Custom Publishing.
Combs, C.C. (2013) *Terrorism in the Twenty-First Century*, 7th edition, Boston: Pearson.
Croitoru, J. (2010, December 28) "Demut und Dschihad. Al Qaidas spirituelle Mobilisierungsschrift," *Frankfurter Allgemeine Zeitung*, no p.
de Vreese, C.H. (2005) "News Framing: theory and typology," *Information Design Journal + Document Design*, 13(1), 51–62.
Entman, R. (1993) "Framing: toward clarification of a fractured paradigm," *Journal of Communication*, 43(4), 51–8.
Entman, R. (2010) "Media Framing Biases and Political Power: explaining slant in news of campaign 2008," *Journalism*, 11(4), 389–408.
Fiske, S.T. and Taylor, S.E. (1991) *Social Cognition*, 2nd edition, New York: McGraw-Hill.
Flood, C., Hutchings, S.C., Miazhevich. G. and Nickels, H. (2012) *Islam, Security and Television News*, Basingstoke and New York: Palgrave Macmillan.
Frankfurter Allgemeine Zeitung (2010a, January 5) "Wohin sich zurückziehen?" no p.
Frankfurter Allgemeine Zeitung (2010b, November 3) "Paketbomben aus dem Jemen. Die Suche nach Tätern und Erklärungen," no p.
Frankfurter Allgemeine Zeitung (2010c, November 3) no title, no p.
Frankfurter Allgemeine Zeitung (2010d, November 9) no title, p. 12.
Frankfurter Allgemeine Zeitung (2010e, December 14) "Glosse Politik," no p.
Frankfurter Allgemeine Zeitung (2010f, December 16) no title, no p.
Ginori, A. (2010, January 3) "Vendetta sul vignettista di Maometto killer tenta di ucciderlo con un'ascia," *La Repubblica*, p. 1.
Glaab, S. (ed.) (2007) *Medien und Terrorismus – Auf den Spuren einer symbiotischen Beziehung*, Berlin: Berliner Wissenschafts-Verlag.
Goffman, E. (1974) *Frame Analysis: an essay on the organization of experience*, Cambridge: Harvard University Press.
Hannemann, M. (2010, January 4) no title, *Frankfurter Allgemeine Zeitung*, no p.
Herrmann, G. (2010, January 12) "Massive Selbstzensur. Dänemark hadert weiter mit den Folgen der Karikaturenkrise," *Süddeutsche Zeitung*, no p.
Hürriyet Gazetesi (2010, December 15) "İsveç 'radikal İslam' raporunu açıkladı," http://hurarsiv.hurriyet.com.tr/goster/ShowNew.aspx?id=16540874, accessed June 11, 2011.
Katzenstein, P.J., Keohane R.O. and Krasner, S. (1998) "International Organization and the Study of World Politics," *International Organization*, 52(4) (Autumn), 645–85.
Kepel, G. (2010, January 3) "L'attentatore della porta accanto," *La Repubblica*, p. 1.
Klein, S. (2010, January 7) "Abgetaucht," *Süddeutsche Zeitung*, no p.

Krell, G. (2004) "Theorien in den Internationalen Beziehungen," in M. Knapp and G. Krell (eds) *Einführung in die Internationale Politik: Studienbuch*, 4th edition, Munich: Oldenbourg Wissenschaftsverlag GmbH.

Kreye, A. (2010, January 4) "Die Wertedebatte läuft falsch. Anschlag auf dänischen Karikaturisten liefert neuen Zündstoff," *Süddeutsche Zeitung*, no p.

Kubálková, V., Onuf, N. and Kowert, P. (1998) "Constructing Constructivism," in V. Kubálková, N. Onuf and P. Kowert (eds) *International Relations in a Constructed World*, Armonk, NY: M.E. Sharpe, Inc.

Laqueur, W. (1976) "The Futility of Terrorism," *Harper's Magazine*, March: 99–105.

Le, E. (2006) *The Spiral of "Anti-Other Rhetoric": discourses of identity and the international media echo*, Amsterdam and Philadelphia: John Benjamins Publishing Company.

Linsky, M. (1986) *Impact: How the Press Affects Federal Policymaking*, New York: Norton.

Lomax Cook, F., Tyler, T.R., Goetz, E.G. Gordon, M.T., Protess, D. *et al.* (1983) "Media and Agenda Setting: Effects on the Public, Interest Group Leaders, Policy Makers, and Policy," *Public Opinion Quarterly*, 47(1), 16–35.

Martin, L.J. (1985) "The Media's Role in International Terrorism," *Terrorism: An International Journal*, 8(2), 127–46.

Nacos, B.L. (2002) *Mass-Mediated Terrorism: the central role of the media in terrorism and counterterrorism*, Oxford: Rowman & Littlefield.

Nacos, B.L., Boch-Elkon, Y. and Shapiro, R. (2011) *Selling Fear: counterterrorism, the media, and public opinion*, Chicago, IL: University of Chicago Press.

Nesser, P. (2006) "Jihadism in Western Europe After the Invasion of Iraq: tracing motivational influences from the Iraq war on jihadist terrorism in Western Europe," *Studies in Conflict & Terrorism*, 29(4), 323–42.

Norris, P., Kern, M. and Just, M. (eds) (2003) *Framing Terrorism: the News Media, the Government, and the Public*, London: Routledge.

Pew Research Center (2005, July 14) *Islamic Extremism: Common Concern for Muslim and Western Publics*, http://pewglobal.org/2005/07/14/islamic-extremism-common-concern-for-muslim-and-western-publics/, accessed September 1, 2011.

Pritchard, D. (1992) "The News Media and Public Policy Agendas" in J.D. Kennamer (ed.) *Public Opinion, the Press, and Public Policy*, Westport, CT: Praeger.

Puglisi, R. (2004) *Being the New York Times: the political behavior of a newspaper*, Working Paper, http://ssrn.com/abstract=573801, accessed May 10, 2011.

Scott, W.A. (1965) "Psychological and Social Correlates of International Images," in H.C. Kelman (ed.) *International Behavior: a social-psychological analysis*, New York: Holt, Rinehart and Winston, Inc.

Steinfeld, T. (2010, January 14) "Unsere Hassprediger. Die Islamkritiker werden selbst zu Fundamentalisten," *Süddeutsche Zeitung*, no p.

Süddeutsche Zeitung (2010, November 3) "Paketweise Ärger. Planung, Zünder und Testlauf deuten darauf hin, dass die Terroristen die Achillesferse des Sicherheitssystems erkannt haben," p. 2.

Sutter, T. (2010) *Medienanalyse und Medienkritik. Forschungsfelder einer konstruktiven Soziologie der Medien*, Wiesbaden: VS Verlag.

Trouw (2010, January 6) "Cartoonist krijgt meer beveiliging," no p.

Truc, O. (2010, January 6) "Les partis danois veulent durcir les lois sur les étrangers après la tentative de meurtre contre un caricaturiste," *Le Monde*, p. 8.

USA Today (2006, August 8) "USA's Muslims under a cloud," www.usatoday.com/news/nation/2006-08-09-muslim-american-cover_x.htm, accessed September 1, 2011.

Watt, N. and Norton-Taylor, R. (2010, December 14) "WikiLeaks Cables: drive to tackle Islamists made 'little progress'," *Guardian*, also online www.guardian.co.uk/world/2010/dec/13/wikileaks-cables-uk-muslim-communities?INTCMP=SRCH, December 13, accessed June 10, 2011.

Wiener, A. (2006) *Constructivist Approaches in International Relations Theory: puzzles and promises*, Constitutionalism Webpapers, ConWEB 5, www.qub.ac.uk/schools/SchoolofPoliticsInternationalStudiesandPhilosophy/FileStore/ConWEBFiles/Filetoupload,52215,en.pdf, accessed January 2, 2007.

Wilkinson, P. (2006) *Terrorism Versus Democracy: the Liberal State Response*, 2nd edition, New York: Routledge.

Weller, C. (2005) 'Perspektiven eines reflexiven Konstruktivismus für die Internationalen Beziehungen' in C. Ulbert and C. Weller (eds) *Konstruktivistische Analysen der internationalen Politik*, Wiesbaden: VS Verlag.

8 Counterterrorism as contested terrain

Performative contradictions and "autoimmune disorder"

Ramaswami Harindranath

The contested terrain of the discourse on terrorism and counterterrorism in India was temporarily obscured on February 9, 2013, when Afzal Guru, the prime accused in the December 2001 terrorist attack on the Indian parliament, was secretly hanged in Tihar jail, a prison in New Delhi (Roy 2013). Following the announcement of this execution, the subsequent cross-party celebration of the Indian judiciary and of Indian democratic values momentarily brought together the major political parties in a show of unity that belied the profound and obdurate differences in their framings of terrorism, the meanings they ascribed to acts of terror, and their advocacy of counterterrorism policies. The concerns voiced by critics such as Arundhati Roy (2013) of the Indian government's anti-terror policies notwithstanding, the case of Afzal Guru attested to the abiding dominance of specific discourses on terrorism and the popular media representations of "the terrorist". "In a moment of rare unity," claims Roy, "the Indian nation, or at least its major political parties – Congress, the Bharatiya Janata Party and the Communist Party of India (Marxist) – came together as one to celebrate the triumph of the rule of law."

For the ruling coalition, Guru's case was seen as a vindication of its counterterrorism strategies, whereas for the opposition, the right-wing Hindu nationalist Bharatiya Janata Party (BJP), it was further evidence of the dangers posed by the Muslim minority in India and of the influence of Pakistan on India's Muslim minority. In other words, as a Kashmiri and a Muslim, in his iconic long beard and cap, Guru filled the profile of a "terrorist" in India. His arrest and imprisonment, the ensuing protracted trial at the Supreme Court, and the death sentence were seen as evidence of the alleged independence of the judiciary.

However, as this chapter will argue, the performativity of counterterrorism discourse in India is indicative of deep and problematic distinctions and disputes in the political arena, and of diverse, and at times contradictory, interests. Implicated here, as we shall see, are the performative dimensions and disparities intrinsic to domestic politics in India. The ruling UPA (the United Progressive Alliance) coalition, attempting to establish its secular credentials, negotiates a complex discursive terrain that includes being sensitive to both Muslim and Hindu religious extremism in India as well as separatist and leftist extremism, while, contradictorily, drawing from the global discourse on terrorism, which highlights the rise in Islamic extremism. The opposition BJP, a Hindu nationalist party, is more overtly concerned with extremist violence and acts of terror carried out by Islamic terrorism, as for instance in the Mumbai attacks of 2008, while the regional state governments, many of which are part of the ruling coalition UPA, are more concerned about sovereignty and autonomy at the state level in terms of counterterrorism policies.

In the West, particularly since 9/11, "radical" Islam has been identified as the key generator of terrorist activity, which in turn has contributed to counterterrorist policies and strategies aimed primarily at particular ethnic groups at home and abroad. The discourses attending to these polices have been, as is well known, much criticized for racial profiling and for contributing to the further radicalization of Muslim populations (Hoskins and O'Loughlin 2007). Al Qaeda has, since 9/11, come to be identified, both by political and security forces as well as in the popular social imaginary, with global terror, against which legal, security, extra-judicial policies have been proposed, debated, and accepted in North America and Europe. India's experience of terrorism however, is markedly different. The subcontinent has, for several decades, been a terrain of multiple terrorist activities, either state-sponsored or practiced by non-state actors, and prompted by ethnic or religious conflict, claims to territorial independence or other kinds of separatist politics, or by Maoist and Marxist–Leninist groups fighting alleged economic exploitation. Over the past few decades terrorism has been recognized as a major force of destablization in the region. As a recent report has observed:

> [T]errorists represent the most serious threat to stability in South Asia. Their capacity to transform the region in accordance with their ideological preferences may be limited, but by their destabilizing influence, they could undermine governance, generate domestic conflicts and trigger another round of tensions between India and Pakistan.
> (Basrur *et al.* 2009: 44)

Consequently, counterterrorism has to recognize and acknowledge the diverse logics that underpin these extremist activities. As the Indian Prime Minister pointed out in his argument for establishing a national counterterrorism centre:

> On the whole, there is broad agreement on the strategy and measures that we must adopt to counter terrorism in all its multifarious dimensions in India, including cross-border terrorism, Left-Wing extremism, terrorism in Jammu and Kashmir, insurgency in the North-East, and religion based terrorism.
> (NDTV 2012b)

However, the majority of counterterrorism discourse in India, as elsewhere, has tended to emphasize Islamic terrorism over other forms of extremism, in keeping with the global discourse on terror.

Counterterrorism is predicated on a shared understanding of what constitutes terrorism. In their attempt to balance rights with risks, security and protection with suspicion, governments in both Western liberal and postcolonial democracies have amended laws, justified policies, increased surveillance, all in an attempt to provide national security. Aligning with the global war on terror has allowed states – democratic, quasi-democratic, and autocratic – on the one hand, to cooperate with other states in establishing counterterrorism strategies and operations across the globe, and on the other hand, to pass laws and other emergency provisions within their borders, which have, at the very least, suspended a few of their citizens' rights. The balance between security and rights has shifted markedly in favor of the former, with states adopting policies that undermine democratic principles. Euphemisms, particularly since 9/11 and the commencement of the global "war on terror," have become a constant presence in official discourse, often used to refer to extrajudicial policies – the "rendition" of suspects, "enhanced interrogation" techniques, and new laws to counter terrorism: the Patriot Act in the United States, the Prevention of Terrorism Act in India, Internal Security Acts in Singapore and Malaysia, and similar emergency provisions in Europe. As Buck-Morss has shown, the rise in unchecked executive power in terms of both legislation and justice is a real threat in Western democracies:

> [w]hat three years ago seemed implausible is now commonplace: the US population has demonstrated its support in free elections for preemptive war, government misinformation, media control, dictatorial executive powers, suspension of human rights, and violation of international and domestic laws.
>
> (Buck-Morss 2006: xi)

These developments have often been theorized as instances of Agamben's "states of exception," in which the executive assumes allegedly temporary emergency powers. As I have argued elsewhere (Harindranath 2009), there is evidence of the state assuming such powers in India.

Focusing primarily on aspects of counterterrorism strategies in India, in particular those motivated by the terrorist attacks in the city of Mumbai in November 2008, this chapter explores the politics of counterterrorism as displayed in both political and media discourses that testify to fundamental disagreements with regard to various significant aspects of the framing of terrorism, and consequently, of counterterrorism policy. The discursive terrain of counterterrorism in India is revealing, not only of profound ideological distinctions between the various political parties, but also of the religious dimensions of national identity formation, the tensions between the national federal government and the state governments, extremist violence in rural areas and separatist politics in specific parts of the country. Counter-terror discourse is therefore, characterized by deep and at times paralyzing differences in understandings of what constitutes terrorism – for instance, for the Hindu nationalist BJP, the main opposition in New Delhi, the murder of Muslim minorities during the riots in Mumbai in 1992 and Gujarat in 2002 by Hindu mobs cannot be characterized as terrorism and consequently falls outside strategies of counterterrorism. Instead, the party subscribes to the idea of terrorism as having a Muslim face and global presence.

Examining these distinctions reveals both the performative dimensions of this discourse, as well as the challenges that Indian democracy encounters in relation to the adoption of anti-terror strategies. Relevant here are Butler's notion of "performativity" (1993, 1994, 1995, 2004), and Derrida's (in Borradori 2003) concern regarding the consequences of counterterrorism for the body politic in democratic societies. This chapter invokes Butler's insights in order to examine the performative contradictions inherent in political and media discourse on terrorism and counterterrorism in India, and builds on this analysis to show how Derrida's concerns are validated in contemporary India. Drawing from Butler, this chapter attempts to demonstrate how the performative iterations in political and media discourse, in this instance, manifest in contestations in discussions of terror and counter-terror, while addressing particular political constituencies and thereby retaining specific ideological positions, and bring into being certain realities with regard to counterterrorism strategies. Bringing about such social and political realities, in turn, has important consequences that include the undermining of the fabric of democracy, its institutions, and its functioning in India. Pertinent here is Derrida's argument that state policies on countering terrorism are an instance of "autoimmune disorder" that weakens the very fabric and existence of democratic societies. This chapter draws from Derrida's thesis to examine the ways in which discursive contestations, the politics that underlie and inform them, and the policies that they produce continue to pose a threat to the body politic in India.

Counterterrorism, performativity, and "auto-immune disorder"

Governments, state institutions, and the media are centrally implicated in ascribing meaning to enactments of terror: "too often what we are told about terrorism is what governments say," claims Susan Moeller (2009: 181). She points to a paradoxical nexus between terrorist acts, the reporting of terrorism, and the relationship between the state and the media in what come to be labeled as terrorist acts. In her view, public perceptions of threat and security are aligned closely with the media's framing of official pronouncements, which are in turn, influenced by government officials and institutions:

> The nature of national security and intelligence policy and crises is such that relatively few people other than those within government can speak with any authority ... As a consequence, how government frames an event or policy becomes the standard way media talk about it – even when media disagree with the government's position.
>
> (ibid.: 183)

The significance of the framing of terrorism, the interpretations of acts of terror and terrorist incidents by the state and its institutions, cannot be overstated. To affirm an obvious truism: counterterror policies are based on these interpretations and understandings of terrorism and its causes. Recent inter-governmental alliances on counterterrorism are premised on an allegedly common cause that unites states and institutions against a perceived common enemy, namely, Islamic terrorism. Much has been written about the declaration of "war on terror" that followed the 9/11 attacks. As argued elsewhere (Harindranath 2009), a consequence of this global war on terror has been the reframing of local conflicts that have persisted for decades as instances of global terror. In other words, there has developed, since 9/11, a consonance in the counterterror rhetoric with regard to conflicts in diverse locations across the globe, in particular those involving Islamic populations and minorities. One major consequence of this has been the strategic re-framing and re-interpretation of longstanding local conflicts through the lens of the global discourse on the war on terror. In a move that foreshortens the history of such campaigns, long-standing insurgencies, as in Kashmir, have been discursively reconstituted as instances of global Islamic extremism, thereby forestalling any possibility of dialogue with separatist movements, installing, in place of dialogue, counterterrorist strategies that have raised concern.[1]

As Svensson notes, "the privileging of global and 'cross-border' traits of terrorism rather than an emphasis on domestic facets, somewhat paradoxically, blurs the fault lines between the external and the internal, as well as between the global and the local" (2009: 30). Universal and universalizing discourses on the rise of Islamic terrorism underpin both the understanding and framing of acts of terror as well as the apologia for special measures to oppose terrorism such as special laws and acts, as exemplified in Indian counterterror policies:

> With the events of 11 September 2001 having been closely followed by the attack on the Indian Parliament on December 13 the same year, the discourse on terrorism in India accommodated itself in the burgeoning idea of *global* risks, pressing for concerted and consensual efforts against *global* terrorism. The debates in Parliament ... show that POTA [the Prevention of Terrorism Act] was being justified as part of

the *international* effort to fight terrorism, and its "statement of object and reasons" clearly identifies the "*global* dimensions" of challenges to "internal security". [Emphasis added]

(Singh 2006: 117)

Butler's formulation and refinement of the notion of "performativity" enables us to consider the discursive dimensions that constitute the contested domain of counterterrorism, including, most importantly, the political and official discourse that underpins state counterterror policies, the disputes between political parties, and the ways in which these are manifest in the media. Performativity for Butler is the process through which the subject, and all its constituent elements, overlapping, contradictory, diverse and multiple, is composed. Even more significant for our purposes is her claim that performative speech acts, through their discursive practices, create that which constitutes those acts. In this Butler borrows from and builds on Austin's distinction between two kinds of performatives: "illocutionary" and "perlocutionary"; while both have effects, the former, as she argues, "characterize speech acts that bring about certain realities," such as pronouncements from a judge or a Minister of Home Affairs, the latter "characterizes those utterances from which effects follow only when certain other kinds of conditions are in place" (2010: 147). The analysis below will demonstrate the significance of both illocutionary and perlocutionary performatives in counterterror discourse. Also significant here is how Butler's conceptualizations of performativity include the idea that it brings into being certain political, social and cultural processes, "to produce what it names" (Butler 1994). In *Precarious Lives* Butler underscores the connection between official speech or state discourse and the media, arguing that many of the official statements are media performances, "a form of speech that establishes a domain of official utterance distinct from legal discourse" (2004: 80). The performativity of political discourse displayed in the media is often a preamble to the enactment of counterterror measures. They enable and justify policies apparently designed to counter terror and offer security. These have included, in recent times, and in North America, Europe, the former Soviet Union, and Asia, the demonization of Islam. Using Butler's conceptualization of performativity in discourse it is possible to locate in Indian political and media discourses on terrorism and counterterrorism both contradictions and iterations that simultaneously bring into being certain realities with regard to national security, and create tensions between different political groups and affiliations.

Derrida's (in Borradori 2003) diagnosis of terrorism and counterterrorism as symptoms of an "autoimmune disorder" is valuable here, as it provides the opportunity to understand and theorize the effects of changes in laws and institutions on democracies in the context of counterterrorism policies. He extends the analogy of a disorder in which an organism's defense mechanism displays an involuntary suicide, thereby threatening its ability to defend against an external aggressor, to locate the consequences of both acts of terror and policies of counterterrorism on the body politic. For him, these include an undermining of democracy and its legal institutions, as well as the demarcation between secular and religious forces within it (see Borradori 2003: 187, fn 7). As will be demonstrated later, this tension between the secular and the religious is particularly valid in India. Among the three distinct "moments" in the autoimmune disorder that Derrida identifies is "the vicious circle of repression" that might result from the "war on terror" precipitated by September 11. That is to say, the various defenses against terrorism could themselves "work to regenerate, in the short or long term, the causes of the evil they claim to eradicate" (ibid.: 100). In the context of counterterrorism policies in India, it can be argued that the enactment and imposition of the Prevention of Terrorism Act (POTA), as well as other Acts that preceded and replaced POTA, exemplify Derrida's contention regarding the cycle of repression inaugurated by counterterrorism, as demonstrated in the alleged arbitrary detention of Muslims in Kashmir by the Indian Army (Human Rights Watch 2011a, 2011b). For instance, as Singh has shown, "[f]rom the Preventive Detention Act, 1950 through TADA (the Terrorist and Disruptive Activities (Prevention) Act, 1985 and 1987), to POTA ... these laws restrict the 'political' by determining who (group/collectivity/individual) belongs to 'the people'" (2006: 116). Given the dominance of anti-Islamic rhetoric in much counterterrorism discourse, this results in the marginalization of Muslim minorities, a consequence of which, he argues, is the further distancing and conflict between these groups or individuals and these laws. The BJP's discourse, in particular, includes in its rhetoric the claim that India is a Hindu country, and its selective interpretation of what constitutes acts of terrorism excludes Hindu extremist violence in which Muslims have been the victims. Particularly pertinent here is the ongoing dispute between the UPA and the BJP regarding the evaluation of acts of terror by Muslim, Hindu, and leftist extremists. As will be shown later, this is extremely pertinent in terms of evaluations of terrorism and counterterrorism, in the sense that the performative distinctions that are manifest in these parties' divergent positions on this are predicated on mutual accusations of the communalization of counterterrorism measures.

The performative iterations and contradictions of counterterrorism discourse

The insights offered by Butler and Derrida, when transferred to the Indian context, carry a particular resonance. For instance, Derrida's argument that responses to terrorist atrocities often depend on a complex set of factors such as history, politics, and media representations is borne out in the current debates in India regarding what constitutes "terrorism" and what is labeled as such, which in turn, influences responses to counter them. The evaluative context is, consequently, of significance, as is the new evaluative vocabulary, which incorporates the performative element as conceptualized by Butler. This section examines media and political discourses in India on terrorism and counterterrorism as manifest in three ways: the global in the local, that is the re-conceptualization of local conflicts with long histories as instances of global terror; the influence of religion and politics, whose performative contradictions are informed by diverse evaluative registers with regard to acts of terror; and the tension between the national government and the various state governments, which is illustrative of the precariousness of Indian democracy.

Seeing the global in the local

In her account of the 2002 "riots" in Gujarat that claimed hundreds of mainly Muslim lives, Martha Nussbaum contends that the BJP, the right-wing Hindu party that was in power at that time, was in many ways complicit in the violence unleashed by the Hindu extremists on the Muslim population in the state. On the remarks made by the then-Prime Minister Vajpayee blaming the riots on the Muslims, she argues that "there is every reason to think that the rhetoric of his speech was artfully constructed to link the well-known idea of Muslim terrorism to the alleged conspiracy in Gujarat" (Nussbaum 2007: 30), and even more tellingly:

> Vajpayee's rhetoric also appeared to position India alongside the United States, reminding people of the real terrorist acts of 9/11, and suggesting to the international business community that the BJP has values very much line with their own (rather than the values involved in ethnic cleansing, which could be, and were subsequently, a definite deterrent to foreign investment).
>
> (Ibid.)

Similarly, Chakravartty (2002), in her account of Indian English language media reports on 9/11, shows how the tragedy was framed in connection to anti-terror campaigns in India. Her analysis underlines the links between reports such as the story in *The Indian Express* on September 12, 2001 headlined "Terror Strikes India: Airfields on Alert, Vigil Up on Border," with proclamations from the then-ruling BJP government ministers. She claims that the party "moved quickly in its attempt to equate terrorism in America with 'Islamic' terrorism in India, particularly with reference to the volatile issue of Kashmir" (Chakravartty 2002: 207).

More recently, Hardeep Puri, the permanent representative of India to the UN, contended at an open debate on counterterrorism in January 2013:

In our globalized world, terrorists are also globalized in their outreach and activities, they recruit in one country, raise funds in another and operate in others and are waging an asymmetric warfare against the international community.... And, indeed, our entire region, South Asia, has been wracked by the activities of the biggest terrorist actors in the world, be they Al Qaida, Lasskar-e-Taiba, Jamat-ud-Daawa, elements of Taliban and others.

Puri's evaluation of terrorism in India includes no account of Hindu, Maoist, or separatist terror. The entire counterterrorism logic seems to be predicated on Islamic terrorism, and countering terrorist activity in India of the kind that is an instance of global terror, against which the "international community" is waging a struggle: "Terrorism today constitutes the most pressing challenge to international peace and security" (*Times of India* 2013).

In an article published in 2011, *The Hindu* quoted from the annual report of the Union Home Ministry records, saying that large investments were made in new measures to "meet the grave challenges posed by global terrorism." The report says that the "MHA's [Ministry of Home Affairs] major achievements include the establishment of new rapid-response hubs for the National Security Guard special forces, and the establishment of an online National Intelligence Grid" (Swami 2011). Similarly, an article in the *Washington Post*, published in 2012, reported:

> Home Minister P. Chidambaram said this month that an umbrella organization is long overdue because India is the target of several militant groups and that "al-Qaeda's shadow falls in this area." The government says it has broken up 51 terrorism cells and foiled 43 plots since the Mumbai attacks in 2008.
>
> (Lakshmi 2012)

The political discourse from the Indian Home Affairs Ministry thus rationalized the introduction of specific policies and the investments made in building the counterterrorism architecture by locating local incidents within the global discourse on terror and counterterror.

This editorial, published in *The Times of India* on November 28, 2008, two days after the Mumbai attacks, exemplifies the media discourse that saw the attacks as of the same genre as other terrorist incidents elsewhere in the world:

> It's War. This nation is under attack. The scale, intensity and level of orchestration of terror attacks in Mumbai put one thing beyond doubt: India is effectively at war and it has deadly enemies in its midst.... On the plus side, there have been unprecedented outpourings of sympathy and offers of cooperation from world governments.

> All the more reason to make the attacks on Mumbai a transformative moment.... *Security must now be seen as an essential element of infrastructure, as vital as power, water, or transport.* [Emphasis added]
>
> (*Times of India* 2008)

Echoing the post 9/11 discourse that identified it as a world historical event that transformed global politics and society, this editorial discerns in the Mumbai attacks aspects that elevate it beyond the national boundaries, placing it alongside other similar acts of Islamic terror elsewhere. The argument here is that India too had become a victim of global terrorism, and therefore the existing counterterror legal and security infrastructure, including institutions, agencies, and special forces, needs to be urgently revised, and that:

> constitutional experts must put their hands [sic] together to see whether under existing laws any special, but temporary, powers can be given to the security agencies.... Besides terrorists coming in from the Arabian Sea, their looking for Americans, Britons, and Israelis give the signal that the attack on Mumbai is a spill-over from the larger war on terror. Al Qaida is, for the first time, feeling the pressure in its Pakistani sanctuaries as it is under Pakistani and American attack.
>
> (*Times of India* 2008)

What is most significant for our purposes are the ways in which global perceptions of terrorism and concepualizations of counterterrorism have affected local counterterror policies in India. It is difficult to disagree with Svensson's (2009) evaluation of how the counterterrorism practiced by the Indian state authorities and the various state institutions such as the army, the police and the judiciary, affect minorities in India, especially the Muslim population. Since 9/11, he argues, the concept of terrorism in India has undergone a "significant metonymic permutation" (ibid.: 29), as a result of India seeing itself as a victim of transnational terror. Examining the ways in which meaning is attributed to terrorism in India, Svensson finds instrumental in this a "*recurring* articulation of a particular logic of blame" (ibid.: 28, emphasis added), which locates the state between blaming domestic Muslim organizations and those facilitating acts of terrorism from across the border in Pakistan. The ramifications of such a position includes, for him, the Muslim population in India being placed in a precarious situation *vis-à-vis* their patriotic and democratic credentials. "Muslims increasingly find themselves situated on the precincts of the Indian 'nation,'" he argues, but they are also "at the very centre of attention" as "the focal point and fetish around which all debates on terror, and many other contentious issues, orbit" (ibid.: 28–9). While several, at times orchestrated, acts of violence by the majority Hindu population are located outside the parameters of the conceptual frame of terrorism, "the distillation of the icon of the terrorist into the silhouette of a Muslim man generates two premises: firstly, terror is defined as equivalent to Muslim terror.... Secondly, terror is viewed as engendered and nurtured in an outside" (ibid.: 30). This outside is conceptualized as both outside the borders of the nation-state, and as "anti-national," that is, those populations (Muslim) who are Indian nationals and yet unpatriotic, mobilized by religious sentiments into supporting the anti-Indian Other outside the national borders. "The index of blame thus institutes boundaries related to the essence and accepted conduct of an Indian" (ibid.: 30).

Svensson's argument exemplifies both the "auto-immune disorder" which, through its counterterrorism policies and practices, is undermining the constitution of the Indian democracy, making its cohesion as a multi-religious and multi-cultural nation more precarious, and the "performativity" intrinsic to the framing of terror and the recurring logic of blame that informs the state's legal apparatus on counterterrorism. The continuing marginalization and criminalization of the Muslim minority in India that results from these policies (as reported in Human Rights Watch 2011a, 2011b) and, more insidiously, from the discourse on national identity that has continued to privilege India as Hindu and locate Indian Muslim communities outside its conception of the nation, is a clear instance of Derrida's assertion. To the Hindu right, the allegiances of domestic Muslim communities are more firmly fixed with transnational Islam rather than with the Indian nation and, as such, "violence targeting Muslims is represented [among the Hindu fundamentalists] as a necessary catharsis" (Svensson 2009: 31). The perceived use of special legal measures such as POTA and its successor Unlawful Activities Prevention Act (UAPA) to target minorities, as argued by Singh (2006) and Svensson (2009), further adds to the criminalization of Muslims, thereby eroding the foundations of the Indian nation-state. The recurrence, iteration, of blame that thus connects the Indian Muslim minority to global acts of terror performatively enacts and re-enacts the global in the local, the universal and transnational in the national. Svensson (2009), building on Singh's (2006) argument, locates in India's counterterrorism laws the mechanisms that position Muslims as liminal within the nation-state, and which, although initially conceived as temporary measures to deal with an extraordinary situation, have become both normal and permanent.

Religion and politics

In her analysis of mediated practice intrinsic to the ascription of meaning to terror and counterterrorism, Kolas employs "scripting" as a core concept with which to interrogate the "wide range of actors who obviously participated in very different ways in the social construction of the 26/11 attacks in Mumbai" (2010: 84). She deploys a discourse analysis approach to the framing of both the November 2008 terrorist attacks in Mumbai and the subsequent counterterrorism strategies employed by the state, with the main focus on tracking the social context in which meaning is attributed to acts of violence and terror. Kolas underlines the communicative aspect of meaning ascription, and the "contours of interdependency between all actors involved in the social construction of 'terrorism' as a meaningful category, i.e. an event and practice that makes sense" (ibid.: 85); and considers the media's complex role in the "scripting" and framing of the attacks and the state's response. While she makes a convincing case regarding the role of the media in attributing interpretative frames on acts of terror and counterterror, it is important to recognize that, particularly in postcolonial, multi-lingual, multi-ethnic and multi-religious regions such as South Asia, political discourse too, through the media, offers similar kinds of "scripting."

In the Indian context, one of the most significant aspects of this "scripting" is in terms of religious distinctions, and the ways in which these collude with diverse conceptualizations of national identity. An instance of this is in the Home Minister's use of the term "saffron terrorism," and the BJP's accusation that the Congress party was "communalizing the war on terror." In a report headlined, "Saffron terrorism – a new phenomenon, says Home Minister Chidambaram," the NDTV website quoted the Minister on August 25, 2010, saying,

> From well-planned terror attacks, to inciting communal violence, the new phenomenon of "saffron terrorism" led by radical Hindu groups, was raised by the home minister at the meeting of state police chiefs on Wednesday. "There is no let up in the attempts to radicalize young men and women in India. There has been a recent uncovered phenomenon of saffron terrorism that has been implicated in many bomb blasts in the past. My advice to you is that we must remain ever vigilant and continue to build, at both Central and state level, our capacities in counterterrorism."
>
> (NDTV 2010)

The report goes on:

> The main opposition party [the BJP] accuses the government of targeting Hindus. "By using the term 'saffron terrorism,' he has directly targeted the Hindus. It is part of the government's appeasement policy," said party spokesperson Rajiv Pratap Rudy.
>
> (Ibid.)

This demonstration of the performative aspect of the discourse on terrorism and the contestation over the scripting of terror mask a vicious politics of communalism and an extreme religious nationalism. As such, it undermines the thesis proffered by Mahajan who, writing prior to the

2008 Mumbai attacks, celebrates the strength of Indian multiculturalism, claiming that:

> [I]n India the multicultural path is being challenged neither by state authorities nor by society. Nor is there a perceptible wave of "Islamisation" in the Indian Muslim community. India seems to have ridden out the challenges posed by terrorism without abandoning its commitment to multiculturalism.
>
> (Mahajan 2007: 319)

Others however, are not so sanguine. As mentioned earlier, Singh, also writing before the 2008 attacks, is concerned about how the state discourse on terrorism in India linked domestic incidents with perceptions of global or transnational Islamic terrorism and, even more tellingly, about how this discourse, and the legal framework that it justified, excluded Hindu fundamentalism. The most damaging consequence, for him, was "the deflection of attention from the communal activities of Hindu fundamentalist organizations while the Act [POTA] continued to be used selectively against the Muslim minority" within India (Singh 2006: 120). At the same time, as demonstrated by the current Home Minister's references to "saffron terrorism" presented above, the ruling coalition, despite the opposition from the BJP, has recently taken a more robust view on counterterrorism that takes into account the activities of Hindu extremists.

Regardless of such recent developments, the concomitant threat this poses for the stability of Indian democracy is fairly obvious. The performative aspect of the BJP's discourse on terrorism and counterterrorism that brings into being and maintains a reality in which acts of terror are confined to those carried out by those from the Muslim minority further marginalizes this minority, questioning their loyalty as Indian citizens while simultaneously condoning enactments of terror by the Hindu majority against the Muslim population. Similar to Butler's arguments regarding the centrality of performative iterations in the formation of gender, the performative elements of BJP's nationalism both stabilize their popular base, re-iterating their construction of India as a Hindu nation, and make the siutation of Indian Muslims more precarious.

National versus state governments

A similarly divisive politics is played out in another domain in which performative contradictions are evident in the discussions between representatives from the national government and state Chief Ministers. The tension here is more secular, between the discourse of national interest and security that is evident in the iterations of central government ministers, and chief ministers of states performing their role of protecting regional interests. This is evident in the dispute regarding the establishment of a National Counter Terrorism Centre (NCTC), championed by the central government and challenged by several state governments through their chief ministers. As revealed on the NDTV website on May 11, 2012, the former's proposal rests on the alleged need for nation-wide coordination of surveillance and intelligence gathering, and for international diplomacy:

> Unfazed by strong opposition, Home Minister P. Chidambaram today said National Counter Terrorism Centre (NCTC) was the need of the hour as threat perception of terrorism continues to be high and delay in setting up the anti-terror hub will increase the risk in the country ... "Given the gravity of the situation, every day we delay NCTC, we increase our risk. We need to counter terrorism not just as a police operation but we need a counterterrorism organization that mobilizes all elements of national power: diplomatic, financial, investigative, intelligence, and police."
>
> (NDTV 2012a)

This position is re-iterated in the Prime Minister's speech to the state chief ministers at the National Counter Terrorism Centre (NCTC) meeting on May 5, 2012, as quoted on the NDTV website: the intention is to improve:

> our counterterrorism architecture and our operational and institutional capabilities to deal with this menace.... It is not our Government's intention in any way to affect the distribution of powers between the States and the Union that our Constitution provides. The establishment of the NCTC is not a State versus Centre issue.... Terrorism is today one of the most potent threats to our national security. There can be no disagreement on putting in place an effective counter terrorism regime with efficient mechanisms and response systems both at the national level and at the State level. Neither the states nor the Centre can fulfill this task alone.
>
> (NDTV 2012b)

The chief ministers' objection to the establishment of the NCTC, on the other hand, rests on concerns that it potentially undermines the federal constitution of the country. According to the NDTV website on May 5, 2012:

> The state Chief Ministers "allege that the counter-terror agency has sweeping powers that violate the autonomy of state governments and has snowballed into a major confrontation ... [Chief Ministers] from 11 more states have registered their stiff opposition to the NCTC which, they claim, is an attack on the principles of federalism.... The Chief Ministers allege that the NCTC has been empowered to search,

seize and arrest without keeping the state government police or anti-terror squad in the loop.

(NDTV 2012c)

In this instance, the conflict is between the performative logics of national security on the one hand and regional autonomy on the other. While the Central government coalition performatively enacts the concerns of a secular State, the discourse of the Chief Ministers, some of whom are supporters of the coalition at the Centre, performatively bring into being and maintain regional interests and the politics of difference based on linguistic and ethnic difference. This contestation thus underlines yet again the precariousness of the multi-ethnic, multi-lingual and multi-religious nature of the Indian nation-state, particularly with regard to counterterrorism institutions, policies, and practice.

Conclusion

Through its analysis of the contradictions, overlaps, and iterations in three sites of the discursive terrain of terrorism and counterterrorism in India this chapter has tried to show how the performative aspects of this political and media discourse both underpin and bring into being tensions between the secular and the religious, and between the central and state governments, thereby jeopardizing the cohesion of the multi-ethnic, multi-lingual, multi-religious nation that is India. As I have argued elsewhere (Harindranath 2009), the collusion between acts of terror and the media has resulted in spectacularizing terrorism on a global stage, for a global audience, and has initiated a novel global social imaginary typified by the suspension of democratic freedoms, enactments of repressive measures, and the suspicion of religious minorities, all of which have had significant consequences for the subsequent imposition of counterterrorism policies and their justifications. The latter, in particular, is revealed in the political fallout that followed the attacks in Mumbai, in which the BJP, the Hindu right opposition party, seized the performative opportunity to frame the attacks as a failure of governance. As Kolas observes, this had chilling and gruesome repercussions:

> [T]he BJP's ideas about the need for strong measures to fight terrorism, including "speedy prosecution of terrorists", were enacted among others through the staging of public "hanging ceremonies" for Ajmal Kasab, the only surviving member of the group of terrorists[,]
>
> (Kolas 2010: 88)

– another instance of both political performance and performance of public affect.

It is easy to see the consequences of these tensions between diverse interests and political affiliations on counterterrorist policies and how ineffective they have been in India. The country has, since independence in 1947, witnessed a variety of insurgencies and acts of terror involving diverse terrorist, fundamentalist and separatist groups, each with its own specific historical and political context, its own demands, trajectory, and tactics. These groups have at times incorporated and at other times transcended religious, separatist, ethnic, and political divides and affiliations, confined themselves to largely rural areas in specific parts of the country or carried out acts of terror in mainly urban centers. In its deliberation of counterterror policies and laws the Indian state has had to recognize sensitivities that reflect the array of religious, ethnic, linguistic, economic, and political affiliations that together constitute the Indian populace. However, as this analysis has shown, counterterrorism discourse in India manifests multiple and at times contrasting interests that have contributed to a lack of coherence in counterterror policy and the development of the state's security apparatus. Moreover, these performative contradictions and tensions have resulted in counterterrorism policies that are either ineffective, excessively brutal, or both, which have, in turn, marginalized religious minorities and can be seen as contributing to the retrenchment of separatist politics in the Northeast of the country, as observed in successive annual reports on the consequences of India's counterterror measures submitted by organizations such as Human Rights Watch and Amnesty International.

The deep cleavages evident in the performativity of counterterror political discourse offer a clear indication of the pressures being placed on the body politic in India. Despite the longevity and the spread of insurgency and terror on the subcontinent, it has been widely accepted that the states' responses have been limited and/or indiscriminate:

> Terrorist attacks throughout South Asia highlight numerous gaps in the region's response capacity. These include a lack of coherent national counterterrorism strategies, which place too much emphasis on the role of the military and security services; underfunded and poorly coordinated national intelligence services; outdated legal architecture; and generally inadequate rapid response networks.
>
> (Rosand *et al.* 2009: 16)

All these were evident in the aftermath of the November 2008 attacks in Mumbai. As this analysis has attempted to demonstrate, one of the main concerns in this regard is the performative tensions and contradictions that characterize counterterror discourse, which were also evident both before and after the 2008 Mumbai attacks.

Note

1 See, for instance, recent annual reports from Amnesty International, which have, over several years, documented concerns regarding the violation of human rights in India.

References

Basrur, R., Hoyt, T., Hussain, R. and Mandal, S. (2009) *The 2008 Mumbai Attacks: Strategic Fallout*, RSIS Monograph no. 17, Rajaratnam School of International Studies, Nanyang Technological University, Singapore.

Borradori, G. (ed.) (2003) *Philosophy in the Age of Terror: Dialogues with Jürgen Habermas and Jacques Derrida*, Chicago, IL: University of Chicago Press.

Butler, J. (1993) *Bodies That Matter: On the Discursive Merits of "Sex"*, New York: Routledge.

Butler, J. (1994) "Gender as performance: an interview with Judith Butler," by P. Osborne and L. Segal, *Radical Philosophy*, 67, Summer. Available at www.theory.org.uk/but-int1.htm accessed February 21, 2010.

Butler, J. (1995) "Burning acts, injurious speech," in A. Parker and E. Sedgwick (eds) *Performativity and Performance*, New York: Routledge, 197–227.

Butler, J. (2004) *Precarious Life: The Powers of Mourning and Violence*, London: Verso.

Butler, J. (2010) "Performative agency," *Journal of Cultural Economy*, 3(2), 147–61.

Chakravartty, P. (2002) "Translating terror in India," *Television & New Society*, 3(2), 202–14.

Harindranath, R. (2009) "Mediated terrorism and democracy in India," *South Asia*, 32(3), 518–32.

Hoskins, A and B. O'Loughlin (2007) *Television and Terror: Conflicting Times and the Crisis of News Discourse*. New York: Palgrave Macmillan.

Human Rights Watch (2011a) *The "Anti-nationals": Arbitrary Detention and Torture of Terrorism Suspects in India*. New York: Human Rights Watch.

Human Rights Watch (2011b) "India: overhaul abusive counterterrorism tactics," February 2. Available at www.unhcr.org/refworld/docid/4d4ba53bc.html (accessed January 4, 2013).

Kolas, A. (2010) "The 2008 Mumbai terror attacks: (re-)constructing Indian (counter-)terrorism," *Critical Studies on Terrorism*, 3(1), 83–98.

Lakshmi, R (2012, May 1) "India's counterterrorism measures remain in disarray," *Washington Post*, Available at http://articles.washingtonpost.com/2012-05-01/world/35458222_1_regional-parties-national-counterterrorism-center-national-security (accessed June 29, 2013).

Mahajan, G. (2007) "Multiculturalism in an age of terror: confronting challenges," *Political Studies Review*, 5(3), 317–36.

Moeller, S (2009) *Packaging Terrorism: Co-opting the News for Politics and Profit*. Chichester: Wiley-Blackwell.

NDTV (2010, August 25) "Saffron Terrorism – a new phenomenon, says Home Minister Chidambaram." Available at www.ndtv.com/article/india/saffron-terrorism-a-new-phenomenon-says-home-minister-chidambaram-47193 (accessed June 29, 2013).

NDTV (2012a, May 11) "Threat perception of terrorism in India continues to be high: Chidambaram." Available at www.ndtv.com/article/india/threat-perception-of-terrorism-in-india-continues-to-be-high-chidambaram-209693 (accessed June 29, 2013).

NDTV (2012b, May 5) "Prime Minister's speech at the National Counter Terrorism Centre Meeting." Available at www.ndtv.com/article/india/prime-minister-s-speech-at-the-national-counterterrorism-centre-meeting-206608 (accessed June 29, 2013).

NDTV (2012c, May 5) "NCTC meet ends without consensus; India needs anti-terror body, says Chidambaram." Available at www.ndtv.com/article/india/nctc-meet-ends-without-consensus-india-needs-anti-terror-body-says-chidambaram-206762 (accessed June 29, 2013).

Nussbaum, M. (2007) *The Clash Within: Democracy, Religious Violence, and India's Future.* Cambridge: Harvard University Press.

Rosand, E., Fink, N.C. and Ipe, J. (2009) *Countering Terrorism in South Asia: Strengthening Multilateral Engagement.* Washington: Center for Global Terrorism Cooperation, International Peace Institute.

Roy, A (2013, February 10) "The hanging of Afzal Guru is a stain on India's democracy," *Guardian.* Available at www.guardian.co.uk/commentisfree/2013/feb/10/hanging-afzal-guru-india-democracy (accessed June 29, 2013).

Singh, U.K. (2006) "The silent erosion: anti-terror laws and shifting contours of jurisprudence in India," *Diogenes,* 53(4), 116–33.

Svensson, T. (2009) "Frontiers of blame: India's 'war on terror'," *Critical Studies in Terrorism,* 2(1), 27–44.

Swami, P (2011, July 14) "Bombings expose India's counter-terror effort," *The Hindu.* Available at www.thehindu.com/news/national/bombings-expose-indias-counterterror-effort/article2224840.ece (accessed June 29, 2013).

Times of India (2008, November 28) "Editorial Comment. It's War." Available at http://articles.timesofindia.indiatimes.com/2008-11-28/edit-page/27928736_1_oberoi-trident-attacks-financial-capital (accessed June 29, 2013).

Times of India (2013, January 16) "Nations using terror as 'state policy' are short-sighted: Hardeep Puri." Available at http://articles.timesofindia.indiatimes.com/2013-01-16/india/36373621_1_taiba-terrorism-asymmetric-warfare (accessed June 29, 2013).

Part III
Anatomy

9 The elusive essence of evil
Constructing Otherness in the coalition of the willing

Jack Holland

Following the end of the Cold War and making use of the intellectual space its demise created, the role of discourse, including its importance in foreign policy, has increasingly been seen as central to the study of International Relations (e.g. Campbell 1992; Der Derian and Shaprio 1989; Doty 1993; Milliken 1999; Weldes 1996). And, frequently, poststructural and critical constructivist contributions have shown that discourse and foreign policy are intimately linked with questions of identity (e.g. Larsen 2007). Constructivist work in International Relations has shown how particular discourses have underpinned the possibility of realizing specific policies (Holland 2012a), including intervention (Western 2005) and enhanced interrogation (Jackson 2005b). And, most recently, discourse analytic approaches have argued, once again, that language has been central to realizing the policies of the War on Terror (e.g. Collins and Glover 2002; Holland 2012b; Jackson 2005a; Silberstein 2002). This chapter builds upon and adds to this literature.

Since 9/11, critical constructivist and poststructural research themes have been fruitfully applied to the War on Terror, analysing the ways in which foreign policy discourse co-constitutes the national identity. Perhaps most notoriously, these analyses have focused upon the peculiar proclivity for Manichean binaries that the War on Terror has re-awakened (Coleman 2003; Jackson 2005a). Not since the Cold War have appeals to good Selves and evil Others received such a high degree of discursive emphases and dizzying repetition (McCrisken 2003). However, then as now, the construction of Otherness has not been a matter of straightforward binary opposition. While dichotomy and juxtaposition have certainly served useful political functions, the argument made here is that, during the War on Terror, the enemy has been constructed in more nuanced terms than pure opposition. Since 9/11, the construction of the enemy's Otherness has been intimately tied to the particular and distinct self-understandings and self-identities of individual states, as pursued by their leaders.

This chapter considers the construction of the terrorist Other, in relation to the fractured Self of the Coalition of the Willing. Despite shared appeals to the essential evilness of enemies in the War on Terror, analysing discursive constructions of threat and Otherness reveal that divergent understandings of self-identity inspired a heterogeneous construction of Osama bin Laden's Al Qaeda and Mullah Omar's Taliban after 9/11, as well as Saddam Hussein's Ba'ath Party from 2002. In making this argument the chapter analyses speeches from political leaders in the United States, Britain and Australia between 11 September 2001 and mid-2003. However, there is a logical focus on language in the days and weeks after 9/11, as new discourses were established, amplified and solidified. All of the speeches and statements of Bush, Blair and Howard, during this period and with a foreign policy dimension (however small), were analysed; producing over 150,000 words of coded material. Speeches were coded inductively with hierarchical nodes using NVivo software. All of the speeches are, or were, freely available online from official government and party websites.

The chapter is structured around three main sections. First, it begins by outlining a theoretical understanding of Self, and Other and how they relate, within a discourse analytic approach. Second, the chapter considers those mutual constructions of Otherness that were so politically important for the possibility of an international military intervention, conducted by a coalition of culturally similar states. Third, the chapter turns to consider the most interesting and often overlooked issue of divergent representations of otherness. American, British and Australian constructions of the enemy Other reveal the heterogeneity that lay at the heart of foreign policy discourse during the War on Terror and was central to ensuring its political potential. Finally, the chapter reflects upon what these differences mean for the possibility and nature of intervention, as well as its alternatives.

Discourse and identity in the war on terror

The importance of language in the realm of foreign policy has long been understood, but has not always been adequately theorized. While politicians are certainly instrumental and deliberate in their uses of language, terms such as rhetoric often fail to grasp fully the role that language plays in constituting that which it claims to dispassionately describe. Language is more than strategy and style; rather, it brings into being that which it claims to deal with but actually constructs. Foreign policy carves up the world, dividing it into zones of greater and lesser danger such as friendly neighbours, troubled regions and distant allies, for example. Foreign policy conducts a mapping – a literal geo-graphing – of friends and enemies. It is a cartographic enterprise, which involves the mapping of world politics for particular audiences, and fills that map with meaning. Perhaps, better than anywhere, this construction of both the 'geo' and 'politics' of foreign policy has been most fully theorized on the borderlands of International Relations and Geography, in the subdiscipline of Critical Geopolitics (e.g. Toal 1994, 1996; Toal *et al.* 2006).

What Critical Geopolitics, as well as poststructural and thicker constructivist accounts in International Relations, has realized is that ideas lie at the heart of a human's interaction with the world. Whether concerning particular values, understandings of identity or a belief in a particular ideology, ideas are seen to sit at that intersection where the material and ideational worlds become irrevocably intertwined. From this starting point of subjectivity, it is a question of considering how some ideas become shared and widespread, perhaps to the extent that they are agreed upon, tacitly and without question, acting as a bedrock upon which more complex mental formulations can be developed. Language is the principal medium through which humans come to share ideas, as they move from the subjective to the intersubjective and back again. Very simply, where language becomes relatively stable, producing meaning in a fairly systematic way, it is possible to observe a discourse. While this systematicity is inevitably partial and incomplete, without the possibility of fixity, it is relatively regular and predictable in its production of meaning. Foreign policy, in large part, is about the production, maintenance and eventual disruption of particular discourses, which serve to generate meanings – about ideas and identities – in a relatively predictable manner.

Consider, for example, the 2003 American-led intervention in Iraq. The meaning of this intervention varies depending upon the discursive field within which one is located when attempting to make sense of it. Was the intervention an act of war, or one of humanitarian assistance? Did the events constitute an invasion and occupation or act of liberation? Alternatively, was this a war for humanity's freedom or easier access to vital resources? In 2003, as now and always, competing discourses serve to produce different answers and different meanings of the apparently mutually acknowledged 'acts' of foreign policy. The 'acts' and 'events' of international affairs are inseparable from the discourses – from the language, ideas and identities – that national leaders put forward as foreign policy.

Understandings of identity, in particular, lie at the heart of foreign policy discourse (e.g. Larsen 1997). The two are, in fact, co-constitutive (e.g. Campbell 1992; Hansen 2007; Jackson 2005a). A policy of 'democracy promotion', for example, helps to construct, whilst being similarly enabled by, a particular American identity, comprising of democratic, benevolent and exceptional traits. A policy of increasing contributions in overseas aid and development funding relies upon and simultaneously can help to establish the national identity of the contributing state as wealthy, altruistic and ethical. At the same time, a pre-existing identity, founded upon notions of altruism and democracy, helps to enable policies such as higher development spending and the promotion of democracy overseas. National identity and foreign policy build upon each other in these moments. They are seamlessly stitched together, as what the state 'does', through its foreign policy, becomes what the state 'is', in terms of its national identity. It is when foreign policy and national identity are seen to de-align and contradict each other that difficulties can emerge for a state and its leadership (for example, Holland 2012b). Consider, for instance, accusations of American torture, which appear to work against a long-established identity of benevolence and a crusading Wilsonian desire to protect and promote human rights. Opposition to this has been vocal, at home and especially abroad.

During the War on Terror, the construction of identity within foreign policy, as well as foreign policy's reliance upon the construction of particular identities, has been a remarkably central feature of international relations. While foreign policy is always about the national identity, and national identity is always influenced and constituted by foreign policy, the War on Terror has been unusual in the centrality of foreign policy discourse and appeals to particularly strong constructions of national identity. Analyses of the Manichean binaries that have underpinned much American foreign policy since 9/11 pay testament to this fact (for example, Coleman 2003). Here, the important point to note is that the identity of the state is always and inevitably constructed vis-à-vis (the) Other(s). As Rob Walker (1993) has shown, the identity of the inside is reliant upon and often defined in opposition to that of the outside. Self and Other relate directly to each other, frequently but not always in juxtaposition.

This binary process of identity formation through foreign policy is perhaps most explicitly recorded in the work of Jacques Derrida, who urged its deconstruction. For Derrida (1997) and many contemporary Derridean analysts (e.g. Bulley 2008), Self and Other are formed in diametric opposition; as the Self constructs its Other the Self in turn comes to be the Other's antithesis. This particular understanding of the role of identity is useful as a starting point for the analysis of foreign policy discourse, but does not necessarily give us a complete picture of the nuanced empirical reality of identity formation. Suggesting that identity forms antithetically, through a fullness, in contrast to its complete and total lack, is problematic when considering the spectral nature of contemporary national identities. Analysts of EU foreign policy have made this point effectively, as it is possible to witness a 'fading gradation' of Europeanness, away from a total core to a more partial periphery, which is not fully European but does not comprise its total opposite either (see Diez 2007; Wæver 1993). This is certainly also true of coalitions, such as during the Cold War and also the War on Terror.

During the War on Terror, the Coalition of the Willing was both united in certain appeals to mutual values, and divided in the diversity of national identities that comprised it. These self-understandings were embedded in long histories of foreign policy and the distinct cultural composition of Coalition states. The events of 11 September 2001 did not wholly wipe the slate clean; rather, the foreign policies of the War on Terror were built upon the foundations of what had gone before in the US, UK and

Australia. Appeals to national identity and constructions of Otherness were conditioned by widely accepted, pre-existing understandings of self-identity in respective states. This fractured coalition Self – comprising the distinct national identities of America, Britain and Australia – inevitably therefore articulated and constituted a fractured enemy Other. Each state emphasized different themes and qualities in the enemy that worked in harmony with particular and divergent understandings of the national Self.

One self, one other?

During the War on Terror the Coalition of the Willing principally comprised three states – America, Britain and Australia – which spearheaded interventions in Afghanistan and Iraq, in terms of troop numbers and dates of deployment.[1] All three state leaders – George W. Bush, Tony Blair and John Howard – were required to justify these interventions to both international and domestic audiences. They converged around a number of narratives and found common ground in several mutual appeals to a Coalition identity, which counterposed important shared constructions of their enemy Other. Often, however, even within mutual appeals to constructions of Otherness, differing slants and degrees of emphasis were evident between coalition states. Here, seven of the most important points of convergence are discussed.

First, all three states made mutual appeals to the notion of a 'barbaric' enemy within their respective foreign policy discourses. This began in the United States, with Bush (2001a, 2001b) hailing the 'civilized world', which he argued denounced the 'barbaric' new enemy. On the eve of Operation Enduring Freedom, Bush (2001c) painted the civilized–barbaric dichotomy in stark terms, with severe political and military consequences:

> The United States is presenting a clear choice to every nation: Stand with the civilized world, or stand with the terrorists. And for those nations that stand with the terrorists, there will be a heavy price.

He insisted in dramatic terms that, faced with these 'uncivilized acts', the 'civilized world' must unite, because this was indeed a 'war for civilization' (Bush 2001d, 2001e). Gradually, this theme became increasingly existential and fundamental, as, rather than justifying a single intervention, it was used to underpin a global war effort. Bush (2001f) argued that 'no civilized nation' was secure in a 'word threatened by terror'. And when faced with the insecurity of this threat, 'every civilized nation' would ultimately resolve to 'keep the most basic commitment of civilization' (Bush 2001g).

In the United Kingdom and Australia, barbarism was also a key early feature of coalition language, as Blair and Howard set about constructing the identity of the enemy. In Britain, Blair (2001a) recurrently portrayed a particular slant on 'barbarism', speaking of Al Qaeda as wearing 'the badge of the fanatic':

> Our beliefs are the very opposite of the fanatics. We believe in reason, democracy and tolerance. These beliefs are the foundation of our civilized world. They are enduring, they have served us well and as history has shown we have been prepared to fight, when necessary to defend them. But the fanatics should know: we hold these beliefs every bit as strongly as they hold theirs.

This subtle difference, as Blair stressed the *fanaticism* of the enemy, is already testament to different understandings of British and American Selves. British national identity, premised on rationality, required the Other to lack the ability to think and act logically. Mired in ideology, Blair's portrayals were centred on terrorist irrationality, in contrast to Bush's appeals to illegitimate violence and Howard's arguments about barbaric brutality.

The second key point of convergence in Coalition constructions of the Other centred on the notion of cowardice. After 9/11, all three coalition state leaders made repeated reference to the 'cowardly' nature of the enemy Other.

> We're facing people who hit and run. They hide in caves. We'll get them out.
>
> (Bush 2001b)

> [The events of 9/11 were] just about the most cowardly, despicable, low-life way of attacking a country imaginable.
>
> (Howard 2001a)

> [We face] an enemy hiding in dark corners of the world.
>
> (Howard 2001b)

Again, however, despite converging around this particular theme, all three states made use of it in slightly different ways with diverging degrees of emphasis. In the US, cowardice was contrasted with American bravery. Repeatedly, the actions of American heroes aboard Flight United 93, which crashed in Pennsylvania, were juxtaposed to the cowardly decision to strike and hide, hit and run, and cower in caves. The juxtaposition of the evil enemy and the good American is a theme to which we return in the following section, since it frequently made use of appeals to American exceptionalism, which were not shared in other coalition states. In the United Kingdom, rather than the bravery and heroism that typified the American response, it was leadership that was offered in opposition to cowardice. In direct opposition to portrayals of the enemy, Blair insisted that the United Kingdom had never been 'a nation to hide at the back' (Blair 2003). The unusual degree of emphasis afforded to narratives of courageous British leadership play testament to the unique geopolitical position of the UK and its cultural predisposition to welcome illusions of continued significance on the world stage. Lastly, it is worth noting that in Australia cowardice also featured, but was a less frequent refrain for John Howard than his coalition allies, perhaps due to the decreased need for Australians to assert the strength of their nation in international affairs. Unlike the US and UK, Australia does not have a history of global leadership. Cowardice, therefore, is less politically useful in constructions of the enemy Other, due to the greater acceptance of a middle power status, into which Australia seems to have grown naturally in recent decades. Challenges to superpower status and resisting imperial decline bring very different political and discursive priorities.

On the third point of convergence, Bush, Blair and Howard all attempted to foster and relied upon a systematic dehumanization of the enemy Other. Again, this occurred in the run-up to intervention in both Afghanistan and Iraq, but was particularly accentuated in the early stages of the War on Terror, as leaders explained the nature of the terrorist threat to their respective domestic publics. Bush (2001h) spoke of 'starving' terrorists out as they 'burrowed deeper into caves', while Blair and Howard both made reference to the 'scourge' of international terrorism. However, in contrast to Bush's recurrent framing of the enemy in animalistic and parasitic terms, Blair spoke repeatedly of the 'machinery' of terrorism and Howard of its 'monstrosity' (see also Devetak 2005). Whereas Bush (2002a) spoke of the need to 'eliminate the terrorist parasites', Blair (2001e) spoke of the need to defeat 'the machinery of terrorism'. Despite these different slants, both appeals underplayed associations of human qualities with the enemy, making a policy of militaristic intervention more likely and arguments in favour of diplomatic engagement difficult to sustain.

The fourth and fifth mutual themes of coalition foreign policy after 9/11 saw the construction of the enemy Other as pure evil, motivated by their 'Absolute Evilness' (Toal 2003). It is perhaps this particular discursive theme of foreign policy during the War on Terror that has received the most widespread and sustained academic analysis to date. Coleman (2003), for example, has analysed the impact that appeals to evil have had in terms of the possibility of counterterrorism, while Jackson (2005b) has gone further still, making explicit the links between language and torture. Such language was most accentuated in the United States, where the largest audience existed for the resonance of these particular framings (Holland 2012b). However, in the United Kingdom, Blair was also able to use the language of evil to great effect, employing bold rhetorical contrasts to create space for grandiose posturing in a quest to defeat it.

Charteris-Black (2005) has noted this strategy and Blair's associated proclivity for 'conviction rhetoric'. Reading his analysis here, in light of variations within the Coalition, shows how particular constructions of Otherness, such as appeals to evil, which were shared by Coalition states, ultimately fed into different and divergent constructions of Otherness, such as a lack of morality (in the US) and fanaticism (in the UK). Moreover, this example shows the inseparability of constructions of the Self and Other, as appeals to evil are pursued in broadly harmonious but notably distinct ways, depending on the cultural context of individual states and the particular national identity, which foreign policy is both simultaneously embedded within and constitutive of.

Sixth and seventh, the Coalition made mutual appeals to the notion that the enemy supported and promoted a perversion of Islam, rather than its true reading, and that the rest of the world stood unified in opposition to such a perversion. The former effectively enabled a dividing line to be drawn between good and bad Muslims (Mamdani 2001), facilitating the claim that this was not a war against Islam and nor were all Muslims culpable.

> Those were people who have no compassion for their fellow human beings. People prepared to kill innocent men, women and children. People prepared to kill indiscriminately, including killing many Muslims. The perpetrators of those attacks in America contravened all the tenets of Islam.
>
> (Blair 2001d)

The latter presented a united front and facilitated the argument that the Coalition represented the views of a unified and correct majority; it granted a basis on which to develop a significant claim of legitimacy. However, unity took on slightly different slants on either side of the Atlantic, as Bush emphasized the national motto – *E Pluribus Unum* ('out of many, one') – and American unity, in contrast to Blair's appeals to international unity, founded on the emerging and solidifying doctrine of international community, of which he had spoken in Chicago in 1999. Here again we see mutual appeals for political reasons, pursued in slightly different ways due to the divergent national identities and cultures of Coalition states. Clearly, appeals to unity served a useful legitimizing function, enabling political leaders to claim to speak for a wide national and international community. However, the need to reassure the nation, combined with the insular tendencies of some parts of the United States, ensured that Bush spoke foremost of domestic unity, whereas Blair's foreign policy discourse was located within the political project he had pursued since 1999.

The above analysis shows that the Coalition converged around each of these seven themes, despite subtle differences remaining evident. And in

The elusive essence of evil 209

each instance, it is possible to understand this convergence based around a combination of political necessity and pre-existing understandings of the national identity in each state, as well as understandings of the wider international community. First and foremost, however, convergence served a political function: helping to make policy conceivable on the world stage (Holland 2012b). Where the Coalition rallied around mutual framings, there was nearly always a political logic at work, whereby shared constructions made preferred policy thinkable and even necessary. Together the shared framings discussed here helped to construct a benevolent, unified coalition, in opposition to an evil, less-than-human enemy, with whom no negotiation was possible. Such shared constructions helped to render military intervention logical and necessary. In the following section, we pick up on the subtle differences in emphasis that were already evident and the distinct slants placed on shared arguments in order to explore important and accentuated appeals to divergent themes, which were informed by the unique contexts and identities of individual Coalition states.

The fractured Self and the elusive essence of evil

American constructions of otherness: evil outlaws

Despite the relatively high degree of convergence that the Coalition pursued in constructing the Other around themes such as barbarism, cowardice and dehumanization, important divergences were also evident. These differences were essential to constructing a resonant foreign policy in the distinct domestic contexts of Coalition states, and helping to legitimize and sustain the interventions of the War on Terror. They also had important implications for the type of policy that could reasonably be adopted and the scope of the policy field within which practitioners and politicians could manoeuvre. First, in the United States the mutually pursued construction of the Other as both being and motivated by a pure form of evil took on a noteworthy distinction from Coalition counterparts.

As the above analysis showed, American appeals to evil were often juxtaposed to claims of American heroism. This heroism included the actions of those on Flight United 93, but also the work of firefighters in the aftermath of 9/11, as well as health workers. And later, Bush frequently contrasted the heroism of the American armed forces with the evil of America's enemies. The narrower narrative of heroism in fact comprised part of a far broader understanding of American exceptionalism, which has a long history in American politics, culture and foreign policy. According to the 'myth' of American exceptionalism, which has been evident since the late eighteenth century (McCrisken 2003), the United States stands alone and isolated, unique and superior, unmarred by the degradations of the Old World and lesser nations. In this understanding, the United States possesses a virginal purity of goodness; America is kindly protected by two great oceans from the corruption that plagues older states (Gaddis 2004). According to the myth, the United States is the ultimate bastion and defender of freedom; in 'her' we see God's ultimate vision for the freedom of all mankind. It is against this cultural backdrop of self-identification and self-understanding that we must locate the binary construction of America's enemies as *pure* evil.

Devoid of these particular self-understandings, British and Australian constructions of the enemy Other as evil lacked the zeal of American counterparts. Part of this zeal was certainly religious – Bush for example turned to Psalm 23 on the evening of 11 September 2001 as he sought to comfort Americans – but it was also a fundamentally cultural construction, which fitted with the domestic American context. This was a context in which Americans believed they were 'untouched and untouchable' (see Holland 2009). Standing alone at the end of the Cold War, Americans understood that they had vanquished the Evil Empire to remain as the world's sole superpower. The events of 9/11 were framed by the Bush Administration as the unexpected and unforeseeable return of evil into the heart of American life. Within American political culture, infused with notions of exceptionalism and unparalleled goodness, appeals to Manichean binaries were exacerbated and accentuated. The War on Terror quickly and readily took on biblical tones and proportions. It was rapidly spoken of as a battle of good and evil, pure positive battling pure negative, and ultimately love versus hate. As well as embedding foreign policy with this particular cultural terrain, such appeals also served to construct and reinforce these themes and the identity to which they were linked.

The second distinct theme of American constructions of the Other revolved around another peculiarly American political and cultural condition. On leaving office, Bush would later lament his use of terms such as 'Dead or Alive', but in September of 2001, appeals to the mythology of the Old Wild West were plentiful and important (West and Carey 2006). Bush spoke of rounding up terrorists, calling their hand and reining them in, as they were smoked out of their caves. Within this discourse, whether they were captured or killed did not really matter: 'whether we bring our enemies to justice, or justice to our enemies, justice will be done' (Bush 2001i). This disregard of terrorist life, through its literal and explicit outlawing, was a logical political consequence of applying a discourse of frontier justice to the War on Terror. Having broken the law, Bush, Rumsfeld and Cheney each spoke in accentuated Western terms about the lack of a need to apply due legal process to enemies on the battlefield and detainees in captivity. It was at Guantánamo Bay, established in January 2002, that this language most obviously received concrete, physical realization. However, it is also possible to trace the conditions of possibility – the background ideas and identities – within which abuse and torture can occur to these initial, folksy and populist appeals to widely understood narratives of 'frontier justice' (Holland 2012a, 2012b; Jackson 2005b; West and Carey 2006).

In the accentuated appeals and reliance on the marker of 'evil' to denote and explain the enemy, as well as the recurrent trope of frontier justice to construct an outlawed Other, American foreign policy discourse was unique and divergent from that of Coalition allies. Both themes 'worked' in an American domestic political and cultural context that was predisposed to hearing them; they resonated with and reproduced key features of American identity. And both themes served important political functions, making particular policies possible, whilst closing down the possibility of alternatives. Appeasing evil, negotiating with those motivated by an unyielding hatred and talking up the need to recognize the human rights of the Other were all made extremely challenging by American foreign policy discourse, which not only resonated but also dominated. Those wary of the Administration's policies were acquiesced, coerced and silenced by the rhetorical force of official language, which stacked the deck in favour of the Bush Administration's arguments and policies (Holland 2012a, 2012b; Krebs and Lobasz 2007).

British constructions of otherness: irrational and undemocratic

As in the United States, at least two peculiarly British framings of the terrorist threat were evident after 9/11. While the United Kingdom shared in Australian and especially American appeals to civilization and barbarism, British foreign policy took on two distinct and divergent slants in making these appeals. First, British foreign policy discourse after 9/11 was unique in the degree of emphasis it placed on democracy as a key marker of the Self and its concomitant lack in the Other. And, second, British foreign policy diverged from Coalition allies in the emphasis that was placed on rationality in the Self and irrationality in the Other. Only three days after 9/11, these themes were already being used together in Blair's mutual construction of Self and Other (2001a):

> And of course it is difficult. We are democratic. They are not. We have respect for human life. They do not. We hold essentially liberal values. They do not. As we look into these issues it is important that we never lose sight of our basic values. But we have to understand the nature of the enemy and act accordingly.
>
> The people perpetrating it wear the ultimate badge of the fanatic: they are prepared to commit suicide in pursuit of their beliefs.
>
> Our beliefs are the very opposite of the fanatics. We believe in reason, democracy and tolerance.
>
> These beliefs are the foundation of our civilized world. They are enduring, they have served us well and as history has shown we have been prepared to fight, when necessary to defend them. But the fanatics should know: we hold these beliefs every bit as strongly as they hold theirs.

On the first theme – democracy – Blair repeatedly made reference to the blatant fact of British and Coalition adherence to democratic values and principles (2001c):

> Look for a moment at the Taliban regime. It is undemocratic. That goes without saying.

It was an appeal that would serve Blair well throughout the War on Terror, as it had before 9/11, and was continued as the terror threat was translated from Afghanistan to Iraq. Blair (2002a) identified Saddam Hussein's Iraq as a threat precisely because of its lack of democratic values. Within British foreign policy discourse, therefore, a lack of adherence to democracy and 'democratic values' was precisely that marker which characterized the Other, but also that marker that denoted the Other as threatening. Indeed, the aims of the Other were articulated within British foreign policy discourse as more than pure evil: they were defined as a desire to destroy democratic values:

> What the terrorist wants to do is to gain their way, not by reasoned argument or by democracy, but by terror. They hope to literally, not just by the act of terror but by the consequences of it, create such a conflagration that they get their way...
>
> [Saddam Hussein is] a clear threat because [he] operate[s] without any sense of democratic values.
>
> (Blair 2002a)

Within this portrayal, the Other – whether terrorist or dictator – was characterized by a lack of democracy, as being motivated by a hatred of democracy and as threatening democracy. With democracy as a core component of the British Self, these constructions had important policy implications, which Blair (2002b) spelt out for the public:

> [W]hen you are dealing, not with another democracy, but when you are dealing with a dictatorship, they don't really understand diplomacy unless they think force is backing it up. Kofi Annan was making this point the other day, diplomacy not backed by force when dealing with a dictator is not merely useless, it is often counter-productive. They have to know that force will be used and that we are prepared to do that.

Force then – military intervention – was presented and rendered a logical policy response against the backdrop of the construction of the Other as lacking democratic values, in direct contrast to the democratic British Self.

Tied to this exaggerated emphasis on democracy, British foreign policy after 9/11 was also noteworthy for its repeated appeals to the notion of British rationality and, again, its concomitant absence in Britain's enemies. At its heart, this argument, like that of appeals to democracy, was about the construction of a particular British national identity that was both democratic and rational. Blair presented one as flowing naturally into the defence of the other:

> it is in our nature to be reasonable, to proceed very cautiously and carefully ... I think that we can proceed in a sensible way ... this is a time for cool heads, for calm nerves.
>
> (Blair 2001e)

> I very much would want those measures to be part of a process that means that we are defending the basic rights and freedoms and those freedoms are essential to our democracy.
>
> (Blair 2001b)

Throughout the run up to intervention in both Afghanistan and Iraq, Blair repeatedly revisited the need for the Coalition response to be sensible, logical and appropriate, with conflict conducted properly. Blair (2001f), for instance, went out of his way to talk up the 'careful, measured' nature of British and Coalition foreign policy. This was, simultaneously, a construction of the rational, careful and measured British Self, in direct opposition to the spectacular destruction of 9/11 and the unwarranted, incalculable atrocities of the Ba'ath Party. Through combined appeals to democracy and rationality, Blair constructed the British Self and enemy Other as antithetical:

> I hope people when they look at Saddam Hussein realize that that is someone who represents the very antithesis of all the values that we stand for.
>
> (Blair 2002a)

Australian constructions of otherness: hateful and divided

Australian constructions of the Other also followed the logic of national identity and its cultural foundations. However, Australian foreign policy during the War on Terror did possess one unusual and less predictable feature. After 9/11, one of the most striking features of Australian foreign policy discourse was the intensity of John Howard's emotional appeals (Gleeson 2001). Howard was in Washington D.C. on 11 September 2001 and watched the smoke rise from the Pentagon out of his hotel window (DeBats *et al.* 2007; Holland 2009). His first press conference remarks were dripping with heartfelt sympathy for Americans:

> [T]he only other thing I can say to you is really on behalf of all the Australians here is to say to our American friends who we love and admire so much, we really feel for you … we feel for our American friends … [they have] been hurt by today's events … like everybody else. I'm numb … I'm unashamedly distressed as a human being about what is happening. It's just awful. And I feel so deeply for the Americans.
>
> (Howard 2001a)

This emotional intensity was retained in the days and weeks to come. It served two important functions. First, it was used to naturalize the offer of military support for the United States in 'anything' they might choose by way of response. This promise came as Howard presented an emotional solidarity as flowing quite normally into the offer of practical support. He also, slowly, evolved the nature of Australian emotional solidarity from a 'sympathy' for American loss to 'empathy' with Americans as shared US–Australian values were presented as having come under attack (Holland 2012a, 2012b; Holland and McDonald 2010). And, second, Howard's emotional language, his repeated talk of love for Americans, helped to construct an especially hate-filled enemy, whom it was difficult to comprehend, let alone engage in dialogue. This was a theme that would remain throughout the War on Terror, as one year on Howard recalled the 'tears', 'compassion' and 'heartache' that defined the constructed experience of 9/11 for Australian and Americans alike (Howard 2002a).

The second divergent theme of Australian foreign policy discourse after 9/11 fed directly out of a mutual appeal to Coalition unity but was inevitable colored and conditioned by a longstanding element of the national identity, which is deeply embedded in Australian culture. Mateship is an enduring feature of Australian popular and political culture. During the War on Terror, John Howard frequently revisited narratives of mateship to naturalize Australian participation in the Coalition of the Willing (e.g. Dyrenfurth 2007; Holland and McDonald 2010). The camaraderie and commitment that the narrative presupposes of fellow Australians was enlarged to the level of the international coalition. And, again, a lack of mateship and a desire to end the values of mateship were seen to define the enemy Other:

> [W]e have to hang onto those values which the terrorists themselves would seek to tear down … we must extend the hand of friendship and the hand of Australian mateship.
>
> (Howard 2001c)

Appeals to mateship tied in explicitly with the broader Coalition constructions of a united international community and an enemy, itself fractured, that sought to divide Australians:

> The things that unite us as Australians are infinitely greater and more enduring than the things that divide us. And the things that unite us, tolerance, fair play, call it, in the Australian vernacular, mateship.
>
> (Howard 2001d)

Howard was clear in spelling out what this meant for fighting the War on Terror with coalition allies that he sought to keep close to Australia. Speaking in the United States, Howard delivered an intensely personal speech, which recounted his own family's and the nation's histories, before reaching a logical climax of 'mateship':

> Most of all, we value loyalty given and loyalty gained. The concept of mateship runs deeply through the Australian character. We cherish and where necessary we will fight to defend the liberties we hold dear.
>
> (Howard 2002b)

Within the context of Australian dependence upon American military security, this was a particularly useful political narrative and national identity to promote. It served to construct a particular image of the enemy Other, with a distinct emphasis on their desire to divide as well as to destroy the values of Australia and its allies.

Conclusion

This chapter has argued that foreign policy is a discursive enterprise; language and identity are integral components of how a state conducts itself in international relations. Two important points can be gleaned from this analysis.

First, this chapter delivers an empirical confirmation of anti-essentialist arguments. Foreign policy should not be formulated on the basis of the inherent nature of the Other, as that nature remains elusive. It is not true that the Others in the War on Terror were essentially evil, but rather that this 'reality' of evilness came to be constructed through foreign policy discourse. We can see the elusive nature of identity in the varying appeals that were evident in different Coalition states as they sought to construct an Other that opposed their own understandings of respective national Selves. At times these variations were a matter of differing emphases, but in other moments wholly distinct constructions were pursued to explain and justify the War on Terror to domestic audiences. The fact that the enemy Other meant different things within a political community as close as the Coalition of the Willing serves as further proof that identity is constructed, incomplete and contestable. The chapter has shown that the identity of enemies in the War on Terror could not be fixed; the notion of an essential evilness in the enemy Other ultimately proved elusive for Coalition states, which pursued divergent framings. Despite concurring on the evil nature of the Taliban, Al Qaeda and Saddam Hussein, the nature and key features of that evilness varied within the Coalition of the Willing. In turn, these variations served important political demands in terms of justifying intervention by creating a resonant foreign policy at home. They also however posed important policy implications for the conduct of the War on Terror, as different identities supposed distinct aims, which required a particular array of policy measures in order to combat them.

Second, this chapter has developed a theoretical argument that builds on the work of constructivist and poststructural scholars in International Relations, as well as those working in the borders of Geography and IR in Critical Geopolitics. Laclau and Mouffe (2001) in particular, as well as those who have made use of their work such as Hansen (2007), have developed important theoretical arguments on identity formation and the language of foreign policy that are reinforced by the findings presented here. For Laclau and Mouffe, as well as Hansen, rather than pure binary opposition, identity formation occurs through a process of linking and differentiation. Identities comprise a number of features and themes that will broadly support and complement each other, such as democracy, rationality and brave leadership in the case of Blair's Britain at the outset of the War on Terror (Holland 2012c). These features of identity only make sense however in opposition to what they are not. Thus the enemy Other becomes defined by the lack of these values, their opposites and as potentially threatening those values. This was the case with the War on Terror. Within the Coalition of the Willing we can see how key features of an American, British and Australian Self were brought together through appeals to construct a Coalition Self, but at times distinct understandings of national identity came to the fore. These were inevitably accompanied by broadly complementary but distinct and divergent constructions of the enemy Other. And these constructions had important political implications, both in terms of selling and fighting the War on Terror.

Note

1 For instance, the Polish contribution to intervention in Iraq, at less than two hundred troops, was ten times smaller than that of Australia, which in turn was over twenty times smaller than that of the UK, and which in turn was about one-fifth that of the US. And, in Iraq and Afghanistan, American, British and Australian forces were committed from the early stages of intervention.

References

Blair, T. (2001a) 'Statement to Parliament', 14 September. Prime Minister's Office. Available at http://webarchive.nationalarchives.gov.uk/20061004085342/http://number10.gov.uk/page1598 (accessed 30 September 2013).

Blair, T. (2001b) 'CNN Interview', 16 September. Prime Minister's Office. Available at http://webarchive.nationalarchives.gov.uk/20061004085342/http://number10.gov.uk/page1599 (accessed 30 September 2013).

Blair, T. (2001c) 'Speech to the Labour Party Conference', 2 October. BBC News. Available at http://news.bbc.co.uk/1/hi/in_depth/uk_politics/2001/conferences_2001/labour/1564434.stm (accessed 30 September 2013).

Blair, T. (2001d) 'Press Conference with Muslim Leaders', 27 September. Reocities.com. Available at www.reocities.com/Athens/Oracle/1722/Lectures/Blair.html (accessed 30 September 2013).

Blair, T. (2001e) 'Statement and Questions and Answers', 12 September. Prime Minister's Office. Available at http://webarchive.nationalarchives.gov.uk/20061004085342/http://number10.gov.uk/page1597 (accessed 30 September 2013).

Blair, T. (2001f) 'Press Interview on Route to New York', 21 September. Prime Minister's Office. Available at http://webarchive.nationalarchives.gov.uk/20061004085342/http:/number10.gov.uk/page1602 (accessed 30 September 2013).

Blair, T. (2002a) 'Interview with NBC', 4 April. Prime Minister's Office. Available at http://webarchive.nationalarchives.gov.uk/20091006031459/http://number10.gov.uk/page1709 (accessed 30 September 2013).

Blair, T. (2002b) 'Press Conference', 3 October. Prime Minister's Office. Available at http://webarchive.nationalarchives.gov.uk/20061004051823/http://number10.gov.uk/page3002 (accessed 30 September 2013).

Blair, T. (2003) 'Address to the Nation', 20 March. Prime Minister's Office. Available at http://webarchive.nationalarchives.gov.uk/20091006031459/http://number10.gov.uk/page3002 (accessed 30 September 2013).

Bulley, D. (2008) 'Foreign Terror? London Bombings, Resistance and the Failing State', *British Journal of Politics and International Relations*, 10(3), 379–94.

Bush, G.W. (2001a) 'National Day of Mourning', 13 September. The White House. Available at http://georgewbush-whitehouse.archives.gov/news/releases/2001/09/20010913-7.html (accessed 30 May 2013).

Bush, G.W. (2001b) 'Remarks to the Press', 16 September. The White House. Available at http://georgewbush-whitehouse.archives.gov/news/releases/2001/09/20010916-2.html (accessed 30 May 2013).

Bush, G.W. (2001c) 'Address to the Nation', 6 October. The White House. Available at http://georgewbush-whitehouse.archives.gov/news/releases/2001/10/20011006.html (accessed 30 May 2013).

Bush, G.W. (2001d) 'US, China stand against terrorism', 19 October. The White House. Available at http://georgewbush-whitehouse.archives.gov/news/releases/2001/10/20011019-4.html (accessed 30 May 2013).

Bush, G.W. (2001e) 'Progress', 8 October. The White House. Available at http://georgewbush-whitehouse.archives.gov/news/releases/2001/10/20011008-3.html (accessed 30 May 2013).

Bush, G.W. (2001f) 'Warsaw Terror Conference', 6 November. The White House. Available at http://georgewbush-whitehouse.archives.gov/news/releases/2001/11/20011106-2.html (accessed 30 May 2013).

Bush, G.W. (2001g) 'Speech to UN', 10 November. The White House. Available at http://georgewbush-whitehouse.archives.gov/news/releases/2001/11/20011110-3.html (accessed 30 May 2013).

Bush, G.W. (2001h) 'Address to the Nation', 7 October. The White House. Available at http://georgewbush-whitehouse.archives.gov/news/releases/2001/10/20011007-8.html (accessed 30 May 2013).

Bush, G.W. (2001i) 'Address to Congress', 20 September. The White House. Available at http://georgewbush-whitehouse.archives.gov/news/releases/2001/09/20010920-8.html (accessed 30 May 2013).

Bush, G.W. (2002a) 'State of the Union', 29 January. The White House. Available at http://georgewbush-whitehouse.archives.gov/news/releases/2002/01/20020129-11.html (accessed 30 May 2013).

Campbell, D. (1992) *Writing Security: United States Foreign Policy and the Politics of Identity*, Minneapolis, MN: University of Minnesota Press.

Charteris-Black, J. (2005) *Politicians and Rhetoric: The Persuasive Power of Metaphor*, New York: Palgrave.

Coleman, M. (2003) 'The naming of "terrorism" and evil "outlaws": geopolitical place-making after 11 September', *Geopolitics*, 8(3), 87–104.

Collins, J. and Glover, R., (eds) (2002) *Collateral Language: A User's Guide to America's New War*, New York: New York University Press.

DeBats, D., McDonald, T. and Williams, M. (2007) 'Mr Howard Goes to Washington: September 11, the Australian–American Relationship and Attributes of Leadership', *Australian Journal of Political Science*, 42(2), 231–51.

Der Derian, J. and Shapiro, M. (eds) (1989) *International/Intertextual Relations: Postmodern Readings of World Politics*, Lexington, KY: Lexington Books.

Derrida, J. (1997) *Of Grammatology*, trans. G. Spivak, London: Johns Hopkins University Press.

Devetak, R. (2005) 'The Gothic Scene of International Relations: Ghosts, Monsters, Terror and the Sublime after September 11', *Review of International Studies*, 31(4), 621–44.

Diez, T. (2007) 'Constructing the Self and Changing Others: Reconsidering Normative Power Europe', *Millennium*, 33(3), 613–36.

Doty, R. (1993) 'Foreign Policy as Social Construction: A Post-Positivist Analysis of US Counterinsurgency Policy in the Philippines', *International Studies Quarterly*, 37(3), 297–320.

Dyrenfuth, N. (2007) 'John Howard's Hegemony of Values: The Politics of Mateship in the Howard Decade', *Australian Journal of Political Science*, 42(2), 211–30.

Gaddis, J. (2004) *Surprise, Security, and the American Experience*, Joanna Jackson Goldman Memorial Lecture on American Civilization and Government, London: Harvard University Press.

Gleeson, K. (2008) *Australia and the Construction of the War on Terror*, Presented at the International Studies Association Annual Conference, San Francisco, CA.

Hansen, L. (2007) *Security as Practice: Discourse Analysis and the Bosnian War*, London: Routledge.

Holland J. (2009) 'From September 11th 2001 to 9-11: From Void to Crisis', *International Political Sociology*, 3(3), 275–92.

Holland, J. (2012a) 'Foreign Policy and Political Possibility', *European Journal of International Relations*, 19(1), 48–67.

Holland, J. (2012b) *Selling the War on Terror: Foreign Policy Discourses after 9/11*, New York: Routledge.

Holland, J. (2012c) 'Blair's "War on Terror": Selling Intervention to Middle England', *British Journal of Politics and International Relations*, 14(1), 74–95.

Holland, J. and McDonald, M. (2010) 'Australian Identity, Interventionism and the "War on Terror"', in A. Siniver (ed.) *International Terrorism Post 9/11: Comparative Dynamics and Responses*, London: Routledge.

Howard, J. (2001a) 'Press Conference', 11 September. Prime Minister of Australia, media interviews. Available at http://pandora.nla.gov.au/pan/10052/20020221-0000/www.pm.gov.au/news/interviews/2001/interview1236.htm (accessed 30 September 2013).

Howard, J. (2001b) 'Address to the Australian Defence Association', 25 October. Prime Minister of Australia, media interviews. Available at http://pandora.nla.gov.au/pan/10052/20020221-0000/www.pm.gov.au/news/speeches/2001/speech1308.htm (accessed 30 September 2013).

Howard, J. (2001c) 'Address in Brisbane', 11 October. Prime Minister of Australia, media interviews. Available at http://pandora.nla.gov.au/pan/10052/20020221-0000/www.pm.gov.au/news/speeches/2001/speech1290.htm (accessed 30 September 2013).

Howard, J. (2001d) 'Campaign Speech', 16 October. Prime Minister of Australia, media interviews. Available at http://pandora.nla.gov.au/pan/10052/20020221-0000/www.pm.gov.au/news/speeches/2001/speech1295.htm (accessed 30 September 2013).

Howard, J. (2002a) 'Address to the National Press Club', 11 September. Prime Minister of Australia, media interviews. Available at http://pandora.nla.gov.au/pan/10052/20021121-0000/www.pm.gov.au/news/speeches/2002/speech1848.htm (accessed 30 September 2013).

Howard, J. (2002b) 'Speech to Congress', 16 June. *Australian Politics*. Available at http://australianpolitics.com/2002/06/12/howard-addresses-us-congress.html (accessed 30 September 2013).

Jackson, R. (2005a) *Writing the War on Terrorism*, Manchester: Manchester University Press.

Jackson, R. (2005b) 'Explaining Torture in the War on Terrorism', *Centre for International Politics (CIP) working paper*, University of Manchester.

Krebs, R. and Lobasz, J. (2007) 'Fixing the Meaning of 9/11: Hegemony, Coercion, and the Road to War in Iraq', *Security Studies*, 16(3), 409–51.

Laclau, E. and Mouffe, C. (2001) *Hegemony and Socialist Strategy: Towards a Radical Democratic Politics*, London: Verso.

Larsen, H. (1997) *Foreign Policy and Discourse Analysis: France, Britain and Europe*, London: Routledge.

Mamdani, M. (2001) 'Good Muslim, Bad Muslim – An African Perspective', *SSRC*. Available at http://essays.ssrc.org/sept11/essays/mamdani.htm (accessed 28 May 2013).

McCrisken, T. (2003) *American Exceptionalism and the Legacy of Vietnam*, Basingstoke: Palgrave.

Milliken, J. (1999) 'The Study of Discourse in International Relations', *European Journal of International Relations*, 5(2), 225–54.

Silberstein, S. (2002) *War of Words: Language, Politics, and 9/11*. London: Routledge.

Toal, G. (1994) '(Dis)Placing Geopolitics: Writing on the Maps of Global Politics', *Environment and Planning D: Society and Space*, 12(5), 525–46.

Toal, G. (1996) *Critical Geopolitics: The Politics of Writing Global Space*, London: Routledge.

Toal, G. (2003) 'Just out Looking for a Fight: American Affect and the Invasion of Iraq', *Antipode*, 35(5), 856–70.

Toal, G., Dalby, S. and Routledge, P. (2006) *The Geopolitics Reader*, London: Routledge.

Wæver, O. (1993) 'Societal Security: the concept', in O. Wæver, B. Buzan, M. Kelstrupand and P. Lemaitre (eds) *Identity, Migration and the New Security Agenda in Europe*, New York: Continuum International Publishing.

Weldes, J. (1996) 'Making State Action Possible: The United States and the Discursive Construction of "the Cuban Problem", 1960–1994', *Millennium: Journal of International Studies*, 25(3), 361–98.

West, M. and Carey, C. (2006) '(Re)Enacting Frontier Justice: The Bush Administration's Tactical Narration of the Old West Fantasy after September 11', *Quarterly Journal of Speech*, 92(4), 379–412.

Western, J. (2005) *Selling Intervention and War: The Presidency, The Media and the American Public*, Baltimore: John Hopkins University Press.

10 The discourse on political Islam and the "War on Terror"
Roots, policy implications and potential for change

Corinna Mullin

The discourse on political Islam as it developed during the "war on terror" years was predicated on what Mamdani (2004) referred to as the "good Muslim/bad Muslim" distinction, in which the latter is viewed as fanatical, uncompromising and anti-Western whereas the former is moderate, modern and Westernised. In recent years, the discourse has adapted to a changed geopolitical context attributable in large part to the "Arab spring uprisings," in which the US has had "no choice" but to engage former enemies (Gerges 2013). Today, it seems more apt to discuss the discursive distinction made between "good" Islamist/"bad" Islamist, based on the relative amenability of the individual, movement or political party to US economic and foreign policy interests in the region. Most important amongst these are adherence to a neoliberal economic agenda, cooperation in "counterterrorism" intelligence and security activities, and maintenance of the regional status quo vis-à-vis Israel. This chapter will explore the discourse on political Islam as it developed in the context of the US declared "war on terror" and, more recently, in light of the Arab revolutions.[1] In doing so, it will consider the ideological and epistemic roots of the discourse in modern rationalism, Orientalism and US exceptionalism, as well as the ideational and material power that has been generated by its hegemonic diffusion. As this chapter also aims to uncover the complex and dynamic relationship that exists between discourse and policy in the context of the "war on terror," it will consider the extent to which this discursive shift has entailed a concomitant shift in policy towards political Islam.

Much has been written in the years following the 9/11 attacks on the various policies that came to be associated with the "war on terror," assessing their failures and successes from both tactical and strategic perspectives and critiquing what many have considered the underlying ideological and material commitments behind these policies (Ali 2003, 2004; Bacevich 2005, 2008; Baxter and Akbarzadeh 2008; Chomsky 2004; Chomsky and Achcar 2008; Cole 2005, 2006, 2009; Scheuer 2008a, 2008b). There has also been a growing body of literature considering the discursive aspects of the "war on terror," and the identity function the "war" has performed in terms of molding the "cultural terrain" and thus impacting upon the parameters of what is considered "possible" and "actual" in the field of international relations in general, and in US foreign policy in particular (Telhami and Barnett 2002). Furthermore, these authors have encouraged a more contextualised and holistic approach to understanding the reasons why certain forms of political violence are chosen by both state and non-state actors at various points in time, calling for "context" to be placed "at the heart of investigation," and "allowing the concept to evolve along with the world, and embedding (counter)terrorism within its wider socio-historical context of social movements, political, societal and economic structures, non-violent social practices, and the like" (Toros and Gunning 2009: 107). Important work has also been written on the way in which popular culture has contributed to constructing and sustaining the "war on terror" discourse (Croft 2006), and on the genealogy of the binary thinking that underpins the "clash of civilisations" discourse, popularised by Samuel Huntington and used to normalise many aspects of the "war on terror," considering the ways in which this discursive construct has been "objectified and disseminated" to enforce certain "political, economic, cultural and social agendas" (Adib-Moghaddam 2011: 12).

However, there has yet to be a comprehensive and systematic assessment of how and why Islamists, or those movements that "mobilise and agitate in the political sphere while deploying signs and symbols from Islamic traditions" (Ismail 2006), came to occupy the space of the enemy Other in post-Cold War US identity construction in general, and in the context of the "war on terror" in particular. It is the aim of this chapter to fill this gap in the literature by examining the relationship between the discourse on political Islam as it has developed in particular over the last decade and the "war on terror" discursive and policy frameworks.

This chapter starts from the premise that a strong correlation exists between state identity, interests and practices. This position is influenced by the constructivist perspective, and views state identity and interests as mutually constitutive, as opposed to the typical realist view, which holds that national interests are objectively defined and impact upon state policies in a direct, and monocausal way (Wendt 1999). The understanding of state identity employed here views it as temporally and spatially contingent; as independent- and dependent-variable, capable of explaining state interests and hence policies, but also in need of explanation itself, often by reference to those same interests and policies. Hence the focus here is on the identity function of the discourse on political Islam in the context of the demise of the Soviet Union, and the concomitant "threat deficit" this entailed to both material and ideational interests in the US (Buzan 2006: 1101). In its dependence upon sets of binary self–other distinctions, the discourse has come to perform an important identity function in (re)producing US' self-identity as a beacon of democracy, progress and modernity in relation to a backward and irrational Islamist Other. In doing so, it also contributed to the (re)production of US material power in the West Asian and North African region by providing it with a seemingly perpetual justification: the need to combat the ongoing threat posed to "our way of life" by the actual or potential violence of the enemy Other. Ultimately, it was the ontological distinction constructed between "their" (indiscriminate and irrational) and "our" (targeted and necessary) violence that allowed for the dehumanisation of the Islamist Other and normalisation of rights violations committed against him in the "war on terror" context.

Considering the above, it is not surprising that for the latter part of the 1990s, with the end of the Cold War and the onset of the "end of history" triumphalism that heralded the US' unipolar moment, US analysts came to exercise such an overwhelming influence on knowledge production associated with political Islam (Fukyama 1992; Krauthammer 1990). In the aftermath of the September 11, 2001 attacks on US soil, and in the context of the policies developed and implemented as part of the US government's attempts to address these attacks and, as many have since argued, to implement a neoconservative agenda that predated them, these analyses gained a distinct, if not always uncontested, authority. Due to the accumulated weight generated by these analyses during the post-9/11 period, they can now be described not merely as dominant or even authoritative perspectives, but rather as constituting a hegemonic discourse. In this sense, the discourse on political Islam has been sanctioned by a time-and-space-contingent "regime of truth," which enables it to, in the words of Foucault, "function as true" (Foucault 1980: 131). As with nineteenth- and twentieth-century European Orientalism, the "regime of truth" that authorises and regulates the discourse on political Islam also determines "the status of those who are charged with saying what counts as true" (ibid.: 131). This means that "no one writing, thinking, or acting" on the subject can do so "without taking account of the limitations on thought and action imposed by" it (Said 1978: 2).

The methodology employed in this chapter borrows from Foucault's "archaeological method" to deconstruct the discourse on political Islam as it has developed during the "war on terror" years and hence uncover both "the fact of acceptance" as well as "the system of acceptability" that underpins it, highlighting along the way the "knowledge–power interplay" (Foucault 2007: 61). In order to explain the intricacies of the construction and maintenance of the discourse, this chapter focuses on its intertextuality, i.e. on the explicit and implicit ways in which authoritative references are made within certain texts and statements to other texts and statements and how, taken together, this body of self-referential discourse constructs and regulates the context in which people make sense of the images and words they come into contact with on a daily basis (Hansen 2006: 54). It also seeks to examine the policy implications of the discourse by examining it as a form of "productive power," capable of producing subjects marked by "asymmetries of social capacities" and "defin[ing] the social fields of action that are imaginable and possible" (Barnett and Duval 2005: 56).

This chapter seeks to examine how certain ideas, language and practices associated with political Islam have become hegemonic in the Gramscian sense, and therefore internalised by the population to the extent that they now appear as "common sense" and the natural order of things, in the context of the US-initiated and led "war on terror" (Gramsci 1971). In recognising Foucault's (1990) observation that "where there is power, there is resistance," this chapter also seeks to understand how this hegemonic order has been contested and challenged by "counter-hegemonic practices, i.e. practices which ... attempt to disarticulate the existing order" (Mouffe 2005: 18).

The discourse on political Islam: roots, development and implications

Alhough the discourse on political Islam has its epistemic roots in Enlightenment-era intellectual, institutional and political developments associated with modern rationalist thought, the discourse gained particular authority in the first decade of the twenty-first century, due to specific political, discursive and institutional conjunctures, including the election of a neoconservative president and the 9/11 attacks, as well as the growing salience of a particular power constellation, including an influential pro-Israel lobby, an increasingly significant Christian right, and a military–industrial complex that emerged and was consolidated in the context of the Cold War. This combination of forces, whose presence continue to act as structural constraints on the discourse today, enabled the modern rationalist paradigm to gain hegemony within the growing corpus of analyses on political Islam that emerged in the post-Cold War period. The modern rationalist approach holds that Islamism "is a reflex reaction to certain political or socio-economic circumstances" that generally arise as a result of the impact of globalisation, outside intervention or internal "modernization" processes (Euben 1999: 23). As such, it precludes a less deterministic, more contextualised and nuanced analysis of the wide variety of movements to which the Islamist label may be applied.

Though US politicians were certainly not the first to employ this approach, their use of the conceptual tools associated with modern rationalism to explain the increasing appeal of Islamist movements in the Muslim world imbued this analysis with an official authority and, by presenting these movements in a way in which their "threat" to the West's security would appear inevitable, contributed to their "securitization" (Buzan *et al.* 1998: 25). As then-US Secretary of State Condoleezza Rice put it, these movements develop in places where freedom and hope are lacking, and, as such, they provide "a fertile ground for ideologies of hatred that persuade people to forsake university educations, careers and families and aspire instead to blow themselves up – taking as many innocent lives with them as possible" (Rice 2003). It was along similar lines that former US President George W. Bush elaborated in his "Proposed Middle East Initiatives" for "Promoting Economic Growth," the stated intention to strengthen and liberalise the economies, media, and educational and judicial systems in the region (Bush 2003). As such, "modernization" and "democracy" are prescribed as generic cures for all ailments associated with the savagery of the "barbarian," deemed to "have declared war on the American people" (Bush 2001).

Similar in substance and rhetoric to other proposals and policies of successive US administrations (regardless of party political affiliation) vis-à-vis the Muslim world, and West Asia and North Africa more specifically, these statements are predicated on a dichotomous understanding of the relationship between Islamist politics and the "modern" world. In this binary construction, the term "modern," despite its cloak of neutrality, actually signifies a specific set of social, economic and political developments and practices that took place across Europe between the fourteenth and twentieth centuries. According to the mainstream Western social sciences narrative, these developments entailed "the ascendancy of reason, science, and statist forms of political organization," including the Enlightenment, the industrial revolution, the emergence of capitalist modes of production, socialism and democracy. More critical analyses take into consideration the foundational role of slavery and colonialism to these (Euben 1999: 22). Despite their geographic and temporal contingency, as well as their idealised depiction in these narrative accounts, all other states in the international system have been expected to emulate these developments. As a result, Ayoob argues that "state making and national building in the Third world" have been inextricably bound to, and limited by, the Westphalian "normative framework," in which secularisation has been equated with "modernization" (Ayoob 2002: 48; Mullin 2010).

The use of sets of binary oppositions, perhaps most importantly the modern/anti-modern one, to define, explain and justify the West's position vis-à-vis its various "others" is hardly a new phenomenon. Although one could reasonably argue that this discursive construction has been somewhat arbitrary in terms of "who at any given time fills the role of other," it is clear that Islam has occupied that role quite consistently throughout the West's modern, and even pre-modern, history (Neumann 1999: 41). Iver B. Neumann, for example, has argued that while the "Turkish other" was vital in the creation and consolidation of a modern European identity that "evolved from the ashes of Western Christendom" between the fourteenth and nineteenth centuries, one can see evidence of the conceived existence of a general Muslim Other over the last 1,300 years of "European" history (Neumann 1999: 52).

While defining the Other in terms of religion served the purposes of Western Christendom throughout the Middle Ages and even into the

Renaissance, by the 1500s, the "Turk" came to be defined less in terms of his religious or cultural deficiencies and more in terms of his temporal distance from a civilised West. Once Europe entered into this new epistmic era in which "reason" is said to have gained ascendancy over religion in the struggle to explain and structure human relations, a new conceptualisation of its adversary was necessary (Hansen 2006: 48). While religion could no longer be employed to explain or confirm the superiority of the European in relation to the Muslim Other, his level of civilisation could. As the former was an enlightened, rational, scientific, progressive – in essence a thoroughly "modern" human being – the latter could justifiably be marginalised or exploited insofar as he/she lacked the various attributes that made the European "modern" (Neumann 1999: 56). A new dichotomy was elaborated in which a "civilized" and modern Europe, "defined by criteria such as 'humanity,' 'law,' and 'social mores,'" stood in stark contrast to a backward, tyrannical and barbarian Turkish Other (Hansen 2006: 48).

It is within this context that the "civilizing missions" of nineteenth- and twentieth-century European colonialism can be seen, with European identity assembled vis-à-vis a discursively constructed backward Arab/Muslim Other (Said 1978), as well as in more recent years the development of US identity as an exceptional state in which a belief in America's uniqueness, "transcendence" and almost God-given role to spread freedom and democracy, or "modernity," throughout the world has led to the US' own civilising missions (Lieven 2004: 35; Morgenthau 1960). Over the last two decades, political Islam, came to replace the general Arab/Muslim, as substantiating the Other in the (re)production of US identity as exceptional state. Related discourses regarding the superiority of American political concepts and modes of governance, such as those that have underpinned the "democracy promotion" agenda, most notably associated with the two George W. Bush administrations, with important elements carried over to the Barack Obama presidency, also came to rely upon this Self/Other binary and the ontological distinctions upon which it claimed to be based. The next section will examine the discursive constructions that came to be associated with maintaining the Self/Other binary in US identity making, as well as their broader policy implications.

Dichotomous distinctions: identity and policy ramifications

While the nations, movements and individuals constituting either side of the modern/anti-modern ("us/them") divide have altered over time, the basis for the existence of the dividing line, as defined by the children of the Enlightenment in their efforts to distinguish between "universal man" and those who refuse, or are unable to see the light, has remained largely the same. On *our* side, with the US at its helm since World War II, you have the democratic, modern, secular states, which participate in international institutions, abide by the rules of an ostensibly "universal" human rights regime, and (at least claim to) comply with "international" law, and which are comprised of law-abiding, rational and civilised citizens. On *their* side, you have the rogue states and the failed/failing states that are antimodern: that fail to respect the individual rights of their citizens, that violate international law (even if this body of law was devised in the context of the imperialist project, at a time when most of these states did not yet exist in their current, sovereign form (Anghie 2004)), that resist neo-liberal economic reforms, that are comprised of human beings who privilege the community over the individual, and that fail to make a clear separation between "church" and state. Although this Manichean thinking is most often associated with Bush's "war on terror" years, Obama, has also employed this language, albeit with a slight tonal shift, to (re)construct distinctions between those deemed worthy of the protection of "universal" rights, of which the US deems itself both originator and guarantor, and those rendered to what Agamben has described as "bare life," a "life devoid of value" in which the "sovereignty of man over his own existence" can be denied (Agamben 2005: 88). As Obama explained in his speech to the United Nations General Assembly's 67th session, only those who make the "right choices" will be afforded "peace and progress":

> We know from painful experience that the path to security and prosperity does not lie outside the boundaries of international law and respect for human rights.... History shows that peace and progress come to those who make the right choices.
>
> (Obama 2012)

Considering the US' ability over the past several decades, due to its extensive economic, political and military might in the world and its ability to influence (both directly and indirectly via proxy "international" institutions) the polities, societies and economies of non-Western states, the West's Other is more often than not non-state actors who reject what are viewed as the illegitimate policies and practices of their governments. These non-state actors often agitate against state power because they desire a state, or an altogether different political configuration, based on some or all of the characteristics that define the "rogue" state. In the context of the "war on terror," Islamist movements, and in the case of Iran, an Islamist state, have been seen to pose the greatest threat to US/Western epistemological and material hegemony in the West Asia and North African region, and hence have occupied the space of Agamben's "political adversaries" that form an "entire categor[y] of citizens who for some reason cannot be integrated into the political system." As such, it is towards them that "the state of exception, of a legal civil war that allows for [their] physical elimination" has been applied (Agamben 2005: 2).

In constructing the exceptional enemy, the "war on terror" discourse has depended upon a false distinction between Mamdani's two "ideal types," where "[o]ne is radical, uncompromising, and bent on a continuous rejection of the West. The other is Westernised and modern" (Messari 2001: 238). By replacing the general Turkish, Arab or Muslim Other that performed a vital function in colonial European, and later neo-imperial American identity and power constellations, as described so eloquently in Edward Said's (1978) work, the former, the "bad Muslim," has been subsumed by what Todorov refers to as the "axiological axis." Having been relegated to this category in the context of the "war on terror," political Islam is subjected to the expression of negative judgment in relation to self (e.g. good/bad, superior/inferior) in order to justify the often violent imposition of the Self on to the Other (Todorov 1984).

The latter ideal type in this discursive construction, the "good Muslim," falls under Todorov's "epistemic axis," in which the Self is defined by either emphasising similarities with the Other, or denying the Other's existence altogether (Messari 2001). If possible, the Other is to be embraced and transformed into an (albeit lesser) version of the West's "modern" Self (Messari 2001). In this case, the Muslim Other is acceptable so long as he assimilates, and hence relinquishes both strategic and ontological challenges. In the context of the "war on terror," the "good" Muslims were those largely secular states that provided military, security and intelligence cooperation, adhered to the "war on terror" discourse, and refrained from challenging other US foreign policy red lines, including in regards to Israel and neoliberal economic policies. Throughout the "war on terror" the Islamist Other came to occupy the axiological axis. On the basis of this categorisation, a wide range of Islamist opposition, including political actors from the Lebanese Shia nationalist–Islamist political party Hezbollah to the Sunni global jihadi Al Qaeda, became the target for ontological and physical elimination (Mullin 2011).

As a result of this distinction, the US government has often turned a blind eye to, or worse, been complicit in, the abuse of power, political repression, and large-scale human rights violations carried out by authoritarian regimes that claim to be acting in the name of their own respective "war[s] on terror," as it did with the actions of right-wing authoritarian regimes across the world throughout the Cold War. As Bush declared in a joint news conference with French President Jacques Chirac on November 6, 2001: "You are either with us or against us" (Bush 2001). Many of the "good Muslim" leaders in the region took this statement to be an implicit endorsement of their repression of political dissent, so long as they provided discursive, intelligence and military cooperation and carried out this repression in the name of fighting "terrorism" (Mullin and Shahshahani 2011). The Bush administration, in turn, depended upon its "war on terror" partners for the outsourcing of "counterterrorism" practices and increased military and intelligence cooperation, much of which resulted in gross human rights violations against the citizens of these states (Hajjar 2011). It is not surprising that US support for repressive, autocratic regimes in the region, including their use of the "war on terror" paradigm to justify the repression of Islamist opposition, has been one of the key grievances expressed by protesters involved in the recent uprisings.

It was under President Bush that the "enemy combatants" label first emerged, "producing a legally unnameable and unclassifiable being," in order to justify the unethical and often illegal treatment of "bad Muslims" caught in the course of the "war on terror" outside the confines of both US and international law (Agamben 2005: 3). All of this is a testament to the US' self-perception as an exceptional state, and its assumption of the position of ultimate "sovereign" in the international system, which entails the power to decide the state of exception where law is indefinitely "suspended" without being abrogated (Agamben 2005). As Mouffe argues, this discursive construction of the "opponent" as "absolute enemy," in which he is "declared criminal and inhuman," locates him beyond the normal boundaries of law and human rights, with "all limits to hostility eliminated" (Mouffe 2005: 80).

Having been relegated to the "axiological axis" Islamist movements and individuals are susceptible to policies associated with the US-declared "state of exception," including invasion, targeted assassination, extraordinary rendition, indefinite detention without charge, and other unethical and, to a large extent, illegal practices associated with the "war on terror." The following section will consider in further detail the discursive processes by which Islamists have been relegated to the "axiological axis" and some of the specific policy implications that have resulted from this discursive placing.

Prominent features: "ideologisation of terror," securitisation and ontological distinctions

In the context of the early years of the "war on terror," a majority of Islamist movements were considered "bad Muslims" and hence relegated to the "axiological axis." As such, they were securitised, and hence constructed as a threat to the national security of individual (Western, or pro-Western) states, or even, occasionally, to the entire international order. When considered solely within this security framework, the diversity that exists between and within Islamist movements is often overlooked. This diversity includes positions adopted on pressing theological, political, economic and social issues, as well as "different conceptions both of the appropriate spheres (political, religious, military) in which to act and of the kinds of action that are legitimate and appropriate" (International Crisis Group 2005). Also disregarded are the more substantive challenges (beyond security) that these movements may actually pose to the "international order" on the epistemic and ideological, as opposed to mere strategic, levels (Mullin 2010). As such, the three most prominent features of the discourse discussed in this section will be: (1) the tendency to "ideologize terror" (Burgat 2005); (2) the tendency to conflate Islamist movements and to view them solely within a security/counterterrorism framework; and (3) the tendency to employ double standards when distinguishing between what is regarded as legitimate and what is regarded as illegitimate use of political violence.

In discursively constructing terrorism as ideology, the first tendency is to assume that the sole aim of Islamist movements is the physical destruction of individuals and symbols associated with the power of a decadent and sinful, or "democratic" and "free" West. This aspect of the discourse is predicated on the construction of an organic and inextricable link between the *raisons d'être* of these movements and the tactics or strategies they employ. Moreover, the "ideologization of terror" perspective implicitly denies issues of power, and the specific political and security contexts in which these tactics and strategies are adopted, often as a last resort. Instead, it either focuses largely on economic factors – assuming that the Islamist is under the influence of "false consciousness," and merely reacting to material frustration caused by underdevelopment, inequality, globalisation, and so on – or, in orientalist fashion, it blames the violence either on some pathological predisposition of Muslims, or on their adherence to *jihad*, patently misconstrued as ideology rather than theological concept. As these movements are reduced to the tactics/strategies they sometimes employ, it is deemed unnecessary to understand the context in which these tactics/strategies are chosen, and hence the motives behind their use. As one prominent Israeli analyst stated: "Motives are entirely irrelevant to the concept of political terrorism.... At best, they are empirical regularities associated with terrorism. More often they simply confuse analysis" (Ganor 1999: 6).

Underlying these ideologisation-of-terror analyses is the assumption that it is pointless to look to the history of Western imperialism, Western support for repressive regimes, or the ongoing Israeli colonisation of Palestinian land to comprehend the actions of these movements, as all of this is mere rhetorical justification for an age-old, irrational hatred of the West/Israel. Dore Gold, the former Israeli diplomat and influential policy analyst, claims to trace the historical roots of the violent tactics employed by national and transnational Islamist movements, while completely overlooking the specific religious, social and political contexts in which these movements developed:

> People do not just decide spontaneously that they are going to hijack an aircraft, crash it into a building, and commit mass murder (and take their own lives) because of some political grievance or sense of economic deprivation. No, there is another critical component of terrorism that has generally been overlooked in the West: the ideological motivation to slaughter thousands of innocent people.
>
> (Gold 2003: 6)

Discourse on political Islam 231

And what is that ideology? The ideology of "martyrdom and its rewards in the afterlife" as if this concept can be viewed outside the religious texts (such as the *Qur'an* and *hadith*) and the long tradition of Islamic jurisprudence and philosophical reflections on the subject, or without taking into consideration the socio-economic and political context in which these movements have developed (Gold 2003: 6).

A recent opinion piece penned for the *New York Times* is emblematic of this tendency. In it, the author compares the political violence employed by presumably Islamist fighters in Gaza to the violence of "rampage shooters," such as Adam Lanza, responsible for the recent attack on an elementary school in Connecticut, in which 26 people were killed (Lankford 2012). Lankford attributes various irrational aims to suicide bombers, including vengeance against those "deemed responsible" for their suffering, irrationally transposed onto an "entire type or category of people," as well as the promise that they "will be honoured and celebrated as 'martyrs' after their deaths," which is why "terrorist organizations produce martyrdom videos and memorabilia so that other desperate souls will volunteer to [similarly] blow themselves up" (Lankford 2012).

This approach results in what Mamdani (2007) calls the "depoliticization of violence," where focus is overwhelmingly placed on the tactics employed by these movements, as opposed to their motivations or desired ends. These often include, contrary to mainstream opinion, very "rational" "cultural demands, in addition to political ones (nationalist, anti-imperialist and even 'democratic')" (Burgat 2005: xvi).

Not only is context and motivation ignored in analyses of Islamist movements discursively relegated to the "axiological axis," but so too is substance. Since these movements and organisations are seen solely in terms of the threat they pose to the West, it is thought unnecessary to attempt to understand their particular histories, paths of development and ideologies in their own terms, resulting in the second tendency, the conflation of diverse Islamist movements. Thus, Hamas, an Islamo-nationlist movement with roots in the Muslim Brotherhood and whose *raison d'être* lies in its effort to end the Israeli occupation of Palestine, can be subsumed within the same category as movements with very different theological, political and strategic outlooks, such as *al-Jama'a al-islamiyya* ("the Islamic Group"), an Egyptian *jihadi* organisation (International Crisis Group 2005: 18) particularly active in the 1990s and influenced by the philosophy of Sayyid Qutb (Kepel 1986), and al Qaeda, a messianic global network which combines Salafi and Qutbist elements in its violent struggle against both external and internal enemies (Esposito and DeLong-Bas 2003: 252–75). This tendency is evidenced most emblematically in the conflation of Al Qaeda and the Taliban, another Islamo-nationalist movement, in discussions around "combating extremism" in Afghanistan and Pakistan. As Gerges (2009) points out: "[Obama] has bought the false, technical claim that the Afghan Taliban, and Osama bin Laden's al Qaeda function more or less as a single entity," as demonstrated in statements made by Harold Koh, a US State Department legal adviser to the Obama administration, justifying the use of drone attacks in the face of criticism challenging their morality and legality under international law (Qureshi 2010; Rogers 2010). According to Koh:

> The US is in armed conflict with al-Qaeda as well as the Taliban and associated forces in response to the horrific acts of 9/11 and may use force consistent with its right to self-defense under international law ... [Individuals] who are part of such armed groups are belligerents and, therefore, lawful targets under international law.
> (Cited in Lobe 2010)

The third tendency of this discourse is to construct an ontological distinction between *our* and *their* violence. Having been relegated to the "axiological axis," instances of political violence employed by Islamist movements are judged by separate, and unequal, criteria. As such, distinctions are made between what the discourse holds is the West's humane and even moral strategies and tactics, on the one hand, and those of their "barbarian" foes, on the other. As Choudhury (2006: 1) argues, this discursive device is used as a means not only to justify particularly grim elements of the "war on terror," which it might otherwise be difficult for the "civilised" world to countenance, but also as a way to construct or consolidate US national identity, similar to the way in which the idea of the backward, violent and irrational Oriental Other was employed during the imperial era. This approach also fails to consider the dynamic nature of political violence, overlooking the ways non-state actor violence often operates in interaction with more sophisticated and brutal state violence. According to this logic, the West, and often Israel as its civilisation proxy, is constructed as "ontologically civilised, humane, reasonable and innocent," in contrast to the Islamist enemy, who is inherently "barbaric, irrational, uncivilised and *a priori* culpable" (Choudhury 2006: 2). The violence of the former is therefore distinguished from the latter in its legitimacy and lawfulness.

Responses to the November 2012 Israeli assault on Gaza, "Operation Pillar of Cloud," are demonstrative of how this logic continues to underpin US discourse and policy vis-à-vis the Palestinian nationalist–Islamist movement Hamas. The asymmetric nature of the November "conflict" between Israel and Hamas-led Gaza was demonstrated by the gross imbalance in deaths and causalities sustained on both sides respectively over the eight days of fighting, with 163 Palestinians killed, including 30 children, and over 1,200 wounded, while, on the other side, six Israelis were killed, four of whom were soldiers, and 224 wounded by Palestinian rocket fire (Bomse and Leas 2012). There has also been widespread agreement that Israel initiated the latest cycle of violence, not only through the ongoing structural violence caused by its long-term blockade of the Gaza strip (Levine 2012), with its harsh restrictions on the movement of people and goods, leading the UN Environment Program (UNEP) in an August report to say that by 2020 Gaza would be unliveable (Alpert 2012), but also through its unprovoked killing of several Palestinian civilians (Levine 2012) as well as the targeted assassination of Hamas security chief Ahmed Jabari, who was involved in negotiating an Egyptian-brokered comprehensive, long-term cease-fire with Israel at the time of his assassination (Baskin 2012). Nevertheless, the Obama administration came out in "full support of Israel's right to defend itself from missiles landing on people's homes and workplaces and potentially killing civilians" (Bruce and Ninan 2012). On the other hand, when it came to Hamas' violence, the administration stressed: "There is no justification for the violence that Hamas and other terrorist organizations are employing against the people of Israel. We call on those responsible to stop these cowardly acts immediately" (Rice 2012). As is the norm in this discourse, Rice went on to conflate diverse Islamist movements, in this case the democratically elected Hamas with generic Palestinian "terrorist organizations."

Another important discursive and foreign policy area where the US ontologically distinguishes between the violence and/or potential violence of an Islamist Other, in this case an Islamist state, and the violence and/or potential violence of its regional civilisational proxy, is the case of Iran's alleged nuclear development. In his 2012 speech to the UN General Assembly, Obama proclaimed: "In Iran, we see where the path of a violent and unaccountable ideology leads.... It would threaten the elimination of Israel, the security of Gulf nations, and the stability of the global economy" (Obama 2012).

The Obama administration has accused Iran of inciting an "arms race" in Western Asia, despite its repeated promises to the international community that its nuclear programme is for peaceful energy purposes only, a position that seems to have been reaffirmed by the consensus view of America's 16 intelligence agencies that "Iran had abandoned its nuclear weapons program years earlier" (Gowan 2012). The picture presented here also confuses cause and effect, a result of Iran's relegation to the "axiological axis" in which its culpability vis-à-vis an ontologically innocent West/Israel, is automatically assumed. Even if Iran were perpetuating the arms race in the region by working to develop nuclear weapons, it certainly would not be responsible for commencing this race. Israel, a state that has consistently demonstrated aggressive tendencies towards its neighbours and threatens to pre-emptively strike Iranian nuclear sites, and, unlike Iran, is not a signatory to the Nuclear Non-proliferation Treaty (NPT), is widely acknowledged to be in possession of between 100 and 200 nuclear warheads.

The double standards entailed by (re)producing the ontological distinction between *their* and *our* violence can also be found in the discourse and policies associated with Yemen, one of the principle geostrategic arenas of Obama's battle against "violent extremists," formerly known as the "war on terror." In justifying the "collateral damage" caused by "our" violence in Yemen in the context of "fighting extremism," Obama's chief counterterrorism advisor and nominee to head the CIA, John Brennan, said of the US drone attacks against Al Qaeda in the Arabian Peninsula (AQAP), the main branch of Al Qaeda deemed to be operating in Yemen: "We're not going to sit by and let our fellow Americans be killed. And if the only way that we can prevent those deaths from taking place is to take direct action against them, we will do so" (Brennan 2012). The most contentious aspect of this policy, according to Yemen expert Gregory D. Johnsen, is the "controversial method for determining how many civilians it has killed, counting all military-age males in a strike zone as combatants" (Johnsen 2012). In overlooking the civilian casualties caused by these unilateral strikes, as all military-aged males have been relegated to the "axiological axis," rendered to "bare life" as a result of their physical proximity to "bad Muslims," an underlying blunt and macabre calculation is revealed: that Yemeni civilian lives are worth less than American civilian and military lives.

Paradoxically, in its dehumanisation of the Islamist Other, it seems that the US is contributing to the very threat that it contends it seeks to reduce, as demonstrated by recent studies showing that the number of Al Qaeda adherents has increased exponentially in Yemen in recent years as a direct result of these policies (Johnsen 2012; Scahill 2012). "Terrorism" in this context may be seen as a response to the US' ontological denial of the Islamist Other's agency, and indeed right to exist, bound up as it is in (re) producing US power in Western Asia and the US' hegemonic position in the "world order." In doing so, the discourse eliminates the possibility of "legitimate political challenges" and "expression of grievances" and creates a geopolitical context in which the "possibility of maintaining sociopolitical models different from Western ones has been drastically reduced" (Mouffe 2005: 61). Furthermore, by overlooking motives, not only are opportunities lost to produce a broader, more in-depth understanding of Islamist movements, but also squandered are opportunities to develop policies capable of breaking these "cycle(s) of violence and counter-violence" (Jackson 2005).

Shifts in discourse on political Islam: impact of Obama's election and "Arab spring" uprisings?

Obama was elected on a platform of change, and promised to amend some of the more odious foreign and domestic policies associated with the "war on terror" and improve US' relations with the Muslim world, so badly damaged during his predecessor's two terms in office. In particular, he vowed "to close Guantánamo, reject the Military Commissions Act, and adhere to the Geneva Conventions" (Baker 2010). Obama's election also signified a significant discursive shift, as it seemed the historic election of the first US black president would lead to a US foreign policy more in areas where legacies of Western intervention and collective memories of Western racism loom large, and help move the country beyond the Manichean "us/them" identity constructions.

It is clear that Obama is more sensitive than Bush to the power of language and its ability to impact perceptions and relations between peoples and states, as he himself noted during an interview with Al Arabiya television: "The language we use matters." Obama has made an effort to avoid the most offensive of the Bush era's discursive constructions, including the "war on terror" label – he claims to view terror as a tactic, "not an enemy" – as well as polemical and poorly defined terms such as "Islamofascism" and "evildoers." His June 2009 speech in Cairo was taken by many to signify a conscious effort to transform US–West Asian relations, characterised for so long by suspicion and animosity. Some argued that it symbolised "a new beginning" for relations between "the US and Muslims" (Saul 2009).

Although his presidency has demonstrated a significant shift in tone, it is not clear that this change will have a lasting impact on the overall discourse on political Islam, and its policy implications are even less clear, as discussed in the section above regarding drone attacks and the continuation of other policies associated with the rendering of Islamists to the "axiological axis." Many have argued (Arquilla 2012; Gerges 2013; Greenwald 2012; Kumar 2012; Mullin 2011) the difference between Bush's and Obama's "war on terror" has been largely at the rhetorical and strategic levels – in form, not substance. Not only has Obama reneged on his promise to close Guantánamo by January 2010, but, with the passage of the 2012 National Defense Authorization Act, the president essentially "legaliz[ed] the arbitrary and military detention of prisoners and, for the first time, including US citizens," effectively "export[ing] the regime at Guantánamo ... to the US mainland by extending detention without trial provisions to all US citizens" (Maniar 2012, 2013). Much to the chagrin of human rights lawyers and activists, and despite veto pledges, Obama also signed into law the 2013 National Defence Authorization Act (NDAA), missing out on an opportunity to fix the indefinite military detention provisions in the previous year's NDAA and making it harder to transfer detainees out of Guantánamo (Sledge 2013). Of the 166 prisoners that remain as Guantánamo prisoners, 86 have reportedly been cleared for transfer by the Obama administration, yet are still kept in a legal limbo. Nine individuals have died since the prison was opened 11 years ago, including six of suspected suicide (Human Rights Watch 2013).

Obama has also failed to address adequately the detrimental "war on terror" legacy, refusing to establish any punitive or deterrence mechanisms, such as an independent inquiry capable of investigating and holding accountable those top-level Bush administration officials responsible for implementing the illegal policies associated with the US' "state of exception," including the torture and "extraordinary rendition" of terror suspects (Shahshahani 2010).

In the aftermath of the Arab revolutions, there seems to have been a dramatic policy shift towards "moderate" Islamist movements, now subsumed under the "epistemic axis," in which they are (reluctantly) embraced in the hopes of their eventual socialisation and transformation. This may be, as Gerges (2012) argues, because the Obama administration "had little choice." With Islamists winning a majority of seats in the new parliaments in Tunisia, Morocco, and Egypt, Obama "reversed two decades of mistrust and hostility toward mainstream Islamists and acknowledged the new political reality in the region" (Gerges 2013: 14). This new engagement "marked a historic shift of US foreign policy," with Secretary of State Hillary Clinton saying that the US would work with the ascendant Islamist parties in Tunisia and Egypt so long as "they played by the rules of the political game" (ibid.: 14). Considering the US had no problem working with dictators in the past, one may assume that these "rules" refer not to the functioning of a democratic polity, but rather to the various red lines the US has established in order to protect its ideational, political and economic interests in the region. These include: maintaining access to natural resources in the region, protecting and promoting Israel's Qualitative Military Edge[2] vis-à-vis its neighbors, and advancing policies associated with the neoliberal economic order, which has facilitated and underpinned the entrenchment of post-World War II US hegemony in the region (Chandler 2000; Gowan 2003), maintaining the Westphalian state order (Mullin 2010).

Today, it seems more apt to discuss the discursive distinction made between "good" Islamists (e.g. those movements influenced by Turkey's 'moderate' and neoliberal AKP) versus "bad" Islamists (e.g. nationalist-Islamist movements, including Hezbollah and Hamas, various Al Qaeda-linked global jihadi movements, as well as a panoply of Salafi groups that have emerged in the region in recent years), based on consideration of the relative amenability of the individuals or movements to US economic and foreign policy interests in the region. Also gaining increasing prominence in the discourse, are the panoply of Salafi Islamist movements, which are, in many ways, a legacy of the repressive security practices and suffocated public spheres that characterised "good Muslim" states allied with the US in the context of the "war on terror" (Merone and Cavatorta 2012). The "good Islamists" in this modified discursive construct are those that refrain from challenging the US and its allies on either ontological or strategic grounds. As such, they abide by neoliberal dictates and respect various US foreign policy red lines, including those vis-à-vis Israel and "war on terror" cooperation. Most prominent amongst the "good Islamist" political parties are the AKP in Turkey, credited by many as being a role "model" for other Islamist parties in the region, along with An Nahda in Tunisia, the Justice and Development Party in Morocco, and the Muslim Brotherhood in Egypt. Rather than examining the subtle shifts in US foreign policy towards Islamist movements, Gerges urges observers to ask instead, "what shifts have the Islamist parties undergone to bring them closer to the American foreign policy priorities?" (Gerges 2013: 189)

Structural change and the emergence of counter-discourses and practices

This chapter has primarily focused on understanding the roots and manifestations of the discourse on political Islam as enemy Other in the context of the "war on terror." It has also considered the policy implications of this discourse. Although it has been argued that there has been more continuity than change, it also must be acknowledged that major challenges have been mounted on both the discursive and policy levels, which could threaten the stability of the "regimes of truth" upon which they have been built and perpetuated. From its inception, there have been critical voices from the realms of academia, journalism, and activism that have challenged various ingrained and distorted views on political Islam, as well as the epistemic foundations in which they are grounded (Mullin 2011). They have also challenged various aspects of the "war on terror," including its discursive violence and the material damage caused, including the deleterious impact that various of its associated policies have had on the human rights of those people caught on the wrong side of the "us/them" divide, as well as on the civil liberties of many Americans themselves (ibid.).

Yet effective change on the discursive and policy levels appears to be limited by several structural obstacles, including those on both the ideational and material levels. Most importantly, there is the imaginative hold of US exceptionalism on state identity formation and its dependence upon the existence of a defective Other in need of assimilation, transformation, or elimination, which reinforces the aggressive side of this identity. Yet for a whole host of reasons, including the current US economic crisis, shifts in the international balance of power due to the decline in US economic might, and the rise of alternative powers, including the BRIC states (Brazil, Russia, India and China), a space has been pried open for counter-hegemonic practices and discourses to emerge (Mullin 2011).

Despite the dynamic nature of US power and its ability to adapt and respond to new forms of resistance, an undeniable space has been created in which counter-hegemonic practices and discourses have already taken hold. Like the forms of power to which they respond, these have taken both material and ideational forms. Within the former category we may include both those forms of resistance emanating from the peoples and states that have been the objects of much of the discourse on political

Islam and associated "war on terror" policies and practices. Most significant are the Arab revolutions themselves, which, even in their incompleteness, have forcefully exposed as farce orientalist tropes regarding the incompatibility of Islam and democracy, as well as cultural explanations for the persistence of authoritarianism and pathologies of Arab "civil society." In one fell swoop, these uprisings not only managed to bring down the wall of fear that divided state and society in the authoritarian contexts where they emerged, but also to expose the international structures of power that underpinned them, in which the US is heavily implicated. As Tariq Ramadan has argued, these uprisings forced the West "to accept that the peoples of the Global South possess the capacity, based on their own referential framework" to construct new modes of governance and frameworks for more equitable international relations. In doing so, they have "challenged existing monopolies" that have entailed "the project[ion] and impos[ition] of a synthesis that glorifies the West and amputates other civilizations of their creative potential" (Ramadan 2012: 19).

These existing monopolies have also been challenged on a juridical level, through civil and criminal litigation occurring in various jurisdictions against Western state actors responsible for human rights violations linked to the "war on terror." Exemplary among these is the case brought against former British Foreign Secretary Jack Straw and the former head of MI6 for their complicity with the US and Libyan governments, in the rendition, torture and detention without trial of two Libyan citizens, Hakim Belhaj and Sami al-Saadi (Norton-Taylor 2012). Another example is the recent case won by German citizen Khaled el-Masri against the Former Yugoslav Republic of Macedonia in the European Court for Human Rights. The court ruled that el-Masri "had been subjected to torture, unlawful detention and other abuses in connection with the CIA's 'extraordinary rendition' programme" (Hafetz 2012). In both cases, these individuals have resisted relegation to the "bare life" category and have demanded a restoration of their agency and rights as human beings through the courts.

One can also include amongst these material counter-hegemonic practices the actions of activists, scholars, politicians, and journalists who have protested the discursive construction of political Islam as enemy Other, as well as the associated policies and structural constraints that have sustained them. For example, the recent protest organised by the anti-war group Code Pink in October 2012 against drone strikes in Pakistan, one of the principle areas where the US declared "state of exception" and ontological distinctions between "their" and "our violence" applies (Khan and Mullen 2012). This protest followed the publication of an investigative report on the impact of drones on civilian lives in Pakistan by scholars at Stanford and New York universities, which empirically challenges the US' official line "that its drone strikes are precise and successful in their mission to attack those deemed to be a threat to the US" ("Living Under Drones" 2012). Instead, the report "Living Under Drones" demonstrates the devastating impact of these drone attacks on the lives of people living in targeted communities. The report also reaffirms the argument made by Johansen and Scahil in relation to drone attacks in Yemen that the drone program is actually "facilitating recruitment to violent non-state armed groups, and motivating further violent attacks" ("Living Under Drones" 2012).

The "Gaza Freedom Flotilla" can also be viewed as a civil-society initiated counter-hegemonic practice, as it has challenged US attempts to maintain the metaphorical wall constructed between an allegedly democratic, secular and law-abiding "us," including the US' Israeli civilisational proxy, and a violent, terrorist "other," allegedly embodied by the Islamist-nationalist movement Hamas (Mullin 2011). In this case, American citizens sailing to Gaza to break the Israeli siege, deliver humanitarian goods, and meet with Palestinian civil society actors, including Islamists, risked conviction under material support provisions of US anti-terrorism laws that have been constructed in such a way to (re)produce these ontological divisions. Their mission also challenged the US' unconditional support for Israel by challenging dominant narratives, and demonstrating the deleterious impact of the US-backed Israeli siege on the humanitarian and human rights situation of Palestinians in Gaza (Mullin 2011).

Also significant in terms of the proliferation of counter-hegemonic voices penetrating even mainstream narrative producers is a recent editorial published by the influential *New York Times*, calling on Obama to fulfil his 2008 campaign promise and finally close Guantánamo prison. By criticising the administration for its "decision to adopt the Bush team's extravagant claims of state secrets and executive power, blocking any accountability for the detention and brutalisation of hundreds of men at Guantánamo and secret prisons, and denying torture victims their day in court," it also challenged the juridical basis for the "state of exception" that has accompanied the "war on terror" (*New York Times* 2012).

On the ideational level, there has emerged a forceful challenge to the types of knowledge production and unequal divisions of intellectual labor that perpetuated this discourse for so long. This movement seeks not only, as post-colonial intellectual movements have, to overcome these power divisions but, more importantly, to transcend them. As Dabashi has argued, in reasserting the region's "cosmopolitan worldliness," the "Arab spring" uprisings have the potential to create a new "liberation geography ... render[ing] useless old categories of 'Islam and the West'" (Dabashi 2012: 25). According to Dabashi's optimistic assessment, we are moving into a "post-post-colonial" moment that entails:

> the suspension of all *regimes du savoir*. No lesser battle thus needs to be fought against manners and modes of inherited knowledge that have

been coterminous with the politics of despair we have lived for the last two centuries. Our interlocutor is no longer "the West," for "the West" is dead.

(Ibid.: 251)

Adib-Moghaddam has described these counter-hegemonic intellectual practices as a post-modern and critical movement in which Enlightenment-derived certainties about what constitutes social, political and economic progress have been fundamentally challenged. Instead we have a new generation of thinkers influenced by the likes of Deleuze, Derrida, Baudrillard, and Guttari who "recognise 'being' as compromised by the interpenetration of different histories, causal systems and temporalities." For Adib-Moghaddam, the "inescapable dialectics of history," and the intellectual movement they have spawned, similarly mark the demise of the "West." "From now on," he declares, "the 'West' is spelled with a lower case 'w'" (Adib-Moghaddam 2011: 287–8). As a "counter discourse to the clash regime," Adib-Moghaddam suggests a "negative dialectics," which, like Said's "contrapuntality," embraces difference, while at the same time acknowledging each individual experience as forming "part of a shared common human experience" (ibid.: 289).

The relative effectiveness of these counter-hegemonic challenges has been facilitated by a more conducive structural context, marked by the gradual diminution of US power in the international system. This subtle, yet tangible, shift has come about as result of various strategic and tactical losses suffered in the numerous "war on terror" battlefields, requiring a rethink on the part of US foreign policymakers vis-à-vis the West Asian region. Similar to the way in which Barkawi (2011: 708) describes the moral, strategic and tactical defeats of the Vietnam war as having "generat[ed] and shap[ed]" the post-Vietnam mobilisation of US power, so too have the wars in Iraq and Afghanistan shaped the type of American power now possible in this transformed geostrategic sphere. The Arab revolutions are both a cause and effect of the radical structural transformations now taking place. These changes will have a significant impact upon the US' continued ability to mold the politics of the region for its own benefit. However, it is possible that, as in the case of post-Vietnam America, tactical and strategic lessons will be learned at the expense of deeper ethical and ontological ones. Already there is evidence that the US military is responding to the new geostrategic reality in a way that will perpetuate rather than transform US relations with this part of the world. In particular, it seems likely from planned budget cuts for 2013 (the first since 9/11, due to amount to a 1.6 per cent cut in the Pentagon's base budget within five years) that the government will seek to maintain its hegemony in the region albeit via different means, and will continue to operate as an "exceptional" state, through the exercise of more clandestine forms of power (Bumiller 2012). There will likely be a greater reliance on the CIA, including the deployment of a "combination of spies and special operation forces," in Iraq and Afghanistan in particular, covert military operations, as well as an increase in the use of targeted assassinations and drone strikes in various "battlefields" in the "war against Al Qaida," where ontological distinctions between *their* and *our* violence, rights and agency, are likely to be maintained (Axe 2012; Miller 2012).

It remains to be seen whether these counter-hegemonic practices, accompanied by significant structural change in international power constellations, will succeed in "disarticulating the existing order" (Mouffe 2005: 18). Yet it is certain that such a radical transformation would necessitate not only tangible discursive and policy shifts, in which the humanity of the ("bad") Islamist Other would be restored and the "state of exception" terminated, but also, and connected, a fundamental alteration of the way in which US identity is constructed and maintained in interaction with other states, nations and peoples of the world.

Notes

1 Throughout this chapter I use the term "Islamist movement" interchangeably with "political Islam" to refer to those movements "whose purpose is to attain political power at the national level," and who "generally accept the nation-state, operate within its constitutional framework, eschew violence (except under conditions of foreign occupation), articulate a reformist rather than revolutionary vision and invoke universal democratic norms." When referring to individuals who belong to such movements, I employ the term "Islamist" (International Crisis Group 2005).
2 Defined as "Israel's ability to counter and defeat credible military threats from any individual state, coalition of states, or non-state actor, while sustaining minimal damages or casualties" (Shapiro 2011).

References

Adib-Moghaddam, A. (2011) *Metahistory of the Clash of Civilisation: Us and Them Beyond Orientalism*, London: Hurst & Company.
Agamben, G. (2005) *State of Exception*, trans. K. Attell, Chicago, IL: University of Chicago.
Ali, T. (2003) *The Clash of Fundamentalisms: Crusades, Jihads and Modernity*, London: Verso Books.
Ali, T. (2004) *Bush in Babylon: The Recolonisation of Iraq*, London: Verso Books.
Alpert, E. (2012) "UN: Gaza to be unlivable by 2020 unless serious action taken," *LA Times*, August 27. Available at http://latimesblogs.latimes.com/world_now/2012/08/un-gaza-to-be-unlivable-by-2020-unless-serious-action-taken.html (accessed January 5, 2013).
Anghie, A. (2004) *Imperialism, Sovereignty and the Making of International Law*, Cambridge: Cambridge University Press.
Arquilla, J. (2012) "Three wars on terror," *Foreign Policy*, September 10. Available at www.foreignpolicy.com/articles/2012/09/10/three_wars_on_terror (accessed January 5, 2013).

Axe, D. (2012) "Clinton Goes Commando, Sells Diplomats as Shadow Warriors," Wired.com, May 24. Available at www.wired.com/dangerroom/2012/05/clinton-goes-commando/#more-81367 (accessed September 17, 2013).

Ayoob, M. (2002) "Inequality and theorizing in international relations: the case for subaltern realism," *International Studies Review*, 4(3), 27–48.

Bacevich, A. (2005) *The New American Militarism: How Americans Are Seduced by War*, Oxford: Oxford University Press.

Bacevich, A. (2008) *The Limits of Power: The End of American Exceptionalism*, New York: Metropolitan Books.

Baker, P. (2010) "Obama's war over terror," *New York Times*, January 17. Available at www.nytimes.com/2010/01/17/magazine/17Terror-t.html?pagewanted=all (accessed September 17, 2013).

Barkawi, Tarak (2011) "From war to security: security studies, the wider agenda and the fate of the study of war," *Millennium Journal of International Studies* 39 (3), 701–16.

Barnett, M. and Duvall, R. (2005). "Power in International Politics," *International Organization*, 59, 39–75.

Baskin, G. (2012) "Israel's shortsighted assassination," *New York Times*, November 16. Available at www.nytimes.com/2012/11/17/opinion/israels-shortsighted-assassination.html?_r=0 (accessed June 10, 2013).

Baxter, K. and Akbarzadeh, S. (2008) *US Foreign Policy in the Middle East: The Roots of Anti-Americanism*, London: Routledge.

Bomse, A. and Marc Leas, J. (2012), "Where's the accountability for Israeli war crimes?" *Counterpunch*, November 28. Available at www.counterpunch.org/2012/11/28/wheres-the-accountability-for-israeli-war-crimes/ (accessed January 5, 2013).

Brennan, J. (2012) "US Policy Toward Yemen," Council on Foreign Relations, August 8. Available at www.cfr.org/united-states/us-policy-toward-yemen/p28794 (accessed January 5, 2013).

Bruce, M. and Ninan, R. (2012) "Obama: 'We are fully supportive of Israel's right to defend itself'," *ABC News*, November 18. Available at http://abcnews.go.com/blogs/politics/2012/11/obamawe-are-fully-supportive-of-israels-right-to-defend-itself/ (accessed January 5, 2013).

Bumiller, E. (2012) "Defense budget cuts would limit raises and close bases," *New York Times*, January 26. Available at www.nytimes.com/2012/01/27/us/pentagon-proposes-limiting-raises-and-closing-bases-to-cut-budget.html?pagewanted=all (accessed June 10, 2013).

Burgat, F. (2005) *Face to Face with Political Islam*, London: I.B. Tauris.

Bush, G. W. (2001) "You are either with us or against us," CNN, November 6. Available at http://edition.cnn.com/2001/US/11/06/gen.attack.on.terror/ (accessed January 5, 2013).

Buzan, B. (2006) "Will the 'global war on terrorism' be the new Cold War?" *International Affairs*, 82(6), 1101–18.

Buzan, B., Wæver, O., and de Wilde, J. (1998) *Security: A New Framework for Analysis*, Boulder. CO: Lynne Rienner Publishers.

Chandler, D. (2000) "International justice," *New Left Review*, 6, 55–66.

Chomsky, C. (2004) *Hegemony or Survival: America's Quest for Global Dominance*, London: Penguin Books.

Chomsky, N. and Achcar, G. (2008) *Perilous Power: The Middle East and US Foreign Policy: Dialogues on Terror, Democracy, War, and Justice*, London: Penguin Books.
Choudhury, C. A. (2006) "Comprehending 'our' violence: reflections on the liberal universalist tradition, national identity and the war on Iraq," *Muslim World Journal of Human Rights*, 3(1), 2, 1–20.
Cole, J. (2005) "The Reelection of Bush and the Fate of Iraq," *Constellations*, 12(2), 164–72.
Cole, J. (2006) "'Shiite Crescent'? The regional impact of the Iraq war," *Current History*, 105 (687), 1–6.
Cole, J. (2009) *Engaging the Muslim World*, New York: Palgrave Macmillan.
Croft, S. (2006) *Culture, Crisis and America's War on Terror*, Cambridge: Cambridge University Press.
Dabashi, H. (2012) *The Arab Spring: The End of Postcolonialism*, New York: Zed Books.
Esposito, J. and DeLong-Bas, N. (2003) "Modern Islam," in J. Neusner (ed.) *God's Rule: the Politics of World Religions*, Washington, DC: Georgetown University Press.
Euben, R. (1999) *Enemy in the Mirror: Fundamentalism and Limits of Modern Rationalism*, Princeton, NJ: Princeton University Press.
Foucault, Michel (1980), *Power/Knowledge: Selected Interviews and Other Writings 1972–1977*, edited by Colin Gordon, London: Harvester.
Foucault, M. (2007) "What is Critique?," in S. Lotringer (ed.) *The Politics of Truth*, New York: Semiotext, 41–83.
Foucault, M. (1990) *The History of Sexuality: An Introduction*, New York: Vintage Books, 1990.
Fukuyama, F. (1992) *The End of History and the Last Man*, New York: Free Press.
Ganor, B. (1999) "Defining terrorism: Is one man's terrorist another man's freedom fighter?" Washington, DC: International Policy Institute for Counter-Terrorism.
Gerges, F. (2009) "Disarray in American policy?," Policy Brief: Institute for Social Policy and Understanding (ISPU), Policy Brief #39: 1–5.
Gerges, F. (2013) "The Obama approach to the Middle East: the end of America's moment?" *International Affairs*, 89(2), 299–323.
Gerges, F. (2013) "What changes have taken place in US foreign policy towards Islamists?," *Contemporary Arab Affairs*, 69(2), 189–197.
Gold, D. (2003) *Hatred's Kingdom: How Saudi Arabia Supports the New Global Terrorism*, Washington, DC: Eagle Publishing.
Gowan, P. (2003) US: UN, *New Left Review*. 24, November–December: 5–28.
Gramsci, A. (1971) *Selections from the Prison Notebooks*, London: Lawrence and Wishart.
Greenwald, G. (2012) "Obama moves to make the War on Terror permanent," *Guardian*, October 24. Available at www.guardian.co.uk/commentisfree/2012/oct/24/obama-terrorism-kill-list (accessed June 10, 2013).
Hafetz, J. (2013) "The importance of European court's ruling against extraordinary rendition," *Al Jazeera*, January 7. Available at www.aljazeera.com/indepth/opinion/2013/01/20131595119662381.htm (accessed January 14, 2013).
Hajjar, L. (2011) "Suleiman: The CIA's man in Cairo," *Al Jazeera*, February 7. Available at www.aljazeera.com/indepth/opinion/2011/02/201127114827382865.html (accessed February 6, 2013).
Hansen, L. (2006) *Security as Practice: Discourse Analysis and the Bosnian War*, London: Routledge.

Human Rights Watch (2013) "US: pledges to end 'war,' close Guantánamo," May 24. Available at www.hrw.org/news/2013/05/24/us-pledges-end-war-close-guantanamo.

International Crisis Group (2005) "Understanding Islamism," *International Crisis Group*, Report, 37, March 2.

Ismail, S. (2006) *Rethinking Islamist politics*, London: I.B. Tauris.

Jackson, R. (2005) *Writing the War on Terrorism: Language, Politics and Counterterrorism*, Manchester: Manchester University Press.

Johnsen, G. (2012) "The wrong man for the CIA," *New York Times*, November 19. Available at www.nytimes.com/2012/11/20/opinion/john-brennan-is-the-wrong-man-for-the-cia.html (accessed November 5, 2012).

Kepel, G. (1986) *Muslim Extremism in Egypt: the Prophet and Pharaoh*, Berkeley: University of California Press.

Khan, S. and Mullen, J. (2012) "American activists in Pakistan to protest US drone strikes," CNN, October 6. Available at: http://edition.cnn.com/2012/10/05/world/asia/pakistan-us-drone-protest/index.html (accessed January 5, 2013).

Krauthammer, C. (1990) "The unipolar moment," *Foreign Affairs*, 70(1), 23–33.

Kumar, D. (2012) *Islamaphobia and the Politics of Empire*, Chicago, IL: Haymarket Books.

Lankford, A. (2012) "What drives suicidal mass killers," *New York Times*, December 17.

LeVine, M. (2012) "After the UN vote, how to stop the rockets for good," *Al Jazeera*, November 30. Available at www.aljazeera.com/indepth/opinion/2012/11/2012113085738863612.html (accessed January 5, 2013).

Lieven, A. (2004) *America Right or Wrong: An Anatomy of American Nationalism*, Oxford: Oxford University Press.

"Living Under Drones" (2012) Stanford/NYU Report. Available at http://livingunderdrones.org/report/ (accessed January 14, 2013).

Lobe, J. (2010) "Legality of drone strikes still in question," *TerraViva/IPS*, April 5. Available at http://ipsnorthamerica.net/news.php?idnews=2966 (accessed June 12, 2013).

Mamdani, M. (2004) *Good Muslim, Bad Muslim: America, the Cold War, and the Roots of Terror*, New York: Pantheon Books.

Mamdani, M. (2007) "The politics of naming: genocide, civil war, insurgency," *London Review of Books*, 29(5), 5–8.

Maniar, A. (2012) "Injustice off the agenda?" *Labour Briefing Newsletter*, February 27. Available at www.labourbriefing.org.uk/index.php?option=com_content&view=article&id=501:injustice-off-the-agenda&catid=37:news-a-views&Itemid=54 (accessed June 12, 2013).

Maniar, A. (2013) "Guantánamo Bay: Second Chance for Obama?," *One Small Window*, January 20. Available at http://onesmallwindow.wordpress.com/category/guantanamo-bay-extraordinary-rendition/ (accessed February 6, 2013).

Merone, F. and Cavatorta, F. (2012) "Salafist mouvance and sheikh-ism in the Tunisian democratic transition," *Working Papers in International Studies, Centre for International Studies Dublin City University*, Vol (7), 1–19.

Messari, N. (2001) "Identity and foreign policy: the case of Islam in US foreign policy," in V. Kubalkova (ed.) *Foreign Policy in a Constructed World*, Armonk, NY: M.E. Sharpe, 227–48.

Miller, G. (2012) "CIA digs in as Americans withdraw from Iraq, Afghanistan," *Washington Post*, February 8. Available at http://articles.washingtonpost.

com/2012-02-07/world/35443385_1_cia-veteran-afghanistan-cia-drones (accessed June 10, 2013).
Morgenthau, H. (1960) *The Purpose of American Politics*, New York: Alfred A. Knopf.
Mouffe, C. (2005) *On the Political*, London: Routledge.
Mullin, C. (2010) "Islamist Challenges to the 'Liberal Peace' Discourse: The Case of Hamas and the Israel–Palestine 'Peace Process'," *Millennium Journal of International Studies*, 39(2), 525–46.
Mullin, C. (2011) "The US discourse on political Islam: is Obama's a truly *post*-'war on terror' administration?" *Critical Studies on Terrorism*, 4(2), 263–81.
Mullin, C. and Shahshahani, A. (2012) "The legacy of US intervention and the Tunisian revolution: promises and challenges one year on," *Interface: a journal for and about social movements*, 4(1), 67–101.
Neumann, I. B. (1999) *Classical Theories in International Relations*, New York: St. Martin's Press.
New York Times (2012) "Close Guantánamo Prison," Editorial, November 26. Available at http://www.nytimes.com/2012/11/26/opinion/close-guantanamo-prison.html?_r=0 (accessed September 17, 2013).
Nietzsche, F. (1968) *The Will to Power*, trans. W. Kaufmann, New York: Vintage Books.
Norton-Taylor, R. (2012) "Jack Straw accused of misleading MPs over torture of Libyan dissidents," *Guardian*, October 10. Available at www.guardian.co.uk/world/2012/oct/10/jack-straw-torture-libyan-dissidents (accessed June 15, 2013).
Obama, B. (2012) Remarks by the President to the UN General Assembly, The White House, Office of the Press Secretary, September 25. Available at www.whitehouse.gov/the-press-office/2012/09/25/remarks-president-un-general-assembly (accessed January 5, 2013).
Qureshi, A. (2010) "The 'Obama doctrine': kill, don't detain," *Guardian*, April 11. Available at www.guardian.co.uk/commentisfree/cifamerica/2010/apr/11/obama-national-security-drone-guantanamo (accessed June 10, 2013).
Ramadan, T. (2012) *The Arab Awakening: Islam and the New Middle East*, London: Allen Lane.
Rice, C. (2003) "Transforming the Middle East," *Washington Post*, August 7. Available at www.iraqwatch.org/government/US/WH/us-wh-rice-wp_oped-080703.html (accessed June 10, 2013).
Rice, C. (2012) "Remarks by Ambassador Susan E. Rice, US Permanent Representative to the United Nations, at a Security Council Private Meeting on Gaza," November 14. Available at http://usun.state.gov/briefing/statements/200564.htm (accessed January 5, 2013).
Rogers, P. (2010) "The AfPak war: failures of success," *openDemocracy*, April 8. Available at www.opendemocracy.net (accessed January 5, 2013).
Said, E. (1978) *Orientalism*, London: Routledge.
Saul, M. (2009) "In Cairo speech, President Obama calls for a new beginning between the United States and Muslims," *New York Daily News*, June 4. Available at www.nydailynews.com/news/politics/cairo-speech-president-obama-calls-new-beginning-united-states-muslims-article-1.372557 (accessed June 15, 2013).
Scahill, J. (2012) "Washington's war in Yemen backfires," *The Nation*. Available at www.thenation.com/article/166265/washingtons-war-yemen-backfires#axzz2WreF0Vx7 (accessed March 5–12, 2013).
Scheuer, M. (2008a) *Imperial Hubris: Why the West Is Losing the War on Terror*, Virginia: Potomac Books Inc.

Scheuer, M. (2008b) *Marching Toward Hell: America and Islam After Iraq*, New York: Simon & Schuster.

Shahshahani, A. (2010) "Time to reckon with torture," *Huffington Post*. Available at www.huffingtonpost.com/azadeh-shahshahani/time-to-reckon-with-tortu_b_634137.html (accessed July 2, 2013).

Shapiro, A. J. (2011) "Ensuring Israel's qualitative military edge," remarks to the Washington Institute for Near East Policy, Washington, DC: US State Department, November 4. Available at www.state.gov/t/pm/rls/rm/176684.htm (accessed June 29, 2013).

Sledge, M. (2013) "Harry Reid on Guantánamo: 'Nobody's fault' prison camp hasn't closed," *Huffington Post*, January 29. Available: www.huffingtonpost.com/2013/01/29/harry-reid-guantanamo_n_2576274.html (accessed September 17, 2013).

Telhami, S. and Barnett, M. (2002) *Identity and Foreign Policy in the Middle East*, Cornell, NY: Cornell University Press.

Todorov, T. (1984) *The Conquest of America: The Question of the Other*, trans. R. Howard, New York: Harper & Row.

Toros, H. and Gunning, J. (2009) "Exploring a critical theory approach to terrorism studies," in R. Jackson, M. Smyth and J. Gunning (eds) *Critical Terrorism Studies: A New Research Agenda*, London/New York: Routledge.

Wendt, A. (1999) *Social Theory of International Politics*, New York: Cambridge University Press.

11 The multiple contexts of Russian counterterrorism frames
The framing process and discursive field

Aurélie Campana

In April 2009, Russian President, Dmitri Medvedev, announced the end of the decade-long "counterterrorist operation" in Chechnya; however, at the time of writing, sporadic fighting continues in the war-torn Republic of Chechnya and the neighboring republics (Dagestan, Ingushetia, Kabardino-Balkaria and Karachay-Cherkessia), especially Dagestan, which has been facing escalating violence since the mid-2000s (Mendelson 2010; Mendelson *et al.* 2010). The "Caucasus Emirate," a decentralized network that has united different insurgent groups under the Islamic banner, has claimed responsibility for most of the violence that occurs daily in the region, as well as for the suicide-bombings that hit Moscow in 2010 and 2011 (BBC News 2011; CBS News 2010). In response, federal security agencies regularly lead "counterterrorist operations" in targeted districts, cities or villages, without being able to put an end to the insurgent-like and terrorist activities (Vatchagaev 2012).

The Russian tandem that governed Russia between 2008 and 2012, namely President Dmitri Medvedev and Prime Minister Vladimir Putin, at first minimized the problems caused by this mounting violence, claiming that the situation has been improving since violence diffused regionally (Medvedev 2008). Confronted with daily news reporting terrorist attacks and insurgent strikes against representatives of federal security agencies and local government bodies, they slowly recognized the "threats" this upsurge of violence posed to the Russian Federation (Putin, 2009). At the same time, they adopted new political and socio-economic initiatives in response to critics of the federal center's inability to stop violence (Omelicheva 2009).

This chapter analyzes the interpretative frames elaborated between 2008 and 2012 by President Medvedev and Prime Minister Putin to justify the decisions taken by the federal center to defeat those defined as "terrorist groups." It argues that they failed to adopt a coherent discourse in a context marked by institutional tensions and a relative sense of urgency owing to the deteriorating security situation in North Caucasus and the forthcoming 2014 Winter Olympic Games in Sochi, located west of the troubled Republics. We intend to show how, in this case, framing has been an erratic process, resulting in discursive ambiguities as the governmental counterterrorism discourse was torn between two definitions of the problem (terrorism as a domestic problem or terrorism as an external mastermind), and two solutions (repression versus socio-economic development). We further trace this to the fragmented nature of the Russian counterterrorism discursive field and the non-hierarchical rules of the game that govern it. Finally, we argue that this permanent hesitation between the military and civil solutions has left room for discursive contestation, both at the discourse and policy levels.

Following Hoffman, we consider terrorism and counterterrorism to be primarily communicative and symbolic enterprises (Hoffman 2006). Discourses on terrorism and counterterrorism are "a constitutive element of the conflict" (Jackson 2005a: 19), as they give sense to practices. The discursive and argumentative dimensions of terrorism and counterterrorism are getting increasing attention from researchers, who have developed a critical approach to terrorism and counterterrorism (see, e.g., Hülsse and Spencer 2008; Jackson 2005a, 2005b, 2006; Zulaika and Douglass 1996), and from those interested in the discursive dimensions of internal conflicts. The former have opened the "black box" of the formation of collective understandings of terrorism and counterterrorism by questioning "the nature and politics of representation" (Jackson 2007: 247–8). Among the latter, students of the Chechen conflicts have mainly emphasized the description of the nature of the threat (Russell 2005a, 2005b; Snetkov 2007). Two more pieces of research examine the discursive strategies used to justify the disastrous assault against school number 1 at Beslan (Tuathail 2009) and the implementation of a new socio-political order in Chechnya (Campana and Légaré 2011). The first shows the incoherence of the Kremlin's discourse on the tragic Beslan hostage taking and violence in North Caucasus. It particularly demonstrates how the Kremlin developed, in the aftermath of the event, a discourse that was disconnected from the memories of the local population. The second one points to the influence of the institutional competition taking place between federal agencies and the chaotic development of a frame legitimizing the rule of Ramzan Kadyrov, the Chechen president backed by Moscow.

Based on a micro-discourse analysis of written and spoken texts produced by Russia's President and Prime Minister, this chapter builds on these last two contributions and expands them in two ways. First, it takes into account the interactions between the cultural and structural contexts and the political environment in which framing is embedded. In so doing, it theoretically relies on the concept of discursive field, which is used to explain frame elaboration and highlight the link between framing and the multiple contexts that shape it. Second, it looks at a period of time, namely Medvedev's presidency, and a context, the regionalization of violence in North Caucasus, which has not yet been addressed in this perspective. Finally, it offers insights into the very fabric of counterterrorism policy in

Russia and sheds new light on understanding why Russia seems to be unable to find a way out of these conflicts.

The chapter proceeds as follows. In the first part, we present our approach. We discuss the concepts of frame and discursive field and briefly expose our methodology. We then analyze the diagnostic and prognostic frames developed by Medvedev and Putin. We finally move to the Russian discursive field and analyze how the three main elements that constitute it (cultural resources, the range of actors and the rules of the game that governs it) shape framing. This leads us to address the main inconstancies underlying framing. Framing counterterrorism in Russia appears to be an erratic process marked by the manipulation of symbols and ideas and institutional competition over the solutions that need to be implemented. The uncertainties underlying the framing process prevent frame crystallization and pave the way for discursive contestation.

Conceptual and methodological discussions: frames and discursive fields

Framing can be broadly defined as "the use of language and ideas to interpret and influence the understandings of others regarding an issue or event" (Benford 2010: 294). Frame analysis encompasses several approaches (Scheufele 1999: 103). While this chapter studies frames articulated by institutional actors with the intention of justifying counterterrorist policies, it relies mostly on the social movements literature as we believe that it provides relevant theoretical and methodological tools to further understand how a problem and the appropriate means for actions are defined, and how the contexts in which framing is embedded shape the whole process and its outcomes.

The social movements scholars have made frame analysis a dominant perspective to conceptualize the cultural and ideational aspects of collective action (Oliver and Johnston 2000). Tackling a wide range of issues, they examine the elaboration of frames and dissemination of ideas, symbols and images, and also consider the different functions of frames and their possible outcomes. The first function of framing is to define an issue. As Goffman put it, frames are "schemata of interpretation" (1974: 21). This definition is not a neutral one, as frames offer strategic interpretations of an issue; they emphasize certain points, organize them into a hierarchy and structure them while overriding others (Benford and Snow; 2000: 614). Frames are therefore goal-oriented; their main objectives are to persuade, mobilize and legitimize the strategy adopted and ultimately make it resonate within the targeted constituency. Resonance is determined by the issue's salience with the public experience and the perceived credibility of the content and sources of frames (Della Porta and Diani 2006: 81). In such a perspective, framing is defined as a strategic process that results in a dynamic process of producing meaning. Framing performs three core tasks: the "diagnostic," the "prognostic" and the "motivational" ones. Diagnostic framing identifies the "sources of causality, blame, and/or culpable agents"; prognostic framing "involves the articulation of a proposed solution to the problem" (Benford and Snow 2000: 616); motivational framing "provides a 'call to arms' or rationale for engaging in ameliorative collective action, including the construction of appropriate vocabularies of motive" (ibid.: 617). We will focus on the first two, as we are not interested in the frames' mobilization potential.

Framing is a process that does not occur in a vacuum. Most social movements' scholars agree that frames are embedded in specific historical and cultural contexts (Oliver and Johnston 2000). They show that political entrepreneurs who take part in the framing process draw on existing cultural stocks and structure their language around available cultural resources and symbolic repertoires. More precisely, cultural resources form as many tools "that groups wield more or less self-consciously in their social and political struggles" (Williams 1995: 126). But the cultural context is not the only one shaping framing. As Oliver and Johnston suggest, one should also link "the social construction of ideas with organizational and political process factors" (2000: 37). While cultural elements are essential to the elaboration and articulation of frames, structural elements also matter (Fiss and Hirsch 2005). By structural elements, we here mean socio-political structures. Many concepts, like organizational, multi-organizational, identity fields and discursive fields (Snow 2008: 7) have been developed to capture the role of structure and its connection with cultural resources theoretically. We contend that the concept of "discursive field," as recently re-conceptualized by Snow (2008), offers a good avenue for analyzing the influence of both cultural and structural contexts on framing in a relational perspective. Snow proposes a definition of this concept, which encompasses three interrelated dimensions: the historical and cultural resources that form the above-mentioned cultural stock and that could ultimately be manipulated and distorted, the range of actors involved in the framing process and the system of relations between them (2008: 10).

Such a definition invites us to think about discursive fields as "dynamic terrain[s]" (Steinberg 1999: 748). In other words, the concept of discursive fields not only highlights the interaction between actors and cultural materials, but also the system of relations between actors involved in framing and actors belonging to the same movement. We propose to go one step further and to identify the nature of the rules of the game from a Bourdieusian perspective. While the concept of the "rules of the game" is not present in Snow's conceptualization, we argue that it offers important insights into understanding how the systems of relations between actors develop and evolve. Snow proposes a very descriptive definition of the concept of "systems of relations" (Snow 2008: 10). By "systems of relations among the actors," he means the degree of field organization, which "var[ies] on a continuum from unstable or unsettled to stable or settled" (2008: 10). But he fails to explain how they develop and how they structure actors' actions and practices. The Bourdieusian concept fills this gap, as the rules of the game facilitate or constrain the practices of actors, including discursive ones. We share Jorgensen and Philips' assumption regarding the dialectical relationships between discourses and non-discursive practices and see discourses and frames as both constitutive and constituted of social practices (Jorgensen and Philips 2002: 61). This means that discourses are neither neutral, nor independent of other social practices. Moreover, they do not only reflect a social and political order but also construct, reproduce, maintain or/and transform power relations, as sites of "social struggle and conflict" (ibid.). In Russia, formal and informal rules intersect, which leads to a constant redefinition of the counterterrorist discursive field.

To grasp the interaction between these elements, we relied on Hank Johnston's methodological proposal and used "micro-discourse analysis" to map and analyze the frame's structure and content (Johnston 1995: 219). This method proposes to include the selected written and spoken texts in their respective contexts while turning to the texts to analyze the language used and "all sources of meaning" (ibid.: 222). These sources can be cultural or psychological, but the discourses can also be influenced by social roles and social interactions. In such a perspective, micro-frame analysis reintegrates cultural, historical, social and structural influences, providing a good avenue to articulate the macro and micro levels of analysis and to study the influence of the discursive field on framing.

Our empirical material is mainly composed of Medvedev and Putin's oral and written texts, available on the official websites of the Russian presidency and the Prime Minister and, for most of them, reproduced in the media.[1] The period under study extends from 2008 to 2012, with a strong emphasis put on the years 2010–12, during which the tandem proved to be the most active in terms of these issues. Approximately 50 to 60 articles dealing expressly with counterterrorism and/or North Caucasus were selected for each year. We first did a content analysis of all texts, selected the passages we found to be the most relevant to our research question, and then analyzed them. We will begin by presenting the Russian counterterrorism frames, as elaborated by the ruling tandem, before turning to analyzing the influence of the discursive counterterrorism field on shaping framing.

Russian counterterrorism diagnostic and prognostic frames

Russian discourses on terrorism and counterterrorism have been strongly associated to the second Chechen war, which started in 1999. Nevertheless, the diffusion of violence into the republics that neighbor Chechnya from the mid-2000s raised new concerns and prompted the Russian leadership to address these issues seriously. The diagnostic and prognostic frames they elaborated served the same purpose as before, namely to delegitimize the ongoing insurgency and depoliticize its claims, play down the significance of its resilience over the years despite quite successful repressive politics,[2] and change the image of the federal center. However, we argue that none are organized coherently and hierarchically; they appear to be more of a catalogue of causes and solutions rather than integrated frames presenting a clear portrait of the situation.

Diagnostic frame

Four main themes formed the backbone of the diagnostic frame: socio-economic problems, widespread criminalization and corruption, radical Islam and international terrorism. None were new as they were part of the discursive repertoires already used during the second Chechen war (1999–2009), but the change in scale and scope of the conflicts and the evolution of the balance of power following Medvedev's election to the Presidency contributed to making the framing process evolve. Russian leaders tended to downplay the two elements that have been pointed at for years as the main sources conducive to violence, namely international terrorism and radical Islam. Instead, they underlined the role of socio-economic factors and corruption, but failed to establish the causes of violence hierarchically or offer a strong diagnosis of the problem, which might have led to a more helpful framing of the problem.

Socio-economic problems

The socio-economic argument, used sparingly since 2004, has been strongly shaping the diagnostic framing since Medvedev took office in 2008. Indeed, Medvedev can be considered as its main proponent, although Putin also employed it quite frequently from 2010 on. According to both leaders, socio-economic difficulties form the conditions for violence. The leaders regard the insurgent groups as being successful in attracting young people because the youth has no future in the region. They believe that the main problem is unemployment, which is much higher in the Muslim Republics of North Caucasus than elsewhere in Russia.[3] As Putin put it, "long-term unemployment is probably the region's most acute social and even psychological challenge" (Premier.gov.ru 2010). Nonetheless, they acknowledged that the range of problems identified as the main destabilizing sources is wider than this. It runs from a lack of essential infrastructure to a low level of industrialization, a poorly modernized agriculture and a deficient education system. Russian officials mostly blamed what they call "poor quality of life" (Premier.gov.ru 2011a) and socio-economic backwardness caused by the legacies of the Soviet Union, the absence of investment during the 1990s and the escalation of violence.

Criminalization and corruption

Many states use the criminalization thesis to delegitimize insurgent or terrorist groups (Bhatia 2005: 12; Oren and Bar-Tal 2007: 114). In Russia, this argument is further supported by an old representation dating back to the 1920s and characterizing opponents to state as bandits and criminals. Putin is one of the main proponents of this argument, which strongly resonates with the discourses on the Chechen separatist leaders (Campana and Légaré 2011: 53–4). In 2010, he declared: "True, extremists continue to stage their terrorist attacks, but they have increasingly degenerated into ordinary criminals. Their political slogans are just a front for robbery and redistribution of property" (Premier.gov.ru 2010). As for Medvedev, he insisted on another related aspect: the influence of widespread corruption in setting the stage for violent practices. Since taking office, he has repeatedly stated that corruption undermines state stability throughout Russia. He considered the problem to be endemic in North Caucasus and regarded corruption as "a fact of direct aid to separatists" (Medvedev quoted in Ria-novosti.ru 2010b). He put constant pressure, at least on paper, on the presidents of the North Caucasus Republics, but with little or no actual result.

Islamization and violence

Russian media has usually emphasized the "Islamist" nature of the insurgency, describing the insurgents as "Wahhabi" radicals or "extremists." They also point out the role of the so-called "Caucasus Emirate" in most of the attacks in the region. Russian leaders proved to be more cautious than they did before and avoided putting blame on Islam and alienating Russia's Muslim population. Medvedev presented himself as the President of all Russians. He often officially acknowledged the historical role of Islam, but he also adopted a more alarmist discourse, recognizing the threats posed by radical Islam: "For centuries, Islam has developed in Russia as one of our traditional religions, but the injections of extremism and radical movements have appeared only recently and they are extremely dangerous" (Kremlin 2011). Putin adopted a similar storyline, insisting on the fact that "Islam is one of the traditional religions of the Russian people" (Premier.gov.ru 2011b). The tandem tried to dissociate Islam from violence, two words that are closely linked according to the Russian collective imaginary (Hunter 2004: 155), especially following the two waves of terrorist attacks, the first one (2000–4) being associated to the second Chechen war (2000–4) and the second one, which occurred in the context of the spillover of the Chechen conflict to the whole North Caucasus region from 2009 onwards.

International terrorism

While Putin's administration often relied on the thematic of international terrorism to describe the evolutions in Chechnya between 2000 and 2008

(Campana and Légaré 2011: 51–2), Medvedev's administration used it more sparingly. However, in the aftermath of each major attack, officials promptly recalled the supposed link between the North Caucasus insurgency and "international terrorism." Putin stated that,

> The region faced open aggression against the people of Russia, aggression incited by international terrorism, and by those who wanted to deal the final blow to an already weakened country, to destroy its territorial integrity and to create a bridgehead for the expansion and implementation of their self-serving plans.
>
> (Premier.gov.ru 2010)

From such a perspective, insurgent groups are said to be masterminded from the outside and to have no legitimate claims over the region. But contrary to what we observed before 2008, Russian officials did not establish a direct link between local insurgent/terrorist groups and Al Qaeda. This discursive strategy contrasts with the one adopted earlier, which made international terrorism the "usual culprit" (Campana and Légaré 2011: 51).

Although the diagnostic framing delimited a range of problems that have been affecting the stability of the North Caucasus region for years, we argue that it failed to organize them into a hierarchy. Moreover, the four themes that form the backbone of the diagnostic frame have never been articulated together and the Russian leadership never showed how they interact with each other. They rather adapted framing to the audiences and the context, bringing confusion to the discursive delimitation of the main problems to be addressed.

Prognostic frames

Russian leaders proposed a wide range of policies to reduce the levels of violence and ultimately quell the insurgency. The solutions they put forward are based on the above definitions of the problem. But, while there is a certain consistency between the diagnostic and prognostic frames, the prognostic frame proposes a catalog of solutions, ranging from repression to socio-economic development, but without explaining how these different parts of the solution should work together. As such, none of the different parts of the Russian solution are coherently articulated together both at the discursive and policy levels.

Since 2008, the federal government has been deploying lots of resources to show Moscow's determination to restore order and stability. Medvedev was the first member of the tandem to call for a "comprehensive" solution to be implemented (Kremlin 2010a). This "comprehensive" solution prioritizes the region's socio-economic development over other policies and makes socio-economic development a counterterrorism tool.

Indeed, the federal center injected billions of billions of rubles (R5.5 trillion since 2000) into socio-economic programs and invested a lot of energy in the initiation and sustenance of investment projects (Parfentyeva 2011). The main intention was to create new jobs, promote the building of infrastructures and develop new industries: Medvedev and Putin made fighting unemployment a priority. As for Medvedev, "only the creation of new jobs can bring hope to young people, who have no jobs and who are first recruited and then brainwashed by the extremists" (Kremlin 2011).

To give this revised approach some legitimacy, both Medvedev and Putin engaged in a persuasive enterprise, trying to show how solutions tailored by Moscow could match the needs of the region. As North Caucasus lacks a leading industry, they first tried to convince the local population, local authorities and potential investors that the creation of a tourism industry might open up new opportunities, given the region's potential and the forthcoming Winter Olympic Games. Nevertheless, its development encountered many difficulties, including an obvious security problem, requiring Russian leaders to intervene personally following all major events that could compromise existing and new projects. For example, at the beginning of 2011, a terrorist attack struck a ski resort in Kabardino-Balkaria. After this event, Medvedev reasserted the need to keep working on this type of project: "Whatever criminals try to do, we will continue to implement projects, including the development of the tourism cluster" (Medvedev quoted in Ria-novosti.ru 2011b). Persuasive efforts were specifically directed at the North Caucasian population, who had not been consulted on these projects. Some people overtly expressed strong criticism of such developments. Answering a question from a young local man about the mentality of the locals who "are proud Mountain people, always ready to fight and not waiting for tourist [*sic*] to come," Putin, adopting a customary paternalist attitude, firmly recalled that:

> Mountain people are proud people, ... but they are not prone to fight. I think you have a wrong idea about waiting on tourists. Tourism is a very important industry for many countries and many local people depend on it. Understand that and you will stop treating it as a minus [i.e., second-rate] service and instead see it as real work.

Putin also added that local men should also "stop pinching female tourists" in order to attract investors in the region (Putin quoted in Ria-novosti.ru 2011c).

The objectives of these programs themselves are intended to distract people from joining the insurgents. They are also intended to change the image of the federal center, but the results are not as immediate as the tandem would like them to be. Since the beginning of 2011, both Putin and Medvedev have recognized that it will take decades to fix the problem.

They consequently attempted to diversify their strategies, both at the discursive and policy levels, and tried to enroll the civil society and particularly the local Sufi clergy loyal to Moscow. They called for Muslim leaders to engage in a "moral" fight to cut the ground from underneath the radical Islam's feet. According to Medvedev, "it is not for state officials to deal with this or, in any case, not only for state officials. This, above all, is a job for the clergy, because this problem exists throughout the Muslim world" (Medvedev quoted in Ria-novosti.ru 2011a). Medvedev and Putin have implicitly recognized that they basically have no control over this issue.

The Russian leadership justified further the implementation of a revised approach by the need to adopt "modern" counterterrorism policies (Granik 2010). The use of this adjective illustrates a change in focus: North Caucasian residents, once considered suspect, are now put at the centre of Moscow's strategy. Two rationales lie behind this shift. First, local inhabitants should benefit from these policies and in return change their opinion about the federal center. From this perspective, Russian leaders insisted on their readiness and decidedness to intervene at all levels. Second, North Caucasians should feel like full Russian citizens. As Putin put it:

> Citizens must truly be able to interact with government officials; only then will they believe that the government understands their needs and can find ways to solve their problems. Once again: making tangible changes in people's public life and attitudes is one of United Russia's major political goals for the North Caucasus
>
> (Premier.gov.ru 2010)

Restoring confidence in state institutions is one of the objectives of the Russian leaders, but they also intended to show that the main interests of local populations are better served by adhering to this new approach, as Moscow is committed to bring back stability and prosperity within the region.

The civil approach only constitutes one part of the solution proposed in the prognostic frame, the military approach representing the other part. The military approach encompasses both a preventive and a repressive component, the second remaining the most heavily used in North Caucasus. Although Medevedev and Putin repeatedly called for forging an integrated response to terrorism that would better integrate the civil and the military approaches together to foster a holistic government response, discourses remain torn between these two approaches. Moreover, a gap persists between discourses and practices on the ground. The Russian leaders' argument splits into two parts that are not integrated. They insisted on the need to adopt the so-called "comprehensive" approach that would not further alienate the local North Caucasian population, reaffirming the need to eradicate the use of indiscriminate violence as well as "to improve the situation in the North Caucasus republics in general with terrorism prevention work, educational campaigns and economic programmes" (Kremlin 2012). But, at the same time, they frequently resorted to striking rhetorical figures, using the terms "destroy" or "blow," and encouraging law enforcement to hit "terrorist" and "bandits," giving them *carte blanche*. In a meeting organized in the Dagestani capital, Medvedev urged law enforcement representatives to "continue to strike sharp blows against terrorists, to destroy them and their safe havens" (Kremlin 2010b). Such a discourse indirectly encourages incumbents involved in counterterrorism to resort heavily to repressive measures. These measures range from the military actions taken against insurgent groups to the arrest of relatives of those suspected of involvement in the insurgency. As impunity reigns in North Caucasus, repression very often translates into indiscriminate violence and massive human rights violations according to many NGOs (Amnesty International 2012).[4] The persistence of this state of violence alienates most efforts to gather the support of local residents for the federal projects, and contradicts the President's and Prime Minister's discourses on the need to implement first and foremost a "comprehensive" solution. The discursive tensions within the prognostic framing generate confusion on the means that need to be implemented to meet the real objective of effective counterterrorism policy. Frame incoherence and discursive inconsistencies not only reflect the badly defined orientations of counterterrorism policies; they also result from the instability of the discursive counterterrorist field.

The Russian counterterrorist discursive field

As underlined above, a discursive field is composed, according to Snow, of three elements that influence and constrain framing. We argue that among these elements of context, the dynamics of Russian politics (the range of actors involved in counterterrorism and the non-hierarchical rules of the game) have certainly played an indirect but decisive role in shaping framing, alongside with cultural and historical contexts. We analyze first the historical and cultural contexts in which framing is embedded before moving more extensively to issues related to the agency and the rules of the game that govern the Russian counterterrorism discursive field. We then show how this dynamic opens up opportunities for counter-framing to emerge.

Cultural resources

On the cultural side, both recent and more distant public memories provide resources, images and symbols. The Russian population has a vivid recent memory of horrific terrorist attacks, mainly the Dubrovka theater hostage taking in 2002 and the Beslan hostage attack in 2004, which strongly shapes their beliefs about what has been going on in the region since the mid-1990s. They conflate these with ancient deep-rooted memories that picture North Caucasus residents as continuously resisting the Russian rule or as state traitors (Russell, 2005a). As pointed out by John Russell, Chechens, who actively resisted Russian rule in the nineteenth century, entered the Russian imaginary as "the epitome of the negative perception" (Russell 2005b: 103). Chechens have often been represented as a rebellious people, fighting invaders to death. The image of resolute warriors meets another representation that took shape at the latest during Soviet times. At that time, any individuals or groups suspected of being a threat to the state's security were said to be "criminals," "bandits" or "traitors" (Fitzpatrick 2000: 11; 53). For instance, the propaganda that spread before, during and after the massive deportations that targeted entire nationalities during World War II only further supported this idea of Chechens being a disloyal people (Denis 2010). Described as "criminal" and "traitors to the State," a supreme offense at a time of national cohesion in a war called "the Great Patriotic War," the Chechens were the only deported people to be accused, alongside with the Ingush, of "terrorist activities" carried out against the rear of the Soviet Army (Pobol and Polian 2005: 458–60). Chechens have also been compared to "Mafioso" and to the "most aggressive criminals living in Moscow" (Glasnost 1991), not to speak of the accusation of religious radicalism that spread just after they returned from deportation. These negative representations, targeting first Chechens, have been extended to the other Muslim North Caucasian populations (especially the Ingush and Dagestani), in the context of the spillover of the Chechen conflict into the neighboring republics.

Medvedev and Putin adopted in this respect a paradoxical position. On the one hand, they kept using these epithets, which have a strong resonance with historical and more recent events; but on the other hand, they called for a dissociation of insurgents and terrorists from the region's local population and for a "reintegration" of North Caucasus into Russia. The two Russian leaders, along with other officials, used a wide range of terms to describe those who have been taking arms to oppose the state in North Caucasus. As the systematic analysis of the collected data shows, the terms "bandits," "terrorists" and "extremists" are the most frequently used among the terms employed to depict North Caucasians. Employed interchangeably, they all refer to the notion of an immediate danger threatening the state's integrity and security. The relentless use of such terms demonstrates their naturalization and internalization. We argue that the adoption of a revised approach to fighting terrorism and the nuances introduced within discourses were in fact not accompanied by a change in the definition of the nature of the threat, leading to more inconsistencies in the framing.

Range of actors and the non-hierarchical rules of the game

Although this chapter focuses on the frames elaborated by the Russian President and his Prime Minister, the range of actors participating in the discursive counterterrorism field is larger. Other federal actors include Aleksandr Khloponin, the Presidential Envoy to the North Caucasus Federal District, who acts on behalf of the federal President; the Interior Minister, who had a lesser role in shaping the official position between 2008 and 2012; the FSB (Federal Security Service), which is in charge of coordinating the counterterrorist operations in North Caucasus; and the Minister of Defense, who consistently promotes a hardline policy (Sukhov 2010). Many local actors also participate in the counterterrorist discursive field. These include the President of each North Caucasus republic and his administration, the Republican Ministries of Internal Affairs, the local police and militias, and representatives of the local sections of the FSB, MVD (Ministry of Internal Affairs), and of the Defence Ministry.

Given the implementation of a vertical power structure that made the Russian president the center of gravity in Russian politics, one would expect the Russian counterterrorist field to be organized hierarchically and to be well constucted and stable. Indeed, the main values dominating Russian politics include "hierarchy, paternalism and clientelism" (Gorenburg 2012: 5). Although they have historically governed the relationships between actors, they have gained new momentum under Putin whose reforms "have ensconced these mechanisms more firmly in Russian politics" (ibid.: 5). The counterterrorist discursive field makes no exception, and both Medvedev and Putin, who held power and had authority within this policy field, were also the main producers of the dominant discourses on terrorism and counterterrorism. Their pre-eminent position gave their interpretations of the conflict more symbolic power (Bhatia 2005: 11). Noticeably, the Prime Minister,[5] who had not usually been involved in the development or implementation of counterterrorist policies before 2008, assumed a key role since Medvedev assigned Putin to this position. This shift was part of a greater informal redistribution of power between both members of the tandem and led to an alteration of the political game's existing rules (Kryshtanovskaya 2012: 7). Although Medvedev and Putin ensured a broad political continuity, their cohabitation did not come without tensions, and Medvedev and Putin publicly disagreed on many issues, including counterterrorism, on several occasions. One unresolved contentious issue between the two men concerned the nature of the conflicts that were tearing North Caucasus apart and the role played by separatism as a political cause to these surges of violence. In 2008, Putin, defending his policy towards the region, stated that "separatism retreated," and that Russia was "successful in ending the war in North Caucasus" (Kremlin 2008). Medvedev apparently never shared his optimism and even declared in September 2011 that "separatism and terrorism had not been defeated" (Medvedev quoted in Vesti.ru 2011).

Other aspects of Russia's political life undermine the centrality of hierarchy as a core value. The most important are certainly informal rules and ties, loyalty, localism and the omnipotence of bureaucracy. Monogham convincingly demonstrates that the establishment of a power vertical in Putin's Russia is far from being complete and that the most important splits are horizontal, due to the failure or reluctance of the other layers of authority to fulfill the Centre's orders (2012). Despite the fact that Putin retained most of the real power through Medvedev's presidency, these persistent horizontal splits seem to have increased the gap between the federal center and federate subjects. The situation in North Caucasus is even worse given the region's reigning institutional and organizational chaos.

The numerous federal and local actors involved in the counterterrorist front have proven to be unable or unwilling to cooperate. Since 2006, the National Anti-terrorism Committee (NAK) has been in charge of coordinating counterterrorist operations, but, according to the President's own words, the coordination between the federal agencies, if not the coordination between federal agencies and local administrations and militias, remains highly problematic (Kremlin 2010c). Both Medvedev and Putin regularly vowed to put energy into solving this problem in a timely fashion (Kremlin 2010a), but they are facing the very same issues as those observed during the second Chechen war: strong competition between the different actors on the ground and a total lack of coordination between the various agencies. Competition between actors, coupled with informality, loyalty and localism, constitutes as many rules of the game that make the discursive counterterrorism field unstable.

As a result, the counterterrorist field appears to be very fragmented and unsettled. It is worth noting that over the years, counterterrorism has become a stake in a larger game between the field's main actors. Competition between incumbents takes different forms, including competition over meanings. Actors involved in the field articulate their proposals and concerns in such a way as to try to advance their own agenda. This fragmentation results, for instance, in different readings of the root causes of terrorism in the region. Indeed, most of the Presidents of the North Caucasian republics have kept blaming "international terrorism" for the upsurge of violence. As Boris Ebzeyev, who led Karachayevo-Cherkessia in 2011, stated: "This force is well organized, well paid and has its own agents inside our country as well" (*Interfax* 2011a). Unlike the Russian leadership, who used the argument of international terrorism depending on the temporality and the type of the attack, local actors repeatedly emphasized this external threat to mask other political developments that may incriminate them (localism and private use of violence) (Campana 2013). This situation gives the impression of a badly orchestrated cacophony as every actor engages in a distinctive discursive enterprise.

Institutional competition and absence of field crystallisation

The Russian framing process is strongly embedded in a context where a discrete yet real competition between actors has been taking place at all levels. The rules of the game that govern the counterterrorist discursive field inevitably reflect the tensions between the actors involved. We argue that this self-perpetuating situation prevents the field from crystallizing. The most vivid competition certainly opposes Khloponin and law enforcement agencies. Indeed, the creation of the North Caucasus Federal District and the nomination of Khloponin at its head represented a political decision that increased tensions among incumbents as a new actor entered the game. These tensions manifested at the policy level, but also at the discursive one as two diverging visions emerged, adding to the stress. When Medvedev announced Khloponin's nomination, some newspapers wrote: "Russia Abandons Use of Military Force in North Caucasus."[6] Indeed, after January 2010, Khloponin was supposedly in charge of all regional affairs. Yet he developed very bad relationships with federal and local law enforcement agencies. Not only did the representatives of the latter frequently bypass him, but they also strongly disagreed on what priorities to implement. Khloponin often noted that the military solution is not a good one. He considered the problem to run deeper than just "criminality" and said that, "today, under the mask of terrorism and religious extremism on the territory of the district [of North Caucasus], bandits try to conduct their activities; they form criminal groups, which capture property and goods. It is not the role of counterterrorist operations to struggle against them" (quoted in Regnum.ru 2010). As a matter of fact though, institutional actors representing law enforcement agencies still considered repression to be the main instrument in fighting terrorism. Targeted districts and regions were regularly put under a counterterrorism regime, which means that special measures were implemented to search and "destroy" militants (*Interfax* 2011b).

Two factors increased the competition between the proponents of a hard line and the supporters of a civil approach. First, the flow of money coming into the region from Moscow created tensions within federal agencies, between federal agencies and the local administrations and within the local administrations themselves. This situation resulted from the widespread corruption and the phenomenon of "interpenetration" between security forces and organized crime, which was sometimes controlled by the insurgents themselves (Baev and Milkop 2006). Second, the ambiguous position of the Russian President added elements of confusion. Roughly speaking, before the Domodedovo airport suicide attack at the beginning of 2011, Medvedev adopted a quite moderate position, favoring a civil approach while calling for firm actions against "militants." Indeed, in the aftermath of the 2010 twin suicide attacks against the Moscow metro, he still recommended that the Kabardino-Balkaria leadership fight insurgent groups "calmly" when he stated that, "[you] need to sort things out quietly and, without hysteria, make tough decisions to uproot bandit manifestations" (Medvedev quoted in Ria-novosti. ru 2010a). That said, since 2011, he has adopted a more vigorous position, speaking of "exterminating" or "destroying" the insurgents, like Putin.

This shift in discourse may have been interpreted as a green light for law enforcement agencies to gain some ground once again on the proponents of the civil approach, increasing the sense of confusion within both the diagnostic and prognostic framing processes. For the most part, it introduced a double temporality. When speaking of improving the socio-economic conditions to win hearts and minds in order to defeat the insurgency, the Russian leadership envisioned a long-term process, but when advocating the reinforcement of repressive measures, they insisted on short-term results. Such a double stance is not specific to Russian operations in North Caucasus.[7] What makes the Russian approach different compared to other situations, however, is the total absence of integrated programs and the tensions between the two options not conceived as the two faces of a same coin. In this context, Putin and Medvedev have been holding the balance since 2008, emphasizing one side over the other depending on the context, the audiences and the balance of power within the field. For instance, their attitudes in front of law enforcement agents varied depending on these factors. When they wanted to advance the civil agenda, they usually first praised the work of the security agencies, reminded them of the need to develop preventive measures and highlighted, on a pedagogical tone, the civil component of counterterrorism, which would be given preference over other measures. In Medvedev's words, stability cannot be imposed by strong-arm methods alone, because violence has not only a "strictly criminal tincture, but also an ideological one" (quoted in Sergeev, 2011). When the context commanded stronger reactions, for example, in the aftermath of a major attack in North Caucasus or in Moscow, they declared military solutions as the most effective ones.

Besides, the "institutional inertia" (Il'chenko 2012) and lack of political innovation led to a strategic and political deadlock and ultimately to a counterproductive framing process, marked by discursive tensions and inconsistancies. This leaves room for counter-framing, which puts into question some of the assumptions supported in the frames developed by the ruling tandem.

Discursive contention and counter-framing process

There is a broad consensus in Russia about how the events in North Caucasus should be interpreted. The label "terrorist" seems to be uncritically used and accepted but some increasingly insistent voices raise concerns about the federal approach to the region. In other words, the incoherence of the frames elaborated by the ruling tandem opened up opportunities for contestation to emerge. The development of counter-frames in the more nationalistic circles shows that the discursive field is growing larger and that actors that initially had no role in it are now getting more and more involved in the discursive contestation of the dominant discourses. This also shows that the resonance of the frames elaborated by Medvedev and Putin is quite limited. Two issues are at the forefront of the contestation: the first one pertains to the diagnostic frame and refers to the interpretation of the role of Islam; the other one pertains to the prognostic frame and relates to the investments granted by the federal center to North Caucasus.

On the one hand, infuriated debates over the place of Islam arise within the Russian political class from time to time, especially after a major terrorist attack attributed to "Islamist" militants. Many politicians do not hesitate to blame Islam. Some also accuse Russian leaders of adopting a harmful position. Rogozin, a vibrant Russian nationalist who was the permanent representative of Russia to NATO in 2011, said in a TV debate that Russia is turning into breeding grounds "of not just Islam but of militant fundamentalist Islam. And this is a direct consequence of pseudo-tolerance, when we just pretend that this is not happening, as if the problem does not exist" (Rossiya 2011). Such discourse meets widespread approval among the Russian population, in particular in a context of growing Russian nationalism.

On the other hand, opponents to the massive aid to North Caucasus emphasize the inefficiency of the socio-economic programs that have shown so little results. In 2011, they created an association called "Stop feeding the Caucasus," which denounces the part of the budget devoted to North Caucasus, especially at a time of economic crisis. Some Russian ultra-nationalists even question the contribution of North Caucasus to Russia and claim for its separation from Russia (*Kyiv Post* 2010). Medvedev believes that these people are "not very smart ... or provocateurs" (quoted in Ria-novosti.ru 2011d). Far from reducing the ethnic tensions within the Federation, the federal policies indirectly increase them. This constitutes an additional challenge for the Russian leadership that seems to be running short of solutions.

Conclusion

The beginning of Vladimir Putin's third term as President of the Russian Federation did not bring drastic changes to North Caucasus. Although the levels of violence vary from one Republic to another, they remain a major cause of concern, especially in Dagestan. Indeed, the problems of armed violence in this region seem to remain a priority on the

President's political agenda even though both the Russian public opinion and political parties showed little interest towards the situation in the region. Moreover, the framing process appears still to be torn between the civil and the military approaches, and Russian leadership proves to be unable to articulate them together. This is not something new: discourses on terrorism before 2008 were plagued with the same kind of tensions regarding the causes of terrorism in Chechnya, even if Putin provisionally succeeded in recasting the fight against Chechen separatists as a struggle against Al Qaeda and its associates (Campana and Légaré 2011: 55). In other words, Russia has not managed to develop a coherent counterterrorism discourse to date.

As showed in this chapter, this can be traced to the fact that the counterterrorist framing process is strongly affected by the discursive field in which it is embedded, and more specifically by a combination of cultural, contextual and structural factors. We showed that the range of actors and the rules of the games that govern the counterterrorist field, marked by an intense competition between actors, tensions and informality, constitute as many mechanisms that prevent frame crystallization. In Russia, the rules of the game of the counterterrorist discursive field lead very much to instability and a high degree of fragmentation. Yet the Russian case demonstrates that the absence of field crystallization inevitably leads to the failure of frame crystallization, leading to inconsistencies and the inability to develop a hierarchy of causes and solutions. Ultimately, this absence of convergence leaves room for discursive contestation both inside and outside the counterterrorist discursive field. Indeed, inter-ethnic relations are becoming more and more an issue as tensions around the future of North Caucasus remain very high and counter-framing is gaining support among the Russian nationalist circles (Putin 2012).

Notes

1 Mainly Ria-novosti.ru, *Interfax*, ITAR-TASS, *Rossiyskaya Gazeta*, Regnum.ru, Lenta.ru and kommersant.ru. Most of our sources are in Russian. Except when indicated, all translations from Russian to English are ours.
2 Many leaders of the Emirate, except the self-proclaimed Chef Doku Umarov, have been killed, inflicting major blows on the insurgency.
3 On the last estimation of the average unemployment rate in North Caucasus (Lenta.ru 2010).
4 See also the daily news on the Memorial website, www.memo.ru/daytoday/index.htm.
5 We are here talking about Prime Minister as a function.
6 See http://gazeta.ru, http://www.vedomosti.ru, www.gazeta.ru, http://kommersant.ru, January 20, 2011.
7 The same observation may be transposed to the NATO COIN (counter-insurgency) operation in Afghanistan (personal observations, Kandahar and Kabul, January 2010).

References

Amnesty International (2012) *The Circle of Injustice Security Operations and Human Rights Violations in Ingushetia.* London: Amnesty International. Available at www.amnesty.org/en/library/asset/EUR46/012/2012/en/15aa2dcf-0b39-43f0-a8b8-658668806212/eur460122012en.pdf (accessed July 5, 2012).

Baev, P. and Milkop A. (2006) "Contre-terrorisme et islamisation du Caucase du Nord," *Politique étrangère*, 1, 167–77.

BBC News (2011) "Chechen warlord Doku Umarov admits Moscow airport bomb," February 8. Available at www.bbc.co.uk/news/world-europe-12388681 (accessed July 30, 2012).

Benford, R.D. and Snow D.A. (2000) "Framing processes and social movements: An overview and assessment," *Annual Review of Sociology*, 26, 611–39.

Benford R.E. (2010) "Framing," in R.L. Jackson II and M.A. Hogg (eds) *Encyclopedia of Identity*. Thousand Oaks, CA: Sage, 294–6.

Bhatia, M.V. (2005) "Fighting words: naming terrorists, bandits, rebels and other violent actors," *Third World Quarterly* 26(1), 5–22.

Campana, A. (2013) "La régionalisation de la violence au Caucase du Nord," in A. Campana and G. Hervouet (eds) *Terrorisme et insurrection. Evolution des dynamiques conflictuelles et réponses des États*, Québec: Presses Universitaires du Québec, 113–135.

Campana, A. and Légaré K. (2011) "Russia's Counterterrorism Operation in Chechnya: Institutional Competition and Issue Frames," *Studies in Conflict and Terrorism* 34(1), 47–63.

CBS News (2010) "Chechen rebel admits Moscow bombings," April 1. Available at www.cbc.ca/news/world/story/2010/03/31/russia-caucasus-blasts.html (accessed July 30, 2012).

Della Porta, D. and Diani, M. (2006) *Social movements: an introduction.* Malden: Wiley Blackwell.

Denis, J. (2010) "De la condamnation à l'expulsion: la construction de l'image de collaboration de masse durant la Grande Guerre patriotique," in A. Campana, G. Dufaud and S. Tournon (eds) *Les Déportations en Héritage. Les Peuples réprimés du Caucase Hier et Aujourd'hui*, Rennes: Presses Universitaires de Rennes, 29–51.

Fiss, P.C. and Hirsch, P.M. (2005) "The Discourse of Globalization: Framing and Sensemaking of an Emerging Concept," *American Sociological Review*, 70(1), 29–52.

Fitzpatrick, S. (2000) *Everyday Stalinism. Ordinary Life in Extraordinary Times: Soviet Russia in the 1930s*, Oxford/New York: Oxford University Press.

Glasnost (1991) Interview of MVD member, N. Shilin, "Cecenskâ mafia vse neprosto," *Glasnost*, 7, February 12, 3.

Goffman, E. (1974) *Frame Analysis.* New York: Harper & Row.

Gorenburg, D. (2012) "The rules of the political game in Russia," *Russian Politics and Law*, 50(3), 3–6.

Granik, I. (2010) "Naša politika na Kavkaze dolžna byt' sovremennoj," *Kommersant*, 55, March 31. Available at www.kommersant.ru/doc/1346076 (accessed August 11, 2012).

Hoffman, B. (2006) *Inside Terrorism*, New York: Columbia University Press.

Hülsse, R. and Spencer, A. (2008) "The metaphor of terror: terrorism studies and the constructivist turn," *Security Dialog*, 39(6), 571–92.

Hunter, S. T. (2004) *Islam in Russia: The Politics of Identity and Security*, New York: Center for Strategic and International Studies.

Il'chenko, M. (2012) "Inertia in Russian politics," *Russian Politics and Law*, 50(3), 70–81.

Interfax (2011a) "Karachayevo-Cherkessia to use Ingush counter-terror experience," *Interfax*, February 8.

Interfax (2011b) "Russians announce additional steps to fight militants in Chechnya, Ingushetia," *Interfax*, July 5.

Jackson, R. (2005a) *Writing the War on Terrorism: Language, Politics and Counterterrorism*, Manchester: Manchester University Press.

Jackson, R. (2005b) "Security, democracy, and the rhetoric of counter-terrorism," *Democracy and Security*, 1(2), 147–71.

Jackson, R. (2006) "Genealogy, ideology, and counter-terrorism: writing wars on terrorism from Ronald Reagan to George W. Bush Jr," *Studies in Language & Capitalism*, 1(1), 163–93.

Jackson, R. (2007) "The core commitments of critical terrorism studies," *European Political Science*, 6(3), 244–51.

Johnston, H. (1995) "A methodology from frame analysis. From discourse to cognitive schemata," in H. Johnston and B. Klandesmans (eds) *Social Movements and Culture*, Minneapolis, MN: University of Minnesota Press, 217–46.

Jorgensen, M. and Philip, L. (2002) *Discourse Analysis as Theory and Method*. London: Sage Publications.

Kremlin (2008) "Speech at expanded meeting of the State Council on Russia's development strategy through to 2020," February 2. Available at http://eng.kremlin.ru/speeches/2008/02/08/1137_type82912type82913_159643.shtml, (accessed May 31, 2010).

Kremlin (2010a) "Neobhodimo rasširim' i užestočit' mery po bor'be s terrorismom," April 1. Available at http://kremlin.ru/news/7307. Official English translation available at http://archive.kremlin.ru/eng/text/news/2010/04/225175.shtml (accessed August 12, 2011).

Kremlin (2010b) "Načalo sovešaniâ s rukovotelâmi respublik Severno-Kavkazskogo federal'nogo okruga, territorial'nyh podrazdelenij Federal'noj služby bezopasnosti i organov vnutrennih del," April 1. Available at http://kremlin.ru/transcripts/7308 (accessed August 12, 2011).

Kremlin (2010c) "Sovešanie o kompleksnyh merah po obespečeniû stabil'nosti na Severnom Kavkaze," November 19. Available at http://news.kremlin.ru/news/9557. Official English translation available at http://eng.news.kremlin.ru/news/1336 (accessed August 12, 2011).

Kremlin (2011) "D. Medvedev provël vo Vladikavkaze zasedanie Nacional'nogo antiterrorističeskogo komiteta," February 22. Available at http://news.kremlin.ru/transcripts/10408 (accessed August 12, 2011).

Kremlin (2012) "Dmitri Medvedev met with the Security Council Members to discuss ways to fight terrorism more effectively," March 31, Gorki, Moscow Region. Available at http://eng.news.kremlin.ru/news/131 (accessed August 12, 2011).

Kryshtanovskaya O. (2012) "Formats of Russian state power," *Russian Politics and Law*, 50(3), 7–17.

Kyiv Post (2010) "Russian nationalists, leftists and Chechens debate future of North Caucasus," *Kyiv Post*, May 19. Available at www.kyivpost.com/news/opinion/op_ed/detail/104819/#ixzz1cnE8zJXs (accessed August 12, 2011).

Lenta.ru (2010) "Hloponin predložil podelim' kavkazskimi bezrabotnymi so bsej Rossiej," Lenta.ru, April 15. Available at www.lenta.ru/news/2010/04/15/jobless/ (accessed June 7, 2010).

Medvedev, D. (2008), "Čečniâ Respublika perešla iz vosstanovitel'noj fazy normal'no, ustojčivogo razvitiâ," *Groznyj Inform*, February 4. Available at www.grozny-inform.ru/main.mhtml?Part=8&PubID=5163 (accessed August 12, 2011).

Mendelson, S. (2010) "Violence in North Caucasus. 2009: a bloody year," *Center for the Strategic and International Studies*. Available at http://csis.org/publication/violence-north-caucasus-5 (accessed February 4, 2010).

Mendelson, S., Malarkey, M. and Moore, L. (2010) "Violence in the North Caucasus. Spring 2010: On the rise, again?," *Center for the Strategic and International Studies*. Available at http://csis.org/files/publication/100513_Violence_in_the_North_Caucasus_Spring_2010.pdf (accessed June 3, 2010).

Monaghan, A. (2012) "The *vertikal*: power and authority in Russia," *International Affairs* 88(1), 1–16.

Oliver P.E. and Johnston, H. (2000) "What a good idea! Ideologies and frames in social movement research," *Mobilization: An International Journal*, 5(1), 37–54.

Omelicheva, M. (2009) "Russia's counterterrorism policy: variations on an imperial theme," *Perspectives on Terrorism*, 3. Available at www.terrorismanalysts.com/pt/index.php/pot/article/view/61/html (accessed July 30, 2012).

Oren, N. and Bar-Tal, D. (2007) "The detrimental dynamics of delegitimization in intractable conflicts: the Israeli–Palestinian case," *International Journal of Intercultural Relations* 37(1), 111–26.

Parfentyeva, I. (2011) "Severnyj Kavkaz ne obojdut šedrost'û gosmonopolij," *Kommersant*, September 20. Available at www.kommersant.ru/doc/1777061 (accessed September 30, 2011).

Pobol, N.L. and Polian, P.M. (eds) (2005) *Stalinskie deportatsii 1928–1953. Dokumenty*, Moscow: Materik Fond Demokratia.

Premier.gov.ru (2010) "Predsedatel' Pravitel'stva Rossijskoj Federacii V.V. Putin prinâl učastie v mežregional'noj konferencii partii 'Edinaâ Rossiâ' na temu 'Strategiâ social'no-ekonomičeskogo razvitiâ Servernogo Kavkaza do 2020 goda. Programma na 2010–2012 gody'," June 6. Available at http://premier.gov.ru/visits/ru/11295/events/11301, official translation in English available at http://premier.gov.ru/eng/visits/ru/11295/events/11301/ (accessed August 9, 2011).

Premier.gov.ru (2011a) "Predsedatel' Pravitel'stva Rossijskoj Federacii V.V. Putin provël zasedanie Pravitel'stvennoj Komissii po voprosam social'no-ekonomičeskogo razvitiâ Severo-Kavkazskogo federal'nogo okruga," January 21. Available http://premier.gov.ru/events/news/13920/ (accessed August 12, 2011).

Premier.gov.ru (2011b) "Predsedatel' Pravitel'stva Rossijskoj Federacii V.V. Putin vstretil'câ s predstavitelâmi konfessij I nacional'no-kul'turnyh obŝestvennyh ogranuzannij," June 19. Available at http://premier.gov.ru/events/news/15972/, (accessed September 19, 2011).

Putin, V. (2009) "Special'n'aâ programma: Razgovor c Vladimirom Putinym. Prodolženie," December 3. Available at http://2009.moskva-putinu.ru (accessed August 12, 2011).

Putin, V. (2012) "Rossiâ. Nacional'nyj Vopros," *Nezavisimaâ Gazeta*, 23 January. Available at www.ng.ru/politics/2012-01-23/1_national.html (accessed June 25, 2012).

Regnum.ru (2010) "Hloponin: Pod mskoj terrorizma i ekstremisma skryvaûtsâ bandity," Regnum.ru, May 27. Available at www.Regnum.ru/news/1287978.html (accessed August 12, 2012).

Ria-novosti.ru (2010a) "Medvedev: bandy na Kavkaze nyžno iskorenât' žestko i 'bez isterik'," Ria-novosti.ru, February 27. Available at http://ria.ru/politics/20100227/211264285.html (accessed August 12, 2011).

Ria-novosti.ru (2010b) "Korrupciâ na Severnom Kavkaze ugrožaet nasbezopasnosti – Medvedev," Ria-novosti.ru, May 19. Available at http://ria.ru/video/20100519/236180881.html (accessed August 12, 2011).

Ria-novosti.ru (2011a) "D. Medvedev provël vo Vladikavkaze zasedanie Nacional'nogo antiterrorističeskogo komiteta," Ria-novosti.ru, February 22. Available at http://news.kremlin.ru/transcripts/10408 (accessed August 12, 2011).

Ria-novosti.ru (2011b) "Medvedev obešal razvivat' turism na Kavkaze vopreki dejstviam bantitov," Ria-novosti.ru, February 22. Available at http://ria.ru/politics/20110222/337393388.html (accessed August 12, 2011).

Ria-novosti.ru (2011c) "Putin posovetoval severokavkascam razvivat' turism i 'ne šipat' turistok," Ria-novosti.ru, August 4. Available at http://ria.ru/video/20110803/411526599.html; English translation available at http://en.rian.ru/video/20110804/165561265.html (accessed September 9, 2011).

Ria-novosti.ru (2011d) "Lozung 'Hvatit kormit' Kavkaz' grozit raskolom, sčitaet Medvedev," Ria-novosti.ru, October 20. Available at http://ria.ru/politics/20111020/465574549.html (accessed October 21, 2011).

Rossiyskaya Gazeta (2011) "Yabloko leaders blame corruption for inter-ethnic conflicts in Russia," *Rossiyskaya Gazeta* 1, September 11.

Russell, J. (2005a) "Mujahedeen, Mafia, Madmen…: Russian perceptions of Chechens during the wars in Chechnya, 1994–1996 and 1999 to date," *Journal of Postcommunist Studies and Transition Politics*, 18(1), 73–96.

Russell, J. (2005b) "Terrorists, Bandits, Spooks and Thieves: Russian demonization of the Chechens prior to and since 9/11," *Third World Quarterly*, Special Issue "The Politics of naming: Rebels, Terrorists, Criminals, Bandits and Subversives," 26(1), 101–16.

Scheufele, D.A. (1999) "Framing as theory of mass media effects," *Journal of Communication*, 49(1), 103–22.

Sergeev, N. (2011) "The 'Caucasus emirate' has reached Moscow," *Kommersant*, July 27.

Snetkov, A. (2007) "The image of the terrorist threat in the official Russian press: the Moscow Theatre Crisis (2002) and the Beslan Hostage Crisis (2004)," *Europe–Asia Studies*, 59(8), 1349–65.

Snow, D.A. (2008) "Elaborating the discursive contexts of framing: discursive fields and spaces," in N.K. Denzin (ed.) *Studies in Symbolic Interaction* 30, 3–28.

Steinberg, M.W. (1999) "The talk and back talk of collective action: A dialogic analysis of repertoires of discourse among nineteenth-century English cotton-spinners," *American Journal of Sociology*, 105(3), 736–80.

Sukhov, I. (2010) "War on terror: North Caucasus Federal District," Agentura.ru, September 3. Available at www.agentura.ru/english/terrorism/ncfd/ (accessed September 22, 2011).

Tuathail, G.O. (2009) "Placing blame: Making sense of Beslan," *Political Geography*, 28(1), 4–15.

Vatchagaev, M. (2012) "Dagestan's Security Situation Remains Problematic Despite Increased Military Presence," *North Caucasus Analysis*, 13. Available at www.jamestown.org/single/?no_cache=1&tx_ttnews%5Bswords%5D=8fd5893941d69d0be3f378576261ae3e&tx_ttnews%5Bany_of_the_words%5D=

COUNTERTERRORISM%20NORTH%20CAUCASUS&tx_ttnews%5Bpointer%5D=4&tx_ttnews%5Btt_news%5D=39558&tx_ttnews%5BbackPid%5D=7&cHash=27faad66d791273d34cb2d0a91ef3ba0 (accessed July 30, 2012).

Vesti.ru (2011) "Medveded: separatism i terrorism ostaûtsâ ser'eznymi vyzovami dlâ Rossii," Vesti.ru, September 8. Available at www.vesti.ru/videos?cid=7&vid=359630 (accessed September 19, 2011).

Williams, R.H. (1995) "Constructing the public good: social movements and cultural resources," *Social Problems* 42(1), 124–44.

Zulaika, J. and Douglass, W. (1996) *Terror and Taboo: The Follies, Fables, and Faces of Terrorism*, London: Routledge.

12 The hunter and the hunted

Metaphors of pursuit, prey and the intractability of difference in post 9/11 American counterterrorism discourse

Deborah Wills and Erin Steuter

Counterterrorism discourse, deeply embedded in the metaphoric frames it draws upon to identify and address threats, is neither purely descriptive nor expositional. Rather, its reiterated representations assume a collective force that diagram a logic of enmity founded in a discourse of intractable difference. This logic shapes conceptual frameworks, influences multiple forms of public speech, and potentially mitigates the effectiveness of attempts to break free of cyclical violence. This chapter identifies a coherent set of counterterrorism metaphors circulated and ratified in political and military speech, analyzing government's rhetorical framing of the military's task in the war on terror as a hunt for prey, involving "smoking out" and "hunting down" terrorists. The chapter documents the extent of the hunt metaphor, with its reliance on the conflation of enemy and animal, and its expansion from specific enemy figures to Arabs and Muslims at large. Collectively, these have consequences for fomenting conflict. By analyzing and dismantling them, however, critical attention to such metaphors offers a means of redirecting such powerful rhetorical tools, subjecting them to a revisionary reframing that can usefully evolve our discursive lexicon, and create broadened strategies for counterterrorism communication.

Rhetoric and the "culture of contention"

As scholars of cognitive metaphor studies have long asserted, both the effectiveness and the performativity of counterterrorism are inherently related to the broad metaphorical schema out of which it speaks. Counterterrorist scholarship and practice must therefore take increased note of the "cultural grammar" expressed in and through the language of the war on terror (Jackson 2005: 391). Remolding the language of the culture of contention, observe Arjun Chowhdury and Ronald Krebs, "requires rhetorical intervention"; since "the success of counterterrorist efforts" depends on more than military force and strategy, and since the state's public rhetoric often rivals military endeavor in consequence and urgency, counterterrorist discourse must recognize representational practice as central to its task (Chowdhury and Krebs 2010: 26). Not to do so risks overlooking the fact that the conflicts central to the "war on terror" are inevitably expressed through a "set of rhetorical and ideational elements" and "an array of material practices," which must be understood not as distinct "variables" but as "mutually constitutive" (Jackson 2005: 392). Since such material and ideational practices are interdependent, the rhetorical devices of the first should be considered in relation to the pragmatic measures of the second, particularly when the former furthers a dehumanizing discourse that shapes the latter (Steuter and Wills 2008).

Among the most pervasive and damaging of these discourses are those that figuratively link the enemy with the less than human; this includes the viral, the reptilian or insect, and the bestial. Rhetorical tropes portraying the enemy as inhuman are reinforced on multiple levels of public discourse and, because they are emotionally amplified through the discourses of popular culture, become rhetorically entrenched (Shaheen 2001). The figuration of the war on terror as a hunt has come to dominate multiple forms of social and cultural expression, ranging from official government speech to social networking sites, film and television, talk radio, and political cartoons (Steuter and Wills 2008). These frames are most significant when they are aligned with existing prejudices and preconceptions: if public policy representations dovetail "with existing threat perceptions in the population" that "depict the alleged terrorist threat as ... fundamentally hostile," especially if these depictions are already "accepted by the majority of the population" (de Graaf 2011: 3), they will be most influential. The "representational force" (Bially Mattern 2001: 350) of such semantic practices speaks to more than their ability to persuade: they point to their often less-visible constitutive, even coercive, import. Thus, for example, the rhetorical shift that corresponded with the shift in 2008 between the Bush and Obama administrations supports, in its conscious movement towards a less inflammatory tone and a less controversial martial framing, a degree of heightened political attention towards these aspects of counterterrorist speech. As part of his efforts to combat terrorist networks more effectively, President Barack Obama deliberately moved away from the most "visible symbols and rhetorical framework" of the previous administration's "Global War on Terror"; however, while the stated intent of the Obama administration is to re-establish relations with mainstream Muslim communities, isolate and marginalize violent extremists, and "undermine extremist narratives," tactics largely overlooked by the Bush administration, there nevertheless remains a "substantial continuity" between Obama's policies and those "adopted by the Bush administration in its final two years" (Lynch 2010: 5). For example, Obama has avoided replicating Bush's framing of "the struggle against militant Islamic radicalism" as "the great ideological conflict of the twenty-first century" (Lynch 2010: 3, 16), distancing his own political speech from this "clash of civilizations" model. Rather than propagate Bush's "war of ideas," or his controversial coining of the term

"Islamofacism," Obama attempted to separate extremist organizations such as al Qaeda from "the Muslim communities of the world" (Obama 2009b), a phrasing that offered a significant rhetorical shift from the earlier, more homogenizing phrase "the Muslim world"; this "evolving approach sought to disaggregate the challenges into specific organizations and ideologies rather than to lump them all together into a specific, coherent adversary" (Lynch 2010: 16). The intent to "disaggregate" the previously undifferentiated enemy is central to creating effective public diplomacy speech; it is, therefore, the often unintentional perpetuation of figurative language that may hinder such disaggregating discourse that this chapter will address, focusing on the resilient and persistent metaphors of undifferentiation, dehumanization, predation, and intractable difference that may limit the effectiveness of counterterrorist speech as part of the larger public conversation surrounding counterterrorism, public safety, and conflict resolution. Counterterrorist strategies will be hampered in achieving their goals unless counterterrorist speech redefines its rhetorical range, substituting new metaphors for those currently in use. Perhaps most crucially, counterterrorism speech must dispense with the persistent hunt metaphor, with its reliance upon the conflation of enemy and animal, and its expansive and homogenizing tendencies. These tendencies work against the dynamic of disaggregation and individuation to re-inscribe the conflation of all Muslims or Arabs with specific enemies. An essential first step in rehabilitating counterterrorism rhetoric is to move away from the ongoing characterization, still present in government and military speech and echoed in multiple forms of media and broadcast journalism, of counterterrorist activity as a hunt in which terrorists (and often their compatriots) are figured as prey to the military's hunter. When such metaphors comprise dominant public understandings of terrorism they limit the possibilities of imagining effective counterterrorism measures and positive policy alternatives: in this sense, as Beatrice de Graaf asserts, "government statements are not mere texts: they create reality" (2011: 3). This is especially important because policy alternatives that are "at odds with underlying discourses" are ultimately "not socially sustainable" (Chowdhury and Krebs 2010: 127). The dominant discourse is thus almost inevitably "the only plausible arena of struggle" (Scott 1990: 102). Chowdhury and Krebs argue that, in order for effective counterterrorist measures to occur, the common assumption among "analysts of counterterrorism in particular" must change from regarding rhetoric as "nothing more than 'cheap talk'" to understanding that "what can be said shapes what policies can be pursued (2010: 127). Rhetorical formulations are thus central to the aspirations of both public policy and counterterrorist discourse. Critical attention to such metaphors offers a means of evaluating and redirecting such powerful rhetorical tools, subjecting them to a revisionary reframing that can usefully evolve the current discursive lexicon and create broadened strategies for effective counterterrorism communication.

Metaphor and the representational project

The language of counterterrorism discourse, like the language of wartime rhetoric in general, is neither merely descriptive nor simply expositional. While it contains an obvious element of persuasive purpose, its intent goes beyond persuasion: it "is not simply an objective or neutral reflection of reality" but a "meticulously composed" rhetorical construction of reality (Jackson 2005: 2). This "representational project" is designed to achieve, justify and institutionalize key political goals, from legitimizing existing counterterrorism activities to containing, limiting, and marginalizing counter-hegemonic dissent (Jackson 2005: 70). Central to this project is the mobilization of certain repeated registers of metaphor, which helps to establish and sustain persistent metanarratives of self and other, citizen and barbarian, human and animal, soldier and prey. These metanarratives simultaneously construct both a struggle and an identity for the contestants implicated in that struggle. While metanarratives such as that of an ongoing tension between civilization and barbarism have received considerable critical and theoretical attention since the "clash of civilizations" thesis was politically revitalized in government discourse following the 9/11 attacks, other sets of potent metaphors, while equally charged, have garnered little critical notice. The hunt metaphor is, crucially, one of these neglected but critical tropes.

Influential theories of metaphor and cognition and critical metaphor analysis suggest that metaphoric speech has the capacity to bypass rational modes of persuasion by augmenting or even replacing the appeal to logic with a powerful appeal to emotion. As Schwarz-Friesel and Skirl note, metaphors are thus "always part of the persuasive strategies contained in a text," and are central to argument because "they combine the cognitive function" of persuasion "with an emotional one" (2011: 2). George Lakoff contends that an estimated 98 percent of human thought operates below the level of consciousness, within the "cognitive unconscious" (Lakoff 2008: 9). Instead of relying on logical persuasion, then, metaphoric speech encodes and confirms suspicions, fears, and assumptions about the nature of the enemy, assumptions that often spread beyond the individual terrorist as criminal actor to implicitly embrace all those of the terrorist's religion, ethnicity or nationality. This is particularly true when it draws upon and re-iterates established but often unexamined conceptual frames that are so common that they shape as much as they articulate thought. Such figures, point out theorists of metaphor, "attempt to redraw semantic boundaries" and, in the process, often "re-define the concept of humanity" itself (Goatly 2007: 120).

Critical metaphors, critical discourse

Our work draws on three approaches to the analysis of political speech. Most broadly, it participates in the modes of discourse analysis developed by Norman Fairclough, who argued that such texts "constitute a sensitive barometer of socio-cultural change," and are therefore "valuable material for researching change" (1995: 52). It is also shaped by two strands of metaphor study: Lakoff and Johnson's groundbreaking work on metaphor and cognition, and Charteris-Black's critical metaphor analysis or CMA. We employ CMA's technique of assembling a textual "corpus" in order to identify the presence of the central metaphor *enemy as animal* and its allied tropes of prey, predator, and pursuit. Our approach is influenced by CMA's nuanced attention to the textuality of metaphor; at the same time, it retains Lakoff and Johnson's emphasis on the cognitive and their proposition that the human mind is inherently "embodied," understanding key abstractions primarily through its choice of metaphorical structuration (Lakoff and Johnson 1980). Our process reflects the alertness to the discursive contexts of metaphoric public speech developed in Lakoff and Johnson's early work and the ideological implications of such speech in the manner of Lakoff's more recent work (Lakoff 2006, 2008).

The critical role of race, we argue, which has often remained implicit or tacit in analysis of counterterrorism speech, must be heightened in scholarly discussion. The recent surge of scholarship that focuses on unpacking political discourse has raised valuable insights; the attention drawn in such work to the import of government counterterrorism rhetoric and its encoding of cultural metanarratives of identity and difference is crucial to the analysis of counterterrorism speech. An analysis of race, however, must be more strenuously inserted into discussions of narratives of cultural difference since it is the fundamental trope of racial difference that solidifies and consolidates the discourse of cultural difference upon which many counterterrorist metanarratives rely. Recognizing the racial dimension of the metaphors inscribed by such tropes is crucial to a productive discussion of counterterrorism speech and policy. Such metaphors, especially those that forcefully identify the racial other as animals, reptiles or vermin, imply that conflict has its basis in incurable, implacable and inherent conditions of difference, and consistently replay those metaphors, reinforcing this intractability of difference. They suggest that there is a "historical inevitability" to the kinds of conflict emerging from such differences (El Fadl 2002), and that there is a fundamental embeddedness to such difference that lies beyond negotiation or resolution. Images emphasizing inherent difference circulate widely across many genres of public representation, from political speech to journalism to popular culture, generating an Islamophobia based on the assumption that, at root, Islam is not only aggressively anti-Western but is innately alien, barbaric, and resistant to change; its difference and oppositionality, in other words, are not only inherent but implacable.

This notion of intractable difference is crucially reinforced by the triple conflation in public discourse of religion, culture and race; frequently the public blurring of distinctions between these three markers creates both a false homogenization of a discursively constructed enemy with a threateningly unified community of difference, and "plays into the idea that Arabs represent a Muslim race, which then mirrors the State's construction of a raced Muslim terrorist" (Choudhury 2006: 25). Film and television portrayals of Arabs and Muslims, for example, offer an unproblematized body of images depicting them as violent, driven by illogical passions and implacable hatreds. These images are so common that they have become part of America's "visual heritage," reinforcing, with each iteration, oppositional metaphors of fundamental difference (Shaheen 2006). The recirculation of this body of images across many discursive venues amounts to a "trafficking in expert Middle eastern lore" (Said 1993: 295). Scholars such as Sherene Razack (2008) and Karim H. Karim (2000) have documented ways in which post 9/11 representations exacerbated the "racial structure of citizenship," rewriting the "cold war script" to feature the "Muslim Other" as the new threat and arguing that government counterterrorist responses employ race "as a proxy for risk"; Razack notes that when such responses are "recast as bureaucracy, it becomes easy to miss the inclining rather than declining significance of race" (Razack 2008: 4, 32, 33).

Our aim is therefore to re-insert into the critical explorations of counterterrorist speech the heightened alertness to racism and its implications initiated by earlier developers of critical metaphor analysis and critical terrorism studies. Using as evidence the US government's persistent likening of their counterterrorist strategy to a hunt for animals rather than a search for humans and their rhetorical framing of the military's primary operational mandate as one of "smoking out" and "hunting down" terrorists, we propose that this body of hunt metaphors has collectively merged the figure of the soldier with that of the hunter. This conflation is significant, since such figurations shape the choices made in pursuing both the mechanisms of conflict and those of resolution, as well as influencing the behavior and self-representation of soldiers operating under the unexamined or naturalized rubric of the hunt metaphor.

Political scripts and rhetorical tropes

The language of the war on terror comprises a "set of words, and assumptions, metaphors" designed to "normalize and legitimate" current counterterrorist approaches (Jackson 2005: 2). Fundamental to this process is the construction of the enemy as non-human (Steuter and Wills 2011); while this technique has historically been a staple of wartime propaganda across a spectrum of national and international conflicts, new wartime technologies have endowed it with an increasingly urgent consequentiality. Thus, the central question of what constitutes the human is not only an instructive issue from the perspective of metaphorical theory, but promises "to be one of the major ideological battlegrounds of the 21st century" (Goatly 2007: 126). When counterterrorism speech relies increasingly on a set of metaphors that is patterned and programmatic, the ideologically charged nature of such discourse becomes clear. While Goatly's work has been exceptionally alert to the importance of the *human as animal* metaphor that diminishes the enemy in public government discourse, it overlooks one aspect of the metaphor's asymmetrical application, that is, the consistent categorization of the enemy as a particular kind of animal: specifically, a lower-order animal or reptile rhetorically figured as prey in the "hunt" for terrorists, prey that must be "flushed out," "smoked out," "snared," or "netted" (National Counterterrorism Center 2005; Department of Defense 2005b). This enemy-prey is metaphorically situated in a low or subterranean habitat, habitually figured as a den, lair, hole, swamp, or cave (Steuter and Wills 2008). Linking the language of hunt and prey to that of verminous hoard or swarm, US Department of Defense publications also regularly employs the terms "breed" or "breeding grounds" for terrorist activities, populations, and locales. Donald Rumsfeld, for example, said the US must pursue "terrorist cells where they breed" (Department of Defense 2003), and referred to Afghanistan as a "breeding ground for radical Islamic militancy" (Department of Defense 2002b). Similarly, Deputy Secretary of Defense Paul Wolfowitz insisted that "we work to destroy the habitat where terrorists breed" (Department of Defense 2004b), and that Americans must no longer "allow the Middle East to breed terrorists on a massive scale" (Department of Defense 2004a). Wolfowitz also memorably merged habitat and swarm language when he noted that the task of the US military was "not only to capture and kill terrorists, but to drain the swamp in which they breed" (Department of Defense 2002a). Noting such rhetorical patterns is crucial not only because such metaphors "embody the constructionist principle in their very logic of operation," but also because collectively this rhetorical repertoire points both to key revelations about the construction of apparently intractable difference and to the extent to which such a stock of metaphors becomes binding even to its chief articulators (Hulsse and Spencer 2008: 578). When we participate in a discourse we must employ its metaphors (Doty 1993), and this process is often automatic, since most metaphors are conventionalized, a rhetorical figure "for which a particular reading has become socially established," thus "constraining other readings" (Charteris-Black 2004: 17).

One of the most provocative examples of this is found in the difference between scripted counterterrorism speech and extemporized counterterrorism speech following 9/11. In his Presidential remarks on September 24, 2001, for example, George W. Bush (2001a) described his administration's latest initiative in "our war on terrorism" as "a strike on the financial foundation of the global terror network." His scripted speech employed strong language promising to "starve" and "rout" the terrorists, but used human-habitat language throughout (referring to the terrorists' "hiding places" rather than dens, swamps, or holes) and referencing human actions (such as "bring them to justice" and "disrupt" their "networks" rather than hunt them down or smoke them out). However, in the President's subsequent unscripted responses to press questions, he employs the hunt motif and commensurate prey-habitat metaphors, promising "we're going to smoke them out of their caves" (ibid.). Similarly, in his October 11, 2001 news conference, Bush's (2001b) scripted speech emphasized habitat-neutral and pursuit-neutral terms, informing Americans that the Armed Forces have "ruined terrorist training camps" and are "pursuing" agents of terror; in his unscripted responses, however, he reverted again to prey-habitat language, promising to "smoke" the enemy "out of his cave," a linguistic formulation that came to characterize the "hunt" for bin Laden in military as well as government speech and subsequently in media headlines (Steuter and Wills 2008) and as reflected in many examples of Bush's later, unscripted public speech. This framing of the hunt came frequently to characterize the rhetoric of key administrative and military figures: for example, Secretary of Defense Donald Rumsfeld described the hunt for al Qaeda as an effort to "chase them to ground and root them out" (Department of Defense 2001). Major General Hertling echoed this hunting terminology in his assertion that "al Qaeda has gone to ground," a term originating in fox hunting; Hertling added, "we are hunting them out where they have gone to ground" (Department of Defense 2008a). Major General Hammond likewise noted that enemies in Iraq had either dispersed or "gone to ground" (Department of Defense 2008b). Senator Joe Lieberman (2007) described the "terror[izing] Mahdi Army" as having "gone to ground;" White House Press Secretary Tony Snow also described al Qaeda as having "gone to ground" (Snow 2006). Journalists began to use the same phrasing in their questions to military leaders, as when CNN's Mike Mount asked Major General Joseph Fil if insurgents who "have essentially gone to ground" might re-appear (Department of Defense 2007). The proliferation of hunt language between speakers and across discursive contexts underlies the powerfully replicating effects of such metaphors, illustrating how such discursive figurations can shape both speakers and actors, "their self-understandings, their purposes, and their practices" (Hulsse and Spencer 2008: 577). When President Bush said, in his remarks to the International CEO Summit, that the enemy "has chosen to live on the hunted margins of mankind" (Bush: 2001c), he articulated a stance drawn from the "cynegetic war," a war based on the hunt for "ontologically disfigured" enemies who are depicted as proscribed not only from law or a particular community but from "humankind in general" (Chamayou: 2011).

The metaphors consistently identifying the terrorist enemy as prey to be hunted is further reinforced not only by the rhetorical identification of enemy bases as animal habitats, but by a similar identification of the soldier as a hunter who does not "fight," "engage with," or even "conquer" the enemy but rather "hunts down," "smokes out," or "flushes out" prey.

In a speech to a domestic audience, President George W. Bush said, "Listen, you've just got to know ... there's no cave deep enough for the long arm of American justice" (Bush cited in Charteris-Black 2004: 171). Charteris-Black's analysis of Bush's comments aptly emphasizes the nature of the specifically American brand of "justice" that the President's speech invokes; it is perhaps even more important, however, to take note of the metaphor of the cave as the site in which Bush's comments locate the enemy. His allusion suggests that these are not merely criminals or outlaws who are evading the penalties of their actions and need to be drawn out of their hiding place and into the justice system: they are, instead, portrayed as creatures who have, instinctively, gone to ground, where animals typically go to hide. The cave metaphor, as part of the larger complex of hunt and predation discourse, is just one example of a network of intersecting metaphors that consolidate to shape and influence public perception. The hunt metaphor has thus, over time, become a remarkably coherent, consistent, and potent collection of complementary linguistic framings.

The resilience of metaphors emerging from the hunted animal trope is exemplified in the way official government speech recirculates them over time, even across different political administrations. In September 2002, for example, the US Senate's Congressional Record documents an early use of a persistent image, the terrorist organization as snake (US Congressional record 2002). Over time, the reptile metaphor re-asserts itself in the public record across multiple fora of government speech. It is noteworthy too, that the snake metaphor shifts and migrates while remaining in broad use: it is employed to describe, variously, specific terrorist leaders, specific terrorist organizations, and entire nations, a flexibility of use that dangerously conflates individuals and their actions with entire populations. For example, in 2004, when a Pentagon press release stated that Afghanistan was the "head of the snake" of global terrorist activity, the snake metaphor is attached not to an individual but to an entire nation (Department of Defense October 2004c). In 2005, the metaphor resurfaces in a comment from Chairman of the Joint Chiefs of Staff Richard Myers, who said that "the nature of an insurgency is that you can cut the head off the snake, but it will grow another one" (Department of Defense 2005a). The snake metaphor continues in use in military and political speech during the Obama administration, as well. For example, on May 2, 2011, John Brennan, US Chief of Counterterrorism, described the killing of Osama bin Laden in a raid by US special operations forces as "decapitating the head of the snake" (Department of Defense 2011a), and described the Defense department and the CIA working together to cut off "the head of the snake known as al-Qaeda" (Department of Defense 2011b). If, as Jackson argues, "the deployment of language by politicians is an exercise of power" that, unchecked, "inevitably becomes abusive," then public interrogation of such dehumanizing rhetoric offers one way to offer a necessary and salutary check – it becomes, in other words, and in both senses of the word, critical.

Metaphor and reconciliation: retiring the hunt metaphor

Taken together, these metaphors effectively conflate the figure of the soldier with that of the hunter, a significant conflation not only in its shaping of the choices made in both conflict and resolution strategies, but in the behaviors it directs, supports, and cultivates. Such metaphors, embedded within the political and social narratives they sustain, are problematic not only because they often articulate fundamentally flawed or limited sets of assumptions, but because they are simultaneously ubiquitous and unexamined. Essentialist characterizations of Arabs and Muslims as embodying an intractable Otherness emerge from what Mahmood Mamdani calls "culture talk;" such talk is dangerous not only in the stereotypes it creates, circulates, and implicitly endorses, but in its ability to evade or distract from meaningful political analysis (Mamdani 2005: 11). By proffering a set of metaphors that emphasized and reinforced the inherently bestial Otherness of the enemy, the clear need for in-depth political analysis is apparently obviated.

The behaviors and public self-representations of soldiers as hunters is one of the most consequential outcomes of such far-reaching metaphorical systems. The "*language* of the 'war on terror' normalizes and reifies the *practice* of the war on terrorism," to the extent that "language and practice" come to "reinforce each other" (Jackson 2005: 2; emphasis added). This is most egregiously reflected in the inhuman treatment following and corresponding to such inhuman representations, or what Chamayou calls the "practical correlates" of counterterrorist activity. Evidence of the success of the metaphoric conflation of soldier and hunter is found in the public self-representations of soldiers who clearly identify with the hunter model, consolidating it with behaviors such as the circulation of souvenir photos that recall hunters' mementos. Such photos feature soldiers in postures of physical and spatial dominance, standing individually or in clusters over the prone body of the enemy. Living or dead, the captured body is almost without exception shown on the ground, often heavily trussed or netted, visually emphasizing its subjugation to the captor. Captives are not photographed bound and standing, an arrangement which would indicate their status as prisoners but would not suggest to the same degree the extent of their subordination; instead, the photographs' narrative displays an iconography of inhumanity and subalterity: captors as triumphant, upright humans, juxtaposed with captives as fallen, prostrate, or supine prey. A recurring visual motif is found in the soldier's stance, which often depicts him with one foot resting on a recumbent captive's body like a big game hunter with his kill. *New York Times* columnist Luc Santé immediately recognized the import of such photographs, provocatively describing the servicemen posed "as if they were standing next to a gutted buck" (Sante 2004). Many soldiers themselves acknowledge the photos' reference to a game hunter's memento through their symbolic and sometimes literal mounting of the kill. One such literal example can be found in soldiers' photos and video footage of Iraqi corpses tied like game to the hoods of army vehicles. US Marine Adam Kokesh describes a photo of himself posed smiling with the body of a shot Iraqi civilian; he notes:

> This is a picture that I'm very ashamed of, having posed with this dead Iraqi as a trophy picture. But what felt awkward to me at the time was not that – not so much that I was taking the picture, but rather that I had not killed this man, and I was almost – I was taking a trophy of someone else's kill.
>
> (Kokesh 2008)

Evidence of defiling and dehumanizing practices among soldiers has continued to appear since the international outcry that followed the release of photographs documenting cases of prisoner abuse at Abu Ghraib, in which inmates were, among other abuses, leashed and ridden like animals (Buncombe and Huggler 2004). Trophy-taking such as the soldiers' circulation of Abu Ghraib photos is perhaps the inevitable conclusion to the rhetorical juxtaposition of the *enemy as animal* metaphor with the *enemy as prey* metaphor. It is not enough, within the hunt metaphor, for the enemy to be an animal; he must also be a defeated animal, stilled, and mounted for the hunter's glorification. The enemy's inferiority must be confirmed by the completeness of his defeat, his subhuman nature confirmed by the extraordinary degree to which he can be brought to heel.

The widespread denunciation of the Abu Ghraib abuses did not prevent subsequent trophy-taking activities on the part of soldiers, some figurative in the form of circulated photographs, some literal in the form of physical body parts. In 2011, for example, newspapers around the world reported "the publication of 'trophy' photographs of US soldiers posing with the dead bodies of defenseless Afghan civilians"; an investigation by *Der Spiegel* unearthed approximately 4,000 photographs and videos taken by a "self-styled 'kill team'" and accounts of the group's leader cutting off fingers and removing a tooth from the corpse of the victim (*Guardian* 2011). While some commentators have likened the mutilations to actions "typical of serial killers" (Escobedo Shepherd 2011), we argue that this behavior finds it origins in the dominance of the hunt metaphor in military rhetoric: as one blogger observes, the pictures released by *Der Spiegel* depict the soldiers standing by the bodies "as if posing for the next issue of *Hunting* or *Outdoor Life*" (Woodgate 2011). In April 2012, against government recommendation, the *LA Times* broke the story of soldiers from the 82nd Airborne posing with the mangled remains of dead suicide bombers, including one holding up a severed hand with its middle finger raised and another with an "unofficial platoon patch" reading "Zombie Hunter" placed adjacent to the human remains (*LA Times* 2012). Desecrating behaviors such as these should not be dismissed as individual or idiosyncratic cases of bad behavior carried out by those suffering from the stress of battle, suggests research released in 2012 by the Economic and Social Research Council. These activities are rooted not in "individual psychological disorders," notes principal investigator Simon Harrison, "but in a social history of racism and in military traditions that use hunting metaphors for war" (Harrison 2012). It is crucial to note that the broader systems of racism that create and sustain the hunt metaphor thus, paradoxically, ultimately create more, rather than less potential threat, since the images of soldiers' desecrating behavior, globally circulated via new media, generate increasing outrage in its witnesses. The difference in the treatment of enemy corpses in combat, in fact, highlights the key role of racism and the hunt metaphor it supports; Europeans and North American soldiers who admitted to mutilating enemy corpses "appear to have drawn racial distinctions" between "close" and "distant" enemies, seeing themselves as "fighting" enemies most like themselves in appearance and leaving these combatant bodies untouched, but as "hunting" distant enemies more visibly inflected with signs of racial difference and defiling these "other" bodies (Harrison 2012).

This kind of trophy-taking has a long tradition, especially in conflicts in which military discourse emphasized the fundamental inhumanity of the enemy, figuring the campaigns as blood sports or hunting expeditions (Andersen 2006; Cannizzo 1991; Chacon and Dye 2007; Harrison 2006, 2008; Spence *et al.* 2004; Weingartner 1992). Certainly, the connection between war and hunting represents both a culturally multi-faceted and historically resonant relationship. As Barbara Ehrenreich observes, there is "little controversy" in the claim that war has its roots in early animal predation; "well into the modern era" foot regiments echoed, in the line of their battlefield advance, the lines of early tribal game hunters (Ehrenreich 1997: 117–18). However, in the war on terror in general and the wars in Afghanistan and Iraq in particular, the metaphor of the hunt has been introduced into the sphere of public speech by the White House and the US military in a particularly patterned fashion. The hunted-animal motif has spread, likewise, to other national discourses, as when British PM Tony Blair observed that "What we have done is put Saddam back firmly in his cage" (Karmi 2002). Gradually, then, much political discourse has come to rely on the rhetoric of the hunt metaphor. Even the names of military operations, carefully chosen to "sell … all sorts of things, to all sorts of people: inspiration to the troops, righteousness to Americans at home, partnership to allied countries" (Davenport 2010), reflect and re-inscribe the hunt metaphor. They often feature initiatives labeled in ways that clearly derive from the hunter/prey dyad, including Operations "Beastmaster," "Snake Hunter," "Cobra Sweep," and most tellingly, "Hunter." Other operation names imply eradication or extermination as the hunt's purpose, as in "Operation Mouse Trap," "Rat Trap," "Tapeworm," and

"Locust."[1] Within such rhetorical and discursive contexts, it is perhaps unsurprising that officially unsanctioned behaviors such as military atrocities and trophy-taking continue to be uncovered.

Mutilation and cadaver defilement, trophy-taking, prisoner abuse and the circulation of abuse mementos are behaviors that exist, we suggest, along a continuum of dehumanization. This continuum connects the debasing metaphors dominating counterterrorist rhetoric with the very behaviors from which military officials attempt to distance themselves even as their official discourse (emblematized through operational names, strategic metaphors and other forms of enemy construction), obliquely or directly invites them. Among the most horrifying examples of such officially repudiated behaviors are instances of attacks on civilian families such as the one carried out by what the *NY Daily News* called a single "deranged" Army Sergeant, who left his Kandahar base in the middle of the night to enter civilian homes and shoot 21 people, including nine children. The *NY Daily News* reports an Afghan survivor describing the armed soldier "stalking" through his home as if "hunting prey" *(NY Daily News* 2012). This language suggests the degree to which, since 2001, the figure of the soldier, always a culturally fluid representation, has coalesced and solidified around the central metaphor of hunter and prey. This is similarly expressed in a potent intersection of cultural forms including political and military discourse, news media, and soldier's self-representations in trophy photos, war memorabilia, social media, and uploads on video-share sites (Wills and Steuter 2009). Such representations suggest a figurative and sometimes literal echoing of the persistent hunt motif. Social discourse thus affects social actions; it does this "not by directly or inevitably determining them but rather by rendering these actions plausible or implausible, acceptable or unacceptable, conceivable or inconceivable" (Yee 1996: 97). The framing of both problems and solutions, then, is shaped, structured and conditioned by rhetorical choices, since "the framing of problems often depends upon the metaphors underlying the stories which generate problem setting and set the direction of problem solving" (Schon 1979: 280). If persistent metaphors such as the hunt motif offer ways of consciously or unconsciously selecting, labeling, filtering, evaluating and understanding "facts," then the consequences of buried, indirect, or hidden metaphors may constrain both the production of social reality and, significantly, possibilities for policy choices and resolutions: they may truncate debate, distorting the search for alternatives, and impede potentially more effective responses to terrorism (Jackson 2007: 234).

Such distortions and impediments, however, even as they illustrate the urgent necessity for a sustained critical intervention into destructive habits of rhetoric, also offer a starting point for analysis and critique. Jennifer Milliken's argument that discursive efforts on the part of "authorized speakers" to exploit and reproduce dominating discourses within the public speech of international relations are "not always successful" points to one starting point: the "open-endedness and instability" of many such discourses implies they may "slip and slide into new relationships via resistances that their articulation and operationalization may engender" (Milliken 1999: 242). Once we "draw attention to the contestable and politicized character" of such dominant narratives, including the ways in which "Islamic terrorism" is socially and linguistically "constructed as an existential threat" we may, by exposing such "ideological effects and political technologies," open up "a critical space for the articulation of alternative and potentially emancipatory" new practices (Jackson 2005: 425). Lakoff suggests that, to accomplish this, progressive political speech must be as deliberate, self-aware, and programmatic as most public speech emerging from governments (and, we would add, adopted and uncritically furthered within media speech, much contemporary terrorism discourse, and military and strategic figurations of counterterrorist activity). One immediate remedy is the jettisoning of the "war" metaphor in all public counterterrorism discourse (Lakoff and Frisch 2006); this might entail, as many scholars advocate, shifting North American public speech to the criminal framing that dominates European rhetoric rather than the martial framing that dominates US counterterrorist speech and activity. Even such attentive scholars, however, with their alertness to dehumanizing figurations, appear to have often overlooked the potentially devastating prominence of the rhetorical figurations of terrorists as prey within the *war as hunt* metaphoric system. Acknowledging and repudiating such figures from all public counterterrorist speech is a clear first step in formulating Milliken's moments of "resistance," and in taking advantage of the "opportune moment" of international outrage following "ongoing revelations of torture and rendition" (Milliken 1999: 242). It could also be valuable to point out the limits endemic to the hunt trope even to those employing it. For example, while the hunter–prey metaphor offers an illusion of potency it also contains less visible constraints and challenges to the hunter's agency. A hunter's choice of actions are limited: he may stalk, track, kill, snare, net, or trap, but cannot negotiate, confer, converse, settle, or otherwise alter or ameliorate the terms of conflict. The hunter trope, then, requires an ongoing critical contestation.

Moreover, the dehumanizing hunt metaphor not only undermines attempts at resolution and reconciliation; like other such discursive formations, it helps to "significantly explain support for aggressive retaliatory practices" (Maoz and McCauley 2008: 93). Such metaphors also fuel domestic public support for "extreme forms" of state policies directed against an "out-group threat" portrayed as "subhuman," policies that risk furthering the global cycle of aggression and assumptions of mutual intractability (Maoz and McCauley 2008: 94).

Meanwhile, such reflections are timely because there is, suggest members of the Council on Foreign Relations, an "opportunity to change minds" and "project a more favorable image of America in the Muslim world" (Charney and Yakatan 2005: iii). The Council's report observes:

> [T]he widely held view that nothing can be done about the spread of negative attitudes toward the United States among Muslims in the Middle East and Asia is incorrect. What we say and how we say it can make a difference... An effort to communicate and the right content for the dialogue can help to change their perceptions.
>
> (Charney and Yakatan 2005: 5)

Any such content, we argue, will not be fully effective until the rhetorical mechanisms of "how we say it" are consciously addressed. This process has already begun in US and other governments with the official shifting away from the term "War on Terror." A memo from the US Defense Department's office of security review to senior Pentagon staff stated that the Obama administration "prefers to avoid using the term ... Global War on Terror" and requests staffers to "pass this on to your speech writers" (*Guardian* 2009). Dismissing the hunt metaphor as a trope equally worth avoiding is a productive place to begin.

The hunter–prey dyad recycles narratives of humanity and inhumanity, superiority and inferiority, triumph and capitulation that are often deeply at odds with the real circumstances and conditions of post-2001 conflict. These narratives support and recapitulate the processes and strategies of the "hostile imagination" (Keen 1991: 25), as it works to construct an enemy who is fundamentally, inherently, and intractably different. As long as the metaphors of public speech endorse rather than repudiate such narratives, the content of such speech, however well meant, risks elision or even negation. Potent metaphors of intractable difference will outweigh, to intended and unintended audiences both domestically and abroad, even restorative or conciliatory intentions in public speech; as Jodi Halpern notes, before any forms of reconciliation can begin, a rehumanization of delegitimized groups must occur, especially since "the dehumanizing of specific groups ... does not stop when conflicts end" (Halpern and Weinstein 2004: 562). Nor did such dehumanization begin with the events of 9/11 and the subsequent wars in Afghanistan and Iraq. Instead, as a considerable body of research has demonstrated, long-time mass media depictions of Arabs and Muslims present them as the "quintessential Other" (Michalek 1988: 3), a social fact so entrenched as to constitute "commonsense knowledge" (David and Jalbert 2008: 23). Such "knowledge," with its tacit and overt inscriptions of the intractability of difference, will always limit even well intentioned attempts at reconciliation. As former CIA analyst Ray McGovern writes:

> [W]e can wish [good luck to] President Obama with his efforts to "communicate clearly to Muslims," but there will be no diminution in the endless cycle of violence unless legitimate grievances are addressed on all sides," including the "root causes" for apparently "irrational actions" by Muslims.
>
> (McGovern 2012)

If counterterrorism speech dispenses with rhetorical language that insists upon intractable difference, it can only become more effective. The roots of the hunt metaphor, especially, must be critically contested, since it is a trope so resilient that it reappears, if in rhetorically softened form, even in the relatively moderate speech of current President Barack Obama, who re-activates the metaphor when he claims that "we cannot respect terrorist organizations ... and we will hunt them down" (Obama 2009a), or pledges to increase pressure on Afghan insurgents in order to "flush them out" (Department of Defense 2009). Even in counterterrorist speech designed to distance itself from the language and tactics of the previous political regime, spokespeople for Obama's administration reveal the persistence of the rhetorical encoding and figurative dehumanization of the enemy. For example, in his speech announcing the plan to close the Guantánamo Bay prison, Attorney General Eric Holder asserted that "Nothing symbolizes our new course more" than this decision (Department of Justice 2009). He describes how, immediately after the events of 9/11, Americans "stood together" with "our shock and grief still raw," and "prepared with solemn purpose to root out terrorism from every crack and crevice of the earth." In a speech rife with sub-text, Holder goes on to say:

> In a page of history never written, we together could have seized that tragic moment to raise liberty's torch brighter and more broadly than ever before. The decisions made in the years that followed have been long debated and will be studied for generations to come.
> (Department of Justice 2009)

Tacitly critical of these early policies that failed to "raise Liberty's torch brighter," Holder claims that "nothing symbolizes our new course more" than the decision to close the prison (a decision announced in 2009 and as of 2013, yet to be enacted). However, while Holder's speech offers an implied repudiation of previous policies and tactics, and an attempt to distance the present regime from its predecessor, there is notably no parallel repudiation of the hunt vocabulary that situates the dehumanized and broadly aggregated enemy in the animal habitats where, apparently, they belong: that is, the "cracks and crevices of the earth." Indeed, these words are linked to and framed by the rhetorical vehemence that calls up the emotive power of phrases such as "raw," "grief," and "solemn purpose." This solemnity rhetorically attaches itself to, and thus validates and valorizes, the hunt imagery and its lexicon, re-enshrining them in the public speech even of a statement intended to repair damaged relationships with our "global community."

As resilient as the hunt metaphor is in public discourse, however, it is not impregnable. As the work of Richard Rorty suggests, to change metaphors is to change the conversation; at the very least, he says, coining a new metaphor can produce a new vivacity of speech, or turn the conversation in a new direction (Rorty cited in Barnes 1991). If we currently face, as Gibson Winter argues, a "crisis of root metaphors," then "a shift in metaphors may open new vistas of human possibilities" (Winter 1981: 484). Freeing ourselves from our "dead metaphors," Orla Schantz asserts, will "free us to develop a talent for speaking differently," a talent that will allow us to discover that it is "rhetorical innovation" that is ultimately the "chief instrument of cultural and political change" (Schantz 2007).

Note

1 From *Multi-National Force – Iraq*, at mnf-iraq.com. This website is now closed; it was a site belonging to the United States Central Command for organization of information regarding coalition forces in Iraq from 2004 to 2010.

References

Andersen, R. (2006) *A Century of Media, a Century of War*, New York: Peter Lang.

Barnes, T. (1991) "Metaphors and Conversations in Economic Geography: Richard Rorty and the Gravity Mold," *Geografiska Annaler*, 73(2), 111–20.

Bially Mattern, J. (2001) "The Power Politics of Identity," *European Journal of International Relations*, 7(3), 349–97.

Buncombe, A. and Huggler, J. (2004) "Iraq: Abuse Crisis: Abu Ghraib: Inmates Raped, Ridden like Animals," *Independent* (London), May 22.

Bush, G. W. (2001a) "Remarks by the President, Secretary of the Treasury O"Neill and Secretary of State Powell on Executive Order, The Rose Garden," The White House, Office of the Press Secretary, 24 September. Available at http://georgewbush-whitehouse.archives.gov/news/releases/2001/09/20010924-4.html (accessed May 31, 2012).

Bush, G.W. (2001b) "President Holds Prime Time News Conference," The White House, Office of the Press Secretary, October 11. Available at http://georgewbush-whitehouse.archives.gov/news/releases/2001/10/20011011-7.html (accessed May 31, 2012).

Bush, G.W. (2001c) "Remarks by the President to the CEO Summit, Pudong Shangri-La Hotel, Shanghai, People's Republic of China," The White House, Office of the Press Secretary, October 20. Available at http://georgewbush-whitehouse.archives.gov/news/releases/2001/10/20011021-5.html (accessed May 31, 2012).

Cannizzo, J. (1991) "Exhibiting Cultures: 'Into the Heart of Africa'," *Visual Anthropology Review*, 7(1), 150–60.

Chacon, R. and Dye D. (2007), *The Taking and Displaying of Human Body Parts as Trophies by Amerindians*, NYC: Springer.

Chamayou, G. (2011) "The Enemy as Prey," *VillaVoice.met*. Available at http://villa-voice.net/2011/02/02/the-enemy-as-prey-exlusive-essay-by-gregoire-chamayou/ (accessed May 31, 2012).

Charney, G. and Yakatan, N. (2005) "A New Beginning: Strategies for a More Fruitful Dialogue with the Muslim World," *Council on Foreign Relation*, 7, i–12.

Charteris-Black, J. (2004) *Corpus Approaches to Critical Metaphor Analysis*, London: Palgrave Macmillan.

Choudhury, C. (2006) "Terrorists & Muslims: The Construction, Performance, and Regulation of Muslim Identities in the Post-9/11 United States," *Rutgers Journal of Law and Religion*, 7(3), 8–48.

Chowdhury, A. and Krebs, R. (2010) "Talking about Terror: Counterterrorist Campaigns and the Logic of Representation," *European Journal of International Relations*, 16(1), 125–50.

Davenport, C. (2010) "Military Chooses Names of Operations Carefully," *Pittsburgh Post-Gazette*, March 21, 2010. Available at www.post-gazette.com/stories/news/us/military-chooses-names-of-operations-carefully-23888/ (accessed May 31, 2012).

David, G. and Jalbert. P. (2008) "Undoing Degradation: the Attempted 'Rehumanization' of Arab and Muslim Americans," *Ethnographic Studies*, 10, 23–47.

de Graaf, B. (2011) "Why Communication and Performance Are Key in Countering Terrorism," International Centre for Counter-Terrorism – The Hague, research paper. Available at www.un.org/en/sc/ctc/specialmeetings/2011/docs/icct-researchpaper-degraaf.pdf (accessed May 31, 2012).

Department of Defense (2001) "DoD News Briefing – Secretary Rumsfeld and Gen. Myers," Office of the Assistant Secretary of Defense (Public Affairs), October 25. Available at www.defense.gov/transcripts/transcript.aspx?transcriptid=2183 (accessed May 31, 2012).

Department of Defense (2002a) "Prepared Statement for the Senate Committee on Foreign Relations: the Situation in Afghanistan," Office of the Assistant Secretary of Defense (Public Affairs), June 26. Available at www.defense.gov/speeches/speech.aspx?speechid=261 (accessed May 31, 2012).

Department of Defense (2002b) "Remarks as Delivered by Secretary of Defense Donald H. Rumsfeld, Pentagon, Washington, D.C.," Office of the Assistant Secretary of Defense (Public Affairs), August 6. Available at www.defense.gov/speeches/speech.aspx?speechid=274 (accessed May 31, 2012).

Department of Defense (2003) "Rumsfeld, Myers Thank Troops, Employees for Their Service," American Forces Press Service, November 21. Available at www.defense.gov/news/newsarticle.aspx?id=27737 (accessed May 31, 2012).

Department of Defense (2004a) "Terror is Losing," as published in the *New York Post* by Deputy Secretary of Defense Paul Wolfowitz, Washington, DC, April 19. Available at www.defense.gov/speeches/speech.aspx?speechid=104 (accessed May 31, 2012).

Department of Defense (2004b) "Remarks as Delivered by Deputy Secretary of Defense Paul Wolfowitz, Washington, DC," Office of the Assistant Secretary of Defense (Public Affairs), September 21. Available at www.defense.gov/speeches/speech.aspx?speechid=155 (accessed May 31, 2012).

Department of Defense (2004c) "Afghan Ops: Major Attack on Terrorism, Fight Not Over," American Forces Press Service, October 6. Available at www.defense.gov/news/newsarticle.aspx?id=25130 (accessed May 31, 2012).

Department of Defense (2005a) "Iraqi Elections Ended Any Insurgent Legitimacy. Myers says," American Forces Press Service, February 24. Available at www.defense.gov/news/newsarticle.aspx?id=25809 (accessed May 31, 2012).

Department of Defense (2005b) "Iraqis, Coalition Combine to Snare Terror Leaders," American Forces Press Service, June 19. Available at www.defense.gov/news/newsarticle.aspx?id=16366 (accessed May 31, 2012).

Department of Defense (2007) "DoD News Briefing with Major General Fil from Iraq". February 16. Available at www.defense.gov/transcripts/transcript.aspx?transcriptid=3891 (accessed May 31, 2012).

Department of Defense (2008a) "DoD News Briefing with Major General Hertling from Iraq," February 11. Available at www.defense.gov/transcripts/transcript.aspx?transcriptid=4141 (accessed May 31, 2012).

Department of Defense (2008b) "DoD News Briefing with Major General Jeffrey Hammond from Iraq," June 2. Available at www.defense.gov/transcripts/transcript.aspx?transcriptid=4234 (accessed May 31, 2012).

Department of Defense (2009) "Obama Pledges Increased Pressure in Afghanistan," August 20. Available at www.defense.gov/news/newsarticle.aspx?id=55556 (accessed May 31, 2012).

Department of Defense (2011a) "Intelligence, Secrecy Drove bin Laden Operation," American Forces Press Service, May 2. Available at www.defense.gov/news/newsarticle.aspx?id=63787 (accessed May 31, 2012).

Department of Defense (2011b) "Official: bin Laden"s Death is 'Defining Moment'," American Forces Press Service, May 2. Available at www.defense.gov/news/newsarticle.aspx?id=63786 (accessed May 31, 2012).

Department of Justice (2009) "Attorney General Eric Holder Delivers Remarks in Berlin on the Closing of Guantánamo Bay," Department of Justice, April 29. Available at www.justice.gov/ag/speeches/2009/ag-speech-090429.html (accessed May 31, 2012).

Doty, R. (1993) "Foreign Policy as Social Construction: A Post-Positivist Analysis of US Counterinsurgency Policy in the Philippines," *International Studies Quarterly* 37(3), 297–320.

Ehrenreich, B. (1997). *Blood Rites*. New York: Henry Holt.

El Fadl, A. (2002) "Four telltale Themes: Anti-Muslim bigotry 'spreading like wildfire'," Haroon Siddiqui, *Toronto Star*, November 24.

Escobedo Shepherd, J. (2011) "More Damaging Than Abu Ghraib? Repugnant Army 'Kill Team' Took Photos, Trophies from Murdered Afghan Civilians," alternet.org, March 21. Available at www.alternet.org/newsandviews/article/534336/more_damaging_than_abu_ghraib_repugnant_army_%27kill_team%27_took_photos,_trophies_from_murdered_afghan_civilians/ (accessed May 31, 2012).

Fairclough, N. (1995) *Media Discourse*, London: E. Arnold Publishing.

Goatly, A. (2007) *Washing the Brain: Metaphor and Hidden Ideology*, Amsterdam: John Benjamin Publishing Company.

Guardian (2009) "Obama Administration Says Goodbye to 'War on Terror'," March 25.

Guardian (2011) "US Army 'Kill Team' in Afghanistan Posed for Photos of Murdered Civilians," March 21.

Halpern, J. and Weinstein, H. (2004) "Rehumanizing the Other: Empathy and Reconciliation," *Human Rights Quarterly*, 26(3), 561–83.

Harrison, S. (2006) "Skull Trophies of the Pacific War: Transgressive Objects of Remembrance," *Journal of the Royal Anthropological Institute*, 12(4), 817–36.

Harrison, S. (2008) "Skulls and Scientific Collecting in the Victorian Military: Keeping the Enemy Dead in British Frontier Warfare," *Comparative Studies in Society and History*, 50(1), 285–303.

Harrison, S. (2012) "ESRC: Soldiers Who Desecrate the Dead See Themselves as Hunters," Politics.co.uk, May 21. Available at www.politics.co.uk/opinion-formers/economic-social-research-council-esrc/article/esrc-soldiers-who-desecrate-the-dead-see-themselves-as-hunte (accessed May 31, 2012).

Hulsse, R. and Spencer, A. (2008) "The Metaphor of Terror: Terrorism Studies and the Constructivist Turn," *Security Dialogue* 39(6), 571–92.

Jackson, R. (2005) *Writing the War on Terrorism: Language, Politics And Counterterrorism: New Approaches to Conflict Analysis*, Manchester: Manchester University Press.

Jackson, R. (2007) "An Analysis of EU Counterterrorism Discourse Post-September 11" *Cambridge Review of International Affairs*, 20(2), 233–47.

Karim, K.H. (2000) *The Islamic Peril: Media and Global Violence*. Montreal: Black Rose Books.

Karmi, G. (2002) "An attack on us all: Saddam is simply the latest focus for the west's racist abuse of Arabs," December 28, *Guardian*, Available at www.guardian.co.uk/world/2002/dec/28/usa.iraq1 (accessed May 31, 2012).

Keen, S. (1991) *Faces of the Enemy: Reflections of the Hostile Imagination*, New York: Harper Collins.

Kokesh, A. (2008) "Winter Soldier on the Hill: War Vets Testify Before Congress," *DemocracyNow*, November 28, Available at www.democracynow.org/2008/11/28/winter_soldier_on_the_hill_war (accessed May 31, 2012).

LA Times (2012) "US Troops with Body Parts of Afghan Bombers," *LA Times*, April 18.

Lakoff, G. (2006) *Thinking Points*, NYC: Farrer, Strauss and Giroux.

Lakoff, G. (2008) *The Political Mind: A Cognitve Scientist's Guide to Your Brain and Its Politics*, NYC: Viking Books.

Lakoff, G. and Frisch, E. (2006) "Five Years After 9/11: Drop the War Metaphor," *Commondreams*. Available at www.commondreams.org/views06/0911-20.htm (accessed May 31, 2012).

Lakoff, G. and Johnson, M. (1980) *Metaphors We Live By*. Chicago, IL: University of Chicago Press.

Lieberman, J. (2007) "Lieberman Floor Speech on Joint Iraq Resolution," lieberman.senate.gov, March 14. Available at http://lieberman.senate.gov/index.cfm/news-events/speeches-op-eds/2007/3/lieberman-floor-speech-on-joint-iraq-resolution (accessed May 31, 2012).

Lynch, M. (2010) *Rhetoric and Reality: Counter Terrorism in the Age of Obama*, Center for a New American Security, Washington, D.C. Available at www.cnas.org/files/documents/publications/CNAS_Rhetoric%20and%20Reality_Lynch.pdf (accessed May 31, 2012).

Mamdani, M. (2005) *Good Muslim, Bad Muslim: America, the Cold War, and the Roots of Terror*, NYC: Random House.

Maoz, I. and McCauley, C. (2008) "Threat, Dehumanization, and Support for Retaliatory Aggressive Policies in Asymmetric Conflict," *Journal of Conflict Resolution* 52(1), 93–116.

McGovern, R. (2012) "The Obama Team Just Doesn't Get It: Us Violence and Occupation Spark Terrorism," alternet.org. Available at www.alternet.org/story/155246/the_obama_team_just_doesn%27t_get_it%3A_us_violence_and_occupation_spark_terrorism (accessed May 31, 2012).

Michalek, L. (1988) "The Arab in America cinema: a century of Otherness," *The Arab Image in American Film and Television*, American-Ethnographic Studies Publications.

Milliken, J. (1999) "The Study of Discourse in International Relations: A Critique of Research and Methods," *European Journal of International Relations*, 5(2), 225–54.

National Counterterrorism Center (2005) VADM John Scott Redd Statement before the Senate Select Committee on Intelligence, July 21, National Counterterrorism Center. Available at www.nctc.gov/press_room/speeches/con_statement.html (accessed May 31, 2012).

NY Daily News (2012) Survivor of Afghan massacre says Army sergeant hunted through house for victims: "He was walking around, taking up positions," *NY Daily News*, March 12. Available at http://articles.nydailynews.com/2012-03-12/news/31156284_1_afghan-forces-nato-military-base-afghan-officials (accessed May 31, 2012).

Obama, B. (2009a) Interview on Al-Arabiya Television, Washington, DC, January 26. Available at www.presidentialrhetoric.com/speeches/01.26.09.html (accessed May 31, 2012).

Obama, B. (2009b) Remarks by the President On a New Beginning, Cairo University, Cairo, Egypt, June 4. The White House, Office of the Press Secretary. Available at www.whitehouse.gov/video/President-Obama-Speaks-to-the-Muslim-World-from-Cairo-Egypt#transcript (accessed May 31, 2012).

Razack, S. (2008) *Casting Out: The Eviction of Muslims from Western Law and Politics*, Toronto: University of Toronto Press.

Said, E. (1993) *Culture and Imperialism*, NYC: Random House Digital, Inc.

Sante, L. (2004) "Tourists and Torturers," *New York Times*, May 11.

Schantz, O. (2007) "Richard Rorty: In Memorium," *The Enlightenment Underground*. Available at http://enlightenmentunderground.blogspot.com (accessed May 31, 2012).

Schon, D. (1979) "Generative Metaphor: A Perspective on Problem Setting in Social Policy," in A. Ortony (ed.) *Metaphor and Thought*, Cambridge University Press.

Schwarz-Friesel, M. and Skirl, H. (2011) "Metaphors for Terrorism in German Media Discourse," *Re-visioning Terrorism*, Purdue University. Available at http://docs.lib.purdue.edu/revisioning/2011/909/21/ (accessed May 31, 2012).

Scott, J.C. (1990) *Domination and the Arts of Resistance: Hidden Transcripts*, New Haven: Yale University Press.

Shaheen, J. (2001) *Reel Bad Arabs: How Hollywood Vilifies a People*, Northampton, MA: Interlink Publishing Group.

Shaheen, J. (2006) Interviewed, in Reel Bad Arabs. [videorecording]. Media Education Foundation.

Snow, T. (2006) "Press Gaggle by Tony Snow," The White House, Office of the Press Secretary. September 10. Available at http://georgewbush-whitehouse.archives.gov/news/releases/2006/09/20060910-1.html (accessed May 31, 2012).

Spence, M. C., White, Longstaffe F. and Law K. (2004) "Victims of the Victims: Human trophies worn by sacrificed soldiers from the Feathered Serpent Pyramid, Teotihuacan," *Ancient Mesoamerica*, 15(1), 1–15.

Steuter, E. and Wills D. (2008) *At War with Metaphor: Media, Propaganda and Racism in the War on Terror*, Lanham, MD: Lexington Books.

Steuter, E. and Wills D. (2011) "Making the Muslim Enemy: The Social Construction of the Enemy in the War on Terror," in M. Ender and S. Carlton-Ford (eds) *Handbook of War and Society*, New York: Routledge.

US Congressional record (2002) "Iraq and Homeland Defense," *US Congressional Record*, 107th Congress, S8965, 20 September 20. Available at http://thomas.loc.gov/cgi-bin/query/R?r107:FLD001:S58965 (accessed May 31, 2012).

Weingartner, J. (1992) "Trophies of War: US Troops and the Mutilation of Japanese War Dead, 1941–1945," *Pacific Historical Review*, 61(1), 53–67.

Wills. D. and Steuter, E. (2009) "The Soldier as Hunter: Pursuit, Prey and Display in the War on Terror," *Journal of War and Culture Studies*, 2(2), 195–210.
Winter, G. (1981) *Liberating Creation: Foundations of Religious Social Ethics*, New York: Crossroad.
Woodgate, L.B. (2011) "Trophy Hunters – A Cruel Mentality Carried Too Far," Woodgatesview.com, March 21. Available at http://woodgatesview.com/2011/03/21/trophy-hunters-a-cruel-mentality-carried-too-far/2011 (accessed May 31, 2012).
Yee, A. (1996) "The Causal Effects of Ideas on Policies," *International Organization*, 50(1), 69–108.

Index

Page numbers in **bold** denote figures.

6 December (6D) Revolutionary Organization 97, 100
9/11 attack 2–3, 29, 33, 36, 40, 80, 86, 142, 143, 148, 151, 156, 182, 185, 201–2, 207, 273
17 November (17N) Revolutionary Organization 97

Abu Ghraib, cases of prisoner abuse at 280; *see also* Guantánamo Bay prison, Cuba
Action Directe in France (1979) 58
acts of terrorism *see* terrorist acts
Adler Mission (German–Afghani operation, 2009) 124, 127, 130, 136n3
Afghanistan 36–7, 40; armed struggle against Soviet Red Army 123–5; as breeding ground for radical Islamic militancy 276; NATO mission 128; under the Taliban and Al Qaeda 127–8, 131; terror attacks 127
al-Jama'a al-islamiyya (the Islamic Group) 231
Almani, Ayyub 124, 128, 130, 132–5
al-Qaeda (AQ) 28, 34, 40, 45, 95, 122, 124, 151, 165–7, 171, 173, 182, 190, 202, 216, 228, 231, 241, 272, 277; global jihadi movements 236; US drone attacks against 234; in Yemen 234
Al-Shabaab (Somali terrorist group) 165
American Indian tribal councils 35
American Revolution 11, 34, 47
America's indigenous populations 4, 28, 32, 35; barbaric nature of 34; transitory lifestyle of 38

Amnesty International 113, 196, 257
Annan, Kofi 212
anticipatory self-defense 45
Anti-Terrorism Bill (2005), Australia 150
anti-terrorist campaign 115
anti-terrorist legislation: Australian Federal Police Act (1979) 156; Australian Security Intelligence Organisation Act (1979) 156; Convention for the Prevention and Punishment of Terrorism (1937) 61; Crimes Act (1914), Australia 156; Criminal Code Amendment (Suppression of Terrorist Bombings) Bill (2002), Australia 151; Export Administration Act (1979), USA 38; Federal Police and Other Legislation Amendment Act (2004), Australia 156; Indian Removal Act (1830), USA 44; Internal Security Acts (Singapore and Malaysia) 183; Legislation Amendment Act (2003), Australia 156; Military Commissions Act, USA 234; Patriot Act, USA 183; Prevention of Terrorism Act (POTA), India 183, 185, 187, 191, 193; Preventive Detention Act, India 187; Security Legislation Amendment (Terrorism) Bill (2002), Australia 151; Suppression of the Financing of Terrorism Bill (2002), Australia 151; Surveillance Devices Act (2004), Australia 156; Telecommunications Interception Legislation Amendment Bill (2002), Australia 152; Terrorist and Disruptive Activities (Prevention) Act, India 187;

Unlawful Activities Prevention Act (UAPA), India 191
Arab civil society 238
Arab revolutions 221, 236, 238, 240
Arab spring uprisings 7, 221, 234–7, 239
Arafat, Yasser 42
Arendt, Hannah 102
assassinations: Fortuyn, Pim (Netherlands, May 6, 2002) 74, 79–81; Lindh, Anna (Sweden, September 10–11, 2003) 74, 79, 81–3; mass bombings *see* mass bombings; political 74, 79
asylum seekers 16, 148–9
Austin's (1962) Speech Act Theory 20
Australia, terrorism in: Anti-Terrorism Bill (2005) 150; anti-terrorism legislation 147, 150–1, 156; asylum seekers and 149; Australian Federal Police Act (1979) 156; Be Alert, Not Alarmed campaign 147–8, 151; Border Security Legislation Amendment Bill (2002) 151–2; Citizenship Test 148–9, 151; constructions of otherness and 213–15; counterterrorist legislation since 9/11 attack 151–2; Crimes Act (1914) 156; Criminal Code Amendment (Suppression of Terrorist Bombings) Bill (2002) 151; criminalization of terrorism *vs* the legitimization of war 153–5; Cronulla riot (2005), Sydney 150; fear of outsiders 144; Federal Police and Other Legislation Amendment Act (2004) 156; foreign policy after 9/11 attack and 213; human surveillance 155; legal and journalistic framing of the war on terror 152–3; level of threat 143; National Security Hotline 147; and need for civil protection 157; policies on citizenship and 148; politics of terror and citizenship post-9/11 147–51; presentism in media reportage of 145–6; and privacy 155–7; reportage of 143–5; Security Legislation Amendment (Terrorism) Bill (2002) 151; Suppression of the Financing of Terrorism Bill (2002) 151; Surveillance Devices Act (2004) 156; Telecommunications Interception Legislation Amendment Bill (2002) 152; zero tolerance policy 149

Australian Federal Police (AFP) 156
Australian Security Intelligence Organisation (ASIO) 151, 154; Legislation Amendment Act (2003) 156
Australian Security Intelligence Organisation Act (1979) 156
axiological axis 228–35
axis of evil 35, 40

Baader-Meinhof group, Germany 58–9
Ba'ath Party 7, 202, 213
balance of power 237, 252, 262
Bali Bombings (October 2002) 147, 149
Balzacq, Thierry 14
Banham, Cynthia 144
barbaric enemy, notion of 205–6
Barbary pirates 4, 28, 38–9, 42–3, 48
Be Alert, Not Alarmed campaign, Australia 147–8, 151
Beastmaster, Operation 281
Bharatiya Janata Party (BJP) 181–2, 184, 187–8, 192–3, 195
bin Laden, Osama 7, 28–9, 36, 41, 202, 231, 277–8
biological warfare 45
Black September Organization 42, 58–9
Blair, Tony 202, 205–8, 211–13, 216, 281
Böses Vaterland (jihadi video) 125, 131, 134–5
Bossio, Diana 147
Breivik, Anders Behring 74, 76, 78–9, 83–5
Brennan, John 234, 278
BRIC states (Brazil, Russia, India and China) 237
Britain: constructions of otherness 211–13; democratic values and principles 212; foreign policy after 9/11 attacks 211–13; national identity 213
Burton, J. 111; theory of the human limits 111
Bush, George H. W. 48
Bush, George W. 27, 33, 36, 154, 205, 229, 276, 278; democracy promotion agenda 226; Proposed Middle East Initiatives for Promoting Economic Growth 225
Butler, Judith 21, 187–8; *Gender Trouble* (1990) 20; notion of performativity 6, 20, 184–6, 188, 193; *Precarious Lives* 186

Button, James 148–9

Carlos the Jackal 31, 59
Carter, Jimmy 30
casualties, from international terrorism **146**
Caucasus Emirate 247, 253
Central Intelligence Agency (CIA) 27, 234, 238, 241, 278, 284
Charteris-Black, J., critical metaphor analysis 208, 274, 278
Chechnya: causes of terrorism in 264; Chechen war (1999–2009) 251, 260; counterterrorist operation in 247–8; Great Patriotic War 258; international terrorism, issue of 253–4; Islamization and violence in 253; poor quality of life 252; religious radicalism 258; socio-economic problems 252–3; unemployment and deficient education system 252
Cheney, Dick 29, 36, 121, 210
Chidambaram, P. 189, 192, 194
children overboard scandal 149
Chirac, Jacques 228
Chomsky, Noam 154
Citizenship Test, Australia 148–9, 151
clash of civilizations 175, 271, 273
Clinton, Hillary 236
Coalition of the Willing 201, 204; America, Britain and Australia 205; American constructions of otherness 209–11; Australian constructions of otherness 213–15; barbaric enemy, notion of 205; British constructions of otherness 211–13; constructions of the Self and Other 205–9; evil enemy and the good American, theme of 206; language of evil 207; point of convergence in 205–9; portrayals of the enemy 205–9; war against Islam 208
Cobra Sweep, Operation 281
Code Pink (anti-war group) 238
Cold War 28, 31, 68, 145, 201, 204, 210, 228; military-industrial complex 224
colonial/anti-colonial warfare 145
Convention for the Prevention and Punishment of Terrorism (1937) 61
Council of Europe 61
counterterrorism 21, 56, 141, 207; in Chechnya 247–8; communalization of 187; Derrida's views on 186; framing and 75–7; intelligence and security activities 221; inter-governmental alliances on 185; legal model of action 60; legislations in Australia 151–2; minimum force, concept of 60; performative iterations and contradictions of 187–95; performativity and auto-immune disorder 184–7; policy in the European Union 76; radicalisation, concept of 121–2; Russian diagnostic and prognostic frames for 251–7; strategies in India 181–4; transnational 61
criminals on the run 105
critical discourse analysis (CDA) 19–21
Critical Geopolitics, notion of 202–3, 216
critical metaphor analysis (CMA) 21, 273–5
cross-border terrorism 182, 185
culture talk 279
cynegetic war 277

Das Konzept Stadtguerilla (1971) 58
democracy promotion, policy of 203, 226
Department of Defense (DOD), USA 29, 276–8, 284–5
depoliticization of violence 231
Derrida, Jacques 2, 16, 187, 191, 204, 240; account of terrorism and counterterrorism 7, 186; concern regarding consequences of counterterrorism 184
Domodedovo airport suicide attack (2011), Russia 261
drone strikes in Pakistan 234, 238–9
Dublin Agreement (1979) 61
Dubrovka theater hostage attack (2002), Russia 257–8

Ebzeyev, Boris 260
Economic and Social Research Council 281
Egyptian: Islamic Jihad 29; *jihadi* organisation 231
Ehrenreich, Barbara 281
Enduring Freedom, Operation 205
English Campaign 57
Enlightenment 32, 224–6, 240
ethos 66–7
Europe, jihadist terrorism in: balancing of security and civil liberties 173; media discourse on 160, 164–73;

media's acts of self-exposure and self-portrayal 162; motives for attacks, messages and broader causes 165–7, 175–7; motives leading to 161; reactions, dimension of 171–3; relationship between media and 163; role of media and 162–4, 173–5; social constructivism and 163; suicide attack in Stockholm (2010) 161, 167, 176; symbolic offences, dimension of 168–9; terrorist attacks 160–1; Westergaard, Kurt (Danish cartoonist), attack on (2010) 161, 167–8, 171; Western troops in Muslim countries, impact of 167; Western–Muslim relations, barriers in 169–71; Yemen cargo plane plot (2010) 161, 165, 172, 175
European Convention on the Suppression of Terrorism (1977) 61
European Court of Human Rights (ECHR) 69n4, 238
European Orientalism 223
European Political Cooperation (EPC) 61
European Union (EU): counterterrorism policies across 76; foreign policy 204; reaction to lone wolf and non-Islamic attacks 79–85; terrorism in the Netherlands, Sweden, and Norway 77–8
Europol 76, 85; *see also* Interpol
Euzkadi ta Askatasuma (ETA), Spain 57, 59
Export Administration Act (1979), USA 38

Fairclough, Norman 19, 274
Federal Security Service (FSB), Russia 259
Fire Cells Conspiracy (FCC) 97, 100, 103–4, 108, 112
foreign policy, politics of 202–4
Foucault, Michel 2, 18–19, 57, 59; on discourse on political Islam 223–4
framing of terrorism, significance of 2, 74, 152, 157, 183, 185
freedom of expression 87n6, 165, 168–9, 174
freedom of press 168
French Revolution 4, 28, 34–5, 48–9
Frey, Bruno 141–2
Front de Libération Nationale (FLN), Algeria 57

Gaza Freedom Flotilla 239
Gelb, Leslie H. 121
Geneva Protocols 63, 70n22, 154, 235
geo-political conflict 146
German Revolutionäre Zellen 59
German Taliban Mujahideen (DTM) 124
global terror network 29, 43, 276
global war on terror 46, 183, 185, 271, 284
Gold, Dore 230
Greek guerrillas, public discourse of *see* urban guerrilla activity, Greece
Greek Penal Code 97
Grenzschutzgruppe 9 (GSG 9), Germany 60
Guantánamo Bay prison, Cuba 43, 144, 155, 210, 234–5, 239, 285
Guru, Afzal 181

habeas corpus 60
hadith (stories of Prophet Muhammad) 135, 231
Halpern, Jodi 284
Hamas (Islamo-nationlist movement) 231–3, 236, 239
Hardaway, Robert 152
Harrison, Simon 281
Hezbollah 228, 236
Hindu fundamentalism 191, 193
Holder, Eric 285
Howard, John 147–51, 202, 205–7, 213–15, 214
human dignity, preservation of 40, 111
human rights violations 122, 228, 257
Human Rights Watch 113, 191, 196
humanitarian law discourse 63
Hunter, Operation 281
hunter-prey metaphor 283–4
Huntington, Samuel 222
Hussein, Saddam 33–5, 37, 40–1, 202, 212, 281

Ibn Taymiyya 135
immigrants, marginalization of 171
India, terrorism in: acts of terror and terrorist incidents, interpretations of 185; acts of terror by Islamic terrorism 182; anti-terror policies 181, 184; Bharatiya Janata Party (BJP) 181–2, 184, 187–8, 192–3, 195; communalization of counterterrorism measures 187; counterterrorism, performativity,

296 *Index*

India *continued*
   and auto-immune disorder 184–7; counterterrorism strategies 181–4, 196; dangers posed by the Muslim minority 181; Gujarat riots (2002) 184, 188; Hindu extremist violence 187, 188; Hindu fundamentalists and 191, 193; Indian parliament, attack on (December 2001) 181, 185; Maoist and Marxist-Leninist groups 182; Ministry of Home Affairs (MHAs) 189; Mumbai attacks (2008) 182, 189–92, 190–2, 193, 195–6; Mumbai riots (1992) 184; Muslim minority in India, criminalization of 191; National Counter Terrorism Centre (NCTC) 194; National Security Guard special forces 189; national *versus* state governments 193–5; performative iterations and contradictions of counterterrorism discourse 187–95; Prevention of Terrorism Act (POTA) 183, 185, 187, 191, 193; Preventive Detention Act 187; religion and politics, issue of 191–3; saffron terrorism 192–3; seeing the global in the local 188–91; significance of framing of 185; Terrorist and Disruptive Activities (Prevention) Act 187; Unlawful Activities Prevention Act (UAPA) 191

Indian Removal Act (1830), USA 44
Indignant movement 95
industrial revolution 225
information and communications technology (ICT) 156
Internal Security Acts (Singapore and Malaysia) 183
International Committee of the Red Cross 63
international community, doctrine of 208
international humanitarian law (IHL) 63
international relations 203, 216
International Relations and Geography 202
Interpol 61; *see also* Europol
intractable difference, notion of 274–5
Iran 40; arms race in Western Asia 233; Iranian hostage crisis (1979–80) 30–1; nuclear development 233; relegation to the axiological axis 233
Iraq: association with al-Qaeda 37; axis of evil nation 40; Iraq War (2003) 35, 203; Persian Gulf War (1990–1) 40–1, 43; weapons of mass destruction 40, 68, 152

Irish National Liberation Army (INLA) 69n1
Islamic identity 170
Islamist movements: aim of 230; axiological axis 228–35; cycle(s) of violence and counter-violence 234; false consciousness, influence of 230; Hamas 231–3, 236, 239; ideologisation of terror in 229–34; Islamic Movement of Uzbekistan (IMU) 29, 124, 125; *jihad* 230; Muslim Brotherhood 231, 237; political violence employed by 232; prominent features of 229–34; Salafi 236; Taliban *see* Taliban
Islamist terrorism: acts of terror by 182; in Chechnya *see* Chechnya; and counterterrorism policy 75; demonization of Islam and 186; in Gaza 231; in India 182, 185; and Islamist extremists 74, 80, 83; Islamist terrorist threat 2; organized Islamist terrorism (OIT) 74–80, 84–6; rise of 185; social and linguistic creation of 283; transnational 193
Islamofascism 235, 272
Islamophobia 151, 274
Israel: assault on Gaza 232–3; Israel–Lebanon war (2006) 145; occupation of Palestine 231; Pillar of Cloud, Operation (2012) 232; right to defend against Hamas' violence 233

Jefferson, Thomas 31, 34, 42, 44
Jemaah Islamiah 147
jihad 122; *Böses Vaterland* video 131, 134–5; communicating 123–5; Egyptian *jihadi* organisation 231; empirical credibility 131–3; framing and data selection 125–7; framing of the enemy and 129–31; Islamist movements and 230; jihadi videos 123–6, 131; Muslim holy warriors 171; occupation of Islamic territories and 127; principles of belief 125; problem and solution 127–9; *Ruf zur Wahrheit* video 135; socio-religious authority 135; soldiers of God (*jund allah*) 135; against Soviet Red Army 123; terrorism in Europe *see* Europe,

jihadist terrorism in; values, symbols and performance 134–5; and war against Islam 127; war theme 133–4
Johnsen, Gregory D. 234
Johnston, Hank 251
Jung, Franz Josef 126, 132–3, 135

Kadyrov, Ramzan 248
Karim, Karim H. 275
Khloponin, Aleksandr 259, 261
knowledge-power interplay 223
Koh, Harold 232
Kokesh, Adam 280

Lakoff, George 273–4, 283
Laqueur, Walter 67, 154, 163
Laura, Bush 33
League of Nations 61, 63
liaison guerrillas 103
Lijst Pim Fortuyn (LPF) 80–1
Lindh, Anna, murder of (Sweden, September 10–11, 2003) 74, 79, 81–3
Living Under Drones report 239
Locust, Operation 282
London bombings (July 7, 2005) 151, 155
Luban, David 156

McGovern, Ray 284
Mamdani, Mahmood 221, 227, 231, 279
Manichean binaries 201, 204, 210
martyrdom and its rewards in the afterlife, ideology of 231
Marxism, decline of 97
mass bombings 63, 74; Bali Bombings (October 2002) 147; London bombings (July 7, 2005) 151, 155; Stockholm bombing (December 11, 2010) 83, 161, 167, 176
media and communication: acts of self-exposure and self-portrayal 162; discourse on jihadist terrorism in Europe 160, 164–73; freedom of press 168; portrayals of Arabs and Muslims 275; relationship with jihadist terrorism 163; role of, in coverage of acts of terrorism 162–4, 173–5; social reality, in social interaction 164
Medvedev, Dmitri 247–8, 249, 251–63
Michaelsen, Christopher 143
Military Commissions Act, USA 234
military tribunals 27, 44
Milliken, Jennifer 282–3

minimum force, concept of 60
modern warfare, reasons for demise of 145
Moeller, Susan 184
money laundering 155
Mouse Trap, Operation 281
Muhammad cartoons 161, 166, 168, 174
Mujahideen 127, 130, 135
Mumbai attacks (2008) 182, 189–92, 193, 195–6
Munich Conference (1938) 43
Munich massacre (1972) 58, 60, 62
Muslim Brotherhood 231, 237
Muslim Republics of North Caucasus 252
Myers, Richard 278

National Counter Terrorism Centre (NCTC), India 194
National Defense Authorization Act, USA 235
national identity 28, 32–3, 49, 148–9, 203–5, 208–9, 214–16; British 206, 213; concept of 16, 192; destabilization of 17; public discourse on 191, 201; religious dimensions of 183; USA 232
national liberation movements 57–8
National Security Strategy (2002), USA 45
Nazi Germany 35, 43, 134
neo-terrorism 98, 101, 103, 114; and theory of inter-generational influence 104
Neumann, Iver B. 225
New Order 47
Nietzsche, Friedrich 66
Nixon, Richard 4, 28; policy of no-concessions/no negotiations 42
non-state terrorism 64
North Korea 40, 46, 130
Nuclear Non-proliferation Treaty (NPT) 233
Nussbaum, Martha 188

Obama, Barack 144, 226, 232–4, 271–2, 285; impact on war on terror 234–7
offenses against children 33–4
Official Irish Republican Army (OIRA) 59, 69n1
oil-for-food program 40
Omar, Mullah 202
ontological culture 106

298 *Index*

Order of Physicians in Athens 113
Organization of Petroleum Exporting Countries (OPEC) 59
organized Islamist terrorism (OIT) 14, 74–80, 84–6
Orientalism (1978) 15, 18

Palestinian Liberation Organization (PLO) 42–3
Patriot Act, USA 183
Patterns of Global Terrorism 2003 Report 146
Pearl Harbor 27–8
performativity, Butler's notion of 184, 186, 188
Persian Gulf War (1990–1) 40–1, 43, 48
Personen, Institutionen, Objekte, Sachen (PIOS), Germany 62
Pillar of Cloud, Operation (2012) 232
Pim Fortuyn, murder of (Netherlands, May 6, 2002) 79–81; Van den Haak report 79–80
political Islam, discourse on: axiological axis 228–35; counter-discourses and practices 237–41; dichotomous distinctions, identity and policy ramifications of 226–9; Islamist movements *see* Islamist movements; knowledge-power interplay 223; roots, development and implications 224–6; shifts in 234–7; structural change and 237–41; during the war on terror 221
political terrorism, concept of 84, 141, 230
political violence 4, 56, 58, 61, 80, 84, 98, 102, 105, 115, 222, 231–2; illegitimate use of 230; by Islamist movements 232; limits of 65; in the Netherlands 78; in Northern Ireland 69n1; public discourse of 96; sources of 145–6; types of 57
Powell, Colin 36–7, 40–1
Prevention of Terrorism Act (POTA), India 183, 185, 187, 191, 193
Preventive Detention Act, India 187
prisoner abuse 280–2
Provisional Irish Republican Army (PIRA) 57, 69n1
proxy wars 145
Pueblo crisis (1968) 31
Puri, Hardeep 188–9
Putin, Vladimir 247, 249, 251–6, 258–60, 262–4

Qadhafi, Muammar 46
Qur'an 135, 231
Qutb, Sayyid 231

raced Muslim terrorist, State's construction of 275
racist violence 78
radicalisation, concept of 121–2
Ramadan, Tariq 238
Rat Trap, Operation 281
Razack, Sherene 275
Reagan, Ronald 4, 28, 30–2, 38–9, 46, 48; handling of terrorism 31
real terrorists 130, 188
Red Brigades, Italy 58–9
regimes of truth 237
reign of terror 34, 49
religious: distinctions 192; nationalism 192
Revolutionary Anti-Racist Action group (RaRa) 78
Revolutionary People's Struggle (RPS) 97
Revolutionary Struggle (RS) 97, 103
Rice, Condoleezza 224–5, 233
right of self-defense 45
right-wing extremism 78, 86
Rohner, Dominik 141–2
Rorty, Richard 285–6
Rote Armee Fraktion (Red Army Faction, RAF), Germany 58–9, 78; May Offensive of 1972 58
Roy, Arundhati 181
Ruf zur Wahrheit (jihadi video) 124–5, 135
Rumsfeld, Donald 32–3, 35–7, 43, 45, 210, 276–7
Russell, John 258
Russia, terrorism in: actors participating in counterterrorism operation 259–60; Beslan hostage attack (2004) 248, 258; Chechnya *see* Chechnya; counterterrorism policy 248–9; counterterrorist discursive field and 257–62; cultural resources and 257–8; diagnostic frame for counterterrorism 252–4; discursive contention and counter-framing process 262–3; Domodedovo airport suicide attack (2011) 261; Dubrovka theater hostage attack (2002), Russia 257–8; Federal Security Service (FSB) 259; framing counterterrorism, frames and discursive fields for 249–51; human

rights violations 257; institutional competition and absence of field crystallisation 261–2; international terrorism, issue of 253–4; Islamization and violence in 253; Kabardino-Balkaria ski resort, attack on 255; Moscow's strategy in dealing with 256; National Anti-terrorism Committee (NAK) 260; prognostic frame for counterterrorism 254–7; socio-economic problems associated with 252–3

saffron terrorism, phenomenon of 192–3
Said, Edward 15, 228, 240
Salafi Islamist movements 236
Sect of Revolutionaries (SR) 97
Snake Hunter, Operation 281
social construction of threat, mechanisms of 115
social revolution 107–8
soldiers of God (*jund allah*) 135
Soviet Union 151, 186, 252; collapse of 222; Communism 35; Red Army 123
Special Permanent Committee on Institutions and Transparency, Greece 113
Speech Act Theory 20
state-sponsored terrorism 61, 64
Stirner, Max 106–8, 111–12, 114
Stockholm, suicide attack in (2010) 83, 161, 167, 176
Strasbourg and Dublin agreements 65
suicide-bombings: in Algiers (2007) 136n1; in Moscow (2010) 247; in Stockholm (2010) 83, 161, 167, 176
Svensson, T. 185, 190–1

Taliban 28, 33–4, 36–7, 40, 125, 127, 129, 133, 202, 216, 231
Tapeworm, Operation 281
tawhid 135
terrorism: abuse of modern technology 68; activities associated with 67; in Australia *see* Australia, terrorism in; casualties from **146**; chemical, biological, radiological and nuclear (CBRN) 68; counterterrorism, performativity, and auto-immune disorder 184–7; criminalization of 153–5; critical discourse analysis (CDA) 19–20; cross-border 185; definition of 21, 63; Derrida's views on 186; and erasing of individual identity 29–32; and erasing of national identity 32–3; and exiled members of the international community 35–9; framing of 185; ideologisation of 229–34; in India *see* India, terrorism in; international 253–4, 260; and Islamist extremists 74, 80; and Islamist movements 229–34; Islamist terrorist threat *see* Islamist terrorism; jihad in Europe *see* Europe, jihadist terrorism in; knowledge on terrorism 66–9; martyrdom and its rewards in the afterlife, ideology of 231; media discourse on 162, 164–73; motives for attacks, messages and broader causes 165–7; murder of Pim Fortuyn (Netherlands, May 6, 2002) 79–81; in the Netherlands, Sweden, and Norway 77–8; as new mode of warfare 68; non-state *see* non-state terrorism; organized Islamist terrorism (OIT) 74; political 230; and privacy 155–7; protection of Western societies from 171; relationship between media and 163; right-wing extremism 78; in Russia *see* Russia, terrorism in; saffron terrorism 192; scope of the enemy in 32; social construction of 192; state sponsorship 39, 61, 68; suicide-bombings *see* suicide-bombings; underlying causes of 64; US response against *see* US response against terrorism; Western science of 66–9
terrorist acts: 9/11 attack *see* 9/11 attack; Bali Bombings (October 2002) 147, 149; Beslan hostage attack (2004) 248, 258; categories of 62–3; definition of 152; difference with acts of violence 154; Dubrovka theater hostage attack (2002), Russia 257–8; Fire Cells Conspiracy (FCC) 97, 100, 103–4, 108, 112; on Indian parliament (December 2001) 181, 185; Kabardino-Balkaria ski resort, Russia 255; London bombings (July 7, 2005) 151, 155; Mumbai attacks (2008) 182, 189–92, 193, 195–6; Munich massacre (1972) 58, 60, 62; Stockholm, suicide attack in (2010) 83, 161, 167, 176; suicide-bombings *see* suicide-bombings; Yemen cargo plane plot (2010) 161–2, 165, 167, 169–70, 172, 174–6

Terrorist and Disruptive Activities (Prevention) Act, India 187
terrorist, identification of 65
terrorist states 33–5
terrorist threat 2, 45, 56–9, 68, 80, 85, 87n3, 150, 207, 211, 271
terror-security nexus 58, 61
Thatcher, Margaret 141
transnational Islamic terrorism 193
TREVI group 61

UN Environment Program (UNEP) 233
United States of America: American identity, features of 211; anti-terrorism laws 239; conflict with al-Qaeda and Taliban 232; constructions of otherness, evil outlaws 209–11; Council on Foreign Relations 283; democracy promotion agenda 226; Department of Defense (DoD) 29, 276–8, 284–5; drone attacks against Al Qaeda 234, 238; exceptionalism on state identity formation 237; foreign policy since 9/11 204; indigenous populations *see* America's indigenous populations; Military Commissions Act 234; myth of American exceptionalism 209–10; National Defense Authorization Act (NDAA) 235; political and cultural condition 210; relations with the Muslim world 234–5; response against terrorism *see* US response against terrorism; self-identity 222
universalized surveillance 152, 156
Unlawful Activities Prevention Act (UAPA), India 191
urban guerrilla activity, Greece: analysis of the public discourse of 98–101; as anarchist-individualist movement 108; armed struggle 110; attitudes towards the state 112–14; campaigns 96, 100; criminal nature of 104–5; current upsurge in 96–8; and ethical considerations 98–9; from the guerrillas' perspective 105–14; ideological positioning of 106–9; incoherence in social construction of threat 101–2; methodological remarks 99–101; motives and objectives of 98; movement and the press 101–5; neo-terrorism 98, 103, 114; origins of 98; public discourse of 114–15; reformist tendencies 115; and relations with society 109–12; revolutionary transformation of society 109; solidarity, idea of 108; subalternity 103–4; uprising of 2008 102

US response against terrorism 39–48; active defense measures, use of 46; assimilation, strategy of 39–43; critical metaphors and critical discourse in 273–5; defiling and dehumanizing practices among soldiers 280–2; enemy removal, strategy of 43–5; extermination of threats 45–6; hunter-prey metaphor 283–4; metaphor and reconciliation 279–86; metaphor and the representational project 273; Patriot Act 183; political scripts and rhetorical tropes 275–8; public communication strategy 39; rhetoric and the culture of contention 270–2; and winning the war on terror 46–8

vicious circle of repression 187
Vietnam War 28, 48, 69n2, 240

Wahhabi radicals 253
Walker, R.B.J. 16
Walker, Rob 204
war against Islam 123, 127, 130, 167, 208
war for civilization 205
war on drugs 151, 155
war on terror 1–2, 22, 35, 154, 187, 201–2, 204, 207, 227, 237–8, 279, 284; Australian government's contribution to 148; construction of identity 204; constructions of otherness 209–15; declaration of 185; depicting the enemy and 28–39; discourse and identity in 202–5; foundational principles of 46; global discourse on 185; impact of Obama's election 234–7; Islamist movements 232; leaders of 40; legal and journalistic framing of 152–3; political Islam, discourse on 221–2; public acceptance/approval of 153; public non-negotiation strategy with terrorists 42; strategy of international exile in 39; US policies on 27–8; US response and 39–48
war without war 65
war-crime frame 153

weapons of mass destruction 40, 68, 152
Westergaard, Kurt (Danish cartoonist), attack on (2010) 161–2, 165, 167–9, 171–6
Western European countries: counterterrorism apparatus 56, 59–62; discourse of terrorism 62–6; legal model of action 60; political violence 56, 57; problem of terrorism 57; security apparatus in 61; terrorist threat 56–9

Western security apparatuses 69
Westphalian state order 236
Winter, Gibson 286
Wolfowitz, Paul 276
World War II 31, 35, 43, 48, 226, 236, 258

Yemen cargo plane plot (2010) 161–2, 165, 167, 169–70, 172, 174–6

Zulaika, J. 121, 248